# Gangs in the Global City

# Gangs in the Global City

## Alternatives to Traditional Criminology

**EDITED BY JOHN M. HAGEDORN**

UNIVERSITY OF ILLINOIS PRESS

Urbana and Chicago

© 2007 by the Board of Trustees
of the University of Illinois
All rights reserved
Manufactured in the United States of America
1 2 3 4 5 C P 5 4 3 2 1
♾ This book is printed on acid-free paper.

Library of Congress Cataloging-in-Publication Data
Gangs in the global city : alternatives to traditional criminology /
edited by John M. Hagedorn.
p.   cm.
Includes bibliographical references and index.
ISBN-13: 978-0-252-03096-3 (cloth : alk. paper)
ISBN-10: 0-252-03096-6 (cloth : alk. paper)
ISBN-13: 978-0-252-07337-3 (pbk. : alk. paper)
ISBN-10: 0-252-07337-1 (pbk. : alk. paper)
1. Gangs.
2. Crime and race.
3. Crime and globalization.
4. Criminology—Philosophy.
I. Hagedorn, John, 1947–
HV6437.G354      2007
364.106'6—dc22      2006000326

# Contents

# Acknowledgments

**JOHN M. HAGEDORN**

In complicated times like these, intellectuals need to question the prevailing wisdom. Edward Said advises, "The intellectual's role is first to present alternative narratives and other perspectives on history than those provided by the combatants on behalf of official memory."[1]

The contributors to this book, though they represent diverse viewpoints, all brought their "alternative narratives" to a working conference in Chicago in the spring of 2002 and revised their essays for this publication. I am grateful to them and their daring, intellectual challenges to official memory and academic orthodoxy.

Contributing both intellectually and financially was Dennis Judd and his Chicago Seminar and David Perry, director of the University of Illinois–Chicago Great Cities Institute (GCI). Dennis first suggested the idea of a working conference, and I especially appreciate his firm belief that this volume was needed. I also owe a debt of gratitude to David Perry and Great Cities, where I have taken residence and have simply refused to leave. The entire staff of GCI, especially Marilyn Ruiz and Christiana Kinder, Joy Pamintuan, Nacho Gonzalez, Denita Johnson, and Chang Lee have made me feel at home and given me both friendship and intellectual support. Brigid Rauch actually organized the conference and pulled it off without a hitch. Karen Colvard of the Harry F. Guggenheim Foundation provided support for my research and encouraged the exploration of broader theoretical perspectives.

It is not easy working in Chicago when my family and I live in Milwaukee, and Mary, Zach, Jess, and Marty had to put up with my frequent absences.

Tracey, Katie, and Mary's daughter Bryna have all flown the coop, but they too have been understanding of my commitments.

Finally, my thanks to the University of Illinois Press and to Joan Catapano, who attended the conference and secured the Rivera print "Frozen Assets" for the cover. Ann Youmans did a painstaking and exemplary job in copyediting the entire volume.

### Note

1. Edward Said, "The Public Role of Writers and Intellectuals," *The Nation,* September 17, 2001.

# Gangs in the Global City

# Introduction: Globalization, Gangs, and Traditional Criminology

## JOHN M. HAGEDORN

This volume, and the 2002 working conference that preceded it, are beginning steps in a process of reframing gangs beyond the criminology literature. While the volume represents widely divergent viewpoints, what unites the authors is a desire to understand gangs in the global era.

The volume brings together an assortment of international scholars who address, from many different perspectives, problems in traditional criminology. They range from the theoretical (Wacquant, Young, Sassen, and my own essays) to the case study (Hazlehurst, Rus and Vigil, Kersten, Pitts) to examining the identities and agency of male and female gang members on the streets (Moore, Barrios, and Brotherton). The book concludes with a sympathetic yet critical review essay by Jim Short.

Individually, none of the papers makes a full critique, though I attempt a synthesis in my concluding essay. But collectively, the chapters present alternatives to three generally accepted propositions of traditional criminology, which are listed in the table below. The authors in this volume, to one extent or another, elucidate the alternatives listed. This introduction intends to outline the contours of the critique as it emerges chapter by chapter throughout this volume.

*Table I.1.*

| Traditional Criminology | This Volume |
| --- | --- |
| 1. Gangs are deviant and temporary adolescent departures from a progressive path of modernization. | 1A. While most gangs are unsupervised teenage peer groups, many others have institutionalized in ghettos, barrios, and favelas across the world. |
| 2. Gangs are paradigmatically an American form, a byproduct of industrialization and urbanization. | 2A. Gangs are found all over the world and today often respond to the changing spaces of globalizing cities. |
| 3. Gangs are mainly youthful products of social disorganization and are not primarily racial or ethnic organizations. | 3A. Gangs are "social actors" whose identities are formed by ethnic, racial, and/or religious oppression; through participation in the underground economy; and through constructions of gender. |

1. While most gangs are unsupervised teenage peer groups, many others have institutionalized in ghettos, barrios, and favelas across the world.

Gangs have been classically constructed as interstitial peer groups, adaptations to immigration and urbanization in the industrial city. The social disorganization paradigm deracialized the study of gangs and described them as transitory adolescent groups rebelling from weak institutions. While the Chicago School's focus on the spaces of the city was a major advance for social science (Hagedorn chapter 1), Wacquant's scathing critique (chapter 2) exposes the limitations of the paradigm and the need for this volume.

While most gangs still remain unsupervised peer groups (for example, Pitts chapter 11; Rus and Vigil chapter 6,) many gangs have older members and have persisted over decades. While authors in the volume use other terms for this process, I argue that some gangs or "street organizations" have *institutionalized* in poor communities. This concept, drawn from the literature on organizations, may be better suited to describe persisting gangs than "organized crime" or other terms drawn from criminology. As explained in chapter 1, this process is not new. Many gangs of the early twentieth century institutionalized as "voting gangs" or adjuncts to political machines. What is new in the global era, however, is the institutionalization of gangs of oppressed minorities.

The underground economy has also played a major role in the institutionalization of gangs, not only in the United States but around the world. Gangs have distinct economic functions as globalization has not narrowed inequalities but has marginalized some areas while valorizing others (Sassen chapter 4). Immigration has accelerated in the global economy, and Chicago School–style "assimilation" is not even on the agenda for many diasporas and ethnic enclaves (see Valier 2003). While some gangs have international criminal ties (Hazlehurst chapter 5), most are local players in drug markets and other informal economic ventures (Rus and Vigil chapter 6).

Most readers will be surprised that Maori gangs in New Zealand have persisted for more than forty years: Cameron Hazlehurst's case study of gangs in a small country (chapter 5) describes an institutionalized group of gangs that appears similar to gangs in the United States. These New Zealand gangs are national in scope with chapters in different cities. They have a Maori identity and are engaged in the drug trade and other underground economic activities. Hazlehurst calls these gangs "self-sustaining, adaptable, and organic," borrowing concepts directly from Philip Selznick, the founder of the institutional school of sociology.

In the United States, institutionalized gangs are more familiar. The Almighty Latin King and Queen Nation in New York City in the 1990s came to resemble a social movement (Brotherton chapter 10) or a religion (Barrios chapter 9). This gang began not on the streets but in prison and was influenced by a migrating Chicago Latin King. The ALKQN developed a written constitution, laws, and prayers and saw itself as a community organization. This gang, whether you accept the persuasive arguments of Brotherton and Barrios or not, is a far cry from Frederic Thrasher's unsupervised peer groups.

The role of prison in gang formation is picked up in my own chapters (1 and 12). Chicago's Blackstone Rangers, as well as the Vice Lords, began their organization in juvenile prison and brought the gang back to the streets. La Eme in Texas and California has also brought its prison gang organization out to the community and has rivaled and even muscled out street gangs. Reports from Rio de Janiero, Puerto Rico, and South Africa have suggested that drug gangs originally formed in prison and only later organized on the streets, a process not consistent with traditional criminological theory.

While institutionalized gangs have become a familiar part of the urban landscape, there is consensus among the authors that most gangs today are not fundamentally different from gangs of the industrial era. Contemporary gangs are not "postmodern" but a product of late modernity, to borrow from the title of my chapter 12, with continuity with the past as well as changes. Just as the method of understanding gangs has been to investigate processes of immigration, urbanization, and industrialization, today the keys to understanding gangs are processes of globalization—the redivision of space, the strengthening of traditional identities, and the underground economy.

2. Gangs are found all over the world and today often respond to the changing spaces of globalizing cities.

In nearly all of the chapters, gangs outside the United States are a major theme. This is an important corrective to the almost entirely American-centered study of gangs. Klein et al.'s *Eurogang Paradox* (2001), for example, while having many chapters on European gangs, has as its central theme the comparison of European gangs with their American prototypes. Klein argues that the Europeans, while attempting to contrast their "peer groups" to the stereotypes of American gangs, in fact demonstrate their similarity,

But is "the gang" an American concept? Certainly London had gangs long before the United States, if Dickens and Elizabethan scholars (for example, Salgado 1977) can be believed. Pearson's influential *Hooligan* (1983) traces a much longer story of British gang life and one predating American influence.[1] And what of the Triads in China, the mafia of Sicily, or the Bo-tsotsi of South Africa? Gangs have a long tradition outside the United States.

This American-centered study of gangs followed from the centrality in the literature of Frederic Thrasher's work on immigrant peer groups in Chicago nearly a hundred years ago. A largely American literature on "gangs" has followed the twists and turns of U.S. gang life into the twenty-first century. Klein's conclusion in *The Eurogang Paradox* is that most European *gangs* (or whatever name they are called) form as unsupervised peer groups, like American gangs, and develop through a definable group process. While this cross-cultural perspective is helpful, it mirrors the narrowness of the U.S. literature and its focus on criminality, and lacks integration with broader literatures on the city and globalization.

The contributors to this volume agree with Klein's point about the continuity of the gangs of today with adolescent gangs of the industrial era (see Rus and Vigil chapter 6; Pitts, chapter 11; Young chapter 3; Moore chapter 7). But if gangs are placed within the spatial and social changes wrought by globalization (Sassen chapter 4, Hagedorn chapter 1), we may come to some different conclusions about their nature. Immigration, as noted earlier, is not the industrial-era process of assimilation, and the increased mobility of immigrants has resulted in the creation of various kinds of ethnic enterprises in the receiving countries, many in the informal or underground economy (Stepick 1989; Sassen 1999). Sassen points out in this volume (chapter 4) that "new economic regimes" in this era and global networks have allowed for the creation of marginalized spaces where gangs and other powerless social actors operate.

It is the concentration of wealth in cities that creates what Marcuse (1997) calls a *citadel* protecting itself against the dark *ghettoes,* that contain Sennett's "night army of the service workers" (1994, 368), and laborers in the underground economy. This spatial imagery resonates with the earlier Chicago School approach. Indeed, rather than reject and replace the insights of the Chicagoans, in both of my essays I advocate updating or supplementing their ecological approach. Jock Young (chapter 3) also cautions against the tendency to see the concept of social exclusion as meaning a complete cultural and spatial divide between the "excluded" and the "excluders." In the spirit of the late Robert Merton, Young powerfully reminds us of the homogenizing global effects of American culture, influencing elites and oppressed alike.

However, Young's incisive analysis should not obscure the real spatial dynamics occurring in cities today. The current redivision of space in Chicago (Hagedorn chapter 1) has pushed gangs from their "interstitial" spaces out toward and into the suburbs, making them more like the banlieue of Paris. The postindustrial spatial dynamics of the city have altered Burgess's concentric zones in many ways (for example, Davis 1998, 364–65). As other literatures have been pointing out, to criminology's neglect, security in the citadel is big business and an integral part of the gentrification of cities (Marcuse 1997). Very little attention in criminology has been paid to the impact of gentrification on gangs and social organization in poor, gentrifying, minority neighborhoods.

The notion of a citadel implies absolute exclusion in a manner Young warns against. After all, the needs of the wealthy require a new servant class (Sassen chapter 4), which inevitably mingles the rich and poor. However, gangs today exist both in marginalized ghettos, as Wacquant argues (chapter 2), as well as in gentrifying areas. Gang activity differs spatially as does the underground economy that provides many gangs today with their prime function. A rich noncriminological literature on the informal economy has looked at how underground economic activities are integrated with the mainstream economy, but in socially excluded spaces, informal goods and service mainly provide survival and relief loosely coupled with the mainstream economy (for example, Portes and Sassen-Koob 1987; Portes 1996). This volume (Sassen; Hagedorn) begins an investigation of the meaning of space in the globalizing city for gangs, but our efforts are introductory and cursory, not conclusive.

Neoliberal policies emphasizing the market and paring down the safety net have also contributed to marginalization and gang activities (Sassen chapter 4). John Pitts's analysis (chapter 11) of Tony Blair's emulation of U.S. criminal justice policy and its effects on gangs will be instructive to readers around the world. Both Hazlehurst (chapter 5) and Rus and Vigil (chapter 6) frame their analysis of contemporary gangs in the particularities of neoliberal national policies. According to these authors, it is the neoliberal policies of the United States, not globalization per se, that have had devastating consequences around the world.

If this volume aspired to representatively sample the current international literature on gangs, the contributors would be quite different. Nothing demonstrates the narrowness of the American paradigm better than looking at major studies of gangs and other groups of armed young men in Rio de Janiero (Dowdney 2003) and Soweto (Glaser 2000). Indeed, Rio and Soweto, as well as São Paolo and Cape Town, represent gang cities that underscore the themes of this volume. Institutionalized gangs also appear to exist, in various forms, in major cities of India, Puerto Rico, Haiti, Russia, Albania, El Salvador, China, Mexico, Nigeria, and cities in many more countries. Another volume would be required to describe the various kinds of interstitial and institutionalized gangs in these cities, their relationship to globalization, and to other groups of armed young men (see Hagedorn chapter 12).

While American research today, like Klein's *Eurogang Paradox,* has begun to look outside the United States, it has yet to shed its American-centered perspective. It is still trying to fit gangs everywhere into a Procrustian, American-made bed. What is clear is that gangs today organize in response not just to industrialization and urbanization but primarily to social exclusion and the changing spaces of globalizing cities worldwide. This volume argues that literatures other than criminology are needed to understand this phenomena. Indeed, I believe U.S. criminology is in a moribund state and in danger of becoming irrelevant to concerns broader than U.S. law enforcement.

> 3. Gangs are "social actors" whose identities are formed by ethnic, racial, and/or religious oppression, participation in the underground economy, and constructions of both masculinity and femininity.

Traditional criminology tends to look at gangs as dependent variables: products of social disorganization, broken families, or street socialization. Gang members, in the traditional argot, are usually troubled boys, limited in social and human capital, or plagued with few resources.

This certainly describes many gangs and their members. However, as many of the chapters explicitly argue (for example, both Barrios and Brotherton) gangs are independent variables as well, *social actors* (Hagedorn) who construct their identities aggressively and in more ways than just as mirrors of others, à la Blumer and Mead. No better example of this process can be found than Joan Moore's look at the construction of female gang identity by Muslim girls (chapter 7). Moore not only provides a global literature review of female gangs (a hint: there isn't much) but also examines how globalization affects the construction of identity for female gang members. She argues that while some studies have looked at how globalization structures male identity, similar investigations have not been extended to women. Female gang members are responding to changing gender roles within traditional communities, like Islamic societies, as well as to economic and social changes.

Joachim Kersten (chapter 8) picks up this theme by looking at Berlin skinheads. Kersten looks at how the reunification of Germany has impacted youth from the East and West and how extremist, racist organizations form under these conditions. Germany has long been the tragic theater for the working out of identity of armed young men, and the skinheads represent another episode. The emergence of racist, anti-immigrant gangs is not restricted on the continent to Germany, however; the coincidence of immigration and economic restructuring pits domestic and foreign workers against one another. Turks in Berlin, Algerians in Paris, and Bangladeshis in London (Pitts chapter 11) all face violence from native gangs and citizens and also from gang rivalries. As Pitts shows, these gangs actively resist oppression. This situation needs much more scrutiny.

Like the skinheads, many of the gangs described in this volume participate in politics. Brotherton and Barrios describe a politicized period in the life of New York's Latin King and Queen Nation, and Hazlehurst describes a long history of politics from Maori gangs. The politics of Chicago gangs (Hagedorn chapter 1) is a century-long tradition, but their early politics were tied to patronage and the Democratic machine. In the 1960s, gangs in Chicago participated in the politics of black and Latino rebellion, and in the last few years some Chicago gangs have returned to ward politics (Rey 2002).

Luis Barrios (chapter 9) will surprise many who are not familiar with his work or with the religious nature of gangs. The religious or spiritual experience has long been a companion of the gang life, particularly in the prisons. From Malcolm X on, Muslims have offered a powerful spiritual alternative to the streets. Among many African American gangs today in New York, Los Angeles, and Chicago, Minister Louis Farrakhan exercises significant influence. Again, these religious ties are not new—recall the scene from the movie *Gangs of New York,* taken from Asbury, where a priest leads the Irish gangs to war against the Protestant mob (see Hagedorn 2003).

Gangs in Chicago, Chiapas, New York, New Zealand, and London all have strong racialized identities, a major theme of the volume. While the sweeping culture of globalization homogenizes all in its path, as Young (chapter 3) argues, it also shapes what Castells calls "resistance identities" (Brotherton chapter 10). These identities are typically ethnoreligious in nature and influence minority communities and their gangs as well.

Wacquant's essay polemicizes against a nonracialized understanding of the ghetto, and indeed this book argues that racial identity is crucial to understanding gangs. Hazlehurst's chilling account of the attempted annihilation of Maori identity will be all too familiar to students of U.S. policies toward Native Americans and Latin American elites' suppression of indigenous peoples.

## Conclusion

This book intends to be the beginning of a theoretical journey. Several major works by conference scholars have appeared since these essays were penned in 2002, including John Pitt's *The New Politics of Youth Crime* and David Brotherton and Luis Barrios's *Between Black and Gold.* My own work has continued to uncover the roots of Chicago's institutionalized gangs but has also moved into an examination of the nature of groups of armed young men around the world. Other participants in the conference are moving in similar, and, significantly, largely noncriminological directions.

Jim Short, in his review essay (chapter 13), argues that the volume challenges traditional criminology, although not with a consistent theoretical critique. As editor of this book, I surely agree. I also agree with Short that "criminology often has been identified with the status quo" (p. 332). The war on drugs, as the prime Justice Department response to incivility in cities, has defined traditional criminology through funding and the shaping of assumptions and research agendas (Chilton 2001). In the post-September 11 world, police investigations of gangs are being subsumed into the war on terror while the gangs themselves flourish in urban areas of weakened nation-states and in socially excluded areas of strong ones. Most current U.S. studies are theoretically trapped by old paradigms that are useful for law enforcement but are unable to understand the complexity of gangs described in this volume and around the world (see Dowdney 2003; Children in Organised Armed Violence). Perhaps the constricted funding opportunities for gang research in the United States Department of Justice will persuade some U.S. criminologists to search for new directions.

The volume does not aspire to unfold a "new criminology" as Jock Young and his colleagues did thirty years ago. Rather, by focusing on the problems of traditional criminology in understanding gangs, our contribution is to provide some evidence that, with an ironical bow to Tennyson, the old order is indeed changing and must surely yield forth to the new. "For God," Tennyson continues, "fulfills himself in many ways, lest one good system should corrupt the world." In less exalted terms, this volume asks whether U.S. criminology will be part of the problem or part of the solution. I believe *Gangs in the Global City* is one sign of the advent of an exciting new era of theoretical discovery.

## Note

1. "From the early 1600s the streets of London and other cities had been terrorized by a succession of organized gangs. . . . The gangs also fought pitched battles among themselves, dressed with coloured ribbons to distinguish the different factions" (Pearson 1983, 188).

## References

Brotherton, David, and Luis Barrios. 2003. *Between Black and Gold.* New York: Columbia University Press.

Burgess, Ernest W. 1925/1961. "The Growth of the City: Introduction to a Research Project" In *Studies in Human Ecology,* George A. Theodorson, 37–44. Evanston, Ill.

Children in Organised Armed Violence. http://www.coav.br.org.

Chilton, Roland. 2001. "Viable Policy: The Impact of Federal Funding and the Need for Independent Research Agendas." *Criminology* 39, no. 1: 1–8.

Davis, Mike. *Ecology of Fear: Los Angeles and the Imagination of Disaster.* New York: Vintage.

Dowdney, Luke. 2003. *Children of the Drug Trade: A Case Study of Children in Organized Armed Violence in Rio de Janiero.* Rio de Janiero: 7 Letras.

Glaser, Clive. 2000. *Bo-Tsotsi: The Youth Gangs of Soweto, 1935–1976.* Portsmouth, N.H.: Heinemann.

Hagedorn, John M. 2003. "Gangs of . . . ." *Chicago Tribune, Perspective,* January 19.

Klein, Malcolm, Hans-Jurgen Kerner, Cheryl L. Maxsen, and Elmar G. M. Weitekamp, eds. 2001. *The Eurogang Paradox: Street Gangs and Youth Groups in the U.S. and Europe.* Dordrecht, Netherlands: Kluwer.

Marcuse, P. 1997. "The Enclave, the Citadel, and the Ghetto: What Has Changed in the Post-Fordist U.S. City." *Urban Affairs Review* 33, no. 2: 228–64.

Pearson, Geoffrey. 1983. *Hooligan: A History of Respectable Fears.* New York: Shocken Books.

Pitts, John. 2000. *The New Politics of Youth Crime: Discipline or Solidarity?* Basingstoke, UK: Palgrave.

Portes, Alejandro. 1996. "The Informal Economy," in *Exploring the Underground Economy,* ed. Susan Pozo, 147–65. Kalamazoo, Mich.: Upjohn Institute.

Portes, Alejandro, and Saskia Sassen-Koob. 1987. "Making It Underground: Material on the Informal Sector in Western Market Economies." *American Journal of Sociology* 93: 30–61.

Salgado, G. Amini. 1977. *The Elizabethan Underworld.* London, Totowa, N.J.: J. M. Dent, Rowman and Littlefield.

Sassen, Saskia. 1999. *Guests and Aliens.* New York: New Press.

Sennett, Richard. 1994. *Flesh and Stone: The Body and the City in Western Civilization.* New York: W. W. Norton.

Stepick, Alexander. 1989. "Miami's Two Informal Sectors." *The Informal Economy: Studies in Advanced and Less Advanced Countries,* ed. A. Portes, M. Castells, and L. A. Benton, 111–34. Baltimore: Johns Hopkins Press.

Sullivan, John P. 2001. "Gangs, Hooligans, and Anarchists: The Vanguard of Netwar in the Streets." In *Networks and Netwars,* ed. John Arquilla and David Ronfeld, 99–128. Santa Monica, Calif.: Rand.

Valier, C. 2003. "Foreigners, Crime, and Changing Mobilities." *British Journal of Criminology* 43, no. 1: 1–21.

# PART I

# Theoretical Perspectives

# 1

# Gangs, Institutions, Race, and Space: The Chicago School Revisited

JOHN M. HAGEDORN

It is time to rethink the way we think about gangs. This essay aims to recast the study of gangs by reviewing, reviving, and revising the Chicago School ecological paradigm.

Just as gangs in Frederic Thrasher's time were closely related to urbanization, immigration, and industrialization, gangs today cannot be understood apart from an analysis of globalization. While contemporary gang research—including my own—has often been framed within a context of deindustrialization, the processes of globalization comprise much more than merely a loss of industry. Gang researchers (for example, Huff 2001; Klein et al. 2001) have paid scant attention, however, to the effects of agglomeration (Friedmann and Wolf 1984; Sassen 1991), informalization (Castells 1996; Portes, Castells, and Benton 1989), gentrification (N. Smith 1996), and geographies of exclusion (Caldiera 2000; Marcuse 1997; Wacquant 2000; Young 1999).

By analyzing how space and race in Chicago have structured gangs, this essay combines traditions of the Chicago School with contemporary urban political economy and institutional theory. A critical overview of three fundamental concepts of the Chicago School will be followed by a description of social processes influencing twenty-first-century Chicago gangs.

## Human Ecology and Gangs in Industrial Chicago

Three fundamental, but contested, concepts are embedded within Frederic Thrasher's *The Gang:* (1) the ecological basis of city life, (2) the interstitial and unreflective adolescent organization of gangs, and (3) the process of ethnic succession.

## THE URBAN ECOLOGICAL SYSTEM

> Gangland is a phenomenon of human ecology. As better residential districts receded before the encroachments of business and industry, the gang develops as one manifestation of the economic, moral, and cultural frontier which marks the interstice.
> —Thrasher, *The Gang*

The gang, for Frederic Thrasher and the Chicago School, was above all to be studied in the context of the physical processes and changing shape of the modern city, with Chicago as the universal model. As Richard Sennett (1969) has pointed out, the Chicago School broke with earlier European urban studies by looking at the city not as an ideal type but as an organism that needed to be understood through direct observation of its parts.

Immigrants lived, and second-generation gangs formed, in "natural areas" near life-sustaining work—Chicago's mills, stockyards, and factories and the central business district. These areas were an "unplanned, natural product of the city's growth" (Zorbaugh 1961 [1929], 46). Gangs, like immigrants, were a temporary, "interstitial" phenomenon, formed as a result of the disorganization of the areas of first settlement and the rebellious culture conflict of second-generation youth with their tradition-bound parents.

For the Chicago School, ganging was not a cultural carryover from the old world but a product of the new. Rather than locate the criminality and violence associated with gangs in an ethnic or racial temperament, Park and his colleagues firmly located these problems in social disorganization. Park, Wirth, and others in the Chicago School were staunch enemies of bigotry and racism.

Many "natural areas," however, proved to be not so natural, and often the result of deliberate policies of real estate interests and politicians (Castells 1979; Molotch 1976). Zorbaugh's notion that railroads, for example, were "naturally" occurring phenomena was simply wrong. Powerful interests decided where railroads or highways should be located with far-reaching consequences (for example, Rast 1999; Cronon 1991). "The city" as Marcuse and van Kempen put it, "is not an actor; it is a place occupied and used by many actors" (2000, 265).

Powerful institutional actors in Chicago, much research has shown (for example, Suttles 1990), created a built environment that had particularly devastating consequences on African Americans and implications for the nature of gangs. Understanding the uses of space was central to Thrasher's perspective on gangs, but his human ecology framework minimized the active role of institutions, particularly the political machine, real estate companies, and the rackets. In order to fully understand Chicago's gangs, the role of the powerful, as well as the powerless, needs to be more fully explored.

## THE INTERSTITIAL VERSUS THE INSTITUTIONAL GANG

> The adult gang, unless conventionalized, is comparatively rare and is the result of special selection . . . the gang appears to be an interstitial group, a manifestation of the period of readjustment between childhood and maturity.
>
> —Thrasher, *The Gang*

One legacy of the Chicago School's study of gangs was to see in gangs the life and liveliness of fun-loving kids, rebelling from the stultifying traditions of their parents and boring routines of school. The gang flourished because the formal institutions of society failed to provide conventional outlets for this boyishness. "The gang, in short," proclaims an admiring Thrasher (3), "is *life.*"

Thrasher argued for the universality of his conclusions about Chicago gangs as a "natural and spontaneous type of organization," citing studies of New York, London, Boston, and other cities (38–41). The adolescent gang was in many ways a social construction of Thrasher's meant to differentiate "the gang" from organized crime, then reigning in Chicago and symbolized by Al Capone. Thrasher also firmly rebutted those who claimed gang formation was an "instinct" or an inbred psychological characteristic of immigrant youth. The gang, he insisted, is the proper study of sociology, not psychology. For Thrasher "the" gang was not a formal organization but a spontaneous peer group (see Short 1963; Short and Strodtbeck 1965).

A careful reading of *The Gang,* however, casts some doubt on the universality of his central idea. At least 20 percent or 243 of Chicago's gangs, Thrasher calculated, were adult or mixed adult gangs (74). He also points out that there were over 500 social athletic clubs "of the gang type" in Chicago (63). These adult clubs, or "conventionalized" gangs, were the result of older teens being "encouraged" to organize by "a politician, a saloon-keeper, or some welfare agency." "Scratch a club man," Thrasher claimed was the conventional wisdom of the time, "and you will find a gangster" (1927, 397). It appears that for some youth gangs, adult institutions played a key role and young adult gangs were widespread.

From the perspective of the institutional school of organizational theory (for example, Scott 1995), many—not all—youth gangs might be seen as functional components of political, ethnic, religious, or illicit economic organizations, with varying degrees of neighborhood legitimacy. To speak of the institutionalization of gangs means that some gangs become "infused with value" (Selznick 1957) and reflect a "rationalized myth" (Meyer and Rowan 1977, 347)[1] of some good to the community.

By the 1920s, Irish, Italian, and Chinese gangs, in this sense, had all become institutionalized in distinct ways. Early Irish gangs had substantial support from the Democratic Party and were loosely based on Catholic parishes (Erie 1988). Politicians nurtured the gangs as politically useful and encouraged them to act as "protectors" of Irish turf, particularly of Bridgeport, which was just across Wentworth Avenue from the Black Belt. Social athletic clubs, Thrasher's map of 1313 gangs showed, lined the Irish side of the black/white divide.

For the Italians, the Irish domination of politics meant Italian young men would not get substantial city patronage (Erie 1988), and many of them were attracted to Capone's "Outfit." Police harassment and political discrimination, coupled with largess and patronage in bootlegging, gave early Italian gangsters an aura of being "defenders of the community" (Lombardo and Lurigio 1995) or Capone "Robin Hoods" (Haller 1984). Similarly, Chicago's Chinese tongs were closely linked to the red light district and protected illicit and licit businesses (Light 1977). Booth adds that by the mid-twentieth century in the United States, "Tongs were institutionalized and thought to be impossible to eradicate" (1999, 302).

Certainly, spontaneous "interstitial" gangs of every ethnic group grew in Chicago's neighborhoods like plants on fertile ground. In many ways, African American gangs may have most closely resembled Thrasher's adolescent peer groups (Perkins 2002). However, a large number of "institutional gangs," structurally related to politics and the rackets, appear to be much less "rare" than Thrasher cared to admit.[2]

## SOCIAL DISORGANIZATION AND THE DECLINING SIGNIFICANCE OF RACE

> The ghetto existed before the riots, and it certainly persisted after they had ended. Yet that is precisely the point. The maintenance of the status quo was an act of great force.
>
> —Arnold R. Hirsch, *Making the Second Ghetto: Race and Housing in Chicago 1940–1960*

One of the primary assumptions, and major contributions, of the Chicago School, is that delinquency and various social processes were not racialized.

Combating the nativism and racism of the day, Park, Thrasher, Burgess, and Shaw and McKay all showed that gangs, delinquency, and crime were products of areas, not ethnic groups. The project of the Chicago School was to dispel stereotypes and humanize immigrants for a sometimes hostile native-born public.

Perusal of Thrasher, or any of the Chicago texts, will find the black experience treated essentially the same as that of any other ethnic group: an ecological and class question, a problem of urbanization and immigration, of ethnic succession, and *not* one of race. Racism toward African Americans may be extreme, they thought, but it was merely a deviant case on the universal road to assimilation. Modernity meant the gradual inclusion of all peoples into the industrial order and a steadily "declining significance of race" (Wilson 1978) as well as other irrational prejudices.

Indeed, Louis Wirth, who would work assiduously for civil rights for decades in Chicago, wrote his classic *The Ghetto* with only Jews in mind and gives no indication that the concept might be applied to African Americans. For Wirth, the "vanishing" Jewish ghetto was merely another illustration of how "land values, rentals, accessibility, and the attitudes of the owners determine, in the last analysis, what type of area a neighborhood shall become" (1928/1956, 285).

But "land values, rentals, and accessibility" did not determine what kind of area the *dark* ghetto would become, as a host of social scientists have found. In 1928, however, Wirth could hardly have failed to note that the Black Belt was the prime example of his notion of the "social isolation" (1928/1956, 4) that had defined the Jewish ghetto.

Thrasher also framed Irish-black hostility as an example of universal ethnic tensions over space. However, consider his description of "the Dirty Dozen," what he calls a "typical" gang: "One night, while the race riots of 1919 were at their height, the gang, armed with revolvers, blackjacks, and knives, started out to get the 'niggers.' After a fight when one boy died, the gang sought revenge: 'They killed two negroes and beat up five more after the death of Shaggy'" (1927, 47). Thrasher also comments on the "Murderers," a solidified gang, which he says took its name from the 1919 riots when they, he says without quotes, "disposed of" several negroes (62–63). Landesco reported that the 1919 race riots would have been much worse but "Ragen's Colts" had been "thinned out" by enlistments into the army (1929/1968, 123). The grand jury and coroner's reports list dozens of white gangs as playing an organized role in the rioting, including Richard J. Daley's Hamburgs, whom Alderman Leon Depres (PBS 1995) claimed were the "chief instigators" of the riot. Ethnic rivalry in industrial-era Chicago *was* universal. Mob violence and race riots, however, were directed almost solely against African Americans.

The Chicago School did not consider an alternative explanation: that racism is normal and the need for a scapegoat is characteristic of the insecurities that accompany modernity (Sennett 1994). Thrasher and Park would have seen as atavistic Winant's conclusion that "in U.S. society, and in many others as well, race is a fundamental organizing principle, a way of knowing and interpreting the social world" (1995, 31).

The urbanists at the University of Chicago curiously seldom cited W. E. B. Du Bois (1899/1967), whose study of Philadelphia Negroes was well known by social scientists at the time, and who had predicted that the "color line" would be the fundamental question of the twentieth century (1902/1989). "Dubois recognized," Silbey points out in his critique of the Chicago School, "that the residential patterns of the black population were structured by racism, contrasting sharply with Robert Park's assimilationist view" (Silbey 1995, 143; see also Greenberg 1980). Drake and Cayton's sober conclusion to *Black Metropolis*—"It is conceivable that the Negro question . . . is incapable of solution" (1970, 766)—scarcely fit into the optimistic worldview of the Chicagoans and even clashed badly with W. Lloyd Warner's odd postscript to their book. African American gangs, it would appear, may be better understood in the context of the permanent ghetto than as just another ethnic successor.

## SUMMARY

The Chicago School has been the most important influence in the social sciences for the study of cities and gangs. Thrasher and Park represented the best of white, progressive urban scholarship, and they had a thoroughly optimistic view of the future of the modern city. This "enlightened" ideology, however, resulted in the Chicagoans' detaching the study of adolescent group process from an understanding of conventional and unconventional institutions and reducing race to "melting pot" assimilationism.

One of the most important aspects of the Chicago School was its study of the real actions of social groups responding to spatial processes. Though Park and his colleagues failed to adequately stress the role of some key institutional actors, they excelled in describing how the particular shape of the industrial city molded its ethnic gangs. Taking into account the Chicago School's weaknesses, their considerable insights can give us guidance today.

## Globalization and Chicago Gangs

Gangs in Chicago can best be understood by analyzing the redivision of space now shaking globalizing cities. Globalization affects our analysis in the following ways: (1) in the impact on gangs of processes of agglomeration, gentrification, and the pacification of the urban frontier; (2) in the relationship of the institutionalization of contemporary gangs to the informalization of the economy; and (3) in the convergence of the ghetto and the prison in the "revanchist" state.

### THE CITADEL AND THE GENTRY

> The effort to recolonize the city involves systematic eviction.
> —Neil Smith, *The New Urban Frontier: Gentrification and the Revanchist State*

Rather than begin by compiling indicators of social disorganization, it might be best to adopt Park's laconic advice to his students and go out and look firsthand at Chicago. The Windy City looks much different in 2002 than it did in 1922. Today Burgess's concentric circles do not represent stages of ethnic succession but, with only a small dose of imagination, might be seen as defense perimeters of an advancing army of gentry occupying what Zukin (1991) calls the "Super-Loop." As Neil Smith (1996) explains, in terms reminiscent of Thrasher's "badlands," gentrification can be compared to the conquering of the global city's "wild frontier."

Land values in Chicago's interstitial slum areas have skyrocketed, and poor black and Latino residents have been evicted, pushed out to what used to be the zone of workers' residences and into the suburbs. Massive spatial upheavals have also accompanied the tearing down of housing projects (J. Smith 1998), creating social disruptions that have powerfully influenced the nature and behavior of gangs. These upheavals, like their industrial-era progenitors, were the result of powerful social actors making profit-driven decisions (for example, Suttles 1990; Rast 1999).

The changing shape of the global city, Saskia Sassen (1991) writes, is determined in part by the agglomeration of producer and other services in a central zone. Despite the mobility that accompanies information technology, technicians and executives huddle together in newly "tamed" consumer spaces near their work in the city center. Friedmann and Wolf (1984) argue that globalization creates new types of "citadels" within cities to protect the gentry as in the old colonial city (see also Caldiera 2000; Davis 1990, 1998; Marcuse 1997).

Rather than modernizing processes working to "include" immigrants and the working class in the industrial order, the postmodern city is an "exclusive society" (Young 1999) where "walls, literal or symbolic, prevent people from seeing, meeting, and hearing each other; at the extremes they insulate and they exclude" (Marcuse and van Kempen 2000, 250). Gentrification *means* the expansion of public surveillance with gated villages, "zero-tolerance" or "community policing," and other policies designed to enhance the "collective efficacy" of neighborhoods against crime (Sampson 2001). These communitarian policies are more often exclusive rather than inclusive processes. As David Harvey says, "The spirit of community has long been held as an antidote to threats of social disorder, class war and revolutionary violence . . . Well-founded communities often exclude, define themselves against others, erect all sorts of keep-out signs (if not tangible walls), internalize surveillance, social controls, and repression. Community has often been a barrier to, rather than a facilitator of, social change" (1990, 170).

The tearing down of Chicago's public housing projects, while cast in terms of crime reduction, also has spawned exclusionary processes. Former housing project tenants have been pushed out of their community and moved west and south with insufficient replacement housing. Rather than resulting in racial integration, the destruction of Chicago's housing projects have essentially resegregated the ghetto (Betancar, Domeyko, and Wright 2001).

These exclusionary processes create different kinds of spaces, and gangs react accordingly (see Stepick 1989). In gentrifying areas, our Chicago field work has found, gangs may at first act as neighborhood defenders as long-time residents are forced out. They may encourage young kids to vandalize Starbucks and other symbols of gentrification. Eventually, gangs in these closely watched areas need to go underground and "lay off" teenage corner kids, who attract unwanted official attention. Some gangs evolve into primarily economic vehicles, often shedding their prior "rationalized myth" of community service.

In more socially isolated spaces, the gang is more likely to be a youth employment agency than merely a social or fighting club. It often has long-standing, if not highly publicized, ties to community institutions such as schools and churches and is seen by some as a semi-legitimate actor. In these spaces, persisting gangs, while mostly concerned with economic survival, may also loudly declare their dedication to the "community" and be seen by some residents as making financial and other positive contributions (Venkatesh 1996).

The current redivision of space also affects immigrant social organization. While African Americans have been steadily pushed away from Chicago's "interstitial" slums, the Puerto Rican community has been uprooted and displaced at least twice (Padilla 1987). Gentrified out of the near west side and then Lincoln Park, Puerto Rican neighborhoods are now under assault for a third time from a rapidly expanding professional invasion of Humboldt Park on the fringes of the "Super-Loop." A forty-year battle against several waves of gentrification, historian Mervin Mendez (2002) says, has defined Puerto Rican gangs.

Mexican immigration, which has greatly increased over the last few decades, has been pushed west from Pilsen and the Little Village and spilled over city lines into fiercely anti-black Cicero. Traditional concepts of ethnic succession may properly be applied to Mexicans in western areas of the city, while many of these areas stay strictly off-limits to blacks. Still, increased mobility to and from Latin America has eroded traditional notions of assimilation and reinforced ethnic enclaves (Valier 2003).

Urban processes of exclusion appear to be universal today, while their geography is unique to each city. Chicago's pattern is quite different than that of less centralized Los Angeles, or more centralized Manhattan, not to speak of cities like Paris (Body-Gendrot 2000; Wacquant 1997) or São Paulo (Caldiera 2000). While some veteran gang researchers seem willing to succumb to the postmodern temptation to proclaim Los Angeles the "new paradigm" (for example, Dear 2000; Maxson and Klein 2000), what should have been learned from the method of the Chicago School is the need to study how the geography of each city influences its gangs.

The fundamental ecological processes in Chicago's industrial era that shaped the nature of its gangs were immigration, industrial concentration, and segregation. Today, among those new ecological processes within Chicago are agglomeration, gentrification, and resegregation. Gangs themselves, however, are not passive observers but institutional actors within this new urban drama.

## INSTITUTIONALIZED GANGS AND INFORMAL ECONOMIES

> There they are.
> Thirty at the corner
> Black, raw, ready.
> Sores in the city
> that do not want to heal.
> —Gwendolyn Brooks, "The Blackstone Rangers"

One of the most important characteristics of the modern world, Portes, Castells, and Benton (1989) tell us, is that informal economies were not undermined by modernization, but persist, and play a functional role in the global economy (Friedmann and Wolf 1984). The informal economy remains as much as half of the GNP of many Latin American nations, even without factoring in the drug trade (Jimenez 1989). The fall of the Soviet Union has also greatly expanded "black markets," not undermined them (Rawlinson 1998), and new Russian gangs have joined an international criminal economy (Castells 1998). Gangs are among those institutions that comprise what Bourdieu and Wacquant call a "field" or "sub-field" of the informal economy with its own "socially structured space," "particular values," and "regulative principles" (Bourdieu and Wacquant 1992, 99–106). Chicago's post–World War II African American gangs institutionalized in this new international environment of permanent informal economies.

The 1960s in Chicago might be seen as a classic case study of competing pressures on street organizations from revolutionary politics and the rackets. Revolutionary groups, like the Black Panthers and Young Lords, competed with the gangs for the allegiance of street youth. At the same time, the new black gangs took control of the drug traffic and other underground services and permanently displaced the Italian Outfit (Lombardo 2002). Black gangs also were politicized, as Jeff Fort led mass demonstrations for black jobs (Perkins 2002; Williams 2001) and Martin Luther King met with the Vice Lords at the beginning of his Chicago open housing campaign. This rapprochement of the gangs and civil rights organizations was viewed as a major threat by the city machine and federal authorities, who used both overt violence and covert means to sow discord between the two (see Fry 1973). The police murder of Black Panther leader Fred Hampton, Euseni Perkins (2002) claims, was the result of Hampton's efforts to unite the gangs and politicize them.

The civil rights movement, in the end, accomplished little for those on the streets (for example, Piven 1973; Venkatesh 2000) who, through riots and militant organizations had emerged as major social actors. Massive housing projects, built to contain Chicago's ghetto, trapped hundreds of thousands of African Americans in third-world-like conditions. The black community became "de-politicized" (Reed 1995), with the black vote declining from 60 percent in 1964 to 37 percent in 1976 (Erie 1988). Daley's "war on gangs" (Chicago Police Department 1969) sent gang members by the hundreds into the prisons, and Chicago's police unleashed a reign of violence against gangs and nationalist organizations alike. One result, as Luis Rodriguez (2001) asserts, was that the political organizations that sought to organize the streets collapsed while the gangs persisted. Disillusionment with the broken promises of civil rights leaders led to a strengthening of a racialized gang identity that was related more to "hustling" than politics, in a process remarkably similar to the post-Soweto student uprising in South Africa (Glaser 2000).

With the 1970s collapse of the industrial economy, so vividly portrayed by Wilson (1987), and feeling abandoned by middle-class allies, Chicago's 1950s "super-gangs" did not fade away. In the 1980s, the cocaine economy prompted the gangs to expand and reorganize. Black Gangster Disciple leader Larry Hoover's "new concept" of a centrally organized economic and political enterprise (Williams 2001) was just one example of the conscious way Chicago's gangs institutionalized in postindustrial conditions. In the twilight years of the twentieth century, Chicago's gangs restructured and prioritized economics over politics (see Hagedorn 1998; Venkatesh and Leavitt 2000).[3]

Centralized organization, despite law enforcement's simplistic notions of gangs as organized crime (for example, Knox 1996), was neither functional nor necessary for the persistence of Chicago's neighborhood-based gangs (see DiMaggio and Powell 1983). The institutionalization of gangs did not automatically mean the construction of hierarchical crime syndicates. Rather, institutionalization meant that the gang provided its members with "basic constructions of reality so that the way a particular activity is organized seems obvious, natural, and appropriate" (Jenness and Grattet 2001, 11).

In other words, as gangs persisted over decades, their symbols, colors, traditions, and rivals all became an expected and "normal" part of the life of the neighborhood, although many residents condemn gang activities. A gang culture orders the world, and its members act in ways that seem "obvious, natural and appropriate." By the 1980s, the drug game had also become "natural" for street organizations, which experimented with a variety of organizational forms in spaces of "conflict and competition" (Bourdieu and Wacquant 1992, 17). Like Capone's bootleggers, the vast sums of money at the command of drug-dealing gangs and their occasional "charity" would promote a rationalized myth of the gang as an organization dedicated to helping the community.

Many of today's gangs are an institutionalized bricolage of illicit enterprise, social athletic club, patron to the poor, employment agency for youth, substitute family, and nationalist, community, or militant organization. This institutionalization of gangs, as we have seen, has a long Chicago tradition. However, black gangs differ from their early Irish and Italian relatives in their social exclusion within segregated ghettoes and in their inability to manipulate the levers of real power.

A postindustrial informal economy, arising to service the ghetto's needs, was essential to the institutionalization of Chicago's gangs. One other institution played an equally prominent role: the prison.

## THE PENAL CITY: GLOBALIZATION AND THE REVANCHIST STATE

> But perhaps one should reverse the problem and ask oneself what is served by the failure of the prison?
>
> —Michel Foucault, *Discipline and Punish: The Birth of the Prison*

It has been a central tenet of the literature that gangs in prison are different than gangs in the community (for example, Fleisher and Decker 2001). But such reasoning misses what is most important about today's relationship between prison, the gang, and the ghetto.

Chicago gangs like the Vice Lords (Dawley 1992) got their start not in neighborhood conflicts but in the St. Charles Juvenile Correctional Facility. As Rev. John Fry put it, the Blackstone Rangers more resembled a "prisoners' organization" than a gang. "As they came out of St. Charles, they were convinced of the idea that America (i.e., the America they knew) is a jail in pretty much the same way St. Charles is a jail. They had gone from one jail, Woodlawn, to another jail, St. Charles, then returned to the Woodlawn jail" (1973, 33).

Jacobs (1977) and Moore (1978) both stressed the importance of the linkage between gangs on the streets and behind bars following extensive repression in Chicago and Los Angeles. Today, all Chicago street gangs' major leaders are incarcerated, and the chain of command, at least formally, always runs from the prison to the neighborhood (Perkins 2002). The vast expansion of incarceration has meant the normalizing of the prison experience for gang youth. The prison is an extension of gang life today, not a radical break. "The prison experience," Venkatesh and Leavitt point out, "became another page in street gang mythology" (2000, 437).

What has occurred in U.S. cities over the past decades has been the consolidation of what Neil Smith (1996) calls the "revanchist state," or the pursuit of vengeful policies that criminalize the urban poor. President Nixon initiated a vast expansion of the criminal justice system with rates of incarceration rising sharply in the 1970s (Mauer 1999). In that same period, a "return to the city" pushed the issue of safety for the gentry to the top of the urban agenda and incarceration became a reliable tool for making "frontier" city spaces safe. Aggressive "community policing" has allowed Cook County jail—with a daily population of more than 10,000—to replace Robert Taylor Homes as the largest residential dwelling in Chicago.

The prison is linked to the ghetto in more ways than as a revolving door for gang members. With a decline in unionized working-class jobs, Wacquant points out, the prison no longer regulates labor, but, like the ghetto, has adopted functions of repression and exclusion. "What makes the racial intercession of the carcereal system different today is that, unlike slavery, Jim Crow and the ghetto of the mid-century, it does not carry out a positive economic mission of recruitment and disciplining of the workforce: it serves only to warehouse the precarious and de-proletarianized fractions of the black working class" (2000, 385).

Any belief that incarceration rates increase in hard economic times and retract in good times (for example, Colvin 1992; Rusche and Kirchheimer 1939) was exploded in the last decades as both the economy and prison populations boomed. While the U.S. industrial economy drew the unskilled labor of millions abroad to fit into urban factories, the global economy locates anywhere it can find cheap "generic labor." Marginal populations, which cannot compete on the global labor market, become economically irrelevant. However, when such socially excluded populations are located in cities, they pose a direct, and immediate, security threat. "The U.S. ghetto today," Marcuse generalizes, "is an outcast ghetto, differing in its definition and role from the historic black ghettoes in that its inhabitants are the excluded and the castaway rather than the subordinated and restricted" (1997, 229).

Thus the control of the poor, as Wacquant argues, is not tied to the regulation of labor but rather unites the ghetto and prison as spaces of social exclusion. The ghetto and prison are both institutions that possess permanent functions of social control. Gangs today might be best defined as organizations of the socially excluded simultaneously occupying the spaces of both prison and ghetto.

## Conclusion

Robert Park and his colleagues brought a change in social science thinking by directly observing how urbanization, industrialization, and ethnic succession were among the spatial processes that gave rise to Chicago's first gangs. Today, direct observation of various social actors in the city is needed to understand how the redivision of space in the global city influences twenty-first-century gangs.

The trope of the central city as citadel, defending the gentry against the natives, may be a useful way to conceptualize gangs and neighborhoods. Lefebvre's (1996) notion of the production of "social space" might profitably be superimposed on Cloward and Ohlin's (1960) concept of licit and illicit opportunity structures, linking urban political economy with criminology. Urban processes such as gentrification, community policing, and the tearing down of housing projects produce "abstract spaces" that have utility for the powerful but also have the unintended effect of producing different kinds of "social spaces" with different modes of gang activity.

In Chicago, the institutionalization of gangs has been historically tied to segregation and the ghetto, but the process of gang institutionalization may, in fact, be more universal. There appears to be a worldwide increase in groups of armed young men. With the advent of globalization, the rise of the drug economy, and the breakup of the socialist camp, many political groups have transformed into gangs. For example, as Michael Manley's PNP failed to deliver the goods, Jamaican "posses" turned decisively toward the criminal economy (Gunst 1995). In Belfast, Protestant militias turned, in their disillusionment, to drug trafficking (Michael Morrissey, personal communication, 2001). The fall of the Soviet Union has meant not only the international rise of the Russian mafia but the expansion of illegal economies in Eastern Europe. The World Bank estimates that up to 25 percent of young men in Albania have become involved in the criminal economy (La Cava and Nanetti 2000).

In Chicago, there has been a historic relationship between gangs, the underground economy, and politics, and this also appears to be the case worldwide. Chinese Triads, as Booth (1999) argues, played political roles with the Kuomintang and were long active in anti-Q'ing and anti-Communist politics. The political history of the Sicilian mafia is well documented (for example, Ianni 1972). Gangs, as armed young men, globally and historically, appear to be politically involved in some conditions and more intent on the underground economy in others (Hobsbawm 1959, 1969; Pinnock 1984).

There appears to be an internal logic to the structure of the postindustrial underground economy. If the network is everywhere replacing solitary corporations (Castells 1996), gangs and other kinds of networks now dominate informal economic ventures. The idea that these underground economic actors will remain forever "demobilized" (Reed 1995) or depoliticized is not in keeping with international experience. In the global era, armed militias with variable ties to state structures are regularly holding center stage. While Chicago's street organizations are not "terrorists" in any way, it must be recognized that, in given conditions gangs as armed young men can play an economic, political, or military role.

Elias's (1939/1994) modernist notion that we are on a steady climb toward civilization finds few adherents in Chicago's gangland. What may be most out of date in social disorganization theory are its not-so-hidden assumptions of the progressive direction of history and the inevitable incorporation of "disorganized" remnants of the old world—and casualties of the new—into a more rational order. Castells's (1998) concept of the dark ghetto as a "black hole" similarly fails to capture the diversity of the processes of institutionalization that shape organizations of the socially excluded in the field of informal economic ventures.

The Chicago School encouraged social scientists for decades to frame gangs through concepts of human ecology, social disorganization, and ethnic succession. This essay proposes we do not discard but update the Chicagoans' ecological framework by looking at globalization and its redivision of urban space in various cities. As in the past, today we find the coexistence of both institutionalized and interstitial gangs. However, the institutionalization of gangs and other organizations of the socially excluded appears to be characteristic of the postmodern era. "Space" and "race" might be good twenty-first-century starting points for a theoretical reconsideration of gangs in the global city.

## Notes

"Blackstone Rangers" excerpt reprinted by consent of Brooks Permissions.

1. "Rationalized myths" are the common understandings people have about institutions, lending them the legitimacy that allows them to persist. Examples are "schools educate," "police protect," and "doctors heal," or in this case, "the gang protects." This differs from Merton's more positive view of "latent functions" of the rackets (1957/1968, 126–36; see also Bell 1960 and Whyte 1943).

2. One final, rather ironical note: When Thrasher moved to New York University, he described how he went off in search of a youth gang that fit his Chicago definition. He finally located a group of kids aged ten through fourteen on a corner in Greenwich Village, took them joyriding in his car, bought them treats, and took them to his apartment. There, he "suggested they take a name" and form a gang, so he could study them (1928). So much for spontaneity.

3. The drug game has also both reinforced gender roles (Maher and Daley 1996) and created new roles for women (Padilla and Santiago 1993), which have become more important as welfare benefits disappear.

## References

Bell, Daniel. 1960. *The End of Ideology: On the Exhaustion of Political Ideas in the Fifties.* New York: Free Press.

Betancar, John J., Isabel Domeyko, and Patricia A. Wright. 2001. "Gentrification in

West Town: Contested Ground." Voorhees Center for Neighborhood and Community Improvement. University of Illinois-Chicago.

Body-Gendrot, Sophie. 2000. *The Social Control of Cities?* Oxford: Blackwell.

Booth, Martin. 1999. *The Dragon Syndicates: The Global Phenomenon of the Triads.* New York: Carroll and Graf.

Bourdieu, Pierre, and Loïc J. D. Wacquant. 1992. *An Invitation to Reflexive Sociology.* Chicago: University of Chicago Press.

Caldiera, Teresa P.. 2000. *City of Walls: Crime, Segregation, and Citizenship in São Paulo.* Berkeley: University of California Press.

Candelero, Dominic. 1984. "Chicago's Italians: A Survey of the Ethnic Factor, 1850–1990." In *Ethnic Chicago: A Multicultural Portrait,* ed. Melvin G. Hollis and Peter d'A. Jones, 229–59. Grand Rapids, Mich.: William B. Eerdmans.

Castells, Manuel. 1979. *The Urban Question: A Marxist Approach.* Cambridge, Mass.: MIT Press.

———. 1996. *The Information Age: Economy, Society, and Culture.* Vol. 1: *The Rise of The Network Society.* Malden, Mass.: Blackwell.

———. 1997. *The Information Age: Economy, Society, and Culture.* Vol. 2: *The Power of Identity.* Malden, Mass.: Blackwell.

———. 1998. *The Information Age: Economy, Society, and Culture.* Vol. 3: *End of Millennium.* Malden, Mass.: Blackwell.

Chicago Commission on Race Relations. 1922. "The Negro in Chicago." Chicago: Chicago Commission on Race Relations.

Chicago Gang History Project. University of Illinois-Chicago.

Chicago Police Department. 1969. "Organized Youth Crime in Chicago." Chicago: Police Department.

Cloward, Richard, and Lloyd Ohlin. 1960. *Delinquency and Opportunity.* Glencoe, Ill.: Free Press.

Colvin, Mark. 1992. *The Penitentiary in Crisis: From Accommodation to Riot in New Mexico.* Albany: SUNY Press.

Cronon, William. 1991. *Nature's Metropolis: Chicago and the Great West.* New York: W. W. Norton.

Davis, M. 1990. *City of Quartz.* New York: Vintage.

———. 1998. *Ecology of Fear: Los Angeles and the Imagination of Disaster.* New York: Vintage.

Dawley, David. 1992. *A Nation of Lords: The Autobiography of the Vice Lords.* Prospect Heights, Ill.: Waveland Press.

Dear, Michael J., ed. 2000. *From Chicago to L.A.: Making Sense of Urban Theory.* Thousand Oaks, Calif.: Sage.

DiMaggio, Paul J., and Walter W. Powell. 1983. "The Iron Cage Revisited: Institutional Isomorphism and Collective Rationality in Organizational Fields." *American Sociological Review* 48: 147–60.

Drake, St. Clair, and Horace R. Cayton. 1970. *Black Metropolis.* New York: Harcourt, Brace, and World.

Du Bois, W. E. B. 1899/1967. *The Philadelphia Negro: A Social Study.* New York: Shocken Books.

———. 1902/1989. *The Souls of Black Folk.* New York: Penguin Books.

Elias, Norman. 1939/1994. *The Civilizing Process: The History of Manners.* Oxford: Blackwell.

Erie, Steven P. 1988. *Rainbow's End: From the Old to the New Urban Ethnic Politics.* Berkeley: University of California Press.

Fleisher, Mark, and Scott Decker. 2001. *Corrections Management Quarterly.*

Foucault, Michel. 1979. *Discipline and Punish: The Birth of the Prison.* New York: Vintage.

Friedmann, John, and Goetz Wolf. 1984. "World City Formation: An Agenda for Research and Action." *International Journal of Urban and Regional Research* 6: 309–44.

Fry, John R. 1973. *Locked-Out Americans: A Memoir.* New York: Harper and Row.

Funchion, Michael E. 1984. "Irish Chicago: Church, Homeland, Politics, and Class: The Shaping of an Ethnic Group, 1870–1900." In *Ethnic Chicago: A Multicultural Portrait,* ed. Melvin G. Hollis and Peter d'A. Jones, 57–228. Grand Rapids, Mich.: William B. Eerdmans.

Glaser, C. 2000. *Bo-Tsotsi: The Youth Gangs of Soweto, 1935–1976.* Portsmouth, N.H.: James Curry, David Philip.

Greenberg, Stanley B. 1980. *Race and State in Capitalist Development.* New Haven, Conn.: Yale University Press.

Gunst, Laurie. 1995. *Born Fi' Dead: A Journey Through the Jamaican Posse Underworld.* New York: Henry Holt.

Hagedorn, John M. 1998. *People and Folks: Gangs, Crime, and the Underclass in a Rustbelt City,* 2nd ed. Chicago: Lakeview Press.

Haller, Mark A. 1984. "Ethnic Crime: The Organized Underworld of Early 20th Century Chicago." In *Ethnic Chicago: A Multicultural Portrait,* ed. Melvin G. Hollis and Peter d'A. Jones, 557–72. Grand Rapids, Mich.: William B. Eerdmans.

Harvey, David. 1990. *The Condition of Postmodernity.* Cambridge, Mass.: Blackwell.

Hirsch, Arnold R. 1983. *Making the Second Ghetto: Race and Housing in Chicago 1940–1960.* Cambridge: Cambridge University Press.

Hobsbawm, E. J. 1959. *Primitive Rebels: Studies in Archaic Forms of Social Movements in the Nineteenth and Twentieth Centuries.* New York: Norton.

———. 1969. *Bandits.* New York: Pantheon.

Huff, C. Ronald, ed. 2001. *Gangs in America.* Thousand Oaks, Calif.: Sage.

Ianni, Fracisca J. 1972. *Family Business: Kinship and Social Control in Organized Crime.* New York: Russell Sage.

Jacobs, James. 1977. *Stateville.* Chicago: University of Chicago.

Jenness, Valerie, and Ryken Grattet. 2001. *Making Hate a Crime: From Social Movement to Law Enforcement*. New York: Russell Sage.

Jimenez, Jose Blanes. 1989. "Cocaine, Informality, and the Urban Economy in La Paz, Bolivia." In *The Informal Economy: Studies in Advanced and Less Developed Countries*, ed. Alejandro Portes, Manuel Castells, and Lauren A. Benton, 135–49. Baltimore: Johns Hopkins University Press.

Klein, Malcolm, Hans-Jurgen Kerner, Cheryl L. Maxsen, and Elmar G. M. Weitekamp, eds. 2001. *The Eurogang Paradox: Street Gangs and Youth Groups in the U.S. and Europe*. Dordrecht, Netherlands: Kluwer.

Knox, George. 1996. *An Introduction to Gangs*. Chicago: Wyndham Hall Press.

La Cava, Gloria, and Rafaella Y. Nanetti. 2000. "Albania: Fight the Vulnerability Gap." Washington, D.C.: World Bank.

Landesco, John. 1929/1968. *Organized Crime in Chicago*. Chicago: University of Chicago Press.

Lefebvre, Henri. 1996. *Writings on Cities*. Oxford: Blackwell.

Light, Ivan. 1977. "The Ethnic Vice Industry: 1880–1944." *American Sociological Review* 42: 464–79.

Lombardo, Robert M. 2002. Lecture to the Chicago Gang History Project.

Lombardo, Robert M., and Arthur J. Lurigio. 1995. "Joining the Chicago Outfit: Speculations about the Racket Subculture and Roving Neighborhoods." In *Contemporary Issues in Organized Crime*, ed. Jay Albanese, 87–109. Monsey, N.Y.: Criminal Justice Press.

Maher, Lisa, and Kathleen Daly. 1996. "Women in the Street-Level Drug Economy: Continuity or Change?" *Criminology* 34: 465–92.

Marcuse, Peter. 1997. "The Enclave, the Citadel, and the Ghetto: What Has Changed in the Post-Fordist U.S. City." *Urban Affairs Review* 33: 228–64.

Marcuse, Peter, and Ronald van Kempen. 2000. "Conclusion: A Changed Spatial Order." In *Globalizing Cities: A New Spatial Order?* ed. Peter Marcuse and Ronald van Kempen, 249–75. Oxford: Blackwell.

Mauer, Marc. 1999. *Race to Incarcerate*. New York: New Press.

Maxson, Cheryl L., and Malcolm Klein. 2000. "'Play Groups' No Longer: Urban Street Gangs in the Los Angeles Region." In *From Chicago to L.A.: Making Sense of Urban Theory*, ed. Michael J. Dear. Thousand Oaks, Calif.: Sage.

Mendez, Mervin. 2002. Interview with the Chicago Gang History Project. http://www.gangresearch.net/latinkings/lkhistory.html.

Merton, Robert K. 1957/1968. *Social Theory and Social Structure*. New York: Free Press.

Meyer, John M., and Brian Rowan. 1977. "Institutionalized Organizations: Formal Structure as Myth and Ceremony." *American Journal of Sociology* 83, no. 2: 340–63.

Molotch, Harvey. 1976. "The City as Growth Machine: Toward a Political Economy of Place." *American Journal of Sociology* 82: 309–32.

Moore, Joan W. 1978. *Homeboys: Gangs, Drugs, and Prison in the Barrios of Los Angeles.* Philadelphia: Temple University Press.

Padilla, Felix. 1987. *Puerto Rican Chicago.* Notre Dame, Ind.: University of Notre Dame Press.

Padilla, Felix M., and Lourdes Santiago. 1993. *Outside the Wall: A Puerto Rican Woman's Struggle.* New Brunswick, N.J.: Rutgers.

PBS (Public Broadcasting Service). 1995. "Daley: The Last Boss." Narrated by Hal Holbrook.

Perkins, Useni Eugene. 1987. *Explosion of Chicago's Black Street Gangs.* Chicago: Third World Press.

———. 2002. Lecture to the Chicago Gang History Project. http://www.gangresearch .net/Courses/history/Perkins.html.

Pinderhughes, Howard. 1993. "The Anatomy of Racially Motivated Violence in New York City: A Case Study of Youth in Southern Brooklyn." *Social Problems* 40: 478–92.

Pinnock, Don. 1984. *The Brotherhoods: Street Gangs and State Control in Cape Town.* Cape Town: David Philip.

Piven, Frances Fox. 1973. "The Urban Crisis: Who Got What and Why," in *1984 Revisited,* ed. Robert Paul Wolff. Amherst, Mass.: Alfred A. Knopf.

Portes, Alejandro, Manuel Castells, and Lauren A. Benton, eds. 1989. *The Informal Economy: Studies in Advanced and Less Advanced Countries.* Baltimore: Johns Hopkins University Press.

Rast, Joel. 1999. *Remaking Chicago: The Political Origins of Urban Industrial Change.* DeKalb: Northern Illinois University Press.

Rawlinson, Paddy. 1998. "Criminal Heirs: Organized Crime and Russian Youth." In *Gangs and Youth Subcultures: International Explorations,* ed. Kayleen Hazlehurst and Cameron Hazlehurst, 94–115. New Brunswick, N.J.: Transaction Publishers.

Reed, Adolph, Jr. 1995. "Demobilization in the New Black Political Regime: Ideological Capitulation and Radical Failure in the Postsegregation Era." In *The Bubbling Cauldron: Race, Ethnicity, and the Urban Crisis,* ed. Michael Peter Smith and Joe R. Feagin, 182–208. Minneapolis: University of Minnesota Press.

Rodriguez, Luis. 2001. *Hearts and Hands: Creating Community in Violent Times.* New York: Seven Stories Press.

Rusche, Georg, and Otto Kirchheimer. 1939. *Punishment and Social Structure.* New York: Columbia University Press.

Sampson, Robert J. 2001. "How Do Communities Undergird or Undermine Human Development? Relevant Contexts and Social Mechanisms." In *Does It Take a Village? Community Effects on Children, Adolescents, and Families,* ed. Alan Booth and Ann Crouter, 3–30. Mahwah, N.J.: Lawrence Erlbaum Associates.

Sassen, Saskia. 1991. *The Global City: New York, London, Tokyo.* Princeton, N.J.: Princeton University Press.

Scott, W. Richard. 1995. *Institutions and Organizations.* Thousand Oaks, Calif.: Sage.

Selznick, Philip. 1957. *Leadership in Administration: A Sociological Interpretation.* Berkeley: University of California Press.

Sennett, Richard, ed. 1969. *Classic Essays on the Culture of Cities.* Englewood Cliffs, N.J.: Prentice-Hall.

———. 1994. *Flesh and Stone: The Body and the City in Western Civilization.* New York: W. W. Norton.

Short, James F., Jr. 1963. Introduction to *The Gang,* ed. James F. Short Jr. Chicago: University of Chicago Press.

Short, James F., Jr., and Fred L. Strodtbeck. 1965. *Group Process and Gang Delinquency.* Chicago: University of Chicago Press.

Sibley, David. 1995. *Geographies of Exclusion: Society and Difference in the West.* New York: Routledge.

Smith, Janet L. 1998. "Cleaning Up Public Housing by Sweeping Out the Poor." *Habitat International* 23: 49–62.

Smith, Neil. 1996. *The New Urban Frontier: Gentrification and the Revanchist State.* London: Routledge.

Stepick, Alex. 1989. "Miami's Two Informal Sectors." In *The Informal Economy: Studies in Advanced and Less Advanced Countries,* ed. Alejandro Portes, Manuel Castells, and Lauren A. Benton, 111–34. Baltimore: Johns Hopkins University Press.

Suttles, Gerald D. 1968. *The Social Order of the Slum.* Chicago: University of Chicago Press.

———. 1990. *The Man-Made City: The Land-Use Confidence Game in Chicago.* Chicago: University of Chicago Press.

Thrasher, Frederic. 1927. *The Gang.* Chicago: University of Chicago Press.

———. 1928. "How to Study the Boys' Gang in the Open." *Journal of Educational Sociology* 1: 244–54.

Valier, Claire. 2003. "Foreigners, Crime, and Changing Mobilities." *British Journal of Criminology* 43, no. 1: 1–21.

Venkatesh, Sudhir Alladi. 1996. "The Gang in the Community." In *Gangs in America,* 2nd ed., ed. Ronald C. Huff, 241–56. Thousand Oaks, Calif.: Sage.

———. 2000. *American Project: The Rise and Fall of a Modern Ghetto.* Cambridge, Mass.: Harvard University Press.

Venkatesh, Sudhir Alladi, and Steven D. Leavitt. 2000. "'Are We a Family or a Business?' History and Disjuncture in the Urban American Street Gang." *Theory and Society* 29: 427–62.

Wacquant, Loïc. 1997. "Urban Outcasts." In *Globalization and the Black Diaspora: The New Urban Challenge,* ed. Charles Green, 331–55. Albany: State University of New York.

———. 2000. "The New 'Peculiar Institution': On the Prison as Surrogate Ghetto." *Theoretical Criminology* 4: 377–89.

Whyte, William Foote. 1943. *Street Corner Society.* Chicago: University of Chicago Press.

Williams, Lance. 2001. Lecture to the Chicago Gang History Project. http://www.gangresearch.net/ganghistory/UrbanCrisis/Blackstone/lance.htm.

Wilson, William Julius. 1978. *The Declining Significance of Race.* Chicago: University of Chicago Press.

———. 1987. *The Truly Disadvantaged.* Chicago: University of Chicago Press.

Winant, Howard. 1995. "Dictatorship, Democracy, and Difference: The Historical Construction of Racial Identity." In *The Bubbling Cauldron: Race, Ethnicity, and the Urban Crisis,* ed. Michael Peter Smith and Joe R. Feagin, 31–49. Minneapolis: University of Minnesota Press.

Wirth, Louis. 1928/1956. *The Ghetto.* Chicago: University of Chicago Press.

Young, Jock. 1999. *The Exclusive Society.* London: Sage.

Zorbaugh, Harvey Warren. 1929/1961. *The Gold Coast and the Slum: A Sociological Study of Chicago's Near North Side.* Chicago: University of Chicago Press.

Zukin, Sharon. 1991. *Landscapes of Power.* Berkeley: University of California Press.

# 2

# Three Pernicious Premises in the Study of the American Ghetto

## LOÏC J. D. WACQUANT

> Now, what led men to consider these mythological
> propositions or beliefs as true? Was it because they had
> confronted them with a given reality? Not at all . . . It is,
> on the contrary, our ideas, our beliefs which confer on the
> objects of thought their reality.
>
> —Emile Durkheim, *Pragmatisme et sociologie*

Three deep-seated proclivities or premises have dominated the recent debate on racial division and urban poverty in the United States. These premises are rooted in long-standing American conceptions of the poor—and particularly the black poor—as morally defective and of the city as a nefarious place that disrupts and corrupts social life, especially among the lower classes (Boyer 1978; Fishman 1988; Katz 1983; Patterson 1986). Endowed with plausibility by the weight of cultural history and intellectual inertia, reinforced by an individualistic national idiom that de-emphasizes class and euphemizes ethnoracial domination, they form the cornerstones of the current *academic doxa* on the topic and therefore typically go unargued and unquestioned.[1] Yet these underlying tenets truncate and distort our understanding of the ongoing (re)articulation of color, class, and place in the American metropolis.

The first, more recent, tendency is the *dilution of the notion of ghetto* simply to designate an urban area of widespread and intense poverty, which obfuscates the racial basis and character of this poverty and divests the term of both historical meaning and sociological content. The second, century-old, tenet is the idea that the ghetto is a "disorganized" social formation that can be analyzed wholly in terms of *lack and deficiencies* (individual or collective) rather than by positively identifying the principles that underlie its internal order and govern its specific mode of functioning. The third, flowing from the idea of disorganization, is the *tendency to exoticize the ghetto* and its residents, that is, to highlight the most extreme and unusual aspects of ghetto life as seen from outside and above, that is, from the standpoint of the dominant. Each of these premises is associated with a series of analytical missteps and slippages that are so commonly effectuated as to go unnoticed or, worse, to appear to be woven into the fabric of the phenomenon itself. Together, they make up a formidable "epistemological obstacle" (Bachelard 1938) to a theoretically rigorous and empirically accurate sociology of racial conflict and urban marginality in contemporary America inasmuch as they converge to efface the boundary between commonsense perception and social scientific analysis, between the contested and complex realities to be elucidated and what people deeply desire to believe about them.[2] The following examination of these pernicious premises is offered as a critical prolegomenon to such a sociology.

## Retrieving an Institutionalist Conception of the Ghetto

Recent discussions of race and poverty in the American "inner city" have tended to equate the ghetto with any perimeter of high poverty irrespective of population and organizational makeup. Paul Jargowski and Mary-Jo Bane offer an exemplar of this common elision of the racial and institutional dimension of the notion of ghetto when they write:

> We have defined ghetto as an area in which the overall poverty rate in a census tract is greater than 40 percent. The ghetto poor are then *those poor, of any race or ethnic group,* who live in such high-poverty census tracts . . . Visits to various cities confirmed that the 40 percent criterion came very close to identifying areas that *looked like ghettos* in terms of their *housing* conditions. Moreover, the areas selected by the 40 percent criterion corresponded closely with the neighborhoods *that city officials and local Census Bureau officials considered ghettos* . . . It is important to distinguish our definition of ghetto tracts based on a poverty criterion from a definition based on racial composition. Not all majority black tracts are ghettos under our definition nor are all ghettos black. (1991, 239, 241; emphasis added)

This (re)definition of the term deserves to be quoted at length because it cumulates nearly all of the flaws that have marred recent such usages of the term: (1) it is perfectly arbitrary (as its authors readily concede on page 239): why exclude rural or even suburban zones and use census tracts as catchment area, the official "poverty line" as measuring rod, and a rate of 40 percent poor persons as cutoff point? (2) it is asociological in that it is pegged on household income (a notoriously unreliable item in standardized surveys, especially among irregularly employed populations) and on the visual state of housing stock, irrespective of the patterning of social and economic relations that determine them; (3) it is ostensibly "deracialized" when in fact it denotes only urban enclaves of colored poverty, to the virtual exclusion of poor white areas; (4) it is essentially bureaucratic, derivative of administrative categories, since the viability of the concept is premised on the existence and availability of government data such as the Census Bureau designation of "poverty area"; finally, (5) it unabashedly conflates a historical-analytical concept with the lay notions held by municipal and state elites ("what city officials and local Census officials considered ghettos") without any possibility of assessing what these folk perceptions might be that serve as warrant for the delineation of the object under study.[3]

This is to forget that most urban areas of "extreme poverty" (however measured) in America's Rust Belt are the direct heirs of yesteryear's urban "Black Belts." To say that they are ghettos because they are poor is to reverse social and historical causation: it is *because they were and are ghettos* that joblessness and misery are unusually acute and persistent in them—not the other way around. To call any area exhibiting a high rate or concentration of poverty a ghetto is not only arbitrary and empirically problematic; it robs the term of its historical meaning and obliterates its sociological import, thereby thwarting investigation of the criteria and processes whereby exclusion effectively operates in it. And it obscures the fact that blacks are the only group ever to have experienced ghettoization in American society, that is, involuntary, permanent, and total residential separation premised on caste as basis for the development of a *parallel (and inferior) social structure.*[4]

As suggested by the historic origins and historiographic usage of the term (Wirth 1928, 11–62; Cooperman and Curiel 1990), a ghetto is not simply a topographic entity or an aggregation of poor families and individuals but an *institutional form*, a historically determinate, spatially based concatenation of mechanisms of *ethnoracial closure and control* (Wacquant 1991).[5] In ideal-typical terms, a ghetto may be characterized as a bounded, racially and/or culturally uniform sociospatial formation based on (1) the forcible relegation of (2) a "negatively typed" population (Weber 1818–20/1978, 385–87), such as Jews in medieval Europe and African Americans in the modern United States, to (3) a reserved, "frontier territory" (Hogan 1980) in which this population (4) develops under duress a set of parallel institutions that serve both as a functional substitute for, and as a protective buffer against, the dominant institutions of the encompassing society (Meier and Rudwick 1976, 232–70; Spear 1968) but (5) duplicate the latter only at an incomplete and inferior level while (6) maintaining those who rely on them in a state of structural dependency (Fusfeld and Bates 1984; Logan and Molotoch 1987; Weaver 1948). Put differently, the ghetto is an ethnoracial formation that combines and inscribes in the objectivity of space and group-specific institutions all four major "elementary forms" of racial domination, namely, categorization, discrimination, segregation, and exclusionary violence (Wacquant 1995).

The fact that ghettos have historically been places of endemic and often acute material misery does not mean that a ghetto has to be poor, nor that it has to be uniformly deprived. Certainly, the "Bronzeville" of the 1940s was more prosperous than southern black communities and contained perhaps the largest and most affluent Afro-American bourgeoisie of its era (Drake and Cayton 1945/1962; also Trotter 1993, for a broader discussion). Conversely, not all low-income areas are ghettos, however extreme their destitution. Declining white cities of the deindustrializing Midwest or of the Appalachian hollows, depressed rural counties of the Mississippi delta, Native American reservations and poor barrios of the Southwest (not to mention vast sections of the United States during the Great Depression) do not present the organizational pattern of the "dark ghetto": they are not, nor have they ever been, "philanthropic, economic, business and industrial colonies" of the wider white society (Clark 1965; also Connolly 1977).[6]

An institutionalist (that is, relational) conception of the ghetto is not only more consistent with the historic root and usage of the term. It foregrounds and interrogates variables that more nominalistic or gradational approaches tend to treat as background conditions requiring no further investigation, such as racial division, whose structural effects may vary over time even when rates remain unchanged, the weak presence and functional inefficacy of those public service institutions that are standard organizational fixtures of other urban neighborhoods, the protrusive role of police and penal institutions, and the absence of "an indigenous exchange value engine" (Logan and Molotoch 1987, 131; Davis 1990, 304–9). In particular, the institutionalist definition problematizes that which a linear, "demographic" perspective takes for granted: the bases and mechanisms of triage that determine relegation within the penalized space of the ghetto. And instead of situating the latter along *continuous* linear distributions of income, housing, segregation, or neighborhood poverty, an institutionalist approach seeks to locate *underlying breaks* in the urban fabric and to trace the (re)drawing of the dividing lines of which the ghetto is the physical manifestation.[7]

Accordingly, the boundaries, form, internal makeup, external linkages, and structural supports of the territory of exclusion considered all become central questions that have to be answered by empirical analysis rather than dissolved by definitional fiat. And each of the traits that compose the ideal type of the ghetto sketched above—constraint, stigma, territorial separation and boundlessness, institutional differentiation and parallelism, functional duplication and dependency—can be turned into a variable subjected to precise measurement, as can their degree of mutual "meshing."

## Forsaking the Trope of "Disorganization"

Anthropologist Arjun Appadurai (1988) has shown that certain places come cumulatively to be represented and discussed in terms of strong tropes, that is, recurrent sets of images and narrative strategies that predetermine and skew the ways in which they are perceived and conceptualized. In American society and social science, the strong trope enveloping the ghetto since its origins at the close of last century has been that of "disorganization."[8]

From the early Chicago school of human ecology to studies of the urban crisis of the 1960s to recent inquiries into the emergence of the so-called underclass and its fearsome implications (for example, Anderson 1991; Banfield 1970; Frazier 1949; Harrell and Peterson 1992; Jencks and Peterson 1991; Park and Burgess 1925; Shaw and McKay 1942; Wilson 1987; Wirth 1928), analysts have accepted as a given that the ghetto can be satisfactorily analyzed in essentially *privative terms,* by pinpointing its shortcomings and those of its residents and by specifying how (and how much) both diverge from "mainstream" society as measured by a putative "middle class" usually left undefined so that their boundaries may be stretched at will to fit the analytic or ideological need at hand.[9] Thus the ghetto is characteristically represented as a place of *disorder and lack,* a repository of concentrated unruliness, deviance, anomie, and atomization, replete with behaviors said to offend common precepts of morality and propriety, whether by excess (as with crime, sexuality, and fertility) or by default (in the case of work, thrift, and family).[10]

This profile in defect—in the twofold sense of portraiture and epistemology—is deeply entrenched in American social science. Historian Alice O'Connor (1995) has shown that the assimilationist framework of the Chicago school consistently depicted "poverty, social 'disorganization' and segregation as inevitable outcomes" of the quasibiotic "processes of city growth" and studiously omitted the strategies of employers and the "role of politics and local government in creating and maintaining ghettos." E. Franklin Frazier, the first African American chair of Chicago's sociology department, all but equated the northern urbanization of blacks with disorganization. His analysis of *The Negro Family in Chicago* (1931) stressed the marital disruption, moral decadence, material destitution, crime and vice into which "Negroes" inevitably sunk upon migrating into the industrial metropolis. Revealingly, he elevated family structure to the rank of cardinal indicator of social disorganization among the African American community—anticipating by a full half-century one of the chief concerns and strategies of his successor William Julius Wilson (1987) in *The Truly Disadvantaged*.[11]

Understanding the ghetto as an institutional form, rather than as an accumulation of pathology, allows one to recognize that it does not suffer from "social disorganization"—a morally loaded concept (see Wirth 1964, 44–49) that is best erased from the sociologist's lexicon, its illustrious intellectual pedigree notwithstanding. As William Foote Whyte noted half a century ago in his classic study of the "street-corner society" of Boston's Italian slum, what appears to outside observers as social disorganization "often turns out to be simply a different form of social organization *if one takes the trouble to look closely*" (1943, 273, emphasis added). But, in the case of the black American ghetto, close-up, firsthand observation is precisely what has been lacking in the recent debate.

Of the twenty-seven authors who contributed to *The Urban Underclass* (Jencks and Peterson 1991), a volume lavishly underwritten and promoted by a consortium of prominent philanthropic and research foundations and claiming to contain "some of the best and most up-to-date research and thinking on the topic," *only one* conducted primary field research in the ghetto. And the one anthropologist invited to present at the conference upon which this "standard reference work" is based saw her critique of the "underclass" problematic from an ethnographic and culture-theoretic standpoint scuttled from the volume.[12] Because research on poverty and race is effectively ruled by economists, demographers, statistically oriented sociologists working with census and survey data, social workers, and social policy experts (or pundits), relevant anthropological research is routinely ignored or, at best, selectively mentioned to play a strictly ornamental function.

Remarkably, a mere handful of field studies of black inner-city life have appeared since the racial uprisings of the mid-1960s, and even the few that have been published are more often than not overlooked—I think for instance of the superb book by Edith Folb, *Runnin' Down Some Lines* (1980), to mention but one. The result is that the same "classic" monographs dating from the War on Poverty era, led by the obligatory quarternity of Oscar Lewis (1996), Elliot Liebow (1967), Ulf Hannerz (1969), and Lee Rainwater (1970), continue to be ritually summoned—and often grossly caricatured to suit current preoccupations (Peterson 1991, 12–13)—as if the basis, structure, and dynamics of the lifeworld of the ghetto (sub)proletariat had somehow been frozen and its patterns remained identical through three decades of massive economic, spatial, and sociopolitical changes.[13]

Yet intensive, ground-level scrutiny based on direct observation—as opposed to measurements effected from a distance by survey bureaucracies utterly unfit to probe and scrutinize the life of marginalized populations—immediately reveals that, far from being disorganized, the ghetto is *organized according to different principles,* in response to a *unique set of structural and strategic constraints* that bear on the racialized enclaves of the city as on no other segment of America's territory (Wacquant 1994a). These constraints include (1) the unrelenting press of economic necessity and widespread material deprivation caused by the withering away of the wage-labor economy, translating into outright deproletarianization for growing segments of the urban poor; (2) pervasive physical and social insecurity, fueled by the glaring failings of public sector institutions and the correlative debilitation of local organizations, fostering in turn irregular sociocultural patterns; (3) virulent racial antipathy conjoined with acute class prejudice resulting in a severe and systematic truncation of life chances and conduits of opportunity; (4) symbolic taint and territorial stigmatization, contaminating every area of social endeavor from friendship and housing to schooling and jobs, reinforced by (5) bureaucratic apathy and administrative ineptness made possible by the electoral expendability of the black poor in a political field thoroughly dominated by corporate lobbies and moneyed interests.

Today's ghetto comprises a Darwinian social order traversed by continual conflict over, a competition for, scarce (and diminishing) resources in an environment characterized by high levels of interpersonal and institutional mistrust, a "dog-eat-dog" worldview, and high densities of "social predators" (Sánchez-Janowski 1991, especially 22–28). This internal order is continually reinforced from without by the routine functioning of state and market, and it is kept structurally peripheral and dependent by the fragmentation of the political-administrative machinery of the American metropolis (Weiher 1991; Weir 1995). The socioanalytic reconstruction of the broken habitus and ambiguous strategies of a professional "hustler" on Chicago's South

Side discloses that the entropy characteristic of street life at the heart of the ghetto is in fact patterned and obeys a distinctive, if unstable, social logic that can be expounded provided one takes pains meticulously to link the ever-shifting game of daily options to the obdurate (and invisible) structure of political, economic, and symbolic domination that predetermines their availability, attraction, and differential payoffs (Wacquant 1993).[14]

The shift from a problematic of disorganization to one of "organization" is not reducible to a simple change in terminology. It implies, rather, a transformation of the *object to be constructed:* it means that the analyst must explicate and display in some detail the concrete mode of structuring of social relations and representations operative within the ghetto—the work of *collective self-production*—whereby its residents endow their world with form, meaning, and purpose, rather than simply reporting that this mode differs from those that hold sway in other sectors of society.[15] It also entails showing how the *activities of dominant institutions,* public bureaucracies and welfare offices, schools and hospitals, private firms and philanthropic associations, police patrols and parole officers, which are so conspicuously absent from the normal social science of the inner city, contribute powerfully to organizing the social space of the ghetto in particular and particularly destabilizing ways. It therefore involves recognizing, and specifying, the institutional bases and limits of the situated agency of ghetto residents so that their practices and life forms emerge not as mere derivations of constraints that can be "read off" structural conditions but as the product of their active engagement with the external and internal social forces that crosscut and mold their world (Abu-Lughod et al. 1994; Bourgois 1995).

## Breaking with Exoticism

The trope of disorganization also has reinforced the exoticizing of the ghetto, that is, the artificial exorbitation of those patterns of conduct, feeling, and thought that differ the most from a norm presumed to represent the broader society and also, too often, from those prevalent and acceptable among ghetto dwellers themselves. This exotic bias is an old and tenacious one, as Swedish anthropologist Ulf Hannerz pointed out long ago: "Ever since the beginnings of the study of black people in the Americas investigators have commented upon the ways in which black men and women—in particular some men and women—differ in their behavior from their white counterparts" (1970, 313).

Following this logic, the most destitute, threatening, and disreputable residents of the racialized urban core are made to stand for the whole of the ghetto, and the dilapidated remnants of the historic Black Belts of America, in turn, are taken to reflect upon, and impugn the civic standing of, the black community in toto (Franklin 1992; Fainstein 1995). The end result is the continual reproduction of stereotypical, cardboard-type, folk images of urban blacks—what Ralph Ellison aptly called "prefabricated Negroes"—that resonate with and perpetuate historic racial prejudice under the impeccable positivist garb of survey categories and the falsely neutral idiom of policy advocacy.

Analysts of the nexus of race and poverty have thus devoted an inordinate amount of attention to the assumed "pathologies" of ghetto residents, namely, to those behaviors that so-called middle-class society considers abnormal, offensive, or unduly costly, from violent crime, school "dropouts," teenage pregnancy, and labor market "shiftlessness" to "welfare dependency." Some have not hesitated to amalgamate these statuses or activities under the pejorative heading of "underclass behaviors," while others have gone yet further and redefined the ghetto itself as an "epidemic of social problems" (Jencks and Peterson 1991, 30, 155–56, 172, 301, 322–23, 397, and passim).[16]

One could show that many (if not most) of these categories, far from reflecting a value-neutral perspective fostering detached analysis and impartial policy prescription, function as thinly disguised *instruments of indictment* of the putatively abnormal conduct of ghetto dwellers. Take the apparently innocuous bureaucratic designation of high school "dropout" touted by many analysts as one variant of "underclass behavior." It insidiously points the arrow of responsibility for educational failure towards students and their "dysfunctional" families and environment when in reality most inner-city public schools in large cities have been transformed into quasi-carceral institutions that devote more resources to security than to teaching (Devine 1995) and actively *push students out* so as to economize on grossly inadequate space, staff, and instructional equipment. "The practice of cleansing the school of 'bad kids' [is] quite widely acknowledged and equally appreciated by administrators, teachers and counselors," reports Fine (1988, 99), based on extended fieldwork in a poor New York City high school. And for good reason: otherwise the schools would be faced with the impossible task of catering to tens of thousands of additional pupils for which physical infrastructure is nonexistent due to the combination of political indifference and fiscal neglect that have turned public schools into warehouses for the children of today's urban outcasts.

Now, every anthropologist is liable "to notice and to report behavior unlike that of his own culture more readily and more faithfully than he tends to notice and report behavior like that of his own culture" and thus to "overlook or underemphasize those elements of the foreign culture which resembles his own" (Naroll and Naroll 1963, 24–26). In the present case, the social and cultural distance between the analyst and the object, the paucity of sustained field observation and the demonic social imagery that enshrouds the ghetto have combined to hide the fact that forms of social action and organization that may appear deviant, "aberrant," or downright inexplicable from afar (and above) obey a *local social rationality* that is well suited to the real-life constraints and facilitations of the contemporary Black Belt.[17]

At the same time, to say that a sociocultural form follows a situated rationality does not necessarily imply that it is *specific* to that particular locale or group: many of the "adaptations" found in the ghetto are not "ghetto-specific" inasmuch as they have been recorded among (sub)proletarians in the industrial townships of Europe or Latin America as well as among working-class youths of white and Latino origins in the United States (for example, Foley 1990; Jones 1992; Leite Lopes 1978; McDermott 1985; McLeod 1994; Robins and Cohen 1978). Which means, again, that invocation of a ghetto culture à la Hannerz (1969) cannot substitute for the empirical dissection of the micro-structures in which social action and consciousness are embedded in today's ghetto. A further irony is that appeals to Hannerz's study of ghetto lifestyles in Washington's Winston Street typically turn its argument upside down since *Soulside* emphasized persistent differentiation among a population now stereotypically represented as homogenous to the point of being faceless. Also, Hannerz viewed ghetto residents as fundamentally "bicultural" and conceded that "much of what has been labelled ghetto-specific here is directly related to poverty" (Hannerz 1969, 192, 182). Such characteristics are therefore more properly conceived as derivative of class position (and trajectory, past and probable) than as effects of caste status and ghetto entrapment.

To guard against this exotic bias, it is indispensable to effect a *moral épochè*, to suspend judgment over the putative (im)morality of ghetto life and to focus, not on the most "spectacular" and publicly salient practices, but on the most banal intercourse and doings of everyday life, the taken-for-granted forms of perception, conduct, and organization that compose the "paramount, wide-awake reality" (Schultz 1962) of the ghetto as an ongoing strategic and interpretive achievement. Now, to assert that the ghetto is a "meaningful, reasonable, and normal" social world[18] is neither to romanticize nor to glorify it. Ethnographic observation establishes beyond dispute that the ghetto is a brutal and crisis-ridden universe, one shot through with abuse, distrust, misery, and despair—how could it be otherwise considering the crushing constraints and multisided compulsions of which it is the expression? It is simply to ask that the same principles of analysis and concepts be applied to it as to any other social system, high or low, glamorous or despised, familiar or alien, harmonious or acrimonious. Studies of war-front atrocities, death camps, rampant ethnocidal conflicts, high-security penitentiaries, or sudden human destruction wrought by man-made or natural calamities (Browning 1992; Pollak 1991; Spencer 1990; Sykes 1958/1971; Erikson 1976) demonstrate that, even in the most extreme of circumstances, social life is patterned, regular, and endowed with a logic and meaning amenable to analytical elucidation.

The task of sociology, then, must be to uncover the *immanent social necessity* that governs the practices and life forms of ghetto residents, not to participate in the fabrication of a new "urban Orientalism"—in Edward Said's sense of the term—of which the "underclass" would be the loathsome figurehead. In short, we should heed Everett C. Hughes's warning in his insightful discussion of "bastard institutions"—of which the ghetto offers a prime example—that they "should be studied not merely as pathological departures from what is good and right, but as part of the total complex of human activities and enterprises. In addition, they should be looked at as orders of things in which we can see the social processes going on, the same social processes, perhaps that are to be found in the legitimate institutions" (1980, 90).

## Notes

Many friends and colleagues have been kind enough to comment on successive versions of this article. Among them a special mention is due to Bill Wilson, who drew me to the topic in the first place and encouraged me to confront these issues even when he disagreed with how I framed them; Godfried Engbersen, Neil Fligstein, Martin Sánchez-Jankowski, Claude Fischer, and Chris Pickvance made pointed suggestions that forced me to clarify my arguments even as I resisted them; and Wilhelm Heitmeyer and Frederico Neiburg supplied the impetus for earlier versions in German and Portuguese. The support of the Russell Sage Foundation, where the initial draft of this paper was written, is gratefully acknowledged. Originally published in *International Journal of Urban and Regional Planning* (1997) 21: 341–53.

1. A large number of works could be cited here. Suffice it to refer to Jencks and Peterson's *The Urban Underclass* (1991), which assembles paradigmatic illustrations of each of these tenets. This is not to imply that the social science literature on race and urban poverty is wholly monolithic (see Devine and Wright 1993; Marks 1991; Wilson and Aponte 1985 for broad surveys) but that what it exhibits are largely contained within the analytic space demarcated by these three preconceptual commitments.

2. As Wittgenstein once remarked, "What makes a subject hard to understand—if it is something significant and important—is not that before you can understand it you need to be specially trained in abstruse matters, but the contrast between understanding the subject and what most people *want* to see. Because of this the very things which are most obvious may become the hardest of all to understand. What has to be overcome is a difficulty having to do with the will, rather than with the intellect" (1977, 17).

3. All of these mistakes are repeated and amplified in Jargowski's *Poverty and Place: Ghettos, Barrios, and the American City* (1996), which effectively equates ghettoization with urban decay.

4. The uniqueness, intensity, and persistence of black segregation and institutional exclusion over the long century of the ghetto's life course is amply documented in the works of Farley and Allen (1987), Hirsch (1993), Jaynes and Williams (1989), Kusmer (1976), Massey and Denton (1993), Osofsky (1971), Spear (1968), and Zunz (1982).

5. In his classic historical overview, Louis Wirth rightly insists that the ghetto is at once "an instrument of control" and "a form of accommodation through which a minority has effectually been subordinated to a dominant group." Where he errs gravely is in portraying ghettoization as a "natural process" that affects "every people and every cultural group" (1964, 84–85). For a cogent delineation of the basic principles of institutionalism (and neo-institutionalism) in the sociological tradition, see DiMaggio and Powell (1992). An exposition of the concept of closure and its usage in (neo-)Weberian theories of class and group inequality more generally is in Brubaker (1991, part 1), Manza (1992), Murphy (1988), and Parkin (1979).

6. For a portrait of the ecological, social, and institutional structure and location of poor Latino neighborhoods in the American metropolis that spotlights differences with the black urban core, see Moore and Pinderhughes (1993). Whether Native American reservations qualify as a subtype of ghetto or are best understood as a distinct mechanism of ethnoracial subordination would require an extensive discussion that is not possible here; materials for an answer can be found in Cornell (1990) and Snipp (1986).

7. For a model study of the sociopolitical production of urban cleavages as an institutional (as opposed to ecological) process, cf. Abu-Lughod's (1980) reconstruction of "urban apartheid in Morocco" and of the transmutation of caste division into class lines in postcolonial Rabat; read also Hirsch's (1983) masterful reconstruction of the paramount role played by the federal and local states in recreating Chicago's "Second Ghetto" between 1940 and 1960.

8. Ward (1989) offers an extended analysis of continuities and changes in the social characterization of slums, ghettos, and other territories of urban relegation in the era of industrial capitalist expansion. Geoffrey Biddle's (1992) *Alphabet City* provides a vivid, up-to-date, photographic illustration of the "disorganization" perspective as applied to Loisada, the Puerto Rican section of New York's Lower East Side. A valuable corrective to this monochromatic picture is Camilio Vergara (1995), who draws a

nuanced visual portrait of different types of ghettos (he uses the term in its common-sensical meaning of segregated and decaying enclaves): the "green ghettos" reclaimed by nature, the "institutional ghettos" that warehouse the undesirable "poorhouses of the twenty-first century" (drug dens and treatment facilities, homeless shelters, soup kitchens, prisons, etc.), and the dynamic and fluid "new immigrant ghettos."

9. A representative usage of this commonsensical duality is Christopher Jencks's excursus on "Underclass versus Mainstream Mothers" (1991, 215–18). Elsewhere, Jencks (in Jencks and Peterson 1991, 28–29) admits that, while "there is widespread agreement that 'underclass' is an antonym for 'middle class,' or perhaps more broadly for 'mainstream' (a term that has come to subsume both the middle class and working class), it remains that 'Americans have never agreed on what it meant to be middle or working class.'" So the key concepts organizing his dissection of the "growth of the American underclass" are marred with epistemic confusion and semantic inde-termination (as well as suffusive moral overtones). Jencks goes on to confess that conformity to scholarly fashion is his only warrant for using this half-scholarly, half-journalistic notion: "In my judgment [relevant social] changes are not large enough to justify substituting the term underclass for the term lower class. But since almost everyone else now talks about the underclass rather than the lower class, I will do the same" (ibid., 28).

10. "The pathology of the ghetto has served as a continuing anomaly tarnishing the ideals of American life," write Goldfield and Lane (1973, 4–5). "The ghetto has sym-bolized poverty in a country of plenty, discrimination in a nation of equals, disease in a country of advanced technology, and crime in a society predicated on law."

11. The large-scale, interdisciplinary, multimethod, empirical research project directed by Wilson at Chicago from 1985 to 1990 to expand and fill in the "theoretical sketch" set forth in The Truly Disadvantaged was officially entitled "The Urban Pov-erty and Family Structure Project." It devoted considerable resources to assessing the correlates and implications of family (de)composition in different "poverty areas." It should be stressed, however, that in Wilson's view family "dissolution" is not an independent causative factor but an *intervening variable* that both reveals, transmits, and amplifies the deleterious impact of precarious (male) labor market status.

12. Her name is not even mentioned in the list of participants and discussants (Jencks and Peterson 1991, v–vi) and her paper had to published elsewhere (Newman 1991).

13. Apart from the works of Elijah Anderson, Mercer Sullivan, Martin Sanchez-Jankowski, and Philippe Bourgois, the most informative accounts of everyday life in today's dark ghetto have been authored not by trained social scientists but by journal-ists: among them, Sylvester Monroe and Peter Goldman's Brothers: Black and Poor (1988), Alex Kotlowitz's There Are No Children Here (1991), Greg Donaldson's The Ville: Cops and Kids in Urban America (1993), Laurie Kay Abraham's Mama Might Be Better Off Dead (1993) and William Adler's Land of Opportunity (1995). (In all fairness it should be pointed out that journalists have also produced the most prejudiced,

lurid, and abjectly distorted depictions of the ghetto.) Also relevant here, though only rarely used, are the works of novelists of urban black America, from books by James Baldwin, Claude Brown, and Piri Thomas to Leon Forrest's *Divine Days* and Jess Mowry's *Six out of Seven*.

14. On the rationality of social structure and action in slums more generally, see also the germinal analyses of Perlman (1976) and Portes (1972) and the research they have spawned on urban marginality in Latin America. In the United States, the works of Gans (1962) and Suttles (1968) bear close rereading.

15. I tried elsewhere to highlight the theoretical and empirical gains made possible by the Copernican shift from disorganization to organization in the case of Sánchez-Jankowski's (1991) long-term participant-observation study of American urban gangs (Wacquant 1994b).

16. Jonathan Crane's (1991) work is a caricatural example of such moralizing, thinly dressed up in social science data and rhetoric that, incredibly, found its way into the pages of the *American Journal of Sociology,* bringing into full light the political-cum-homiletic import of such research. As Sassier (1990) has shown, from the sixteenth to the twentieth century, discourses on poverty have always been reflective not of the condition and state of the poor themselves but of the key political disorders of the period *as perceived by social and intellectual elites.*

17. See, for instance, Fernandez-Kelly's (1993) effective rebuttal of Christopher Jencks's (1991) pseudo "cultural explanation" of teenage pregnancy among ghetto adolescents (an ad hoc postulation arrived at by default, for lack of a more obvious causative factor, and supported by commonsense inference instead of reasoned observation), and Katheryn Edin's (1997) devastating empirical critique of the oxymoronic notion of "welfare dependency."

18. As Erving Goffman reminds us in the introduction to *Asylums:* "Any group of persons—prisoners, primitives, pilots, or patients—develop a life of their own that becomes meaningful, reasonable and normal once you get close to it" (1961, 7). To say that a social world is "normal," however, does not imply that those who participate in it experience or accept it is such, as the case of concentration camps readily demonstrates. For an ethnographic narration that tries to convey the forms of sociability and the tissue of expressive cultural forms through which ghetto residents actively produce the "normality" (or "social structure" in the ethnomethodological sense) of their daily world in spite of the dilapidation and insecurity surrounding them, cf. Wacquant (1996).

## References

Abraham, L. K. 1993. *Mama Might Be Better Off Dead: The Failure of Health Care in Urban America.* Chicago: University of Chicago Press.

Abu-Lughod, J. L. 1980. *Rabat: Urban Apartheid in Morocco.* Princeton, N.J.: Princeton University Press.

Abu-Lughod, J. L., et al. 1994. *From Urban Village to East Village: The Battle for New York's Lower East Side.* Oxford: Basil Blackwell.

Adler, W. M. 1995. *Land of Opportunity: One Family's Quest for the American Dream in the Age of Crack.* New York: Atlantic Monthly Press.

Anderson, E. 1991. *Streetwise: Race, Class, and Change in an Urban Community.* Chicago: University of Chicago Press.

Appadurai, A. 1988. "Putting Hierarchy in Its Place." *Cultural Anthropology* 3, no. 1 (February): 36–49.

Bachelard, G. 1938. *La formation de l'esprit scientifique. Contribution à une psychanalyse de la connaissance objective.* Paris: Libraire Philosophique J. Vrin.

Banfield, E. C. 1970. *The Unheavenly City.* New York: Free Press.

Biddle, G. 1992. *Alphabet City.* Berkeley: University of California Press.

Bourgois, P. 1995. *In Search of Respect: Selling Crack in El Barrio.* Cambridge: Cambridge University Press.

Boyer, P. 1978. *Urban Masses and Moral Order in America, 1820–1920.* Cambridge, Mass.: Harvard University Press.

Browning, C. R. 1992. *Ordinary Men: Reserve Police Battalion 101 and the Final Solution in Poland.* New York: Harper Perennial.

Brubaker, W. R. 1991. "Traditions of Citizenship and Nationhood in France and Germany." PhD diss., New York, Columbia University.

Clark, K. B. 1965. *Dark Ghetto: Dilemmas of Social Power.* New York: Harper.

Connolly, H. X. 1977. *A Ghetto Grows in Brooklyn.* New York: New York University Press.

Cooperman, B., and R. Curiel. 1990. *The Venetian Ghetto.* New York: Rizzoli International.

Cornell, S. 1990. "Land, Labor, and Group Formation: Blacks and Indians in the United States." *Racial and Ethnic Studies* 13, no. 3: 253–72.

Crane, J. 1991. "The Epidemic Theory of Ghettos and Neighborhood Effects on Dropping Out and Teenage Childbearing." *American Journal of Sociology* 96, no. 5 (March): 1226–59.

Davis, M. 1990. *City of Quartz: Excavating the Future in Los Angeles.* London: Verso.

Devine, J. 1995. "Can Metal Detectors Replace the Panopticon?" *Cultural Anthropology* 10, no. 2: 171–95.

Devine, J. A., and J. D. Wright. 1993. *The Greatest of Evils: Urban Poverty and the American Underclass.* New York: Aldine.

DiMaggio, P., and W. W. Powell 1992. Introduction to *The New Institutionalism in Organized Analysis,* ed. W. W. Powell and P. J. DiMaggio, 1–38. Chicago: University of Chicago Press.

Donaldson, G. 1993. *The Ville: Cops and Kids in Urban America.* New York: Ticknor and Fields.

Drake, St. C., and H. R. Cayton. 1945/1962. *Black Metropolis: A Study of Negro Life in a Northern City,* revised and enlarged ed. 2 vols. New York: Harper and Row.

Durkheim, E. 2001. *Pragmatisme et sociologie.* Paris: Vrin.

Edin, K., and L. Lein. 1997. *Making Ends Meet: How Single Mothers Survive Welfare and Low-Wage Work.* New York: Russell Sage Foundation.

Erikson, K. T. 1976. *Everything in Its Path: Destruction of Community in the Buffalo Creek Flood.* New York: Simon and Schuster.

Fainstein, N. 1995. "Black Ghettoization and Social Mobility." In *The Bubbling Cauldron: Race, Ethnicity, and the Urban Crisis,* ed. M. Smith and J. Feagin, 123–41. Minneapolis: University of Minnesota Press.

Farley, R., and W. R. Allen. 1987. *The Color Line and the Quality of Life in America.* New York: Russell Sage Foundation.

Fernandez-Kelly, P. 1993. "Social and Cultural Capital in the Urban Ghetto: Implications for the Economic Sociology of Immigration." In *The Economic Sociology of Immigration: Essays on Network, Ethnicity, and Entrepreneurship,* ed. Alejandro Portes, 213–47. New York: Russell Sage.

Fine, M. 1988. *Framing Dropouts.* Albany: State University of New York Press.

Fishman, R. 1988. *Bourgeois Utopias: The Rise and Fall of Suburbia.* New York: Basic Books.

Folb, E. A. 1980. *Runnin' Down Some Lines: The Language and Culture of Black Teenagers.* Cambridge, Mass.: Harvard University Press.

Foley, D. 1990. *Learning Capitalist Culture: Deep in the Heart of Texas.* Philadelphia: University of Pennsylvania Press.

Franklin, R. 1992. *Shadows of Race and Class.* Minneapolis: University of Minnesota Press.

Frazier, E. F. 1931. *The Negro Family in Chicago.* Chicago: University of Chicago Press.

———. 1949. *The Negro in the United States.* New York: Macmillan.

Fusfeld, D., and T. Bates 1984. *The Political Economy of the Ghetto.* Carbondale: Southern Illinois University Press.

Gans, H. 1962. *The Urban Villagers.* New York: Free Press.

Goffman, E. 1961. *Asylums: Essays on the Social Situation of Inmates.* Harmondsworth, UK: Penguin.

Goldfield, D. R., and J. B. Lane, eds. 1973. *The Enduring Ghetto.* Philadelphia: J. B. Lippincott.

Hannerz, U. 1969. *Soulside: Inquiries into Ghetto Culture and Community.* New York: Columbia University Press.

———. 1970. "What Black Males Are Like: Another Look." In *Afro-American Anthropology: Contemporary Perspectives,* ed. N. E. Whitten and John F. Szwed, 313–27. New York: Free Press.

Harrell, A. V., and G. E. Peterson 1992. *Drugs, Crime, and Social Isolation: Barriers to Urban Opportunity.* Washington, D.C.: Urban Institute Press.

Hirsch, A. 1983. *Making the Second Ghetto: Race and Housing in Chicago, 1940–1960.* Cambridge: Cambridge University Press.

———. 1993. "With or without Jim Crow: Black Residential Segregation in the United States." In *Urban Policy in Twentieth-Century America,* ed. A. Hirsch and R. A. Mohl, 64–94. New Brunswick, N.J.: Rutgers University Press.

Hogan, R. 1980. "The Frontier as Social Control." *Theory and Society* 14: 35–51.

Hughes, E. C. 1980. *The Sociological Eye.* New Brunswick, N.J.: Transaction.

Jargowski, P. 1996. *Poverty and Place: Ghettos, Barrios, and the American City.* New York: Russell Sage Foundation.

Jargowski, P., and M. J. Bane. 1991. "Ghetto Poverty in the United States, 1970–1980." In *The Urban Underclass,* ed. C. Jencks and P. E. Peterson, 235–73. Washington, D.C.: Brookings Institution.

Jaynes, G. D., and R. M. Williams Jr. 1989. *A Common Destiny: Blacks and American Society.* Washington, D.C.: National Academy Press.

Jencks, C. 1991. *Rethinking Social Policy: Race, Poverty, and the Underclass.* Cambridge, Mass.: Harvard University Press.

Jencks, C., and P. E. Peterson, eds. 1991. *The Urban Underclass.* Washington, D.C.: Brookings Institution.

Jones, J. 1992. *The Dispossessed: America's Underclasses from the Civil War to the Present.* New York: Basic Books.

Katz, M. 1983. *Poverty and Policy in American History.* New York: Academic Press.

Kotlowitz, A. 1991. *There Are No Children Here.* New York: Doubleday.

Kusmer, K. L. 1976. *A Ghetto Takes Shape: Black Cleveland, 1870–1930.* Urbana: University of Illinois Press.

Leibow, E. 1967. *Tally's Corner: A Study of Negro Streetcorner Men.* Boston: Little, Brown.

Leite Lopes, J. S. 1978. *O Vapor do Diabo: O Trabalho dos Operarios do Acucar.* Rio de Janeiro: Paz e Terra.

Lewis, O. 1966. *La Vida: A Puerto Rican Family in the Culture of Poverty—San Juan and New York.* New York: Random House.

Logan, J. R., and H. L. Molotoch. 1987. *Urban Fortunes: The Political Economy of Place.* Berkeley: University of California Press.

Manza, J. 1992. "Classes, Status Groups, and Social Closure: A Critique of Neo-Weberian Social Theory." *Current Perspectives in Social Theory* 12: 275–302.

Marks, C. 1991. "The Urban Underclass." *Annual Review of Sociology* 17: 445–66.

Massey, D., and N. Denton. 1993. *American Apartheid: Segregation and the Making of the Underclass.* Cambridge, Mass.: Harvard University Press.

McDermott, K. 1985. "All Dressed Up and Nowhere to Go: Youth Unemployment and State Policy in Britain." *Urban Anthropology* 14: 91–108.

McLeod, J. 1994. *Ain't No Makin' It,* 2nd ed. Boulder, Colo.: Westview Press.

Meier, A., and E. Rudwick. 1976. *From Plantation to Ghetto.* New York: Hill and Wang.

Monroe, S., and P. Goldman 1988. *Brothers: Black and Poor—A True Story of Courage and Survival.* New York: William Morrow.

Moore J., and R. Pinderhughes, eds. 1993. *In the Barrio: Latinos and the Underclass Debate.* New York: Russell Sage Foundation.

Murphy, R. 1988. *Social Closure: The Theory of Monopolization and Exclusion.* Oxford: Claredon Press.

Naroll, R., and F. Naroll. 1963. "On Bias of Exotic Data." *Man: A Monthly Record of Anthropological Science* 63 (February): 24–6.

Newman, C. 1991. "Culture and Structure in 'The Truly Disadvantaged.'" *City and Society* 12, no. 3: 67–83.

O'Connor, Alice. 1995. "Race and Class in Chicago Sociology." Paper presented to the Social Science History Association Meetings, November.

Osofsky, G. 1971. *Harlem: The Making of a Ghetto—Negro New York, 1890–1930,* 2nd ed. New York: Harper.

Park, R. E., and W. Burgess. 1925. *The City.* Chicago: University of Chicago Press.

Parkin, F. 1979. *Marxism and Class Theory: A Bourgeois Critique.* New York: Columbia University Press.

Patterson, J. 1986. *America's Struggle against Poverty,* 2nd ed. Cambridge, Mass.: Harvard University Press.

Perlman, J. 1976. *The Myth of Marginality.* Berkeley: University of California Press.

Peterson, P. 1991. "The Urban Underclass and the Poverty Paradox." In *The Urban Underclass,* ed. C. Jencks and P. E. Peterson, 3–27. Washington, D.C.: Brookings Institution.

Pollak, M. 1991. *L'expérience concentrationnaire.* Paris: A.-M. Métaillé.

Portes, A. 1972. "Rationality in the Slum: An Essay in Interpretive Sociology." *Comparative Studies in Society and History* 14, no. 3 (June): 268–86.

Rainwater, L. 1970. *Behind Ghetto Walls: Black Families in a Federal Slum.* Chicago: Aldine.

Robins, D., and P. Cohen. 1978. *Knuckle Sandwich: Growing Up in the Working-Class City.* Harmondsworth, UK: Penguin Books.

Sánchez-Jankowski, M. 1991. *Islands in the Street: Gangs in Urban American Society.* Berkeley: University of California Press.

Sassier, P. 1990. *Du bon usage des pauvres. Histoire d'un theme politique, XVIe-XXe siecle.* Paris: Fayard.

Schutz, A. 1962. *Collected Papers I: The Problem of Social Reality.* The Hague: Marinus Nijhoff.

Shaw, C., and H. McKay. 1942. *Juvenile Delinquency in Urban Areas.* Chicago: University of Chicago Press.

Snipp, C. M. 1986. "The Changing Political and Economic Status of American Indians: From Captive Nations to Internal Colonies." *American Journal of Economics and Sociology* 45, no. 2 (April): 145–57.

Spear, A. H. 1968. *Black Chicago: The Making of a Negro Ghetto, 1890–1920.* Chicago: University of Chicago Press.

Spencer, J. 1990. "Collective Violence and Everyday Practice in Sri Lanka." *Modern Asian Studies* 24, no. 3: 603–23.

Suttles, G. D. 1968. *The Social Order of the Slum: Ethnicity and Territory in the Inner City.* Chicago: University of Chicago Press.

Sykes, G. M. 1958/1971. *The Society of Captives: A Study of a Maximum Security Prison.* Princeton, N.J.: Princeton University Press.

Trotter, W. J., Jr. 1993. "Blacks in the Urban North: The 'Underclass Question' in Historical Perspective." In *The Underclass Debate: Views from History,* ed. M. B. Katz, 55–81. Princeton, N.J.: Princeton University Press.

Vergara, C. 1995. *The New American Ghetto.* New Brunswick, N.J.: Rutgers University Press.

Wacquant, L. J. D. 1991. "What Makes a Ghetto? Notes toward a Comparative Analysis of Modes of Urban Exclusion." Paper presented at the Working Conference on Poverty, Immigration, and Urban Marginality in Advanced Societies, Paris, Maison Suger, May 10–11.

———. 1993. "'The zone': le métier de 'hustler' dans le ghetto noir américain." In *La misère du monde,* ed. Pierre Bourdieu et al., 181–204. Paris: Editions du Seuil. 181–204. [Translated as "Inside the Zone." In *The Poverty of Society,* ed. P. Bourdieu et al. Oxford: Polity Press, 1997].

———. 1994a. "Le gang comme prédateur collectif." *Actes de la recherche en sciences sociales* 101–2 (March): 88–100.

———. 1994b. "The New Urban Color Line: The State and Fate of the Ghetto in Postfordist America." In *Social Theory and the Politics of Identity,* ed. C. J. Calhoun, 231–76. Oxford: Basil Blackwell.

———. 1995. "Elementary Forms of Racial Domination." Rockefeller Lecture presented to the Nucleo da Cor, Instituto de Filosofia e Ciências Sociais, Universidade federal do Rio de Janeiro, Brazil, October 10.

———. 1996. "Un mariage dans le ghetto." *Actes de la recherche en sciences sociales* 113 (June): 63–84.

Ward, D. 1989. *Poverty, Ethnicity, and the American City, 1840–1925.* Cambridge: Cambridge University Press.

Weaver, R. 1948. *The Negro Ghetto.* New York: Russell and Russell.

Weber, M. 1818–20/1978. *Economy and Society.* Berkeley: University of California Press.

Weiher, G. 1991. *The Fractured Metropolis: Political Fragmentation and Metropolitan Segregation.* Albany: State University of New York Press.

Weir, M. 1995. "The Politics of Racial Isolation in Europe and America." In *Classifying by Race,* ed. P. E. Peterson, 217–42. Princeton, N.J.: Princeton University Press.

Whyte, W. F. 1943. *Street Corner Society: The Social Structure of an Italian Slum.* Chicago: University of Chicago Press.

Wilson, W. J. 1987. *The Truly Disadvantaged: The Inner City, the Underclass, and Public Policy.* Chicago: University of Chicago Press.

Wilson, W. J., and R. Aponte. 1985. "Urban Poverty." *Annual Review of Sociology* 11: 231–58.

Wirth, L. 1928. *The Ghetto*. Chicago: University of Chicago Press.

———. 1964. *On Cities and Social Life*, ed. and with an introduction by Albert J. Reiss Jr. Chicago: University of Chicago Press.

Wittgenstein, L. 1977. *Vermischte Bermerkungen*. Frankfurt: Suhrkamp.

Zunz, O. 1982. *The Changing Face of Inequality: Urbanization, Industrial Development, and Immigrants in Detroit, 1880–1920*. Chicago: University of Chicago Press.

# 3

# Globalization and Social Exclusion: The Sociology of Vindictiveness and the Criminology of Transgression

## JOCK YOUNG

> The tendencies towards economic division and social exclusion now characteristic of America do seem to be hardening both in Britain and Western Europe. The racial and ethnic element here is prominent. In cities such as London, Manchester, Rotterdam, Frankfurt, Paris and Naples the position of the urban poor is worsening. Hamburg is Europe's richest city, as measured by average personal income, and has the highest proportion of millionaires in Germany. It also has the highest proportion on welfare and unemployment—40 per cent above the national average. A third of industrial jobs in and around the city have disappeared in the fifteen years up to 1994.
>
> —Anthony Giddens, *Sociology*

> There are imaginary geographies which place imperfect minorities in marginalized locations: in a social *elsewhere*. These locations consist of protected zones which ensure the reproduction of those who inhabit them, who are separated from the majorities living outside. These geographies of exclusion associate *elsewhere* with that which is contaminated, filthy, offensive to morality and olfaction.
>
> —Vincenzo Ruggiero, *Crime and Markets*

In *The Exclusive Society* (1999), I contrast the inclusive world of the postwar period of the 1950s and 1960s with the more exclusionary social order of late modernity in the last third of the twentieth century and beyond. Eric Hobsbawm's (1994) "Golden Age" of high employment, job security, and stable marriage and community is contrasted with a more insecure and divided society that followed it. For whereas the Golden Age granted social embeddedness, strong certainty of personal and social narrative, and a desire to assimilate the deviant, the immigrant, the stranger, late modernity generated both economic and ontological insecurity, a discontinuity of personal and social narrative, and an exclusionary tendency towards the deviant.

In my research, I started from the most immediate and apparent manifestations of social exclusion in late modern societies. I subdivided these exclusions into three layers: the labor market, civil society, and the State. Within the labor market, I noted the decline of the primary labor market, the expansion of a secondary labor market characterized by insecurity, short-term contracts and multiple career trajectories, and a penumbra of those on the margins, an underclass of those who are structurally unemployed and spend a lifetime idle or working for poverty wages. It is, in short, what Will Hutton has characterized as "the 40:30:30 society" (1995).

Corresponding to this exclusion from the labor market was the exclusion from civil society: an underclass left stranded by the needs of capital on housing estates either in the inner city or on its periphery. This includes those who because of illiteracy, family pathology, or general disorganization were excluded from citizenship, whose spatial vistas were those of constant disorder and threat, and who were the recipients of stigma from the wider world of respectable citizens; the welfare "scroungers," the immigrants, the junkies and crack heads: the demons of modern society. And lastly, such a second-class citizenship was demonstrated and exacerbated by the focus of the criminal justice system, by their existence in J. A. Lee's (1981) graphic phrase as "police property" and by the extraordinarily disproportionate presence of the immigrant and the poor within the penal system.

Such a dualism is captured by John Galbraith's (1992) contrast between the "contented majority" and an underclass of despair, with respectability on the one hand and stigma on the other, a world of civility and tranquillity over against that of crime and mayhem. It underscores much of the contemporary usage of the phrase "social exclusion." But it soon became clear to me that such a dualism was fundamentally misconceived. It echoed the conventional wisdoms of the subject, to be sure, but it did not adequately grasp the social and spatial terrain of the late modern city nor the dynamics of the actors who traverse it. It rightly suggests barriers and divisions but wrongly exaggerates their efficacy and solidity: it mistakes rhetoric for reality; it attempts to impose hard lines on a late modern city of blurred demarcations and crossovers. Furthermore, it neither captures the intensity of the exclusion—the vindictiveness—nor the passionate resentment of the excluded while painting a far too calm picture of the fortunate citizens—the included.

Let us first examine the components of the social exclusion thesis:

1. The Binary: that society can be divided into an inclusive and largely satisfied majority and an excluded and despondent minority;

2. Moral Exclusion: that there exists a vast majority with good habits of work, virtuous conduct between citizens, and stable family structures and a minority who are disorganized, welfare dependent, criminal and criminogenic, who live in unstable and dysfunctional families;

3. Spatial Exclusion: that the excluded are isolated from the included, that stronger and stronger barriers occur between them, and that these borderlines are rarely crossed. Furthermore, that the fortunate classes create gilded ghettos from which to systematically exclude the poor;

4. The Dysfunctional Underclass: that the underclass is a residuum that is dysfunctional to itself and to society at large, both in its cost in taxes and in its criminogenic nature. It is the "dangerous classes" of the Victorians underwritten by the taxes of the welfare state;

5. Work and Redemption: that the provision of work will transform the underclass: changing their attitudes of mind, habits of dependency, cultures of hedonism, criminal tendencies, and dysfunctional families and transport them into the ranks of the contented and the law abiding.

This thesis is held by writers of various theoretical and political dispositions: whether it is the "social isolation" of William Julius Wilson (1987), the "hyperghettoization" of Loïc Wacquant (2001), the warnings of "Indian style reservations" by Richard Herrnstein and Charles Murray (1994), "the New Bantustans" of Mike Davis (1990), the language and rhetoric of New Labour's Social Exclusion Unit (1999), "the dual city" of Manuel Castells (1994), "the geographies of exclusion" of David Sibley (1995), or the New York of nightmares and dreams portrayed in Tom Wolfe's *Bonfire of the Vanities* (1988). And parallel to the segregation of the poor is the self-imposed isolation of the middle classes whether it is in "the gated communities" of Los Angeles, so well publicized by Mike Davis (1990), or "the fortress city" of Susan Christopherson (1994), or "the hyper-anaesthetized play zones" that are the "flip side narrative of the 'jobless ghetto'" (2000, 91) of Christian Parenti.

I wish to contest this thesis not from a perspective that there are no wide-scale disparities in late modern society nor that areas of the city are not particularly blighted by crime and that their inhabitants experience social exclusion and stigmatization. Surely all of this is true and should be a target and priority of any progressive policy. But the construction of the problem in a binary mode obfuscates the issue, while the notion of social exclusion ironically exaggerates the degree of exclusion while underestimating the gravity of the problem (see table 3.1).

The danger of the concept of social exclusion is that it carries with it a series of false binaries: it ignores the fact that problems occur on both sides of the line, however much one has clusters in one area rather than another and, more subtly, it conceals the fact that the "normality" of the majority is itself deeply problematic.

Thus in the first respect, unemployment, poverty, economic insecurity are scarcely unknown outside the designated areas—indeed quantitatively they are overall more prevalent in the supposedly secure majoritarian heartlands of society than they are in the selected minority of "excluded" areas. And the same, of course, is true of illicit drug use, community disorganization, unstable family structures, and so forth. In the case of the notion of "the normal majority," it assumes that, in this world, class differentials are somehow insignificant, that paid work is an unambiguous benefit, that "stable" family life is unproblematic, licit psychoactive drug use is less a problem than illegal drug "abuse," and so on. Furthermore, it assumes that the transition from the social excluded to the majority via the vehicle of work will miraculously solve all these problems.

But we can go further than this, for there is widespread evidence that the culture of contentment—which John Galbraith (1992) talks of: a "contented majority" who are all right thank you, doing fine and sharing little in common or concern for the excluded minority—is a myth. Note, first of all, Will

Table 3.1. Blurring the Binary Vision

| The Binaries of Social Exclusion | |
| --- | --- |
| Society at Large | The Underclass |
| The Unproblematic | The Problem |
| Community | Disorganization |
| Employment | The Workless |
| Independence | Welfare Dependency |
| Stable Family | Single Mothers |
| The Natives | The Immigrants |
| Drug Free | Illicit Drug Use |
| Victims | Criminals |

Hutton's figures, 40:30:30, where the secure primary labor market is reduced itself to a minority, but it would be foolish to suggest that even this island of seeming certainty was secure, serene, or self-satisfied. The demands for a more and more flexible labor force coupled with the leap forward in automation and the sophistication of computer software caused great reverberations of insecurity throughout the employment structure. Redundancy, short-term contracts, multiple career structures have become the order of the day. Furthermore, as the recent Joseph Rowntree Foundation Report, *Job Insecurity and Work Intensification,* discovered, redundancy not only causes chronic job insecurity but the workers who remain have to work longer hours and expand their skills to cover the areas of those dismissed (B. Burchell 1999, 60). For those in work, the length of the working day increases: it is, of course, easier for the employer to ask more and more time when security of employment is uncertain. *The market does not compete in hard places, it goes for the soft tissue of time and vulnerability.* Moreover, while in the past the income of one wage earner was sufficient to maintain a family, the dual-career family has now become a commonplace where both partners are immersed in the labor market. And if in the economic sphere precariousness and uncertainty are widespread, so too in the domestic sphere: divorce, separation, single parenthood are endemic, with the pressures of work merely adding to the instability of the late modern family.

## Bulimia: Not Exclusion but Inclusion/Exclusion

There is a strange consensus in recent writings about the underclass. Both writers of the right and the left concur that what one has is not a separate culture of poverty as earlier conservative and radical writers presumed (for example, Edward Banfield 1968 on the right or Michael Harrington 1963 on the left), but rather that what has occurred is a breakdown of culture. Thus William Julius Wilson (1987) in his influential "social isolation" thesis points to the way in which whole areas of the inner city, having been formed around the previous needs of manufacturing industry, are left stranded as capital wings its way to more profitable dividends elsewhere in the country or abroad. While the middle and respectable working classes escape to the suburbs, the less skilled remain behind bereft of work and, indeed, role models that display work discipline and the values of punctuality and reliability. The loss of work, in turn, leads to a lack of "marriageable men" who can earn a family wage and engenders the rise of single mothers in the ghetto—and the role model of the family, parallel to that of work, is likewise diminished.

Charles Murray (1984), writing from the opposite political perspective, comes to surprisingly similar conclusions. His causal sequences are, of course, very different: it is not lack of work that causes the problem but lack of willingness to work, engendered by an "overgenerous" welfare state that creates "dependency" among the poor. Such a dependency manifests itself in a lack of motivation to work and single mothers. Thus the effects on attitudes to work and the family are similar and the perceived consequences, a high rate of crime and incivilities, identical.[1]

All of these assessments of the morals of the poor are those of *deficit:* in the recent writers they lack our values, in the earlier writers they have different values that are seen as deficient. And all of them describe a fairly similar value system or lack of it, namely short-term hedonism, lacking in restraint, unwillingness to forgo present pleasures, aggressiveness, and willingness to use violence to achieve desired goals. In short, a spoiled, petulant, immature culture at the bottom of the social structure.

In *The Exclusive Society,* I set out to examine this picture of mores at the bottom of the social structure. I decided to look at the American black underclass as a test case, for surely, if this thesis were true, it would be among these supposed outcasts of the American Dream that this distinct, localized, and anomic deficit culture would be found. In particular I looked at Carl Nightingale's brilliant ethnography of the black ghetto of Philadelphia, *On the Edge* (1993). What Nightingale discovered confounded such an image. For instead, the ghetto was the apotheosis of America. Here is full immersion in the American Dream: a culture hooked on Gucci, BMW, Nikes, watching television eleven hours per day, sharing the mainstream culture's obsession with violence, backing, at the time of the study, Bush's involvement in the Gulf War, lining up outside the cinemas, worshipping success, money, wealth, and status—even sharing in a perverse way the racism of the wider society. The problem of the ghetto was not so much the process of it being simply excluded but rather of it being one that was all too strongly included in the culture but, then, systematically excluded from its realization. All of this is reminiscent of Merton—but where, in a late modern context, the implosion of the wider culture on the local is dramatically increased. We have a process that I likened to bulimia of the social system: a society that choruses the liberal mantra of liberty, equality, and fraternity yet systematically practices exclusion in the job market, on the streets, in day-to-day contacts with the outside world. It brands as "losers" those who had learned to believe that the world consisted of "winners" and "losers."

## Crossing the Borderline: The Dual City Thesis

Thus the underclass is constructed as an Other, as a group with defective norms who contrast with the normal majority. And here in this region lie all sorts of crime and incivilities. From this perspective of essentializing the other, the demand is to locate the problem areas: where exactly *are* the demons, so to speak? The powerful seek, in Todd Gitlin's poignant phrase, "to purge impurities, to wall off the stranger" (1995, 233). Thus the underclass is said to be located within the clear-cut ghettos of the inner-city sink estates or the long-lost satellite slums at the city's edge (see Byrne 1999). But, in fact, there is no such precision here: the poor are not as firmly corralled as some might make out. Thus, as Gerry Mooney and Mike Danson write in their critique of the "dual city" concept based on their research in Glasgow—a city, some would say, of extreme cultural and economic contrasts:

> The conclusion which is drawn from the analysis of poverty and deprivation in contemporary Glasgow presented here is not one which lends support to the dual city model. . . . This is not to deny, however, that there is an uneven distribution of poverty in the city or that poverty is concentrated in certain areas. What is being contested is the usefulness of the dual city argument for our understanding of such distributions and the processes which contribute to it. . . .
>
> The language of the two city/dual city argument is one which is seriously flawed by definitional and conceptual difficulties. Despite the continuing use of concepts such as polarisation, underclass, exclusion and marginalisa-tion, we are little clearer about the underlying factors which are viewed as contributing to such processes. In this respect the dual city perspective and its implicit arguments about growing socio-spatial polarisation are plagued by ambiguity and vagueness.
>
> In discussions of the emerging "tale of two cities" in Glasgow, the attention which the peripheral estates received does not relate directly to the levels and proportions of poverty to be found there. In part this is a consequence of reluctance to define adequately the areas or social groups concerned. Further *within* peripheral estates there is a marked differentiation between the various component parts in terms of unemployment, poverty and deprivation. This is almost completely neglected in the dominant picture of these estates which has emerged in recent years which stereotypes the estates as homogeneous enclaves of "despair" or "hopelessness." (1997, 84–85)

Similarly, John Hagedorn points to the variegated neighborhoods in Mil-waukee that he studied: "a checkerboard of struggling working class and poor families, coexisting even in the same block, with drug houses, gangs and routine violence" (1991, 534). Maybe urban geographers of all political persuasions would like more of a clear-cut cartography than is healthy, but, in reality, the contours of late modernity always blur, fudge, and cross over (see Young 2001).

Manuel Castells advocates the concept of dual city as the fundamental urban dualism of our time: "It opposes the cosmopolitanism of the elite, living on a daily connection to the whole world . . . to the tribalism of local communities, retrenched in their spaces that they try to control as their last stand against the macro-forces that shape their lives out of their reach. The fundamental dividing line in our cities is the inclusion of the cosmopolitans in the making of the new history while excluding the locals from the control of the global city to which ultimately their neighbourhoods belong" (Castells 1994, 30). In this conception, the rich live in late modernity whereas the poor are trapped in locality, tribalism, and the past. Such a notion of a class divide based on information fails to grasp the cultural penetration of globalization. For, as John Tomlinson points out:

> those marginalized groups for whom "locality is destiny" experience a *trans-formed* locality into which the wider world intrudes more and more. They may in all sorts of ways be the "losers" in globalisation, but this does not mean that they are excluded from its effects, that they are consigned to cultural backwaters out of the mainstream of global modernity. Quite to the contrary, it seems to me that the poor and marginalized—for example those living in inner-city areas—often find themselves daily closest to some of most turbulent transformations, while it is the affluent who can afford to retire to the rural backwaters which have at least the appearance of a preserved and stable "locality." (1999, 133–34)

Thus in terms of mass communication, they are exposed to messages and commodities from all over the world, while the inner-city area in which they live becomes multiethnic and diverse due to labor immigration. They are exposed to what Dick Hebdidge (1990) calls a "mundane cosmopolitanism" just as real or perhaps more significant than the rich tourist who travels the world in a fairly sanitized fashion from chain hotel to chain hotel, from airport lounge to airport lounge. And cultures of distant places either through the media or on the streets become incorporated in the local cultures particularly of the youth (see Back 1996; Young 2001).

## The Functional Underclass

> What is not accepted, and indeed is little mentioned, is that the
> underclass is integrally a part of the larger economic process and, more
> importantly, that it serves the living standard and the comfort of the more
> favored community . . . The economically fortunate, not excluding those
> who speak with greatest regret of the existence of this class, are heavily
> dependent on its presence.
>
> The underclass is deeply functional; all industrial countries have one in
> greater or lesser measure and in one form or another. As some of its mem-
> bers escape from deprivation and its associated compulsions, a resupply
> becomes essential. But on few matters, it must be added, is even the most
> sophisticated economic and social comment more reticent. The picture
> of an economic and political system in which social exclusion, however
> unforgiving, is somehow a remediable affliction is all but required. Here, in
> a compelling fashion, the social convenience of the contented replaces the
> clearly visible reality.
>
> —John Galbraith, *The Culture of Contentment*

It is common to portray the underclass as not wanted, as a social residuum.
They are the people who were left behind in the urban hinterlands as capital winged its way to places where labor was cheaper, they are those whose
labor is no longer required and who, furthermore, are "flawed consumers"
as Zygmunt Bauman (1998b) would have it, whose income is insufficient to
render them of any interest to those selling the glittering commodities of
late modern society. They are the casualties of globalization and the new
technology: they are the useless class, a segment of society that has become
detached and irrelevant. As Ralf Dahrendorf put it, "They are, if the cru-
elty of the statement is pardonable, not needed. The rest of us could and
would quite like to live without them" (1985, 20). They are not simply of
little use because their presence has dysfunctions for the rest of society: they
have no uses but great costs. These dysfunctions take two forms. Firstly, the
underclass is a source of crime and incivilities, so it is viewed as a dangerous class; secondly, the residuum are costly, an ever-increasing burden on
the hard-pressed taxpayer. Nor, for that matter, are they separate in such a
strict spatial sense as is frequently suggested. Thus Zygmunt Bauman writes
of Washington, D.C.:

> One difference between those "high up" and those "low down" is that the
> first may leave the second behind—but not vice versa. Contemporary cities
> are sites of an "apartheid à rebours": those who can afford it, abandon the
> filth and squalor of the regions that those who cannot afford the move are
> stuck to. In Washington, D.C. . . . there is an invisible border stretching along
> 16th Street in the west and the Potomac river in the north-west, which those

left behind are wise never to cross. Most of the adolescents left behind the invisible yet all-too-tangible border never saw downtown Washington with all its splendours, ostentatious elegance and refined pleasures. In their life, that downtown does not exist. There is no talking over the border. The life experiences are so sharply different that it is not clear what the residents of the two sides could talk to each other about were they to meet and stop to converse. As Ludwig Wittgenstein remarked, "If lions could talk, we would not understand them." (1998a, 86)

This eloquent expression of the dual city thesis is wrong, not in its sense of division but in its sense of borders. For the borders are regularly crossed and the language spoken on each side is remarkably similar. The most obvious flaw in the argument is that of gender: maids, nurses, clerical staff move across into work every day. Women, as William Julius Wilson argues in *When Work Disappears* (1985), are more acceptable to the world outside of the ghetto than their male counterparts. It is after all "home boys" who stay at home. But bell-hops, taxi drivers, doormen, maintenance men regularly ply their way across the invisible borders of Washington, D.C. It is not, therefore, just through television that the sense of relative deprivation of the poor is heightened, it is in the direct and often intimate knowledge of the lives of the affluent.

David Rieff in *Los Angeles: Capital of the Third World* (1993) writes of the close physical proximity of the professionals and the underclass in Los Angeles, their interdependence yet the chasm that separates their lives. Frank Webster captures this well when he comments:

> Illustrations of this are easy to find. On the one hand, maids are an essential element of the professionals' lifestyles, to cook, to clean, to look after children, to prepare for the dinner parties held in the gaps found in the frenetic work schedules of those deep into careers in law, corporate affairs, trading and brokerage. The maids, generally Hispanics, ride the infamously inadequate public transit buses to points in the city where their employers may pick them up in their cars to bring them home to clean up breakfast and take the children off to school. On the other hand, visitors are often struck by how verdant are the gardens of those living in the select areas of LA. Often they make the assumption that "anything grows here in this wonderful sunshine." But they are wrong: Los Angeles is a desert and gardens need most intensive care to bloom. They get it from an army of mainly Chicano labourers which arrives on the back of trucks very early in the mornings to weed, water and hoe—for a few dollars in wages, cash in hand.
> In spite of this dependence, which obviously involves a good deal of personal interaction, the lives of the two groups are very far apart. Of course this is

largely because they occupy markedly different territories, with members of the poor venturing out only to service the affluent on their terms as waiters, valets, shop assistants and the like the underclass also inhabit areas which the well-to-do have no reason (or desire) to visit. (1995, 205–6)

The dual city where the poor are morally segregated from the majority and are held physically apart by barriers is a myth. The borderlines are regularly crossed; the underclass exists on both sides anyway, but those who are clustered in the poorer parts of town regularly work across the tracks to keep the well-off families functioning. *The work poor keep the work rich going: indeed, it is only the availability of such cheap "help" that enables the dual career families to continue.* The situation of the dual-income family and their need for support is well documented in Nicky Gregson and Michelle Lowe's *Servicing the Middle Class* (1994). The class relations of this emergent form were well summarized by the Hunts when they wrote, "Hired help on a single-family basis involves a category of workers that must be paid out of the take-home earnings of the nuclear unit. Consequently, the dual-career family is premised upon the increased use of a class of workers locked into a standard of living considerably lower than their employers . . . it would provide the 'liberation' of one class of women by the continued subjugation of another" (Hunt and Hunt 1977, 413). Neither are the poor excluded morally. They are far from socially isolated; the virtues of work and the stable nuclear family are daily presented to them. For not only do they actually directly physically experience it in their roles of nannies, kitchen help, as waiters in restaurants and cleaners and bell boys in hotels—they receive from the mass media a daily ration of these virtues, indeed one that is in excess of that consumed by those who work in the primary labor market.

## Redemption through Labor

Work is central to the Government's attack on social exclusion. Work is the only route to sustained financial independence. But it is also much more. Work is not just about earning a living. It is a way of life. . . . Work helps to fulfil our aspirations—it is the key to independence, self-respect and opportunities for advancement . . . Work brings a sense of order that is missing from the lives of many unemployed young men. . . . [The socially excluded] and their families are trapped in dependency. They inhabit a parallel world where income is derived from benefits, not work; where school is an option, not a key to opportunity; and where the dominant influence on young people is the culture of the street, not the values that bind families and communities together. There are some estates in my constituency where the common currency is the giro; where the black economy involves much more than moonlighting—it involves the twilight world of drugs; and where relentless anti-social behaviour grinds people down . . .

—A speech by Harriet Harman, then Minister for Social Security, at the opening of the Centre for the Analysis of Social Exclusion at the London School of Economics, 1997

The worker . . . feels only outside of work, and during work he is outside himself. He is at home when he is not working and when he is working he is not at home. His work, therefore, is not voluntary, but coerced *forced labour*. It is not the satisfaction of a need but only a *means* to satisfy other needs. Its alien character is obvious from the fact that as soon as no physical or other pressure exists, labour is avoided like the plague. . . . Finally the external nature of work for the worker appears in the fact that it is not his own but another person's, that in work he does not belong to himself but to some one else . . . It is the loss of his own self.

—Karl Marx, *Economic and Philosophic Manuscripts*

To suggest that any work is better than no work and that work has this essential redeeming quality is bizarre in the extreme. Work, as John K. Galbraith so wryly commented in *The Culture of Contentment,* is largely repetitive and demeaning, the use of "work" by the "contented classes" to describe their highly paid, creative, and self-fulfilling activities in the same breath as the low-paid, oppressive chores of the working poor is a fraud of the first order. And to add to this the notion of the majority of work as an act of redemption, a liberation of the self, and a role model to one's children, as our New Labour politicians and their Democratic cousins would maintain, is to add insult to injury.

Even for the working majority, the main virtues of work are the coffee break, the wage packet, and the weekend. In fact the inherently boring and tedious nature of work seems to many people to be precisely the reason that one is paid to do it. It is what you *definitely* would not do if you were not being paid. Yet providing the hours are not too long and the wages high enough, a deal of some sort is being made based much more on the perceived obdurate, difficult, and unchanging nature of reality rather than any ideas of redemption. There is always the teenagers' Saturday night, the forty-somethings' house and car, the "real" world of home, kids, and television. But such a realpolitik of desire is far from redemption. The confusion arises, of course, as Galbraith points out, that for the contented classes work is indeed redemptive: it is

enjoyable, socially reputable and economically rewarding. Those who spend pleasant, well compensated days say with emphasis that they are "hard at work," thereby suppressing the notion that they are a favored class. They are, of course, allured to say that they enjoy their work, but it is presumed that such enjoyment is shared by any *good* worker. In a brief moment of truth, we speak, when sentencing criminals, of years at "hard labor." Otherwise we place a common gloss over what is agreeable and what, to a greater or lesser extent, is endured or suffered. (1992, 33)

The elite workers of stage, screen, and song, the sportsmen and women and the sizable segment of the contented middle classes for whom the day is never long enough—for all of these, their identity is based upon work. Take work away from them and they flounder hopelessly: their ontology *is* work. But if one part of society defines work as what they are, the other very definitely defines it as what they are not.

Below the contented top of society, the broad mass of people are, if anxious about job security, reconciled to the wage deal. But below that, for the working poor, the deal breaks down; the equivalence of selling time and buying leisure is frayed and insubstantial. To take family life as an example: the politicians' rhetoric about work sustaining the family and providing role models for the children is hollow if not downright cruel. In fact, the type of work available to many of the poor leaves little time for stable family relationships either to partners or to children and has wide repercussions for community instability. As Elliott Currie puts it, "Less often discussed [than lack of work] but not less important, is the effect of *overwork* in poorly-paid jobs on the capacity of parents to provide a nurturing and competent environment for childrearing and on the capacity of communities for self-regulation and the maintenance of networks of mutual support and care" (1997, 155).

To force people to work long and antisocial hours undermines the very "basic" morality of family and community that the politicians of all persuasions are constantly harping about. The way in which, for example, single mothers are forced into work at rates that scarcely makes affordable the child care that long hours at work necessitate, suggests ideology at work rather than any genuine care for people. The single mother looking after her children is dependent, the same mother paid to look after your children is by some miracle independent and resourceful. The true motive, the reduction of the tax burden of the well-off, is, as Galbraith suggests, thinly concealed by the rhetoric. Furthermore, the notion that such work provides role models for the children of the neighborhood is implausible: much more likely is that they make crime and the illicit markets of drug dealing all the more attractive. If there are indeed "seductions of crime," as Jack Katz (1988) suggests, then these seductions are all the more sweet given the misery of the alternatives.

## Including the Excluded

What I am suggesting is that both the unemployed and the working poor—
what one might call the overemployed—experience exclusion from social
citizenship, the first because they are denied basic economic substratum concomitant with the widespread expectations of what citizenship implies, the
second because they experience the nature of their work, the hours worked
and the remuneration, as unfair, as being outside of the norms of the wage
deal—a fair day's work for a fair day's pay. They are, of course, part of the
labor market but they are not full citizens. The dragooning, therefore, of
people from one category of exclusion to another ("getting the people to
work," as the Social Exclusion Unit [1999] put it with its cheerless double
entendre) is experienced all too frequently not as inclusion but as exclusion,
not as the "free" sale of labor, but as straightforward coercion.

The "New Deal," therefore, is not the solution but the problem; it is not
inclusion but palpable exclusion. The solution to the New Deal is engaging
in the hidden economy, drug dealing, becoming a single mother—the solution is what the aptly named Social Exclusion Unit sets out as the problem
(see Willis 2000, 89–91).

## Boundaries of Bulimia

Physical, social, and moral boundaries are constantly crossed in late modernity. As we have seen, they are transgressed because of individual movement,
social mobility, the coincidence of values and problems on both sides of any
line, and the tremendous incursion of the mass media that presents citywide
and indeed global images to all and sundry while creating virtual communities and common identities across considerable barriers of space. Boundaries
are crossed, boundaries shift, boundaries blur and are transfixed.

The socially excluded do not, therefore, exist in some "elsewhere" cut off
spatially, socially, and morally from the wider society. To suggest this is not to
say that physical barriers do not occur. Traffic is often routed so as to cut off
parts of town, transport systems leave whole tracts of the city dislocated from
the rest, and gated communities occur both in the fortunate and unfortunate
parts of the city. It is not to deny that a characteristic of late modern society
is the setting up of barriers, of exclusion. Nor is it to suggest that cultural
divisions are set up with society propelled by misconception and prejudice.
Indeed the discourse about social exclusion with its binary structure is itself
part of such an attempt to construct moral barriers and distinctions. Rather,

it is to say that such physical parameters are exaggerated, that the virtual communities set up by the mass media easily transcend physical demarcations, and that values are shared to a much greater extent than social isolation theorists would suggest. Of course subcultural variations exist within society but that is what they are, *sub*cultural: a variation in accentuation of core values rather than a deficit or difference in value.

The binary language of social exclusion fundamentally misunderstands the nature of late modernity. Here is a world where borders blur, where cultures cross over, hybridize, and merge, where cultural globalization breaks down, where virtual communities lose their strict moorings to space and locality. The late modern city is one of blurred boundaries; it was the Fordist city of modernity that had a segregated structure, a division of labor of specialized areas, a Chicago of concentric rings. Now the lines blur: gentrification occurs in the inner city, deviance occurs in the suburbs. It is a world of globalization not separation, of blurring not strict lines of demarcation; it is culturally a world of hybrids not of pedigrees, of minor not major differences—the very decline in the physical community and rise of its virtual counterpart means that it is impossible for an underclass to exist separately.

Once again none of this is to suggest that considerable forces of exclusion do not occur, but the process is not that of a society of simple exclusion that I originally posited. Rather it is one where both inclusion and exclusion occur concurrently—*a bulimic society* where massive cultural inclusion is accompanied by systematic structural exclusion. It is a society that has both strong centrifugal and centripetal currents: it absorbs and it rejects. Let us note first of all the array of institutions that impact the process of inclusion: the mass media, mass education, the consumer market, the labor market, the welfare state, the political system, the criminal justice system. Each of these carries with it a notion of universal values, of democratic notions of equality and reward and treatment according to circumstance and merit. Each of them has expanded throughout the century and has been accompanied by a steady rise in the notion of citizenship encompassing greater and greater parts of the population in terms of age, class, gender, and race. And within the period of late modernity, the mass media, mass education, and the consumer and labor markets have, in particular, increased exponentially. Each of these institutions is not only a strong advocate of inclusive citizenship, it is also paradoxically the site of exclusion. The consumer markets propagate a citizenship of joyful consumption, yet the ability to spend (and sometimes even to enter) within the mall is severely limited. The labor market incorporates more and more of the population (the entry of women into paid work being the prime example), yet, as André Gorz (1999) has so astutely stressed, precisely at the time when work is seen as a prime virtue of citizenship, well-paid, secure, and meaningful work is restricted to a tiny minority. The criminal justice system is on paper a paragon of equal rights. The British *Police and Criminal Evidence Act,* for example, governs amongst other things the powers of stop and search. It is a veritable cameo of neoclassicist notions of equality of citizens in the face of the law and the need for "democratic" suspicion, yet on the streets, in practice, policing is indisputably biased in terms of race and class (see Mooney and Young 2000). Politics is an hourly interjection of radio and television, the mass media speak on our part for "the common good," and "the average" man and woman—they even parade and interview Joe Public with regularity—yet the vast majority of people feel manifestly excluded from political decision making. Indeed even the tiny minority of active party members often feel impotent and uninfluential. Mass education is the major transmission belt of meritocratic ideas, it is the nursing ground of equal opportunity; yet, as subcultural theorists from Albert Cohen to Paul Willis have pointed out, its structures serve to reproduce class divisions and to exacerbate resentment. Lastly the mass media has a pivotal role. It has grown immensely and occupies a considerable part of waking life. In 1999, for example, the average person in England and Wales watched twenty-six hours of television, listened to nineteen hours of radio every week, and read, on top of that, mass circulation newspapers and magazines. That is, 40 percent of one's waking life is spent watching TV or listening to the radio, rising to 60 percent of your free time if you are lucky enough to be in work. The lower down the class structure—the more socially excluded, if you want—the citizen, the more mass media is consumed. Thus, paradoxically, cultural inclusion is the inverse of structural inclusion. The media carry strong notions of the universal citizen, and they, of course, depict the other institutions: the world of consumption, work, education, politics, and criminal justice. Yet despite this overall commitment to social order, the very stuff of news is the opposite: disorder, breakdown, mayhem, injustice (see Young 1981). To take the criminal justice system as an example: crime and police stories are a staple of both factual and fictional mass media, and the miscarriage of justice is a major theme. From the murder of Stephen Lawrence to the Cincinnati riots, from the Guildford Four to Rodney Hill, police prejudice, corruption, and incompetence is paraded daily. The mass media is a spectacular noticeboard of exclusion—it has all the characteristics of a bulimic narrative: it stresses order, justice, and inclusion (the backcloth of the news) yet it highlights disorder, injustice, and exclusion (the foreground).

The contrast between a bulimic society and an exclusive society can be seen if one compares Western liberal democracies (and perhaps the new South Africa) with an explicitly exclusive society, the South Africa of Hendrik Verwoerd and P. W. Botha. Here one had explicit spatial and social exclusion, a multiculturalist apartheid based on racist distinctions, a controlled mass media that refused (on the whole) to report police brutality and that extolled divisions. It was both exclusivist culturally and exclusivist structurally (see Dixon 2001).

The phenomenon of cultural globalization fundamentally ratchets up this process of bulimia. Television drama, news, advertisement contains not only plot, story, and product but a background of expectancies and assumptions. First world culture permeates the globe and carries with it notions of equality, meritocratic values, civil liberties—it proselytizes not only expectancies of standard of living but notions of freedom and citizenship.

I want to suggest that it is the bulimic nature of late modern societies that helps to explain the nature and tenor of the discontent at the bottom of the social structure. It is rooted quite simply in the contradiction between ideas that legitimate the system and the reality of the structure that constitutes it. But the tensions between ideals and reality exist only because of the general and manifest awareness of them. Both the punitive anger of the righteous and the burning resentment of the excluded occur because the demarcation lines are blurred, because values are shared and space is transfixed, because the same contradictions of reward and ontology exist throughout society, because the souls of those inside and those outside the "contented minority" are far from dissimilar, sharing the same desires and passions, and suffering the same frustrations, because there is no security of place nor certainty of being and because differences are not essences but mere intonations of the minor scales of diversity.

The very intensity of the forces of exclusion is a result of borders that are regularly crossed rather than boundaries that are hermetically sealed. No caste-like social order would be as transfixed with crime nor so ready to demonize and pillory the other. For it is an altogether unsatisfactory exclusion: borders and boundaries are ineffective; they create resentment but do not achieve exclusivity. The "excluded" regularly pass across the boundaries whether physically or virtually: they sense injustice, they *know* about inequality, whereas those "lucky" enough to be "included" are not part of the "culture of contentment" that John Galbraith famously alludes to. Rather, they are unsure about their good fortune, unclear about their identity, uncertain about their position on the included side of the line.

But to understand the nature of the forces of exclusion, the barriers set up to man the social structure, we must look at the predicament of the "included."

## The Precariousness of Inclusion

We have discussed in the process of bulimia how the excluded are included in the norms and social world of the wider society. But we can blur the binaries further, for we must now understand how the social predicament and experience of the insiders parallel those of the outsiders and how this process is the key to understanding some of the most fundamental antagonisms in late modern society.

In order to understand this, we must first of all distinguish the two basic facets of social order within advanced industrial societies. First of all, there is the principle that rewards are allocated according to merit, that is, a meritocratic notion of distributive justice. Secondly, we maintain that people's sense of identity and social worth is respected by others, that is, justice of recognition. When the first is infringed we speak of relative deprivation and when the second is violated we talk of misrecognition and ontological insecurity (see Young 2001; Fraser 1997). If we examine the terrain of late modernity in these key areas of distributive justice and justice of recognition, we find a high degree of uncertainty. My assessment is that in both these areas late modernity brings with it a sense of randomness: a chaos of reward and a chaos of identity. To take distributive justice first of all, the unraveling of the labor markets and the lottery of who finds themselves in each sector, the rise of a service industry consisting of diverse and disparate units, the seemingly random discontinuities of career, the profligate and largely unmerited rewards in the property market and in finance, all give a sense of rewards that are allocated by caprice rather than by the rules of merit. A generation that has been extensively instructed in the values of meritocracy are confronted with chaos in the market of rewards, and this engenders a feeling of relative deprivation that does not have the easy comparative points of position in industry within standardized careers characteristic of Fordism, mass manufacturing industry, and the Golden Age but is instead more individualistic in its envy, more internecine in its rivalry.

Secondly, in the area of recognition, of sense of worth and place, of ontology, there has been a parallel chaos. This is fueled by the widespread discontinuities of personal biography both in the world of work and within the family coupled with the undermining of a sense of locality—of physical place of belonging (see Young 2001). This disembeddedness (see Giddens 1991) creates an ontological insecurity—an identity crisis—with the most ready response being the evocation of an essentialism that asserts the core, unchanging nature of oneself and others. This consists of two stages: firstly an insistence of some essential and valued qualities (whether cultural or biological) that are associated with the individuals in question (whether of masculinity, "race," class, religion, or ethnicity), and secondly the denigration of others as essentially lacking these virtues (see Young 1999). Furthermore, such a process of mobilizing negative essences with regards to others creates prejudices, exclusions, and stereotypes within society that further fuel the feelings of ontological insecurity of others.

Both crime and punishment are areas greatly affected by these uncertainties. Relative deprivation especially when coupled with misrecognition and disparagement can readily lead to crime. The classic instance is economic marginalization of a group accompanied by police harassment. But relative deprivation can also occur where someone higher in the class structure looking down can see undeserved rewards unmatched with the disciplines of work and restraint. Just as the relative deprivation of the poor can lead to crime, the deprivation of the more wealthy can lead to feelings of punitiveness.

## The Focus on the Underclass

As we have seen, the hardworking citizen of the majority perceives a world where rewards seem allocated in a chaotic fashion. These rewards have become so diffuse that it is difficult to see rhyme or reason in society at large; hostility at this chaos of rewards tends to focus on the very rich or those at the bottom of the structure. That is, hostility focuses on those who are very obviously paid too much for the amount of work they do and those who are paid for doing no work; it fastens on the more obvious violators of meritocratic principle, namely the super rich and the underclass. The antagonism towards the idle rich and, for example, members of the royal family or company directors who allocate themselves incommensurate rewards, I have documented elsewhere (see Young 1999).

The underclass, although in reality a group heterogeneous in composition and ill defined in their nature, is a ready target for resentment (see Gans 1995, 2; Bauman 1998b, 66–67). Reconstituted, rendered clear-cut and homogenous by the mass media, they became a prime focus of public attention in the sense of stereotypes—"the undeserving poor," "the single mother," "the welfare scrounger," and so forth—and an easy focus of hostility. Such stereotypes derive their constitution from the process of essentializing, so prevalent because of the prevalent crisis of identity, which results in a ready pool of negative images, the opposite of the "virtues" of the included. Thus if the chaos of reward creates ready hostility towards the underclass, the chaos of identity grasps upon them as a phantasmagoric Other with all the opposite characteristics of the world of honest hardworking citizens and a ready prop to ontological security.

But note the paradox, here: an underclass that is, in fact, very similar to the rest of society generates antagonism and distancing. The poor become more like the more wealthy at the same time as they are "othered" by them; the degree to which the poor become more like the rest, the more they resent their exclusion. Indeed, as we shall see, it is the narrowing of cultural differences that allows resentment to travel both ways along this two-way street. Zygmunt Bauman insightfully notes how it is the very similarity of aspiration that the underclass has that exacerbates the dislike of them just as it is this self-same aspiration, thwarted, that creates discontent among the excluded. Thus in his critique of Laurence Mead, he writes:

> "The underclasses offend all the cherished values of the majority while cling-ing to them and desiring the same joys of consumer life as other people boast to have *earned*. In other words, what Americans hold against the underclass in their midst is that its dreams and the model of life it desires are so uncannily similar to their own." Further, and the other side of the coin, "it is logic of consumer society to mould its poor as unfilled consumers [yet] it is precisely that inaccessibility of consumer lifestyles that the consumer society trains its members to experience as the most powerful of deprivations." (1998b, 73)

## Crime and the Narrowing of Differences

Feelings of discontent, of unfairness both in terms of material reward and recognition, are experienced either when cultural differences diminish or when those that were once similar began to be regarded differently. That is because discontent relates to relative, not to absolute, deprivation (see Run-ciman 1966). Thus discontent rises: when migrants are assimilated or when lower classes are granted citizenship or when ethnic groups, once separate, become part of the mainstream; coupled with blockages of social mobility, limited access to privileged labor markets, and public prejudice and denigra-tion—we have, in short, an incomplete meritocracy. The importance then of the ethnographies of Carl Nightingale (1993) on the black underclass of

Philadelphia and Philippe Bourgois (1995) on the Puerto Ricans of the East Harlem barrio of New York City is that they root discontent in the *narrowing* of cultural differences. In the first case, Nightingale traces how much of African American culture of the South is lost in the assimilated generation growing up in the northern cities. Bourgois shows how it is the second-generation Puerto Rican immigrants becoming more "American" who experience the greatest discontent.

Thus the breakdown of spatial and social isolation in late modernity, which I have documented: globalization, the mass media, the consumer market, mass education leads to a diminishing of cultural differences and a rise in discontent both within nations and between nations.

## Toward a Sociology of Vindictiveness

> Oh tell me brave Captain why are the wicked so strong? How do the angels get to sleep when the devil leaves his porch light on?
> —Tom Waits, "Mr. Siegal," *Heartattack and Vine*

Relative deprivation downwards, a feeling that those who work little or not at all are getting an easy ride on your back and your taxes, is a widespread sentiment. Thus whereas the "contented" middle classes may well feel sympathy towards the underclass and their "relative satisfaction" with their position translates into feelings of charity, those of the much larger constituency of discontent are more likely to demand welfare-to-work programs, stamping down on dole "cheats," and so forth. Such a response, whatever its rationality, is not in itself punitive: it is at most authoritarian, but it is not necessarily vindictive. But tied to such a quasi-rational response to a violation of meritocratic principles is frequently a much more compelling subtext that seeks not only to redress a perceived reluctance to work but to go beyond this to punish, demean, and humiliate (see Pratt 2000; Hallsworth 2000).

The key features of such resentment are disproportionality, scapegoating, and stereotyping. The group selected is seen to contribute to the problems of society quite disproportionally to their actual impact (for example, teenage mothers, beggars, immigrants, drug users), and they are scapegoated and depicted as key players in the creation of social problems. Their portrayal is presented in an extraordinarily stereotypical fashion that bears little relationship to reality. In *The Exclusive Society,* I note how there seems to be a common narrative in such depictions of late modern folk devils that is common from "single mothers" to "drug addiction" (see Young 1999, 113).

Svend Ranulf in his pathbreaking book *Moral Indignation and Middle Class Psychology* (1938/1964) was intrigued by the desire to punish those who do not directly harm you. Such "moral indignation," he writes, is "the emotion behind the disinterested tendency to inflict punishment [and] is a kind of disguised envy" (1964, 1). He explores this emotion using the concept of resentment, which was first used by Nietzsche in his condemnation of the moral basis of Christian ethics and developed by Max Scheler in his "Das Ressentiment im Aufbau der Moralen" (1923). Resentment has within it the impulse, as Merton put it, to "condemn what one secretly craves" (1957, 156). Ranulf's innovation was to locate resentment sociologically and to tie the source of envy to restraint and self-discipline. Thus, he writes, "the disinterested tendency to inflict punishment is a distinctive characteristic of the lower middle class, that is, of a social class living under conditions that force its members to an extraordinarily high degree of restraint and subject them to much frustration of natural desires" (1938/1964, 198).

It cannot be an accident that the stereotype of the underclass—with its idleness, dependency, hedonism, and institutionalized irresponsibility, with its drug use, teenage pregnancies, and fecklessness—represents all the traits that the respectable citizen has to suppress in order to maintain his or her lifestyle. Or as Albert Cohen famously put it, "The dedicated pursuit of culturally approved goals, the eschewing of interdicted but tantalizing goals, the adherence to normatively sanctioned means—these imply a certain self-restraint, effort, discipline, inhibition. What effect does the propinquity of the wicket have on the peace of mind of the virtuous?" (1965, 7). Such a social reaction is moral indignation rather than moral concern. The demons are not the fallen and the pitiful that fixate the philanthropist; rather they at once attract and repel: they are the demons within us that must daily be renounced. Thus the stereotype of minorities is not a wholly negative identity, for as Homi Bhabha reminds us, in a telling phrase, it is a "complex, ambivalent, contradictory mode of representation as anxious as it is assertive" (1993, 70).

The rigors of late modernity extend such restraints and insecurities far beyond a narrow class band. A large part of the population is subject to relative deprivation and ontological uncertainties, and the pressures and restraints necessary to function exacerbate this even further. To survive in the late modern world demands a great deal of effort, self-control, and restraint. Not only is the job insecure and poorly paid, the hours worked are long—extra hours are expected as a sign of commitment and responsibility—children are often not seen for long after the long commute home—*people talk of "quality time" as a euphemism for "little"*—the weekends seem short and enjoyment has to be snatched often with the liberal aid of alcohol. The dual-career family more and more becomes a norm with the planning both of adults' and children's schedules that this entails.

Let us summarize the restraints:

- increased working hours (see Gorz 1999; Schor 1993)
- increased intensity of work (see Burchell 1999)
- increased commuting (see Knox 1995)
- dual-career family (see Gregson and Lowe 1994; Taylor 1999)

It is the experience of restraint and sacrifice that turns simple displeasure (a sense of unfairness) into vindictiveness. Furthermore, the climate of work pressure and job uncertainty pervades a wide swathe of the class structure: it is not restricted to the lower middle classes, which Ranulf pinpointed, in line with much of the thinking at the time with its concerns about the rise and social basis of fascism (see also Luttwak 1995). Moreover, this climate of restraint exists on the top of the problems of job security and fairness of rewards and the crises of identity—we thus have a three-layered process, each layer contributing to the process of the demonization of the underclass:

1. Sense of Economic Injustice: the feeling that the underclass unfairly live on our taxes and commit predatory crime against us fuels the dislike and fear of them;
2. Crisis of Identity: The underclass readily become a site for establishing identity by asserting the binary them and us where "us" is normal, hardworking, decent and "them" is lacking these essential qualities. It is such essentialism that demonizes the underclass—constituting them as a homogenous, clear-cut, dysfunctional entity;
3. The Situation of Restraint: It is the projection of all the problems of restraint that supplies the *content* of the demonization: the various supposed facets of underclass life; teenage pregnancy, single motherhood, substance abuse, criminogenic cultures, highly racialized (immigrants, asylum seekers).

Such a process is, of course, not that of simple envy. The lawyer does not want to be a junkie, the professional woman certainly did not want to be a teenage mother, the bank manager could not countenance being a street beggar, the life of the new wave traveler does not instantly draw the careful couple from Croydon (an English suburb). Certainly not: for both real and imagined reasons, the lives of such disgraced "Others" are impoverished and immiserized. No one would want to swap places with them. But their very existence, their moral intransigence, somehow hits all the weak spots of our character armor. Let us think for one moment of the hypothetical day of the hypothetical "included" citizen on the advantaged side of the binary: the traffic jam on the way to work, the hours that have been slowly added to the working day, the crippling cost of housing and the mortgage that will never end, the need for both incomes to make up a family wage, the delay in having children so that the woman's career can get established, the fear of biological clocks and infertility, the daily chore of getting the children to school across the crowded city, the breakdown of locality and community, the planning of the day of two careers and two children (thank God for the mobile phone!), the lack of time with the children, the fear of missing out—"they've grown up before you knew it"—the temptations and fears of the abuse of alcohol as a means of enjoyment, in the time slots between the rigors of work . . .

It is surely not difficult to see how an underclass who, at least in stereotype, are perceived as having their children irresponsibly early, hanging around all day with their large families, having public housing provided almost free, living on the dole, staying up late drinking and taking exotic, forbidden substances, and on top of all that committing incivilities and predatory crimes against the honest citizen, are an easy enemy. They set off every trigger point of fear and desire.

## The Change in the Focus of Reward

Resentment is more than just unfairness when someone receives a reward disproportionate to their merit. Resentment is when someone short-circuits the whole marketplace of effort and reward, when they are perceived as getting exactly what they want without any effort at all—or more precisely exactly what *you* want and can only achieve with great effort. But there is an extra twist to this: an additional ratchet up of the situation. The equation of merit and reward has shifted in late modernity from an emphasis on merit to a focus on reward. Effort, delayed gratification, meriticious progress towards a goal has given way to immediacy, gratification now, short-term hedonism. Work may well be valued, as André Gorz suggests, but hard graft is not. The whole tenor of a society, based on a lavish underwriting of credit, an economy based on the exhortation to possess *now,* is that of a consumer society based on instant gratification. The old values of hard work leading to a deserved reward—the Keynesian formula of working hard and playing hard, characteristic of the Golden Age of modernity (see Young 1971) has given way to a society where the consumer is the paragon and spontaneity the king. Restraint, planning, and control of behavior may be the necessary undergirding of the included citizen, but there is no one out there to admire or congratulate such sacrifices. Furthermore, there is a strange irony here because, whatever the political perspective on the underclass, whether they are seen to have alternative values or lack them, their behavior is seen to epitomize spontaneity, short-term hedonism, lack of planning, immediacy. All the classic statements regarding lower-class culture highlight this combination, whether it is Walter Miller writing in the 1950s or Charles Murray writing today. And if those on the right see this as a collation of individual failures, those on the left see it as a fairly rational plan of action given the unpredictability and insecurity of any long-term future. For if everything is uncertain, you might as well enjoy yourself while you can.

The circle becomes nearly complete: just as the excluded absorb the values of the wider society that both incorporates them and rejects them, the values of the wider society and the margins begin to converge. The central ethos of late modern capitalism becomes like the ethos of the ghetto. Conservative commentators of some acuity have noted this convergence. Myron Magnet, the author of *The Dream and the Nightmare* (1993) and reputedly a great influence on President George W. Bush, locates the problem of the underclass not in their individual failings but in the influence of the new middle-class values that have devalued all the things that would get you out of poverty (such as hard work and marital stability) and valued all of the things that keep the poor in poverty (taking drugs, personal liberation, valuing leisure rather than work). What these writers fail to do is relate these values to changes in late modern capitalism and to the exigencies of life today. Not only do such market values of immediacy permeate all corners of society, the predicament of all people, included and excluded, becomes more similar and favors short-term solutions and immediate pleasures. Thus Gabriel and Lang, in their insightful study of the late-modern consumer society, note how

> The weakening of the Fordist Deal suggests to us that Western consumerism has entered a twilight phase. During the high noon of consumerism, the face of the consumer was clear . . . The pursuit of happiness through consumption seemed a plausible, if morally questionable, social and personal project. Today, this is far more problematic. The economic conditions have become fraught . . . insecurity is experienced across social classes . . . Proponents of consumerism live in the hope that tomorrow will see another bright day. We think this vision is the product of wishful thinking . . .

A far more realistic picture is that casualization of work will be accompanied by casualization of consumption. Consumers will lead precarious and uneven existences, one day enjoying unexpected booms and the next sinking to bare subsistence. Precariousness, unevenness and fragmentation are likely to become more pronounced for ever-increasing sections of Western populations. Marginality will paradoxically become central. (1995, 189–90)

## Toward a Criminology of Transgression

But what of the underclass? The same forces that shape the resentment of those higher in the structure to those below serve to constitute the feelings of exclusion in the lowest point of the structure. Thus relative deprivation and a crisis of identity affect both parts of society although the direction of the hostility so conjured up and the poignancy of its impact are very different indeed.

In the case of the underclass, the acute relative deprivation forged out of exclusion from the mainstream is compounded with a daily threat to identity: a disrespect, a sense of being a loser, of being *nothing,* of humiliation. The source of this systematic disrespect lies, of course, in the dynamics of deprivation, identity crisis, and restraint among those in the secondary labor market—the precariously included that I have outlined above. It is crystallized in particular in the institutions of policing, where the poor become the overwhelming focus of police attention, a "police property," which serves to help constitute collections of youths, street gangs as a group, and where the police become central characters in the narrative of the streets. It is important to underline how the humiliation of poverty and the humiliation of lack of respect interact—that is, problems of gross economic and status inequality—both on a day-to-day level and on an ideological level. To take the latter, first as Bauman has pointed out (2001), income inequality and status inequality (and in turn the politics of redistribution and recognition) are not separate arenas, but misrecognition and disrespect *justifies* income inequality. Thus the poor are seen to be inadequate, dependent, have the wrong personal skills and attitudes as if in a social vacuum. In more extreme cases poverty is simply rationalized as a product of biology or culture.

It is the double stigma of poverty and lack of respect that shapes the life and cultural resistance of the underclass. And all of this, of course, is not in a situation of alienation from the mainstream society but the very reverse. For social bulimia involves the incorporation of mainstream social values of success, wholehearted acceptance of the American (or First World) Dream,

and a worship of consumer success and celebrity. It is this cultural incorporation that puts the sting into the humiliation of exclusion—it is much
easier to ignore a system one despises than one that one believes in.

How is such a double stigmatization reacted to? Let us first note that the
situation of poverty in late modernity would seem to be qualitatively different
than that in the past. Bauman (Bauman and Tester 2001), for example, contrasts the dignity, solidarity, and self-respect of many working-class people in
the Great Depression of the thirties. And as for crime, accounts of that time
stress its utilitarian nature (to tackle directly material needs) and the external
targets of crime rather than crime within the group (see Hood and Jones
1999). Further, as John Hagedorn (1991) has indicated, a shift in the nature
of youth gangs has occurred from ones that were a popular and functional
part of the community to ones that are conflictful and dysfunctional.

Today the poor seem to exist in self-blame and mutual hatred (see, for
example, Seabrook 1988; Sennet and Cobb 1972). Wacquant talks of the
Hobbesian nature of the ghetto poor ("You just gotta be alert Louie in this
neighbourhood here. *You gotta be alert*—know what it is? It's the *law of the
jungle.* Louie: *Bite or be bitten.* And I made my choice long time ago: *I'm not
gonna be bitten, by no one.* Which one do you choose?" Wacquant 1998, 133),
which is reiterated in Philippe Bourgois's harrowing "Just Another Night in
a Shooting Gallery" (1998).

And crime, of course, becomes internecine rather than directed at the
wealthy. There is no shortage of punitive violence among the poor. The
homicide rate, for example, for blacks in the United States is 8.6 times that
of whites and one must remember that the vast majority of black homicides
(94 percent) are intraracial—black upon black (see Mann 1993; DeKeseredy
and Schwartz 1996). In Donald Schwarz's study of inner-city Philadelphia
over a four-year period (1987–90), a staggering 40 percent of black men in
their twenties had been to a hospital emergency room at least once for some
serious injury resulting from violent assault (Currie 1996; Schwarz et al. 1994).
It would be more precise to use statistics by class but these are few and far
between, and while undoubtedly blacks are much poorer than whites, the
existence of a not inconsiderable black middle class in the United States,
with a considerably lower homicide rate, serves to significantly soften these
figures—dramatic as they are. The poor predate the poor quite apart from
their markedly unfavorable predicament as victims of corporate, white-collar, and state crimes.

It is not only, therefore, that the included, the more comfortably off, are
punitive and blaming of the underclass; the poor are self-blaming and puni-

tive to each other. How does this come about? I would point to two factors: the chaos of reward, which I have mentioned previously, and the shift from a politics of class to a politics of identity and with it the rise of celebrity.

In any other society, the chaos of reward might be experienced merely as the arbitrary nature of destiny and fate: the random allocations of Lady Luck. But in a society where meritocracy is pronounced in every television program, media, and schoolyard, such a chaos is felt as an unfairness. In the Fordist structures of high modernity, such unfairness involved comparisons between the serried ranks of roughly equivalent jobs in industry, in the public bureaucracies. The rise of the service industries, of part-time contracts, of outsourcing to myriad small firms, the short-term nature of any job, and the decline of the lifelong narrative of work, each stage with a predictable increase in income, make such large-scale comparisons less possible. Relative deprivation—once in Runciman's (1966) phrase "fraternal," comparisons between individuals on equivalent level or disputes between levels of reward—becomes "egoistic," comparisons between atomistic individuals.

The effect of the chaos of reward is, of course, exerted throughout the social structure. For the included, however, there is one frontier that seems clear and distinct, that between those that work and those who are "work shy"—the chaos of reward, therefore, underwrites the targeting of the underclass. But for those at the bottom of the structure, lack of work looks like self-failure and the allocation of the meager state handouts and provisions on the basis of need rather than "merit" generates divisions between individuals and frequently between ethnic groups.

While poverty is deplored, success is celebrated. The rise of celebrity, the extent to which it replaces notions of class and traditional conceptions of authority is a key transformation in late modernity. Laurence Friedman in his brilliant book *The Horizontal Society* (1999) points to the distinguishing features of celebrities. They are famous, of course, but also they are ordinary and familiar. People feel they know them, that they can speak directly to them. Above all, "a celebrity society [is one] of mobility. The boy from the ghetto can earn millions as a basketball player. The kid next door can become a rap star or a talk-show host. The girl down the block can become another Madonna or a Hollywood star. Celebrities can communicate easily with ordinary people. They do not speak an arcane, élitist language. This is because they *are* ordinary persons" (1999, 34–35). Friedman stresses the sense of accident or fate seemingly behind celebrity. Anyone might become a celebrity: "Fixity has vanished. Lightning can always strike. Anything can happen. Anything does" (35). The celebrity is like us, is talented but lucky, is chosen by us not imposed upon us—but most important of all, the celebrity *deserves* their money and their prestige. The success of celebrity echoes the chaos of reward. As Bauman puts it:

> No longer the moral tales of a shoeshine boy turning into a millionaire through hard work, parsimony and self-denial. An altogether different fairy tale instead, of chasing moments of ecstasy, spending lavishly and stumbling from one stroke of luck to another, with both luck and misadventure being accidental and inexplicable and but tenuously related to what the lucky and unlucky did, and seeking luck, as one seeks a willing lottery ticket, in order to chase more fun and have more moments of ecstasy and spending more lavishly than before. (Bauman and Tester 2001, 118)

And, of course, the luck of celebrity is enacted in the instant fame of *Big Brother* or the speedily fabricated success of *Pop Idol*.

There seems little doubt that the poor celebrate the celebrity. The conspicuous consumption of the ghetto, the immersion in the mass media, the values of luck and excitement, and even the fact that a *few* of their number escape to become stars of music, sport, and entertainment—all make for a close attraction. As for the wider society, I have more reservations: the need for daily restraint, the valuing of meritocratic achievement, the emphasis on hard work *despite* the general debt-based accentuation on consumption now all make for a certain ambiguity rather than undiluted enthusiasm. Despite this, the preeminence of the politics of status and identity and the emergence of celebrity as the apex point of stratification over the older politics of class and arguments over redistribution is a general phenomenon (see Bauman 2001; Fraser 1997). It is detrimental in several ways: it conceals the massive divisions in society between on the one hand the super-rich, and on the other those that sell their labor or are unable to do so and the possible alliance between them. By collating wealth and celebrity, it presents as *natural* that only a few people are the focus of overwhelming financial and status privilege.

Let us conclude this section with the astringent comments of Laurence Friedman on celebrity:

> Very little seems to be left of the old class-based rage—rage at the cruel, unfair way the world distributes its goods; it has been extinguished, except for a few dying embers. Not many people, it seems, connect their own sufferings and privations, their own hunger and longings, with the wealth they see all around them. To the contrary, the money of the rich smells sweet to them. For Marxists, capitalist wealth was blood money, money squeezed from the sweat and muscles of starving workers, money poisoned by poverty, disease, and death; money was greed, exploitation; it was man's oppression of man.

Contemporary money is radically different; magically, it has been washed clean of these bad associations. The public mind connects it with fun: with the world of sports and entertainment. The new (and glamorous) rich are movie stars, rock-and-roll musicians, baseball and soccer players, heroes of TV sitcoms. These are indeed the most visible rich. They breed no resentment. Indeed, the masses seem all too eager to contribute their share of the rents and the tributes. . . .

All this has a profound effect on politics as well as on policies. It explains why, in the 1990s, a politics of low taxes, flat taxes, or even no taxes has become so popular; the progressive income tax has been radically flattened out; death taxes are cut or (in California) eliminated; yet masses of people, who themselves barely scrape by, who have no job security, let alone an estate to worry about, go to the polls and reelect the rich and the representatives of the rich. They refuse to throw the rascals out or to storm the Bastille. Indeed, these masses direct their hatred and disgust, in the main, not against the blatant rich but against those who are worse off than they are: the poor, racial minorities, immigrants, and everyone who is the total inverse of a celebrity. The lifestyle of the rich and famous is the opium of the masses. (1999, 46–47)

## Humiliation and Rebellion

> I'll chill like Pacino, deal like De Niro, Black Gambino, die like a hero.
>
> —Rakim, "Juice (Know the Ledge)" in Carl Nightingale, *On the Edge*

Carl Nightingale's ethnography of the black Philadelphian underclass makes the brave, almost audacious leap of understanding that the culture of the ghetto is not one of isolation and alienation but involves a wholehearted yet desperate embracing of mainstream American values. And indeed all the portfolio of values are available out there: the stress on consumption and immediacy, on machismo, on the use of violence as a preferred means of settling problems both in movies and in military adventures (and more recently in movies about military adventures), and in racist stereotypes and divisions. Nightingale sees such a process as an overaccentuation of the mainstream (rather like Matza and Sykes's [1957] celebrated depiction of juvenile delinquency and subterranean values)—and that this is *compensatory*, easing the pains and humiliations of poverty and racism. Although I think this description of ghetto values is perceptive and accurate, I worry about the psychologistic causality here, with, for example, the invocation of "psychic relief" and the notion that further psychological pain comes from relegitimating the very values that "created their hurtful memories" (see, for example, Nightingale 1993, 218, 55n). In this it is remarkably similar to the "reaction formation" invoked forty years earlier by Albert Cohen in his classic *Delin-quent Boys: The Culture of the Gang* (1955). It might be useful if we return to the two stigmas that the underclass confront, that of relative deprivation (poverty and exclusion from the major labor markets) and misrecognition (lower status and lack of respect). Both of these are forms of humiliation with poverty amid abundance the most humiliating stigma of all: as Bau-man puts it, "a meta-humiliation of sorts, soil on which all-round indignity thrives, a trampoline from which multiple humiliation is launched" (Bauman and Tester 2001, 154). Such a crisis of identity, a need to combat a feeling of being a "nobody," a "loser," a worthless person, produces precisely the same process of essentialization that I described earlier, experienced by those who are part of the socially included—however precariously and tenuously. But it is done with a much a greater intensity and with a different context and outcome by the excluded. That is the generation of a notion of hardness, a fixity, a difference of self based on gender (for example, hypermasculinity), ethnicity, "turf" (locality), and age (for example, the gang). This is seen most in hypermasculinity where, as Nightingale points out, by the fifth or sixth grade, "the bright eyes of the boy students start to glaze over in prepa-ration for assuming a tough look" (1993, 47). The children metamorphose before one's eyes. Such a process of essentializing oneself is greatly facili-tated by essentializing others—but not the rich and the celebrated, as we have seen, not vertical but horizontal divisions: by men against women, by ethnic group against ethnic group, by gang against gang, by locality against locality. Even the essentializing projections of the better off, the othering of the poor, becomes used by the poor to essentialize themselves. The result is widespread self-referral as "nigga," the cult of "badness," the ethical inver-sion of "motherfucker," "pimp," or "b-boy."

The humiliation of poverty finds its "magical" solution in the cult of con-sumerism, in children who learn the trademarks BMW, Nike, Gucci from an early age, who value designer labels, watches, and blatant jewelry. For, unlike the labor market, the consumer society allows easy and universal entry—the sneakers and gold chains are within reach. The American poor eat their way to obesity in pursuit of the American Dream. Although they are flawed con-sumers, the market welcomes micro-consumerism just as it flaunts wealth while excluding the poor. The response of consumerism merely exacerbates relative deprivation rather than alleviating it. As for the hardened response of hypermasculinity, such cultures of toughness, as Paul Willis pointed out in his classic *Learning to Labour* (1977), merely trap them in the lowest part of the structure. Philippe Bourgois details with grim fascination in *In Search of Respect* (1995) how the street identity cultivated by the men from El Barrio—that incorporates limited social skills, assumed gendered arrogance, and an intimidating physical presence—rendered them well nigh unemployable in the burgeoning FIRE service sector of Manhattan. In the office, they appear clumsy and illiterate to their often female supervisors: "They cannot walk down the hallway to the water fountain without unconsciously swaying their shoulders aggressively as if patrolling their home turf. Gender barriers are an even more culturally charged realm. They are repeatedly reprimanded for offending co-workers with sexually aggressive behavior" (Bourgois 1995, 143; see also the discussion in Jay McLeod's *Ain't No Makin' It*, 1995). The major point of all these ethnographers who work in social reproduction theory is that it is not simply that structures oppress the agents, but the social agents themselves contribute in a pyrrhic fashion to their exclusion and oppression: "In the process, on a daily level [of searching for respect] they become the actual agents administering their own destruction and their community's suffering" (Bourgois 1995, 143).

## The Criminology of Transgression

> He looked at the briefcase filled with money, the grocery bag filled with cocaine, the briefcase and the bag side by side in the corner of the room. Funny how neither one meant a damn thing to him. The money couldn't buy him anything better than he had right now, than he had felt that afternoon: the risk of just taking something you decided was yours, the head-up feeling in your stride afterward when you were walking away. *The ride* . . . It was all about the ride.
>
> . . . Cooper was going to take this ride as far as it would go 'cause it *felt* good. Course, he knew the way it was going to end, the same way it always ended for guys like him who never had no chance, and didn't give a good fuck if one came along. The point of it all was to walk like a motherfuckin' man; if you had to, go down like one, too.
>
> —George P. Pelecanos, *King Suckerman*

> As a criminal I have been a lamentable failure. Whatever money I have gained by crime, I could have earned as a labourer in half the time I have spent in prison. My character, which is uncompromising and addicted to taking risks, was a guarantee that I could not be a success as a thief or a bandit. But money has always been a secondary goal; crime has always been directed to more powerful objectives. I took to crime as a course which was dictated by life itself; success or failure in the actual commission of criminal acts was never a matter of much concern to me, nor did they stand in the way of what I was really seeking, which was a particular kind of life style.
>
> Also I am not a really materialistic person. Money has never been, or ever will be, my primary object. Inside or outside, I was always liked by my

own kind. My life was always exciting and dramatic; wherever I was, I was part of the action. Psychologically, I had the satisfaction of personifying the counter-culture with which I identified myself, and I found this was confirmed by my notoriety and prestige. I embodied the supreme virtue of the criminal underworld, and I revelled in the greatest compliment it can bestow—gameness

—John McVicar, *McVicar: By Himself*

I have noted how the response of the included to the poor is more than simply a meritocratic desire to ensure that benefits are drawn fairly and work is not actively avoided. There is a vituperative quality posited on the back of the rationale of control. Similarly with regards to crime, the punitive turn has a vindictiveness that goes beyond the principles of neoclassicism and deserved punishment. Just so with crime: the criminality of the underclass is not simply a utilitarian affair involving the stealing of money or property for food or drink or drugs, for that matter—although all of these devices are part of the motivation. Violence is not a just simple instrument for persuading people to part with their cash nor a management technique in the corporate world of organized crime. Drug use is not a prosaic matter of the pleasures of the poor—an alternative psychoactive experience to gin and tonic or a light and bitter after a hard day at the office. Rather it has, all of these have, a transgressive edge. They are driven by the energies of humiliation—the utilitarian core is often there, but around it is constructed a frequent delight in excess, a glee in breaking the rules, a reassertion of manhood and identity. It is this that the cultural criminologists—Ferrel (1997), Presdee (2000), and Hayward (2002), for example—have highlighted in their critique of neoliberal criminology (for example, Felson 1998; Garland 2001) with its depiction of crime as an outcome of rational choice that occurs in a situation of easy opportunity within a rubric of institutions of weak control (see Young 2002).

In this revision of the conventional liberal wisdoms of the causes of crime, we need to look back at the classic texts. For Robert Merton (1938), crime was an alternative route to the American Dream. In his famous typology, it was an "adaption" or an "adjustment" where the "strain" of not having access to legitimate opportunities led to recourse to illegitimate avenues. The goals of success were unaltered; the cash to achieve them merely was achieved by illegal means. Jack Katz in his *Seductions of Crime* (1988), the major influence on the new cultural criminology, points out that the Mertonian vision of crime simply does not fit the phenomenology of crime: the versatility, the zest, the sensuousness of the criminal act. He points to the attractions of evil, the ways of the "badass," the transformative magic of violence. All of this is very much to the point, but in his correct emphasis on the neglected foreground of infraction, the heightened mental state of the offender, he rejects the structural background. Any such determinism he sees as a gross materialism, a liberal apologia that attempts to link too easily structural poverty to crime—bad background to bad behavior. I think Katz throws the baby out with the bathwater, to simply invert the conventional wisdom by highlighting agency and rejecting structure. Yet we have already seen in our discussion of social reproduction theory and the ethnographies of the underclass how structure and agency interplay. Our job is to emphasize both structure and agency and trace how each constitutes the other (see Giddens 1984 for a discussion of structuration). The structural predicament of the ghetto poor is not simply a deficit of goods—as Merton would have had it—but a state of humiliation that often overwhelms cultural and political resistance. And crime, because it is driven by humiliation rather than by some simple desire to redistribute property, is transgressive. The theory of bulimia that I have proposed involves incorporation and rejection, cultural inclusion and structural exclusion, as with Merton, but it goes further than this, emphasizing that this combination of acceptance followed by rejection generates a dynamic of resentment of great intensity. It is Merton with energy; it is Katz with structure.

## The Humiliation of Exclusion

For Merton (1938), crime was an alternative route to the American Dream, and this prognosis was developed by Richard Cloward and Lloyd Ohlin, so that for the citizen cut off from legitimate opportunities and where illegitimate chances were readily available, criminal behavior was as normal as going out to work. The rich subcultural tradition that followed Merton, represented today by theorists such as William Julius Wilson (1987, 1985), carry forward this analysis presenting forcefully the notion of crime occurring where there is "social isolation" from the world of work.

Wacquant's hustlers, for example, "do not . . . experience . . . rejection from the labour market as a major trauma. This is because holding a stable and well paid portion, a 'legit job' liable to guarantee a modicum of security, has never been part of his horizon of expectations: where marginalization becomes part of *the order of things*, it deprives one even of the consciousness of exclusion" (1998, 13). Anyway, legitimate jobs simply do not compete with the criminal. "What good would it be to take the 'legit route' when the resulting rewards are so meager and almost as uncertain as those more immediate and palpable even if they come at high risks, offered by the street economy?" (Wacquant 1998, 14).

Contrary to this, I have argued throughout that marginalization does have an impact. Bourgois's crack dealers, for example, were far from unaware of the world of legitimate work. They were ridden with self-doubt about their exclusion, had fantasies about being a "normal working nigga," had been in work, and had been humiliated by the world of work. They simultaneously wanted to be legitimate and despised it, but they were far from being oblivious of it (see 1995, chapter 4). It is this humiliation that leads to the transgressive nature of much crime, however utilitarian its core. It is this transgression that means that although crime may be a substitute for work, it is rarely *like* work as many theorists would like us to believe. It is not just the psychotropic qualities of cocaine that make cocaine dealing an erratic, violent, and irascible affair, nor do the international aspects of its trade make the cartels like the corporations that deal in margarine or aluminum.

## Hip Hop across the Borders

I have argued against the use of binaries, against the current discourse on social exclusion that contrasts an included citizen who is contented, secure, and ontologically certain over against the excluded member of the underclass who lacks all of these positives. I have criticized the notion of the dual city where lines are not crossed and where each part of the binary inhabit different moral universes. None of this dismisses the very real physical and social exclusions that rack late modern societies and the system-driven stigmatization and othering that characterize these relations. But such an intensity of exclusion—and the corresponding resentment of the excluded—is propelled by the similarities of values and the transgression of borders. The world of late modernity abhors separateness just as it avidly sets up barriers. Globalization means nothing if it does not imply transgression: of a world brought closer together and the diminishing of cultural differences. How often does one have to say there are no strict lines of demarcation in late modernity? Even in the most ethnically segregated cities of the West—Washington, Philadelphia, and Los Angeles—the barriers are daily breached by the mobility of labor and the all-pervasive penetration of the mass media. The values of the majority constitute the normative life of the minority and generate the bulimia that fuels their discontent. The very similarity of the underclass, indeed its overidentification with the values of consumerism and hedonism, sets itself up almost like an unwitting target for the resentment of the included. Each facet of underclass behavior mocks the daily restraints of the included. Yet there is fascination here as well as disliking and fear. The culture of the underclass—its compensatory masculinity, resorts to violence, and rampant individualism—is marked by overaccentuations of the wider culture, which then influences film, fashion, and popular music. The culture of the excluded becomes the culture of the included, or at least the young and those precariously included who grow to be a larger and larger part of the population. Hypermasculinity resonates far out of the ghetto: the swagger and misogyny of rap stirs the resentment of the white poor and extends further to the swathes of young men in the respectable and lower middle classes who no longer can feel continuity and certainty in their lives. The borders are transgressed, the boundaries are criss-crossed, the center begins to resemble the margins just as the margins the center.

## Note

The theme of this article was developed in Jock Young, *Crossing the Borderline: The Vertigo of Late Modernity*. London: Sage.

1. Charles Murray, often criticized as a "culturalist" in the underclass debate, explicitly denies that this is his position. Thus in his rejoinder to critics, he rejects the culture of poverty thesis, noting, "How can people read my extensive descriptions of causation, all of which focus on the way in which members are responding sensibly (at least in the short term) to policies that have been put in place around them [i.e., the welfare state and thus dependency] and then cite surveys regarding a 'culture of poverty' to refute me? The burden of my argument is that members of the underclass are *not* sunk in a cultural bog" (1996, 83).

## References

Anderson, E. 1999. *Code of the Street*. New York: W.. Norton.
Banfield, E. 1968. *The Unheavenly City*. Boston: Little, Brown.
Back, L. 1996. *New Ethnicities and Urban Culture*. London: UCL Press.
Bauman, Z. 1998a. *Globalization*. Cambridge: Polity.
———. 1998b. *Work, Consumerism, and the New Poor*. Buckingham: Open University Press.
———. 2001. "The Great War of Recognition." *Theory, Culture, and Society* 18, no. 2/3: 137–50.
Bauman, Z., and K. Tester. 2001. *Conversations with Zygmunt Bauman*. Cambridge: Polity.
Bhabha, H. 1993. *The Location of Culture*. London: Routledge.
Bourgois, P. 1995. *In Search of Respect*. Cambridge: Cambridge University Press.

———. 1998. "Just Another Night in a Shooting Gallery." *Theory, Culture, and Society* 15, no. 2: 37–66.

Burchell, B. 1999. *Job Insecurity and Work Intensification.* York: Joseph Rowntree Foundation.

Byrne, D. 1999. *Social Exclusion.* Buckingham: Open University Press.

Castells, M. 1994. "European Cities, the Informational Society, and the Global Economy." *New Left Review* 204 (March–April): 19–35.

Christopherson, S. 1994. "The Fortress City: Privatized Spaces, Consumer Citizenship." In *Post-Fordism,* ed. A. Amin. Oxford: Blackwells.

Cloward, R., and L. Ohlin. 1961. *Delinquency and Opportunity.* London: Routledge and Kegan Paul.

Cohen, A. 1965. "The Sociology of the Deviant Act: Anomie Theory and Beyond." *American Sociological Review* 30: 5–14.

Currie, E. 1996. *Crime and Punishment in America.* New York: Metropolitan Books.

———. 1997. "Market Society and Social Disorder." In *Thinking Critically about Crime,* ed. B. Maclean and D. Milanovic. Vancouver: Collective Press.

Dahrendorf, R. 1985. *Law and Order.* London: Stevens.

Davis, M. 1990. *City of Quartz.* London: Vintage.

DeKeseredy, W., and M. Schwartz. 1996. *Contemporary Criminology.* Belmont, Calif.: Wadsworth.

Dixon, W. 2001. "Exclusive Societies: Towards a Critical Criminology of Post-Apartheid South Africa." Institute of Criminology, University of Capetown.

Faludi, S. 1999. *Stiffed: The Betrayal of Modern Man.* London: Chatto and Windus.

Felson, M. 2002. *Crime and Everyday Life.* Thousand Oaks, Calif.: Sage.

Ferrel, J. 1999. "Cultural Criminology." *Annual Review of Sociology* 25: 395–418.

Fraser, N. 1997. *Justice Interruptus: Critical Reflections on the Post-Socialist Condition.* New York: Routledge.

Fraser, N., and L. Gordon. 1997. "A Genealogy of 'Dependency.'" In *Justice Interruptus,* ed. N. Fraser. New York: Routledge.

Friedman, L. 1999. *The Horizontal Society.* New Haven, Conn.: Yale University Press.

Gabriel, Y., and T. Lang. 1995. *The Unmanageable Consumer.* London: Sage.

Galbraith, J. K. 1992. *The Culture of Contentment.* London: Sinclair-Stevenson.

Gans, H. 1995. *The War against the Poor.* New York: Basic Books.

Garland, D. 2001. *The Culture of Control.* Oxford: Oxford University Press.

Giddens, A. 1991. *Modernity and Identity.* Stanford, Calif.: Stanford University Press.

———. 1997. *Sociology,* 3rd ed. Cambridge: Polity.

Gitlin, T. 1995. *Twilight of Common Dreams.* New York: Henry Holt.

Gorz, A. 1999. *Reclaiming Work: Beyond the Wage-Based Society.* Cambridge: Polity Press.

Gregson, N., and M. Lowe. 1994. *Serving the Middle Classes.* London: Routledge.

Hagedorn, J. 1991. "Gangs, Neighborhoods, and Public Policy." *Social Problems* 38, no. 4: 529–42.

Hallsworth, S. 2000. "Rethinking the Punitive Term." *Punishment and Society* 2, no. 2: 145–60.

Harrington, M. 1963. *The Other America.* New York: Macmillan.

Hayward, K. 2002. "Consumer Culture and Crime." In *The Blackwell Companion to Criminology,* ed. C. Sumner. Oxford: Blackwell.

Heath, A. 1992. "The Attitudes of the Underclass." In *Understanding the Underclass,* ed. D. J. Smith. London: Policy Studies Institute.

Hebdidge, D. 1990. "Fax to the Future." *Marxism Today* (January): 18–23.

Herrnstein, R., and C. Murray. 1994. *The Bell Curve.* New York: Free Press.

Hobsbawm, E. 1994. *The Age of Extremes.* London: Michael Joseph.

Hood, R., and K. Jones. 1999. "Three Generations: Oral Testimonies on Crime and Social Change in London's East End." *British Journal of Criminology* 31, no. 1: 136–60.

Hunt, J., and L. Hunt. 1977. "Dilemmas and Contradictions of Status: The Case of the Dual-Career Family." *Social Problems* 24: 407–16.

Hutton, W. 1995. *The State We're In.* London: Cape.

James, O. 1995. *Juvenile Violence in a Winner-Loser Culture.* London: Free Association Press.

Katz, J. 1988. *The Seductions of Crime.* New York: Basic Books.

Knox, P. 1995. *Urban Social Geography,* 3rd ed. Harlow, UK: Longman.

Lee, J. A. 1981. "Some Structural Aspects of Police Deviance in Relations with Minority Groups." In *Organisational Police Deviance,* ed. C. Shearing. Toronto: Butterworth.

Levitas, R. 1996. "The Concept of Social Exclusion and the New Durkheimian Hegemony." *Critical Social Policy* 16, no. 46: 5–20.

Luttwak, E. 1995. "Turbo-Charged Capitalism and Its Consequences." *London Review of Books* 17, no. 21 (November 2): 6–7.

MacLeod, J. 1995. *Ain't No Makin' It.* Boulder, Colo.: Westview.

Magnet, M. 1993. *The Dream and the Nightmare.* New York: William Morrow.

Mann, M. 1993. *Unequal Justice: A Question of Color.* Bloomington: Indiana University Press.

Marx, K. 1844/1967. *Economic and Philosophic Manuscripts.* In *Writings of the Young Marx on Philosophy and Society,* ed. L. Easton and K. Guddat. New York: Anchor Books.

Matza, D., and G. Sykes. 1961. "Juvenile Delinquency and Subterranean Values." *American Sociological Review* 26: 712–19.

McVicar, John. 1979. *McVicar: By Himself.* London: Arrow.

Merton, R. 1938. "Social Structure and Anomie." *American Sociological Review* 3: 672–82.

———. 1957. *Social Theory and Social Structure,* rev. ed. Glencoe, Ill.: Free Press.

Miller, W. 1958. "Lower Class Culture as a Generating Milieu of Gang Delinquency." *Journal of Social Issues* 14, no. 3: 17–23.

Mooney, G., and M. Danson. 1997. "Beyond Culture City: Glasgow as a Dual City." In *Transforming Cities,* ed. N. Jewson and S. MacGregor. London: Routledge.

Mooney, J., and J. Young. 2000. "Policing Ethnic Minorities." In *Policing after the Stephen Lawrence Inquiry,* ed. B. Loveday and A. Marlow. Lyme Regis, UK: Russell House.

Moore, J. 1985. "Isolation and Stigmatisation in the Development of an Underclass: The Case of Chicano Gangs in East Los Angeles." *Social Problems* 33, no. 1: 1–12.

Morris, L. 1993. *Dangerous Classes: The Underclass and Social Citizenship.* London: Routledge.

———. 1995. *Social Divisions: Economic Decline and Social Structural Change.* London: UCL Press.

Murray, C. 1984. *Losing Ground.* New York: Basic Books.

———. 1996. "Rejoinder." In *Charles Murray and the Underclass,* ed. D. Green. London: Institute for Economic Affairs.

Nightingale, C. 1993. *On the Edge.* New York: Basic Books.

Parenti, C. 2000. *Lockdown America.* London: Verso.

Pelecanos, George P. 1998. *King Suckerman.* London: Serpent's Tail.

Pratt, J. 2000. "Emotive and Ostentatious Punishment: Its Decline and Resurgence in Modern Society." *Punishment and Society* 2, no. 4: 417–40.

Presdee, M. 2000. *Cultural Criminology and the Carnival of Crime.* London: Routledge.

Ranulf, S. 1938/1964. *Moral Indignation and Middle Class Psychology.* New York: Schocken.

Rieff, D. 1993. *Los Angeles: Capital of the Third World.* London: Phoenix/Orion.

Ruggiero, V. 2000. *Crime and Markets.* Oxford: Clarendon.

Runciman, W. 1966. *Relative Deprivation and Social Justice.* London: Routledge and Kegan Paul.

Scheler, M. 1923. "Das Ressentiment im Aufbau der Moralem." In *Van Umsturz der Werte* I, Leipzig.

Schor, J. B. 1993. *The Overworked American.* New York: Basic Books.

Schwarz, D. F., J. A. Grisso, C. G. Miles, J. H. Holmes, A. R. Wishner, and R. L. Sutton. 1994. "A Longitudinal Study of Injury Morbidity in an African-American Population." *Journal of the American Medical Association* 271, no. 10 (March 9): 755–60.

Seabrook, J. 1988. *The Race for Riches: The Human Cost of Wealth.* Basingstoke, UK: Marshall Pickering.

Sennett, R., and J. Cobb. 1972. *The Hidden Injuries of Class.* New York: Knopf.

Sibley, D. 1995. *The Geographies of Exclusion.* London: Routledge.

Social Exclusion Unit. 1999. *Bringing Britain Together: A National Strategy for Neighbourhood Renewal.* London: Stationery Office.

Taylor, I. 1999. *Crime in Context.* Oxford: Polity.

Tomlinson, J. 1999. *Globalization and Culture.* Cambridge: Polity.

Wacquant, L. 1998. "Inside the Zone: The Social Art of the Hustler." *Theory, Culture, and Society* 15, no. 2: 1–36.

———. 2001. "Deadly Symbiosis: When Ghetto and Prison Meet and Merge." *Punishment and Society* 3, no. 1: 95–134.

Webster, F. 1995. *Theories of the Information Society.* London: Routledge.

Willis, P. 2000. *Common Culture.* Milton Keynes: Open University Press.

Wilson, W. J. 1987. *The Truly Disadvantaged.* Chicago: Chicago University Press.

———. 1985. *When Work Disappears.* New York: Knopf.

Wolfe, T. 1988. *The Bonfire of the Vanities.* New York: Bantam Books.

Young, J. 1971. *The Drugtakers.* London: Paladin.

———. 1981. "Beyond the Consensual Paradigm." In *The Manufacture of News,* ed. S. Cohen and J. Young. London: Constable.

———. 1999. *The Exclusive Society.* London: Sage.

———. 2001. "Identity, Community, and Social Exclusion." In *Crime, Disorder, and Community Safety,* ed. R. Matthews and J. Pitts. London: Routledge.

———. 2002. "Crime and Social Exclusion." In *The Oxford Handbook of Criminology,* ed. M. Maguire, R. Morgan, and R. Reiner. Oxford: Oxford University Press.

# PART II

# Spaces of Globalization

# 4

# The Global City: One Setting for New Types of Gang Work and Political Culture?

## SASKIA SASSEN

While still rare, there are indications in the literature on gangs that particular conditions in global cities may explain some current features of gang formation and activity (Hagedorn 2001, 2003; Papachristos 2002; Nashishibi, in progress; various chapters this volume). This essay is written in that exploratory spirit and by invitation from the editor, as the author is not a researcher on gangs. Its focus is on the global city rather than on gangs as such. Two major dynamics come together in global cities that might illuminate some of the propositions and puzzles in the literature on gangs, especially questions about a new type of gang, the postindustrial gang, and, secondly, the emergence of translocal gang networks.

One of these dynamics is the consolidation of new employment regimes in these cities. A key characteristic of these regimes is that they cut off what was historically a bridge from low-wage jobs and poverty into a reasonable work-ing-class or middle-class life. Low-wage jobs are now increasingly dead-end jobs. To move on requires a massive leap in educational attainment and in job experience. As a result, a growing body of research for both North America and Western Europe shows that youths are increasingly seeking meaning and identity in their lives outside the sphere of regular work even when they hold jobs (for example, on disadvantaged youth generally, see Body-Gendrot 1999; Munger 2002; and Roulleau-Berger 2002; on gangs specifically, see Chesney-Lind and Hagedorn 1999; Van Gemert 2001; Moore 1998). These findings on youth resonate with the findings in the gang research literature about members seeing themselves as political and community workers. Another feature of the new employment regimes that might be significant for gang formation is the development of novel types of informal economies that are part of advanced urban service economies rather than, as is typically thought, an anachronistic leftover from an older economy. These informal economies are often interpreted as imported from the global south via immigration. In my reading of the evidence, this is a mistake: they are deeply articulated and enabled by the current forms of economic restructuring centered in the ascendance of high-level services. In the case of gangs, it might take the form of participation in the criminal economy; of interest here is the fact that gang members see this participation as work and often evince the same motivations as workers in the regular economy (see Bourgois 1995; Padilla 1992; Sullivan 1989; see also Levitt and Venkatesh 2000).

The second of these dynamics is the multiplication of global circuits connecting cities across borders and involving both what we might think of as the top end and the bottom end of these urban economies: the new transnational professional classes and minoritized workers and non-workers, usually but not exclusively immigrants. One way of conceiving of these transnational circuits is as localizations of specific global conditions and dynamics in cities. As they become localized in cities, they become accessible to or part of the life and imaginaries of disadvantaged and often largely immobile individuals and groups. These localizations of the global may include a variety of global circuits for the circulation of people, ideas, and cultural productions, but also ideational spaces of globality (Sassen 2006a, chapters 6 and 7). Significant for the purposes of this discussion is, then, that these circuits and localizations now also involve growing numbers of disadvantaged and minoritized people in these cities (see generally Cordero-Guzman et al. 2001; Green 1997; Hamilton and Chinchilla 2001; Nashishibi, in progress).

The term *global city* captures a partial condition: much of what happens in these cities may have little to do with globalization. The key economic features of global cities are presented first in this discussion. The second section examines the new employment regimes in these cities and their implications for disadvantaged individuals and groups. The third section examines the global city as a space for the formation of new types of politics and contestatory practices at both the urban and transnational levels.

## Place and Work in a Global Economy

In developing my model of the global city, the concern was to recover the importance of place and work processes for a global economy usually described in terms of flows, placelessness, and professional talent. The question regarding gangs would then be whether there are today urban conditions linked to globalization, either directly or indirectly, that become articulated with gangs, whether as objective conditions or ideational spaces, and whether they contribute to new types of gang work and gang cultures and to cross-border gang networks. These are questions that only those with extensive knowledge about gangs can answer. My effort here is merely to construct an analytic space that can facilitate understanding the connections between some of these global dynamics and particular features of gangs today, such as the postindustrial gang examined in several of the chapters in this volume. Possibly some of the existing evidence on gangs today, collected with none of these questions in mind, may well point to such articulations with global dynamics. But to see these articulations requires a particular analytics. It is, then, within this broader framing that the materials on the global city are examined here.

If the global economy were indeed largely a matter of flows and networks that make place irrelevant and that need only specialized professionals, then much of what constitutes the daily life of minoritized citizens, disadvantaged immigrants, and gangs would be completely left out. Having worked for a long time on immigration and having learned much about the sharp changes during the 1980s in New York City from immigrants, it seemed to me enormously important politically and theoretically to recover the connections between global dynamics, places, and the growing inequality evident in major cities around the world. The model of the global city is one way of understanding these connections. Crucial to the model is demonstrating that global capital really needs a network of cities for even its most globalized and electronic markets, and that many of the low-wage workers in these cities, both formal and informal, are actually working in the global economy, even though it may not look that way. It is the necessity of that particular moment in the development and operation of global capital that repositions particular components of cities (groups and spaces) in networks that are, or are becoming, global. This specific type of connectedness at the heart of the global city model should allow us to register or see if perhaps some gangs, or some types of gang work and gang culture, are part of such networks. The model should then serve as an analytic tool to detect forms of connectedness deep inside a complex city, forms usually rendered invisible by the dominant ways of thinking about globalization. In the brief discussion that follows, I can touch only on some aspects (for a full account, please see Sassen 2001).

Global cities are centers for the *servicing, managing,* and *financing* of international trade, investment, and headquarter operations. That is to say, the multiplicity of specialized activities present in global cities are crucial to the functioning of the global operations of firms and markets. In this sense, they are strategic "production" sites for today's leading economic sectors.[1] Whether at the global or regional level, urban centers—central cities, edge cities—are adequate and often the best production sites for such specialized services.

When it comes to the production of services for the leading globalized sectors, the advantages of location in cities are particularly strong due to the level of complexity of these sectors and their need for quick access to multiple highly specialized services and professionals. Specialized service firms need and benefit from proximity to kindred specialized firms—financial services, legal services, accounting, economic forecasting, credit rating and other advisory services, computer specialists, public relations, and other types of expertise in a broad range of fields.

The growing digitization of economic activities has not eliminated the need for major international business and financial centers and all the material resources they concentrate, from state-of-the-art telematics infrastructure to brain talent (Garcia 2002; Graham 2002).[2] Telematics and globalization are fundamental forces reshaping the organization of economic space. This reshaping ranges from the spatial virtualization of a growing number of economic activities to the reconfiguration of the geography of the built environment for economic activity. Whether in electronic space or in the geography of the built environment, this reshaping involves organizational and structural changes. The vast new economic topography that is being implemented through electronic space is one moment, one fragment, of an even vaster economic chain that is in good part embedded in nonelectronic spaces. There is no fully dematerialized firm or industry. Even the most advanced information industries, such as finance, are installed only partly in electronic space. And so are industries that produce digital products, such as software design services. It is precisely because of the territorial dispersal facilitated by telecommunication advances that agglomeration of centralizing activities has expanded immensely. This is not a continuation of old patterns of agglomeration but, one could posit, a new logic for agglomeration. Many of the leading sectors in the economy operate globally, in uncertain markets, under conditions of rapid change in other countries (for example, deregulation and privatization), and are subject to enormous speculative pressures. What glues these conditions together into a new logic for spatial agglomeration is the added pressure of speed.

A focus on the *work* behind command functions, on the actual *production process* in the finance and services complex, and on global market*places* has the effect of incorporating the material facilities underlying globalization and the whole infrastructure of jobs not typically marked as belonging to the corporate sector of the economy. This points to an economic configuration that is very different from that suggested by the concept information economy. We recover the material conditions, production sites, and place-boundedness that are also part of globalization and the information economy. And we recover the broad range of types of firms, types of workers, types of work cultures, and types of residential milieux that are also part of globalization processes though not recognized or represented as such. Nor are they valorized as such. This is perhaps particularly evident in global cities. It sets in motion a whole series of new dynamics of inequality (Sassen 2001, chapters 8 and 9).

The global economy materializes in a worldwide grid of strategic places, uppermost among which are major international business and financial centers. We can think of this global grid as constituting a new economic geography of centrality, one that cuts across national boundaries and across the old North-South divide. It signals the emergence of a parallel political geography, a transnational space for the formation of new claims by global capital.

The most powerful of these new geographies of centrality at the interurban level binds the major international financial and business centers: New York, London, Tokyo, Paris, Frankfurt, Zurich, Amsterdam, Los Angeles, Sydney, Hong Kong, among others. But this geography now also includes cities such as São Paulo, Buenos Aires, Bangkok, Taipei, and Mexico City. But we also see the formation of more elementary transnational geographies, such as those binding Silicon valley with Bangalore and Madras (and, it would seem, Los Angeles with San Salvador when it comes to gangs). The intensity of transactions among these cities, particularly through the financial markets, transactions in services, and investment has increased sharply, and so have the orders of magnitude involved. At the same time, there has been a sharpening inequality in the concentration of strategic resources and activities between each of these cities and others in the same country.

Alongside these new global and regional hierarchies of cities is a vast territory that has become increasingly peripheral, increasingly excluded from the major processes that fuel economic growth in the new global economy. Many formerly important manufacturing centers and port cities have lost functions and are in decline, not only in the less-developed countries but also in the most advanced economies. The formation of these new geographies of marginality is yet another meaning of economic globalization.

But also inside global cities, we see both new geographies of centrality and marginality. The downtowns of cities and key nodes in metropolitan areas receive massive investments in real estate and telecommunications while low-income city areas and the older suburbs are starved for resources. Highly educated workers see their incomes rise to unusually high levels while low- or medium-skilled workers see theirs sink. Financial services produce superprofits while industrial services barely survive. These trends are evident, with different levels of intensity, in a growing number of major cities in the developed world and increasingly in some of the developing countries that have been integrated into the global financial markets (for example, Ciccolella and Mignaqui 2002; Cohen et al. 1996; Marcuse and van Kempen 2001; Schiffer 2002).

The new urban economy is highly problematic. This is perhaps particularly evident in global cities and their regional counterparts. It sets in motion a whole series of new dynamics of inequality. The new growth sectors—specialized services and finance—contain capabilities for profit making vastly superior to those of more traditional economic sectors. Many of the latter remain essential to the operation of the urban economy and the daily needs of residents, but their survival is threatened in a situation where finance and specialized services can earn superprofits and bid up prices.[3] Polarization in the profit-making capabilities of different sectors of the economy has always existed. But what we see happening today takes place on another order of magnitude and is engendering massive distortions in the operations of various markets, from real estate to labor (for example, Fainstein 2001 on real estate; Munger 2002 on labor; Massey and Denton 1993 on the accentuation of segregation in large cities; Jargowsky 1996 on poverty and place in large cities; Wilson 1991 on the urban disadvantaged).[4] This has sharply increased the distance between the valorized, indeed overvalorized, sectors of the economy and devalorized sectors even when the latter are part of leading global industries (Chang and Abramovitz 2000; Ehrenreich and Hochschild 2003). This devalorization of growing sectors of the urban economy has been embedded in a massive demographic transition towards a growing presence of women, African Americans, and "third world" immigrants in the urban workforce (Green 1997; van Kempen and Ozuekren 1998; Sassen 2001, chapter 9; Valle and Torres 2000).

We see here an interesting correspondence between great concentrations of corporate power and large concentrations of "others." Large cities in the highly developed world are the terrain where a multiplicity of globalization processes assume concrete, localized forms. A focus on cities allows us to capture not only the upper but also the lower circuits of globalization.

## New Employment Regimes in Global Cities

Cities are a nexus where many of the new organizational tendencies of econo-mies and societies come together in specific localized configurations. We can identify at least three processes in the current economic phase that produce an institutional setting for some of the outcomes described in this book. These three processes contribute to new, and possibly accentuate older, forms of inequality/distance between firms and workers at the bottom of the economic system and those who prosper.

One overall effect is the production of urban marginality, particularly as a result of new structural processes of economic growth. The produc-tion of marginality through abandonment also continues, but it is helpful to distinguish it analytically from the forms of marginality resulting from new forms of growth as these may have a particularly negative impact on youth and their desire to participate in the new economy. It might contrib-ute to explaining the shift from industrial era to postindustrial era gangs as described by Hagedorn (2001) and the disproportionate concentration of the latter in major cities (Papachristos 2002).

While not necessarily mutually exclusive, it is helpful to distinguish these three processes analytically. One is the expansion and consolidation of advanced services and corporate headquarters as the urban economic core, especially in global cities. While the corporate headquarters and services complex may not account for the majority of jobs in these cities, it estab-lishes a new regime of economic activity and the associated spatial and social transformations evident in major cities. What matters for the purposes of illuminating some of the issues about gangs is the extent to which this sector contributes to a sharp and visible demand for highly educated workers and the ways in which it projects itself as radically separate from other sectors of the urban economy. It thereby signals its special, exclusive, and inaccessible character; it turns its back on the rest of the city, feeding into understandings that it does not offer work options to those growing up in low-income areas, in the unglamorous parts of town. At the same time, this new urban core actually produces an effective demand—through its firms and the lifestyles of the expanded professional class—for products and services that low-wage workers, low-profit firms can deliver. This also includes a demand for goods and services from the informal and criminal economy.

A second process is the downgrading of the manufacturing sector, a notion I use to describe a mode of political and technical reorganization whereby some manufacturing sectors become incorporated into the "postindustrial" economy but on terms reminiscent of second-class citizenship. This process of downgrading is to be distinguished from the obsolescence of many manufacturing activities to the urban economy. Downgrading is actually a form of adaptation to two facts. One is an effective demand for manufactured goods in these high-end urban service economies. The other is the pressure of cheap imports and low-profit-making capacities in manufacturing overall are modest compared with those of leading sectors such as telecommunications or finance and other corporate services.[5] It is the downgrading of manufacturing that has played a crucial role in cutting off the bridges that used to enable low-income youths to move into reasonably paying jobs in a world of expanding, mostly unionized factories. Now many of these jobs are gone or have been downgraded to sweatshop work, often drawing on immigrant workers. This cuts off one of the key ways for youth to mainstream themselves out of gang life. The result has been that gang members stay longer in gangs and are more likely to participate in the criminal economy (Hagedorn 1998, 2001; Howell, Moore, and Egley 2002; see also Fagan 1996 and Hagedorn 1998 on gangs and criminality).

The third process is the informalization of a growing array of economic activities. It includes certain components of the downgraded manufacturing sector, notably sweatshops in a growing range of manufacturing. Also informalization is a mode of adapting to new pressures. It entails reorganizing the production and distribution of goods and services when firms have an effective local demand for their goods and services but cannot compete with cheap imports or cannot compete for space and other business needs with the new high-profit firms engendered by the advanced corporate service economy. Escaping the regulatory apparatus of the formal economy enhances the economic opportunities of such firms. It does so by reducing costs and by avoiding regulatory constraints, for example, locating a commercial or manufacturing operation in an area zoned exclusively for residential use or in a building in violation of fire and health standards.[6] The criminal underground economy has also grown in advanced urban economies, partly supported by the resources of these cities and the effective demand by its expanding high-income professional class for drugs. It would seem that both the informal economy (Roulleau-Berger 2002) and the criminal economy (Bourgois 1995) provide youths, including gang members, with economic opportunities and, more concretely, jobs. Youths in low-income areas emerge as a kind of workforce in these criminal economies (Bourgois 1995; National Youth Gang Center 2000; Venkatesh 1997).

The three processes described above are far more interlinked than is commonly assumed or understood (for a detailed analysis, see Sassen 2001, chapters 8 and 9). The changes in the job supply evident in major cities are a function both of new sectors and of the reorganization of work in both new and old sectors. The shift from a manufacturing to a service-dominated economy, particularly evident in major cities, destabilizes older forms of correspondence between the features of jobs and sectors. Today, much more so than twenty years ago, we see an expansion of low-wage jobs associated with growth rather than declining sectors. A second, partly related trend, is that a large array of activities that in the recent past were part of standardized work arrangements today are increasingly informalized, for example, going from unionized factories to sweatshops and industrial homework. Distinguishing the characteristics of jobs from their sectoral locations allows us to see that highly dynamic, technologically advanced sectors may well contain low-wage, dead-end jobs requiring almost no formal education. Conversely, it allows us to see that low-wage dead-end jobs and backward sectors can be part of major growth trends in a highly developed economy. It is often taken for granted that the opposite is the case—to wit, that backward sectors express decline trends, and that advanced sectors, such as finance, have mostly good white-collar jobs (while in fact, finance for one contains a good number of blue collar-jobs such as cleaners, low-level technicians and stock clerks, as well as a number of low-paid jobs in both white- and blue-collar occupations).

This suggests we need to rethink some of the basic propositions about the postindustrial economy. This holds especially for the notion that it needs largely highly educated workers and for the notion that informalization and downgrading are just a third-world import of backwardness or an anachronistic remnant of an earlier era. We are seeing new employment regimes in these services-dominated urban economies that create low-wage jobs with no particularly high education requirements. Many of these jobs have few advancement opportunities, and many often pay little for what is actually very demanding work (for example, Munger 2002).

In the day-to-day work of the leading sectors in global cities, a large share of the jobs involved are lowly paid and manual, many held by immigrant women. Even the most advanced professionals will require clerical, cleaning, repair workers for their state-of-the art offices, and they will require truckers to bring the software but also the toilet paper. These types of workers and jobs are never represented as part of the global economy even though they are in fact part of the infrastructure involved in running and implementing the global economic system, including such an advanced form of it as international finance. Further, the similarly state-of-the art lifestyles of the professionals in these sectors have created a whole new demand for a range of household workers, particularly maids and nannies (Ehrenreich and Hochschild 2003).

The presence of a highly dynamic sector with a polarized income distribution has its own impact on the creation of low-wage jobs through the sphere of consumption (or, more generally, social reproduction). The rapid growth of industries with strong concentrations of high- and low-income jobs has assumed distinct forms in the consumption structure, which in turn has a feedback effect on the organization of work and the types of jobs being created. The expansion of the high-income workforce in conjunction with the emergence of new lifestyles have led to a process of high-income gentrification that rests, in the last analysis, on the availability of a vast supply of low-wage workers.[7] High-price restaurants, luxury housing, luxury hotels, gourmet shops, boutiques, French hand laundries, and special cleaning services are all more labor-intensive than their lower-price equivalents. This has reintroduced—to an extent not seen in a very long time—the notion of the "serving classes" in contemporary high-income households.[8] Very prominent in this market are the International Nanny and Au Pair Agency, headquartered in Britain, Nannies Incorporated, based in London and Paris, and the International Au Pair Association (IAPA) based in Canada.[9] The immigrant woman serving the white middle-class professional woman has replaced the traditional image of the black female servant serving the white master. All these trends give these cities an increasingly sharp tendency towards social polarization.

These are not attractive options for young people who, even when poor, are raised in ideological contexts that emphasize success, wealth, career. Politically and theoretically this points to an employment context that can create both a growing demand for immigrant workers and alienation of native workers.

## A Nexus for New Politico-Cultural Alignments

One of the issues about youths that stands out in several of this volume's chapters and in research on work generally is their growing orientation to peer cultures rather than the world of work and "adulthood" (Young and Moore, this volume). As the world of employment is increasingly fragile and unrewarding for a growing number of young people, other social spheres begin to replace employment as anchors (see also Moore 1998; Munger 2002; Roulleau-Berger 2002; Short 1996). The current situation of many of these young people spells the limitations of their future trajectories. One result is the emergence/production of new trajectories that relocate to the world of peers and the imaginary what in the past or among adults is centrally located in the world of regular work. Analytically this expands the terrain within which to situate the condition of youths in the transition from school to what is usually understood as self-reliant adulthood.

Global cities are environments that bring some of these contradictions into the open and do so in particularly politicized ways. On the one hand, they concentrate a disproportionate share of global corporate power and are one of the key sites for its overvalorization. On the other, they also concentrate a disproportionate share of the disadvantaged and are one of the key sites for their devalorization. This joint presence happens in a context where (1) the globalization of the economy has grown sharply and cities have become increasingly strategic for global capital; and (2) marginalized people have found their voice and are making claims on the city as well. This joint presence is further brought into focus by the sharpening of the distance between the two. The center now concentrates immense power, a power that rests on the capability for global control and the capability to produce superprofits. And marginality, notwithstanding little economic and political power, has become an increasingly strong presence through a proliferation of new types of politics and emergent transnational circuits partly embedded in or enabled by the new geography of economic globalization (for example, Green 1997; Nashishibi, in progress; Sassen 2006a, chapter 6 and 7).

The city emerges as a site for new claims: by global capital that uses the city as an "organizational commodity," but also by disadvantaged sectors of the urban population, who often find their own way of using the city as an organizational tool for their politico-cultural objectives. We can think here of the variety of forms assumed by the politics of claim making—for the rights of the homeless, immigrants, queers and gays—and of contestation—against gentrification, against police abuse.

The space of the immigrant community, of the black ghetto, and of the old decaying manufacturing district emerges as a devalued, downgraded space in the dominant economic narrative about the postindustrial urban economy. It is in terms of the corporate economy and the new transnational corporate culture that economic globalization is represented in the urban landscape. Corporate culture and mass media collapse the differences—some minute, some sharp—among the different sociocultural contexts into one amorphous otherness, an otherness that has no place in the economy, or is, supposedly, only marginally attached to the economy. It therewith reproduces the devaluing of those jobs and of those who hold the jobs. By leaving out these articulations, by restricting the referent to the centrally placed sectors of the economy, the dominant narrative about the urban economy can present the economy as containing a higher-order unity when in fact it is sharply segmented and involves multiple economies and work cultures.

The city concentrates diversity. Its spaces are inscribed with the dominant corporate culture but also with a multiplicity of other cultures and identities (King 1996; on how this plays out with gangs, see Vigil 2002; Short 1996). The slippage is evident: the dominant culture can encompass only part of the city. And while corporate power inscribes noncorporate cultures and identities with "otherness," thereby devaluing them, they are present everywhere. The immigrant communities and informal economy in cities such as New York and Los Angeles are only two instances. It would seem that the different types of spaces that gangs construct for their operations are yet other instances (for example, Jankowski 1991; Simon and Burns 1997; Vigil 2002).

How can we expand the terrain through which we understand the new urban political economy so as to incorporate those other conditions? The global city is a strategic site for these insertions of the global in urban space in a double sense. These cities make some of these less legible localizations of global dynamics more concrete than do other types of spaces, such as suburbs and rural areas. Secondly, they enable the formation of many of these dynamics; urban space is productive space.

Many of these less legible localizations of globalization are embedded in the demographic transition evident in such cities, where a majority of resident workers are today minorities, immigrants, and women, particularly women of color. Further, many of these localizations of the global, such as the expansion of dead-end low-wage jobs and the new serving classes, do not fit the master images about globalization yet are part of it. Their embeddedness in the demographic transition evident in all these cities, and their consequent invisibility, contribute to the devalorization of these types of workers and work cultures and to the "legitimacy" of that devalorization.

This can be read as a rupture of the traditional dynamic whereby membership in leading economic sectors contributes conditions towards the formation of a strong labor movement—a process long evident in western industrialized economies. "Women and immigrants" come to replace the Fordist family wage category of "women and children" (Sassen 1998, chapter 5).[10] This happens amid an explosion in the wealth and power concentrated in these cities—that is to say, in conditions where there is also a visible expansion in high-income jobs and high-priced urban space. "Women and immigrants" emerge as the labor supply that facilitates the imposition of low wages and powerlessness under conditions of high demand for those workers and the location of those jobs in high-growth sectors. It breaks the historic nexus that would have led to empowering workers, and it legitimates this break culturally. The evidence that suggests that a strong safety net may deter long-term intergenerational gang longevity (for example, Gordon 1999) is of interest here.

Another localization that is rarely associated with globalization, informalization, reintroduces the community and the household as an important economic space in global cities. We can see informalization in this setting as the low-cost (and often feminized) equivalent of deregulation at the top of the system. As with deregulation (for example, as in financial deregulation), informalization introduces flexibility, reduces the "burdens" of regulation, and lowers costs, in this case especially the costs of labor. Recapping some of the discussion in the preceding section, informalization in major cities of highly developed countries—whether New York, London, Paris, or Berlin—can be seen as a downgrading of a variety of activities for which there is an effective demand in these cities; informalization also devalues these activities and raises the competition among producers given low entry costs and few alternative forms of employment. Going informal is one way of producing and distributing goods and services at a lower cost and with greater flexibility. Immigrants and women are important actors in the new informal economies of these cities. They absorb the costs of informalizing these activities.

The reconfiguration of economic spaces associated with globalization in major cities has had differential impacts on women and men, on male-typed and female-typed work cultures, on male- and female-centered forms of power and empowerment. The restructuring of the labor market brings with it a shift of labor-market functions to the household or community, and the feminization of urban labor demand brings with it a changed relation between men and women. Both of these can be particularly problematic in low-income areas where men have few options. In this regard, this book's focus on how postindustrial gangs develop informal economic functions adds an important set of issues to the research literature on economic informalization: the research has largely focused on its implications for immigrants and for women immigrants in particular.

What makes these types of localization possibly significant—even though they involve powerless groups and what are often invisible workers—and potentially constitutive of a new kind of politics is that these same cities are also the strategic sites for the valorization of the new forms of global corporate capital, as discussed in the first section. The increased localization of politico-economic power in cities due to deregulation, privatization, and globalization may well make out of the global city a space that can bring voice and visibility to the growing masses of disadvantaged whose home it also is.

Generally, the space of the city is a far more concrete space for politics than that of the nation (Dunn 1994; Drainville 2005; Fincher and Jacobs 1998; Isin 2000; Magnusson 1994). It becomes a place where informal or nonformal political actors can be part of the political scene in a way that is much more difficult at the national level. Nationally, politics needs to run through existing formal systems: whether the electoral political system or the judiciary (taking state agencies to court). Nonformal political actors are rendered invisible in the space of national politics. The space of the city accommodates a broad range of political activities—squatting, demonstrations against police brutality, fighting for the rights of immigrants and the homeless, the politics of culture and identity, gay and lesbian and queer politics. Much of this becomes visible on the street. Much of urban politics is concrete, enacted by people rather than dependent on massive media technologies. In this sense, then, street-level politics make possible the formation of new types of political subjects that do not have to go through the formal political system.

There is something to be captured here—a distinction between powerlessness and a condition of being an actor even though lacking power. I use the term presence to name this condition in the case of the types of actors I have focused on—a variety of activists in familiar struggles such as anti-gentrification, immigrant rights, against police brutality. In the context of a strategic space such as the global city, the types of disadvantaged people described here are not simply marginal; they acquire presence in a broader political process that escapes the boundaries of the formal polity.[11] This presence signals the possibility of a politics. What this politics will be will depend on the specific projects and practices of various communities. Conceivably these dynamics may operate in the case of gangs that consider themselves political (Brotherton and Barrios, this volume).

In this combination of trends lie conditions for the production of new kinds of politics among youths involved with gangs. The current shortage and shortcomings of jobs, especially for young men and the growing numbers who are re-anchoring their identities in non-work worlds can bring with it a different sense of the political and of themselves as political actors. This is not a fully developed theme in this book, but it is present in some of the chapters that show that some gangs see themselves as community organizers (Barrios and Brotherton, this volume). The sharper fragmenting of urban areas, including hyperghettoization (Wacquant 1997), and the associated contestations around questions of space and access to specific places, can all be interpreted as practices that have the capacity to produce political subjects (Sassen 2006a, chapter 6). In my reading of the broader evidence on these conditions, we are seeing the formation of operational and rhetorical openings for new political subjects that stand outside the formal political system as epitomized in the voting citizen. What I find enormously important in the material presented in this book is that the particular types of youths described in some of the chapters instantiate these dynamics in a very sharp and focused fashion (Barrios, Brotherton, and Hagedorn, this volume).

Insofar as the sense of membership of these communities is not subsumed under the national, it may well signal the possibility of a transnational politics centered in concrete localities. I do not know how this would or not hold for gangs. There is some research signaling that there are some instances of a transnationalizing of activities and sense of identity (Hazlehurst, this volume; Nashishibi, in progress). Elsewhere I have argued that the Internet has enabled a new type of cross-border politics that can bypass interstate politics (for example, Cleaver 1998; Mele 1999).[12] That even small, resource-poor organizations and individuals can become participants in global networks signals the possibility of a sharp growth in cross-border politics by actors other than states.

Papachristos (2002) finds that while we may speak of a global ghetto and ghetto culture, gangs remain decidedly local. The particular feature that interests me here is that through the Internet, *localized* initiatives by *local* actors can become part of cross-border networks. This produces a specific kind of activism, one centered in multiple localities yet intensely connected digitally. Activists can develop networks for circulating not only information (about environmental, housing, political issues, and so forth) but also political work and strategies. There are many examples of such a new type of cross-border political work. For instance, SPARC (Society for Poor Areas Resources), started by and centered on women, began as an effort to organize slumdwellers in Bombay to get housing. Now it has a network of such groups throughout Asia and some cities in Latin America and Africa. Their struggles are still local and concern local issues, but they have gained a kind of political clout from being part of a global network of similar groups and struggles. This is one of the key forms of critical politics that the Internet can make possible: a politics of the local with a big difference—these are localities that are connected with each other across a region, a country, or the world. Because the network is global does not mean that it all has to happen at the global level.

## Conclusion

There may well be particular economic-political conditions in global cities that are shaping some of the current features of gang formation and activity. Global cities concentrate global corporate power and become one of the key sites for its overvalorization. But they also concentrate the disadvantaged and likewise become one of the key sites for their devalorization. In this context, (1) cities have become increasingly strategic for global capital as the economy globalizes; and (2) marginalized people must find their voice and make claims on the city if they are to survive. This joint presence is highlighted by the increasing distance between the two. Many of these trends are embedded in the demographic transition evident in such cities, where a majority of resident workers are today minorities, immigrants, and women, particularly women of color.

To what extent the kinds of socioeconomic and spatial dynamics I describe for the global city are feeding the formation of postindustrial gangs and the partial transformation of older types of gangs remains to be established. But bringing together changes in gang culture and practice with these changes in the economic, social, and spatial configuration of a growing number of cities around the world is an intriguing hypothesis for further research. The fact that the networks connecting cities are intensifying and that we are seeing the elements of transurban systems may also be facilitating the formation of translocal gang networks. The latter is incipient, and it is not clear how far it can go. But there is evidence that this is happening.

The two major dynamics in global cities I focused on might be contributing to the formation of a new type of gang, the postindustrial gang, and, secondly, to the emergence of gangs and gang cultures in a growing number of cities around the world. There are various processes that contribute to new, and possibly accentuate older, forms of inequality/distance between the disadvantaged and the advantaged. One overall effect is the production of distinct forms of disadvantage even as there are growing sectors in these cities with very high incomes and high-profit firms. It is important to specify that the types of disadvantage that are emerging result from new structural processes of economic growth rather than from decline. One of these dynamics is the consolidation of new employment regimes in these cities. A key characteristic of these regimes is that they cut what was historically a bridge from low wages and poverty into a reasonable working-class or middle-class life. Low-wage jobs are now increasingly dead-end jobs. To this should be added the growth of new types of informal economies that are part of advanced urban economies. These trends have the effect of repositioning the world of work for disadvantaged people generally, including youth. They make alternatives to regular work more compelling, both for making a living and, perhaps especially, for producing identity.

The second dynamic that matters for the analysis here is the multiplication of global circuits connecting cities across borders and involving both what we might think of as the top end and the bottom end of these urban economies: the new transnational professional classes and minoritized workers and non-workers, usually but not exclusively immigrants. These transnational circuits localize the global inside cities, thereby making it accessible also to those who are not mobile. They can gain access to instances of the global that may not involve their own movement but rather the global circulation of cultural elements and ideational forms. What circulates will be different for the top than the bottom, and in that sense we can detect a process of cumulative causation that strengthens the differences in these global circuits and localizations for the top and for the bottom of the social system. If we add to this the questions of race and power analyzed by Wacquant, these differences become even more significant.

One overall outcome is an increasingly sharp tendency towards social and spatial polarization, partly because power and disadvantage assume some of their strongest forms in global cities. Wealth and power in global cities today are not the discreet wealth and power of older elites, who often recirculated some of it through civic projects. In the global city, wealth is very visible, especially through the expanded high-income professional strata who find in the highly public aspects of individual consumption what the older, much smaller elites found in civic projects. In this regard, one of the issues that stands out in some of the literature on youths is the growing orientation to peer cultures rather than the world of work. With the world of employment increasingly unreliable and unrewarding for a growing number of young people, other social spheres begin to replace employment as sources for rewards and identity. The world of peers and of the imaginary are critical in producing such alternatives to mainstream cultures of "adulthood."

The increased localization of corporate politico-economic power in cities due to deregulation, privatization, and globalization may well have consequences for gangs especially in economic terms and for new kinds of political projects. In economic terms, the large high-income professional strata are clearly a market for some gangs involved in drugs. But this increased localization of politico-economic corporate power also can make the global city into a space that can bring voice and visibility to the growing masses of disadvantaged whose home it also is. Generally, the space of the city is a far more concrete space for politics than that of the nation. In this regard it may be an enabling space for politicized gangs. An important distinction here for me is that between powerlessness as such and a condition of being an actor even though lacking power. What the politics coming out of this condition can be will depend on the specific projects and practices of various communities.

My question is to what extent these conditions produce some of the features of postindustrial gangs and, obversely, to what extent such postindustrial gangs are an enactment of this larger context. The current constraints on youth when it comes to the world of work and their reanchoring in non-work worlds can bring with it a different sense of the political and of citizenship, especially perhaps in global cities, given both their sharp polarizations and their articulations in translocal networks. The fragmenting of public space, the new spatial polarizations evident in cities, and the associated contestations around questions of space and access to specific places, all of these can be interpreted as practices that have the capacity to produce political subjects. In my reading of the broader evidence on these conditions, we are seeing the formation of operational and rhetorical openings for new political subjects that stand outside the formal political system—the formal epitomized in the voting citizen. What I find enormously important in some of the new research on gangs and disadvantaged youth is that these youths instantiate these dynamics in a very sharp and focused fashion.

## Notes

1. In my analysis, what is specific about the shift to services is not merely the growth in service jobs but, most importantly, the growing service intensity in the organization of advanced economies: firms in all industries, from mining to wholesale, buy more accounting, legal, advertising, financial, and economic forecasting services today than they did twenty years ago (Sassen 2001, chapter 5). Thus cities that are not necessarily global are also emerging as production sites for the broad range of specialized services that national firms and markets require.

2. The proposition that the new technologies eliminate agglomeration advantages has proven itself only partly correct. Many sectors do get routinized and leave cities. But the most strategic functions in a global economy evince extremely high agglomeration economies.

3. These new inequalities in profit-making capacities of economic sectors, earnings capacities of households, and prices in upscale and downscale markets have contributed to the formation of informal economies in major cities of highly developed

countries. These informal economies negotiate between these new economic trends and regulatory frameworks that were engendered in response to older economic conditions.

4. For data sources and data analysis on income inequalities in global cities, see Sassen 2001, chapter 8, 2006b, chapter 6.

5. The key issue here is a type of manufacturing that needs an urban location because it is geared to urban markets and functions as part of developed and intense networks of contractors and subcontractors. We have called this type of manufacturing "urban manufacturing" to distinguish it from sectors that respond to very different constraints and advantages. Among its components are crucially design-linked manufacturing typically done on contract: jewelry, woodwork and metalwork for architecture and real estate firms, fashion furniture and lamps, and so on. Many components of urban manufacturing are not downgraded, or at least not yet. One major policy implication for city governments is to support this type of manufacturing and cease to subsidize the kind that will sooner or later leave the city anyhow (Mitchell 1996; Harvard University 1996). Immigrant women and men are a key labor force in urban manufacturing in many U.S. cities.

6. I distinguish the informal from the criminal economy (Sassen 1998, chapter 8). I want to emphasize that among the features of the advanced urban economy is the informalization of what are actually licit activities. These do not have to be underground. We then need to ask why they are informalized. One answer is the new set of pressures coming out of the growth of a high-profit-making sector that casts an enormous shadow on the competitive possibilities of lower-profit sectors and thereby produces a massive distortion in the functioning of land and labor markets. For a broader treatment of the informal economy, including a focus on its reemergence with the end of the so-called Pax Americana, see Tabak and Chrichlow (2000).

7. As for the consumption needs of the growing low-income population in large cities, these are also increasingly met through labor-intensive rather than standardized and unionized forms of producing goods and services: manufacturing and retail establishments, which are small, rely on family labor, and often fall below minimum safety and health standards. Cheap, locally produced sweatshop garments and bedding, for example, can compete with low-cost Asian imports. A growing range of products and services, from low-cost furniture made in basements to "gypsy cabs" and family day care, are available to meet the demand for the growing low-income population. There are numerous instances of how the increased inequality in earnings reshapes the consumption structure and how this in turn has feedback effects on the organization of work, both in the formal and in the informal economy.

8. Some of these issues are well illustrated in the emergent research literature on domestic service (Ehrenreich and Hochschild 2003; Hondagneu-Sotelo 2000; Parrenas 2000) and in the rapid growth of international organizations catering to various household tasks. Catering to these types of professional households, there is now a growing range of global staffing organizations whose advertised services cover vari-

ous aspects of day care, including dropping off and picking up, as well as in-house tasks, from child minding to cleaning and cooking.

9. One international agency for nannies and au pairs (EF Au Pair Corporate Program) advertises directly to corporations urging them to make the service part of their employment offers to potential employees to help them address household and child care needs.

10. This current situation brings out more brutally than did the Fordist contract the economic significance of these types of actors, a significance veiled or softened in the case of the Fordist contract through the provision of the family wage.

11. There are multiple forms this can take, including for instance the definition of certain types of activities and individuals as criminal (for example, Body-Gendrot 1999; Wacquant 1997) and the accumulation in cities of occasions for unjust treatment and biased definitions (Merrifield and Swyngedouw 1997).

12. Such political activities can also thrive without this particular type of connectivity as Keck and Sikkink (1998) have shown us.

## References

Body-Gendrot, Sophie. 1999. *Controlling Cities*. Oxford: Blackwell.

Bourgois, Phillipe. 1995. *In Search of Respect: Selling Crack in El Barrio*. Cambridge: Cambridge University Press.

Chang, Grace, and Mimi Abramovitz. 2000. *Disposable Domestics: Immigrant Women Workers in the Global Economy*. Boston: South End Press.

Chesney-Lind, M., and J. M. Hagedorn, eds. 1999. *Female Gangs in America: Essays on Girls, Gangs, and Gender*. Chicago: Lakeview.

Ciccolella, Pablo, and Iliana Mignaqui. 2002. "Buenos Aires: Sociospatial Impacts of the Development of Global City Functions." In *Global Networks, Linked Cities*, ed. Saskia Sassen, pp. 309–26. London: Routledge.

Cohen, M., B. Ruble, J. Tulchin, and A. Garland, eds. 1996. *Preparing for the Urban Future: Global Pressures and Local Forces*. Washington, D.C.: Woodrow Wilson Center Press (distributed by John Hopkins University Press).

Cordero-Guzman, Hector R., Robert C. Smith, and Ramon Grosfoguel, eds. 2001. *Migration, Transnationalization, and Race in a Changing New York*. Philadelphia: Temple University Press.

Dunn, S., ed. 1994. *Managing Divided Cities*. Stafford, UK: Keele University Press.

Ehrenreich, Barbara, and Arlie Hochschild., eds. 2003. *Global Woman: Nannies, Maids, and Sex Workers in the New Economy*. New York: Metropolitan Books.

Fagan, J. 1996. "Gangs, Drugs, and Neighborhood Change." In *Gangs in America*, 2nd ed., ed. R. C. Huff, 39–74. Thousand Oaks, Calif.: Sage.

Fainstein, S. 2001. *The City Builders*. 2nd ed. Lawrence: University of Kansas Press.

Fincher, Ruth, and Jane M. Jacobs. 1998. *Cities of Difference*. New York: Guilford Press.

Garcia, Linda. 2002. "Architecture of Global Networking Technologies." In *Global Networks, Linked Cities,* ed. Saskia Sassen, pp. 39–70. London: Routledge.

Gordon, I. R. 1999. "Internationalisation and Urban Competition." *Urban Studies* 36: 1001–16.

Graham, Stephen. 2002. "Communication Grids: Cities and Infrastructure." In *Global Networks, Linked Cities,* ed. Saskia Sassen, pp. 71–92. London: Routledge.

Green, C., ed. 1997. *Globalization and the Black Diaspora: The New Urban Challenge.* Albany, N.Y.: SUNY Press.

Hagedorn, John. 1998. "Post-industrial Gang Violence." In *Youth Violence,* ed. M. Tonry and M. H. Moore, 365–419. Chicago: University of Chicago Press.

———. 2001. "Globalization, Gangs, and Collaborative Research." In *The Eurogang Paradox: Street Gangs and Youth Groups in the U.S. and Europe,* ed. Malcolm Klein et al., 41–58. Boston: Kluwer.

———. 2002. "Gangs and the Informal Economy." In *Gangs in America III,* ed. C. Ronald Huff, 101–20. Thousand Oaks, Calif.: Sage.

Hamilton, Nora, and Norma Stoltz Chinchilla. 2001. *Seeking Community in a Global City: Guatemalans and Salvadorans in Los Angeles.* Philadelphia: Temple University Press.

Harvard University. 1996. "Manufacturing Cities: Competitive Advantage and the Urban Industrial Community." A Symposium Given by the Harvard Graduate School of Design and the Loeb Fellowship, May 1996.

Hondagneu-Sotelo, Pierrette. 2000. *Doméstica: Immigrant Workers Cleaning and Caring in the Shadows of Affluence.* Berkeley: University of California Press.

Howell, James C., John P. Moore, and Arlen Egley Jr. 2002. "The Changing Boundaries of Youth Gangs." In *Gangs in America III,* ed. C. Ronald Huff, pp. 3–18. Thousand Oaks, Calif.: Sage Publications.

Isin, Engin F., ed. 2000. *Democracy, Citizenship, and the Global City.* London: Routledge.

Jankowski, Martin Sanchez. 1991. *Islands in the Street: Street Gangs and American Urban Society.* Berkeley: University of California Press.

Jargowsky, P. 1996. *Poverty and Place: Ghettos, Barrios, and the American City.* New York: Russell Sage.

Keck, Margaret E., and Sikkink, Kathryn. 1998. *Activists beyond Borders: Advocacy Networks in International Politics.* Ithaca, N.Y.: Cornell University Press.

King, A. D., ed. 1996. *Representing the City: Ethnicity, Capital, and Culture in the Twenty-first Century.* New York: New York University Press.

Knox, George W., and Andrew V. Papachristos. 2002. *The Vice Lords: A Gang Profile Analysis.* Peotone, Ill.: New Chicago School Press.

Levitt, Steven D., and Sudhir Alladi Venkatesh. 2000. "An Economic Analysis of a Drug-Selling Gang's Finances." *Quarterly Journal of Economics* 115, no. 3: 755–89.

Magnusson, Warren. 1994. *The Search for Political Space.* Toronto: University of Toronto Press.

Marcuse, Peter, and Ronald van Kempen. 2001. *Globalizing Cities: A New Spatial Order?* Oxford: Blackwell.

Massey, Douglas S., and Nancy Denton. 1993. *American Apartheid: Segregation and the Making of the Underclass.* Cambridge, Mass.: Harvard University Press.

Mitchell, Matthew. 1996. "Urban Manufacturing in New York City." Paper presented for the Graduate School of Architecture, Planning, and Preservation, Columbia University, April.

Moore, Joan W. 1998. "Understanding Youth Street Gangs: Economic Restructuring and the Urban Underclass." In *Cross-cultural Perspectives on Youth, Radicalism, and Violence,* ed. M. Watts, 65–78. Stamford, Conn.: JAI Press.

Munger, Frank, ed. 2002. *Laboring under the Line.* New York: Russell Sage Foundation.

Nashishibi, Rami. In progress. "Ghetto Cosmopolitanism." Ph.D. dissertation. Department of Sociology, University of Illinois at Chicago.

National Youth Gang Center. 2000. *1997 National Youth Gang Survey: Summary.* Washington, D.C.: Office of Juvenile Justice and Delinquency Prevention, U.S. Department of Justice.

Padilla, Felix. 1992. *The Gang as an American Enterprise.* New Brunswick, N.J.: Rutgers University Press.

Papachristos, Andrew V. 2001. *A.D., After the Disciples: The Neighborhood Impact of Federal Gang Prosecution.* Peotone, Ill.: New Chicago School Press.

———. 2002. "Rethinking the Economics of Gang Life: Measuring Gang Organization and Gang Participation." Paper presented at the Annual Meeting of the American Society of Criminology, Chicago, November 14.

Parrenas, Rhacel Salazar, ed. 2001. *Servants of Globalization: Women, Migration, and Domestic Workers.* Stanford, Calif.: Stanford University Press.

Roulleau-Berger, Laurance, ed. 2002. *Youth and Work in the Postindustrial City of North America and Europe.* Leiden: Brill.

Sassen, Saskia. 1998. *Globalization and Its Discontents.* New York: New Press.

———. 2001. *The Global City: New York, London, Tokyo,* 2nd ed. Princeton University Press. (Originally published in 1991).

———. 2004. "Local Actors in Global Politics." Special issue on Social Movements and Globalization. *Current Sociology* 52, no. 4: 649–70.

———. 2006a. *Territory, Authority, Rights.* Princeton, N.J.: Princeton University Press.

———. 2006b. *Cities in a World Economy.* 3rd ed. Thousand Oaks, Calif.: Pine Forge/Sage.

Schiffer, Sueli Ramos. 2002. "São Paulo: Articulating a Cross-Border Regional Economy." In *Global Networks/Linked Cities,* ed. Saskia Sassen, pp. 209–36. London: Routledge.

Short, James F., Jr. 1996. "Foreword: Diversity and Change in U.S. gangs." In *Gangs in America,* 2nd ed., ed. R. C. Huff, vii–xviii. Thousand Oaks, Calif.: Sage.

Simon, David, and Edward Burns. 1997. *The Corner: A Year in the Life of an Inner-City Neighborhood.* New York: Broadway Books.

Sullivan, Mercer. 1989. *Getting Paid: Youth Crime and Work in the Inner City.* Ithaca, N.Y.: Cornell University Press.

Tabak, Faruk,and Michaeline A.Chrichlow (eds). 2000. *Informalization: Process and Structure.* Baltimore: Johns Hopkins University Press.

Valle, Victor M., and Rodolfo D. Torres. 2000. *Latino Metropolis.* Minneapolis: University of Minnesota Press.

Van Gemert, Frank. 2001. "Crips in Orange: Gangs and Groups in the Netherlands." In *The European Paradox: Street Gangs and Youth Groups in the U.S. and Europe,* ed. Malcolm Klein et al. Boston: Kluwer.

van Kempen, Ronald, and A. Sule Ozuekren. 1998. "Ethnic Segregation in Cities: New Forms and Explanations in a Dynamic World." *Urban Studies* 35, no. 10 (October): 1631–57.

Venkatesh, Sudhir A. 1997. "The Social Organization of Street Gang Activity in an Urban Ghetto." *American Journal of Sociology* 103, no. 1 (July): 82–111.

Vigil, James Diego. 2002. *A Rainbow of Gangs: Street Cultures in the Mega-City.* Austin: University of Texas Press.

Wacquant, L. J. D. 1997. "Urban Outcasts." In *Globalization and the Black Diaspora: The New Urban Challenge,* ed. C. Green, 331–55. Albany: State University of New York Press.

Wilson, William J. 1991. *The Truly Disadvantaged: The Inner City, the Underclass, and Public Policy.* Chicago: University of Chicago Press.

# 5

## Observing New Zealand "Gangs," 1950–2000: Learning from a Small Country

### CAMERON HAZLEHURST

Consider the history of a small sovereign nation in the South Pacific. One thousand six hundred kilometers long and never more than 450 kilometers wide, surrounded by ocean, it is more than a thousand kilometers from its nearest substantial neighbor. The Maori (Polynesian indigenous) population settled centuries before the Pakeha (Europeans), who arrived in numbers only in the nineteenth and twentieth centuries. The settler colonial society is now properly characterized as "post-colonialist"' (Nash 1990). Tiny and isolated, New Zealand/Aotearoa is "the most transnationalised in the OECD" (Kelsey 2002, 37), a test bed of globalization.

For over a hundred years, New Zealand has been a unitary state. It has one parliament, one national government, and one police force. For sixty years, it has enjoyed high standards of living, "astonishing advances" in material well-being as one scholar noted in mid-century (Miller 1950, 130–33). Until recent decades, it was "a one-crop economy, depending essentially on grass" (Mitchell 1968, 70): agricultural exports, high tariffs, and a negligible manufacturing sector. Its welfare system provided a strong safety net for the urban unemployed and the rural poor—Maori and Pakeha subsisting in relatively tranquil coexistence. But, as late-twentieth-century global pressures dislocated the economy and rendered borders more porous, waves of Pacific Islander and Asian immigration were to transform the social fabric of New Zealand's larger cities.

After extensive intermarriage and in an evolving regime of benefits and opportunities, contemporary Maori and Pakeha identities are fluid, transient,

sometimes instrumental self-ascriptions.[1] Several decades of ideological conflict and political adjustment have produced a society highly sensitized to
inequities and inequalities. But in the mid-twentieth century, most Pakeha
and many Maori subscribed to the comfortable belief that they lived in a
society free from racism, discrimination, and racial tension. The Department
of Justice remarked on the "generally docile nature of New Zealand society"
(1968, 11). "Why," New Zealand's best-known historian asked seminar audiences overseas in the same year, "are race relations in New Zealand better
than in South Africa, South Australia or South Dakota?" (Sinclair 1971, 121).
The truth that Maori lived in "a relatively favourable environment" of course
masked a coexisting reality of unequal opportunities and outcomes (Bedggood 1980).

In 1965, 85 percent of Maori children left school with no formal qualifica-
tion (Walker 1990, 208).[2] A Dutch psychologist at the University of Canter-
bury noted in 1969 the tendency to attribute differences in educational attainment to lesser achievement orientation or lack of scholastic ability: "Social
scientists have only recently become aware of the impact of other factors on
the school achievement of Maori pupils, such as their family background
and rural environment" (Vellekoop 1969, 253). A professor of international
education at Boston University, who should have known better, wrote that
the issue was really one of Maori resistance to educational integration, which
threatened assimilation and the extinction of tradition: "The *pakeha* community can only regard this as a quarrel between the Maori and civilization
itself, and no longer feels a sense of guilt in confrontation with arrested development which is so largely of Maori choice" (Melvin 1968, 117). It was not
until the late 1980s that "evidential grounds for the application of a concept
of institutional racism" began to be assembled (Peters and Marshall 1990).
Whatever the underlying factors, the economic consequences for the youthful
Maori population were predictable: concentrated in less skilled and unskilled
occupations, spreading smaller incomes over more dependents, they constituted nearly a third of the registered unemployed during the recession
of the late 1960s (Butterworth 1974). They and their children were to be the
major casualties of the free-market neoliberal era of dissolving economic
sovereignty in the last decades of the twentieth century.

## Discovering Gangs

Social science was in its infancy in New Zealand in the 1960s. As late as the end
of the decade, Cora Vellekoop could assert, "No attempts have been made to

investigate the occurrence of crime, delinquency, mental illness, and illegitimacy among the various social strata" (Vellekoop 1969, 254). Unsurprisingly, the quiet South Pacific nation had already become a happy hunting ground for Fulbright scholars and other North American social scientists. Explaining Maori crime, a subject to which little attention had been paid, was a topic that invited cross-cultural rumination. Thus the sociologist Albert Morris reflected in 1955 "that a higher percentage of Maoris than Pakehas should be found guilty of conversion [car theft] and wilful damage and of burglary and of theft might be expected of those who have not been brought up in a tradition that stresses the inviolability of private property" (Trlin 1971, 404).[3]

David P. Ausubel of the University of Illinois, after a year as a research scholar in psychology at Victoria University of Wellington, devoted a thoughtful nineteen pages of his 1960 book *The Fern and the Tiki* to "juvenile deviancy." Ausubel's analysis was largely confined to Pakeha youth. But he noted in passing that "although slum conditions and racial problems are still relatively benign in New Zealand, they are rapidly becoming more significant factors in the causation of juvenile deviancy" (Ausubel 1960, 129–48). Acknowledging the existence of "hard-core delinquents" who were "aggressive and anti-social, are often vicious and vindictive, and are sometimes organised in gangs," Ausubel insisted that such gangs were much smaller, less highly organized, and under "less despotic leadership" than comparable American gangs. Nor were they what would later be called "ethnic."

What was unusual about Ausubel's conclusions was his hypothesis about the paradox of widespread adolescent revolt "in a prosperous Welfare State with a predominantly agricultural economy, with no very large cities, and, by American standards, with no large-scale urban slums or racial problems." The answer, he thought, was that there was an unusual predisposition toward adolescent rebelliousness in New Zealand. And, to explain what could not be explained by economic conditions or city environments, there was a psychological key: "inappropriately repressive discipline" (Ausubel 1960, 142).

Ausubel evidently was not privy to what appear to have been the first two "substantial, but rather loose" (Donnell 1981) studies on New Zealand gangs, prepared for the guidance of an interdepartmental committee on adolescent offenders. The reports by A. E. Levett and J. G. Green were later characterized as resembling early accounts of gangs in America, emphasizing the same background features—"broken or disharmonious homes, poor educational attainment, truancy, the concentration of gang behaviour in certain areas, and the lower class origins of many gang members." What was different, it was thought, was their conclusion that gang members seemed to be "disturbed individuals." For both authors, concentrations of low-cost state housing were seen as causes of gang formation, "but their studies were not of sufficient scope or rigour for them to be able to demonstrate this in a conclusive way" (Donnell 1981, 1).

As for the Maori, in a shrewd half paragraph Ausubel accounted for their supposedly three to four times greater incidence of delinquency with "readily apparent reasons"—cultural dislocation and dissonance, inexperience of urban "hazards and temptations," the stress of slum life, racial prejudice, poor education, and absence of traditional parental and tribal social control (Ausubel 1960, 140). In a separate study of Maori youth derived from the same period of fieldwork in 1957–58, Ausubel wrote of a "youthful urban proletariat" whose crime and delinquency he attributed primarily to "urban acculturational stress." Unlike Pakeha offending, however, Maori deviance was traced not to rebellion against excessively authoritarian families and schools but to excessive parental permissiveness and "release from the restraining influence of village elders and community opinion" (Ausubel 1977, 113–14).

Ausubel's understanding of what was happening in Auckland had been informed by the research of a young social anthropologist, Joan Metge, whose doctoral fieldwork on Maori migrants to the city had been conducted a few years earlier. In the published version of her thesis—one of the most cited of New Zealand monographs—Metge had written of "gangs":

> Many young people formed what they called "gangs," informal associations of friends who were in the habit of "going around together." The term was a carry-over from school-days. It was not generally indicative of criminal tendencies, though some did become involved in anti-social behaviour. Those who belonged to a gang had other friends outside it and special intimates within it. They did not all act together on every occasion, merely most of them on most occasions. The typical "gang" consisted of between twelve and twenty young Maoris between the ages of sixteen and twenty-five, of varied tribal background, and in most cases of both sexes . . . A "gang" rarely lasted more than a couple of years without radical changes in personnel. Members married, moved away, quarrelled, or became involved in other activities. New members, often younger siblings of existing or retiring members, were drawn in, until eventually the entire membership had changed. (Metge 1964, 201)

Metge admitted that she had done no research on crime and delinquency. And, such was the rapidity of change in the interval between her fieldwork and publication in 1964 that she reported her research in the past tense (Metge 1964, 5).

Ausubel had been in New Zealand at the height of community debate over the wayward activities of "bodgies and widgies," "milk-bar cowboys," and "mods and rockers" (Yska 1993). He believed it was unfortunate that juvenile delinquency had become a subject of public controversy, stimulated by sensational press reports of American "blackboard jungles." The fact was, he insisted, that the worst American behavior, the "highly organized predatory gang," was confined to small areas, untypical of the United States and so different from New Zealand as to render comparisons pointless. To put the reports from New York in context, he said, one had to appreciate that the vast majority of pupil offenses "are committed in the ten per cent of the schools located in the worst slum areas, largely inhabited by newly arrived and culturally unassimilated Puerto Ricans and Negroes living under indescribably wretched conditions." How could any one in New Zealand translate this into their own world? They would have to "conceive of some of the school problems that would arise if, for example, 100,000 Hungarians and Pacific Islanders were to settle in the slum districts of Auckland within less than a decade" (Ausubel 1960, 132).

Ten years later, Dane and Mary Archer proclaimed to the Polynesian Society that race relations had recently become a "fledgling public issue." The development was hardly surprising when the available data showed that, compared with the 8 percent of the population thought to be Maori, "white" New Zealanders were "healthier, better educated, 'criminal' less often, in higher status jobs, wealthier and in less crowded homes" (Archer and Archer 1970, 201, 215). Unsurprisingly too, the Archers' research on stereotypes and identity found what American studies led them to expect: "Maori share the racial stereotypes held by whites . . . the Maori must liberate himself not only from the prejudice of whites, but from himself as well" (Archer and Archer 1970, 216). As if overcoming stereotypes might not be difficult enough, the Canadian-trained anthropologist Eric Schwimmer had already speculated that mental maladjustment among young Maori might be causally associated with delinquency. "There is a good case," he urged, "for a research project linking the study of Maori delinquency and schizophrenia so that their interconnection, if it exists, can be established" (Schwimmer 1968, 59). What policy might have been pursued had such a connection been established was another matter. The Department of Justice admitted in 1968 that it was "meaningless to talk of psychotherapy or group therapy for offenders when there are no trained psychotherapists or psychologists who can perform such skilled tasks" (Department of Justice 1968, 404).[4]

## Denial

If it made sense to suggest that it might be worthwhile to undertake research into the links between delinquency and schizophrenia, it did so in the context of a state of denial about the danger of gangs. The official government line in 1968 (and apparently unchanged as late as 1974, by which time there had been police/gang clashes in the national capital of "near-riot proportions" [O'Reilly 1979]) was that the nation was as yet relatively free of the "ugly trades" practiced by "criminal syndicates" or of "serious gang violence." Admittedly, "groups of young people have occasionally shown aggressive tendencies." There were two schools of thought. One held that serious and disturbing "group" violence existed, and that it was less cultural than "situational and accidental—at least at the outset—later developing into characteristic gang aggressiveness." The alternative view was that such group violence as had occurred in Auckland and some provincial cities was "involuntary and related to the time, place, and other circumstances. The isolated incidents cannot be ascribed to gangs, as in some overseas cities" (Department of Justice 1968, 12, 203). The Justice Department said nothing of what it knew or suspected about the implications of a Hells Angels chapter in Auckland, founded in 1961, the second outside the United States. Young adult street gangs and outlaw motorcycle groups were as yet in taxonomic silos.

Apart from the disarming quotation marks around the word "criminal," there had been no comment by the Archers on the two relevant statistics they presented: "Maoris are three times as likely as whites to be arrested and three times as likely to be imprisoned" (Archer and Archer 1970, 215). New Zealanders were soon to be in earnest debate about whether the rates of arrest and incarceration of Maori were better construed as evidence of discrimination or as evidence of an as yet unexplained "criminality" (*Evening Post,* April 10, 1971).[5] When could it be said that isolated incidents were, or might become, part of a pattern? Maori community leaders had been quick to draw the Stormtroopers gang, fresh from a much publicized street battle with a Pakeha group in South Auckland, into a Young Maori leaders' conference. The focus then, and for much of the 1970s, was on cultural, educational, and political solutions to preempt a drift into the kind of alienation that would turn good ethnic group engagement into unwanted gang aggressiveness—teaching the Maori language, diminishing bias and stereotyping in the media and history textbooks, promoting Maori welfare officers, and increasing Maori representation in Parliament and local government (Walker 1990, 208). This was an optimistic agenda. But it demonstrated a conviction that a nation that wanted to ameliorate social strains in partnership with those most affected could find ways of doing so.

There were alternative perspectives. John Forster of the University of Alberta prophesied the growth of a universal "problem," "a segment of the population . . . which is incompletely involved in the economic and social life of the community." For Maori, as for those similarly circumstanced elsewhere, there was a simple if elusive solution: "cease to be poor" (Forster 1969, 109–10). Quite how this might be achieved would inevitably be controversial when determinants of poverty had "not yet been studied to any great extent" (Vellekoop Baldock 1977, 138). Forster and his collaborator Peter Ramsay had turned to Gunnar Myrdal for an understanding of the "cumulative causative" effect of Maori disadvantage in education and employment. But they had hastened to assure their colleagues that they were not "suggesting that the condition of the Maori population is as disastrous, or as hopeless, as that of many recent urban migrants in other countries. Our cities are not big enough, nor are opportunities so restricted, that we are likely, in the foreseeable future, to build up ghettos of unskilled and semi-skilled urban workers for whom escape is impossible" (Forster and Ramsay 1969, 201).

Conditions might be worse elsewhere, but no social scientist, no politician, could ignore the phenomenon of the rapid urbanization of the Maori that was transforming both cities and the countryside. In 1945, only 15 percent of the Maori population lived in the nation's eighteen main urban centers. By 1966 it was 41 percent (O'Malley 1973, 392). If the time span was stretched a further fifteen years, the change was even more striking. Official statistics, admittedly beset by definitional inconsistencies (Bull 2001), indicated that the percentage of Maori living in the main urban areas had risen from 11 in 1936 to 50 percent in 1971 (Trlin 1979, 191).

A second important development was the immigrant influx from Tonga, Samoa, and the Cook Islands. By the mid-1960s, New Zealand's largest city, Auckland, with just over half a million residents, had nearly 34,000 Maori and just over 16,000 Islanders (Whitelaw 1971, 66). The Auckland Maori population, augmented by a wave of young migrants from the country, had grown from less than 2 percent to more than 6 percent of the city in twenty years (Rowland 1971, 22, 27). It was about half the nightmare number of Ausubel's scenario, and very few central Europeans to compound the potential for disaster, but a formidably expanding presence nevertheless. Geographers and demographers noticed the residential mobility of the youthful new city dwellers, and remarked on lengthy journeys to work—four out of five travelling five miles or more. But credit for the "progress" made by Maori in "adapting to and advancing within" the city environment was given to the state for its housing loan, rental support, and welfare programs and for the imaginative scheme that allowed family benefits to be capitalized (Rowland 1972, 14, 20).

## Observations and Models

When local social scientists attempted to understand what was happening to their society, many not unnaturally turned to American models for guidance (Rowland 1972). The ideas of the Chicago ecologists of the 1920s had long been influential (McGee 1969). But they did not account for the patterns of mobility and settlement discernible in the New Zealand metropolises. For Auckland in particular, the theory that suggested that there would be "ghetto-like development" with strongly visible minorities concentrated in the central city did not fit the burgeoning reality. Predictably, inner-city populations might swell in future, but the danger such growth might presage would not be the result of Maori concentration: "a situation which must be carefully avoided is that our central cities become ethnic ghettos of foreign-born groups, as has occurred in many cities overseas" (McGee 1969, 154). Maoris and Islanders were increasingly clustering in peripheral suburbs where cheaper state-subsidized housing was available.

The respected Maori educationist and commentator Ranginui Walker took a positive view of the growth of a "brown proletariat" in outer suburbs. Deracinated individuals could only benefit from the development of ethnic subcommunities with "their own social organisations to ensure continuance of their own cultural patterns and adequate socialisation of their children. The formation of Maori cultural clubs, family clubs, benevolent societies, Maori committees, women's welfare leagues, and warden's associations have all proved to be integrative rather than separatist mechanisms. They give the Maori his identity, ensure cultural transmission, and help members to adjust to the wider society" (Trlin 1977, 124).

These putatively benign developments were partly attributed to the absence of the overt segregation and discrimination familiar from American literature. According to the demographer Ian Pool, the "suburban drift" of the Maori followed the "firm precedent" of non-Maoris. And until the 1960s, there were "few marked residential concentrations of Maoris." Quoting the research of Jane Ritchie on a sample of Wellington mothers, Pool suggested that the "significance normally accorded kinship and other traditional ties may have been overstated." Maori were choosing suburbia, foregoing kinship ties in the inner city, in the hope of jobs and social betterment on the fringes (Pool 1977, 206).

Nevertheless, the comparative sparseness of community organizations, corner stores, and churches, as well as a lack of family support, prompted apprehension about what was delicately described as "greater difficulty in adjusting to urban life" (Whitelaw 1971, 71, 74). With New Zealand's puny economy inextricably dependent on international commodity, financial, and capital markets, the nation was among the first "western" societies to have intimations of globalization. There were those who could sense at least something of the future: "socio-economic segregation has had a similar effect to racial segregation" (Rowland 1971, 36). Bureaucrats were meanwhile struggling to assimilate what they knew about local gangs into the portfolio of theory available from international literature (Jensen 1970). With little knowledge of the actualities underlying the works of Albert Cohen, Walter Miller, and other scholars, New Zealand students were ill equipped to filter parochial American elements from the crystallizing paradigms. Professionals engaged in intervention programs had less difficulty in finding inadequately evaluated American precedents to adopt or adapt. Social workers and probation officers, proponents of "detached" social work to modify gang behavior from within, had the advantage over those who advocated vastly more costly and politically problematic schemes of social improvement.

Whatever the preferred and possible remedial strategies, there was a reality to be understood. Little aided by the sociological and anthropological research community, government and law enforcement officers perforce made what they could of their own observations. The chief welfare officer of the Department of Maori Affairs warned that schools even in the smaller towns of the prosperous Waikato region were experiencing "racial fights as gangs of Maoris attacked groups of Europeans. Headmasters didn't know what to do and his department had no solutions" (*Thames Star*, April 28, 1971). Officials in Internal Affairs and Maori and Islander Affairs had linked increasing localized violence on the fringes of the capital city Wellington to "the failure of the policy to pepper-pot housing for Maoris throughout Pakeha housing" (Joint Committee on Young Offenders Working Sub-committee, Minutes, June 11, 1971, Department of Maori Affairs Papers, 36/15/4, National Archives of New Zealand). Yet it was to be some time before either scholars or town planning and housing authorities began to express alarm about the social pathologies that were germinating. J. D. Howman, a postgraduate law student at Auckland University, advised the Maori Affairs

Department in 1971 on the location and nature of Auckland gangs: "There seems to be no gang organised for criminal activity; however the tendency of gang members to commit crimes may be high, whether this is a result of membership or not cannot be determined . . . the Police do not view the gangs as potential criminal bases, although they will not deny the fact that a lot of gang members have individually offended"[6] (Howman 1972). Ironically, while concerned about problems arising from immediate growth of the urban Maori population, Pool's demographic forecast was for a likely decline in Maori fertility, a consequent "ethnic imbalance," demands for immigrant labor, and the challenge this would present for the nation's commitment to biculturalism (Pool 1977, 224–27).

To an extent not at first obtrusive, the failure of state foresight was veiled by an orthodoxy that viewed symptoms of cultural stress as impermanent, likely to be responsive to enlightened social policy, determined efforts to find employment for young Maori men, and sustained economic growth. Civic authorities hopefully fostered recreational facilities and "events of interest to those who might, without such interests, be drawn into unruly youth groups" (*New Zealand Herald,* June 10, 1971). "There is a widespread belief, perhaps because some progress has been achieved in education, housing, health, and employment that the present situation of both Maoris and Pacific Islanders can and will be corrected by the design and application of further compensatory measures" (Trlin 1979, 200).

This was a belief that flew in the face of New Zealand's growing vulnerability to overseas economic fluctuations as well as the destabilization of mood and policy brought by feminist, environmental, and civil rights movements (Pearson 1991, 207–9). There were in any case well-documented barriers to upward social mobility. The issue had preoccupied the research unit of the government's Joint Committee on Young Offenders. The existence of "a relationship" between race, socioeconomic status, and juvenile offending had been established in the mid-1970s. Later analysis indicated that it was a durable relationship, extending to adult as well as juvenile offenders. But the researchers concluded that "improvements in Maori socio-economic status are unlikely to lead to a reduction in crime and other social problems unless they are sufficiently large to advance the relative position of Maoris" (Fifield and Donnell 1980, 52). Trlin put it emphatically: "New Zealand has indeed an emergent Polynesian eth-class" (1979, 201).[7] In any case, world events were to render the belief in amelioration, whether relative or absolute, untestable. The collapse of export income and the catastrophic impact of international oil price escalations of the 1970s ensured that the vulnerable in New Zealand society, the majority of them Maori and Islanders, would be mired in low-income jobs (Brosnan 1984) or unemployment and welfare dependency (Pearson 1990, 106–43).

## Hopes and Fears of the 1970s

In the last years of prosperous optimism, the respected and influential Joan Metge completed a revised edition of her text *The Maoris of New Zealand,* first published in 1967. Metge's section on "'gangs' and other youth movements" grouped gangs like Black Power and the Mongrel Mob with political action groups like the radical and recently visible Nga Tamatoa and university student associations. For Metge, "much of the gangs' apparent alienation is in reaction to a society they see as materialistic, selfish and uncaring." Embrace them, find them jobs, recognize their need for identity, pride, and comradeship, and the "normal processes of maturation" might well produce better outcomes than "trying to make them over in another image" (Metge 1976, 174–77).

If ever a cohort of scholars were to be caught wearing rose-tinted spectacles, this was the time. Too often, ethnographers garnered self-serving rationalizations. A miasma of white guilt shielded many a miscreant from scrutiny. Senior Maori welfare officers argued that "Maori gangs could become community assets instead of liabilities . . . with financial backing and sound counselling, the average Maori gang could become indistinguishable from other service organisations" (*Waikato Times,* July 28, 1971). Sympathetic as they rightly were to the plight of so many trapped in poverty and seeking the warmth of groups that might be a surrogate for the family or clan from whom they were separated, a generation of officials and writers downplayed the purposeful criminal enterprises that were replicating in their midst.

A Department of Internal Affairs review of the research on "juvenile gang membership"—the "juvenile" label serving implicitly to diminish the menace of dominant groups with mature leadership—concluded in 1979, "Most of the literature on gangs in New Zealand has been written by persons who have had some personal experience with gang members, primarily in their official capacities. This however does not mean that observation is less satisfactory than research but it has meant that the analytical side of the question has suffered" (Steadman 1979).

Yet sociologically fluent gang apologists in fact produced some persuasive commentary. The gang, said the "patched" Black Power member Denis O'Reilly (1979), "rejects a society based on 'success,' in which its members fail, and creates a counter culture based on 'failure,' in which its members succeed—a culture of alienation." Civil libertarians excoriated provocatively harsh law enforcement and the flaws of legislation designed to strengthen police powers or make judicial punishments more credible and effective. Endemic brutality was seen as an aberration rather than a defining characteristic. Gazes were averted from the beachhead of international organized criminality that steadily, albeit unadvertisedly, accompanied the other mixed blessings of a globalizing economy. For much of the 1970s and later, many politicians were still in denial about gang criminality. Even allowing for the unemployed, the principal victims of globally influenced structural economic adjustment, it was possible, though tendentious, to argue from the vantage point of the end of the century that the post-1970s Maori population was "in absolute terms larger, per capita materially wealthier, and has a higher life expectancy than at any other time in New Zealand's history" (Chapple 2000, 29).[8] Surely such improvements would diminish the attractiveness of gang lifestyles?

It was easy to point to evidence that some gangs were forming themselves into incorporated societies, setting up companies, opening bank accounts, and taking up work contracts with local authorities (Thomas 1980). The Race Relations Conciliator reached out to four major gangs, arranged work schemes for their members, and mediated between gangs themselves and with the community (Trlin 1982, 189). As a report to the New Zealand Psychological Society suggested in 1980, "the establishment of interventions which encourage self-sufficiency and relative economic independence among gangs may be the most effective technique of reducing anti-social behaviour by gang members" (Thomas 1980, 7). This was an approach in harmony with a new Tu Tangata ("stand tall") policy of participatory community development that saw gang members recruited into an "indigenised" Maori Affairs department (Fleras 1985).

What was more politically salient than gang crime in the 1970s was the efflorescence of pan-Maori ethnic consciousness. Perhaps the most remarkable consequence of urbanization had been the success of entrepreneurs of ethnicity in shaping a sense of shared identity among a people historically divided by tribal loyalties. Protest politics, the prospect of racial unrest, and the outbreak of public disorder over the visit of a racially exclusive touring South African rugby team, therefore, seemed more immediately disturbing than a surge of gangsterism (Hazlehurst 1993). Radical theorists and activists made explicit the connection between the oppressed status of Maori and Polynesians and the social relations of the capitalist system. Their analysis was disturbing less for its theoretical elegance than for its potential impact. It might convince restless gangs to make common cause with radical groups whose rhetoric signaled a revolutionary mission. Government and security authorities' fears that gangs might be politicized were fueled by the efforts of the Polynesian Panthers (modeling themselves on what little they knew of Huey Newton and the Black Panthers) to promote "black" pan-ethnic unity. Labour Party Maori spokesmen spoke of gangs as symptomatic of "a general urban crisis that Maori and Island people face" (K. Hazlehurst 1993, 45).

The rapid growth of a gang calling itself Black Power, and of the more violent and nihilistic Mongrel Mob and Headhunters, seemed proof that New Zealand was in danger of going down an essentially foreign path.[9] But Maori academic theorists at first furnished reassuring commentary:

> Gangs are a creative attempt by rejected youths to establish a sense of identity and belonging. Their defiance of society that has misunderstood and failed them is symbolised by their adoption of uniforms and negative symbols such as names with anti-social connotations like Stormtroopers and Black Power . . . But Black Power is not, as Pakehas think, the seeds of revolution. If Black Power is pushed into becoming an anti-social force then the adoption of that stance will be due to Pakeha paranoia and not the failure of responsible Maori leadership . . .
>
> Although at present they operate at an apolitical, low level of human endeavour—namely drinking, "scoring" women and fighting over territory—within these gangs is enormous potential to burn New Zealand's cities the way the Blacks did in Watts and Detroit. The missing variable in the New Zealand scene is political awareness among the gangs. (Walker 1978, 218–19)

Black Power leaders heard the message. In spite of their adoption of American radical symbols, they had no ambition to be the urban guerrilla spearhead of protest. Their aims were limited and their willingness to enter into dialogue with government agencies revealed a political sophistication that was to discommode a floundering police force for the next decade. When a left-wing Maori political party was launched in 1980 by a tribal kinsman of the Black Power leader Rei Harris, the gang's thirty-seven chapters were summoned to a national conference and told to mobilize votes for the new Mana Motuhake party (Kayes 1995). The party did not prosper (K. Hazlehurst 1993).

The Panthers' dream foundered on the twin rocks of Maori antipathy and gang indifference to pan-ethnic solidarity and "liberation." Neither radicals nor liberal sympathizers in the universities had been quick to realize the extent to which most gang members were alienated both from their own communities and from political action of any kind.[10] A style shift from American black power language to a third- or fourth-world liberation ideology left gangs cold (Greenland 1991). "Attempts have been made by intellectuals and political activists to harness the 'oppressed' . . . The gangs are not interested in the anti-white sentiments of the protesters" (Inspector Philip Keber, interview, March 28, 1981). But when gangs became manifestly more violent in the late 1970s, and police and government responded to a media-inflamed public with initiatives to contain the threat to "law and order," academic activists were to the fore in condemning the "moral panic."

Media and political exploitation of public fears made a "moral panic" diagnosis plausible (Kelsey and Young 1982). But the panic had been some time coming. Research by the Justice Department into "Violent Offending," published late in 1971 and attracting newspaper headlines, concluded that New Zealand "may now be confronted for the first time with a sub-culture of violence in its larger cities" (*The Dominion,* January 5, 1972). Examination of a sample of offenders in 1968 revealed that nearly half of them had committed their offense in a "group" of two or more; and for offenders up to twenty-four years of age, the group percentage was over 60 percent (Schumacher 1971, 50–51, 30–34). The word "gang" did not at first appear. Yet behind closed doors in police headquarters, officials from the Internal Affairs and Maori and Island Affairs departments were already anxiously debating how to deal with "problems arising from the activities of the Mongrel Mob." Late in the same year, they were to take comfort from the observation that other gangs that had once been seen as a social menace had evolved into more constructive groups. If only the police would stop talking about the Mob, or indeed stop referring to any gang by name, their appeal to the young and impressionable would be diminished.

## Diverging Paradigms

No amount of rhetorical economy would keep the gangs at bay. Police progressively gathered intelligence, assessed what they saw as a mounting threat to public order, and tried to deploy themselves in the major cities and across the nation more effectively. It was evident by the end of the 1970s that there were dysfunctional gulfs of understanding and interpretation between police intelligence and investigations, prison and probation officer observations, judicial assumptions, research sponsored and often conducted by government agencies, and the exiguous independent scholarly work that had been published. A 1979 Parliamentary Select Committee on Violent Offending, strongly influenced by academics and community leaders who deplored media sensationalism and stigmatization, treated "the problem of gangs" in the words of a later committee, "almost as a non-event" (Report of Ministerial Committee of Inquiry into Violence 1987). In 1981, prompted by a prime minister who took a personal interest in gangs (Gustafson 2000), an ad hoc committee of officials directing its attention primarily to preventive measures noted in passing that gangs were "developing naturally in New Zealand's social structure, and they will probably always exist since they arise from a particular set of social and economic conditions." The brief report, compiled in little more than a month under the chairmanship of an astute government MP, candidly acknowledged one of the crucial gang puzzles: "There is no satisfactory explanation as to why delinquent gangs form in some situations and not in others where there might be considerable individual delinquency" (Committee on Gangs 1981, 6, 10). Simultaneously, Maori community leaders were admitting privately that "all their efforts to stem the tide of crime and gang recruitment had failed . . . Searching for an old pattern in a phenomenon unlike any seen before in New Zealand some speculated that the gangs represented 'new Maori tribes' in the urban setting" (Hazlehurst 1989). But this dubious analogy was soon discarded in favor of the increasingly flexible concept of whanau—originally understood as the basic descent or kinship unit into which individuals are born and socialized, but latterly extended to describe groups, irrespective of family relationships, that have a common purpose (Metge 1995).

In spite of repeated recommendations that government action needed to be better coordinated and targeted and to have continuing consultation between agencies, little progress was made in the 1980s towards a common understanding or an integrated policy. Demographic forecasts that one in four New Zealanders might be Polynesian by 2011 led to politically incorrect anxieties (Spoonley 1990). Educational, welfare, and employment programs came and went. Community initiatives were encouraged and supported. Governments took what comfort they could from temporary drops in reported crime figures and evidence that the numbers of gang members, associates, and prospects had apparently stabilized by the mid-1980s at around 2,200. While academic commentators were inclined to portray aggressive policing as a potent catalyst of gang growth and criminality, most of what was known about gangs was the product of police surveillance and undercover operations. Perhaps the high-water mark of complacency was the report of a sympathetic committee appointed by the minister of justice in 1986 that admonished the police, recommending that they "review their whole attitude to the question of gangs": "It is our belief that despite the attention periodically given them, gangs are one of the least of this country's worries and, to some extent, they are a result of those more serious concerns" (Report of Ministerial Committee of Inquiry into Violence 1987, 88, 91).

The following year, a report on the Maori perspective on the criminal justice system gave substance to some "more serious concerns." Moana Jackson, a prominent Maori lawyer and scholar commissioned by the Department of Justice, affirmed that gangs "must be seen as part of the Maori community, and their conduct as but an extreme manifestation of the pressures that have shaped that community" (Jackson 1988, 31). Jackson concluded that "existing research has not provided adequate explanations or solutions for Maori offending," and without a "culture-specific criminology" rather than a "monocultural methodology" there could not be an understanding of Maori behavior (Jackson 1988, 25–26). He suggested an explanation for much Maori offending in the undermining of Maori "spiritual strength." Racial and economic inequalities create "an imbalance in the social, cultural and emotional harmony of many young Maori lives" and "an environment in which they are vulnerable to criminal involvement . . . the lack of a positive cultural identity may lead to identification with peer groups and an initiation into the solidarity and sub-culture of a gang" (Jackson 1988, 92, 100).[11]

The idea of spiritual impoverishment, so alien to Western criminology, had been implicit in much of the argument since the 1970s about the need to revive or invent cultural institutions. It was to be the great paradox of the last decades of the twentieth century that the efflorescence of Maori culture, and the introduction of community justice, crime prevention and "restorative" programs, and family group conferencing for young offenders, was accompanied by a renewed surge of gang criminality.[12] Few had appreciated the extent to which ethnic gangs had come to represent a choice against the political expression of ethnicity as much as a symptom of cultural deprivation.[13] Nor was there a realization that internationally connected organized crime groups would successfully nurture and nourish ethnic gangs as partners in drug distribution and other profitable unlawful enterprises. If there were identities to be created and affirmed, respect to be earned, their domain was a potentially boundless global criminal economy rather than an inhibiting world of traditional authority, reverence for elders, and multiple obligations to distant kin.

Acknowledging that gang members had been consulted in the preparation of his report was almost the full extent of Jackson's consideration of gangs. It was hardly surprising. As one senior Justice Department researcher, himself the author of the first work on gangs in prisons, lamented in 1992, "Despite their prominence and significance in New Zealand society gangs have seldom been the subject of academic research or serious consideration" (Meek 1992, 272).[14] The stalled quest for understanding was in part a consequence of a tacit suspension of academic inquiry "in deference to what many accepted as the prerogative of Maori themselves" (Bull 2001, 55). It also reflected an American hiatus in gang research: "after little consideration for almost 20 years, gangs have been resuscitated as an explanation for crime by young people" (Dukes, Martinez, and Stein 1997, 139). Meanwhile rates of unemployment for teenage Polynesians ran between 40 percent and 70 percent, the predominantly Samoan King Cobras flourished, and street gang turf battles continued to erupt despite a variety of programs designed to compensate for disadvantage, provide recreational alternatives, and foster cultural pride (New Zealand Planning Council 1989). Through the 1980s, there was also episodic warfare between the two largest gangs. Black Power recruited vigorously, earning the contempt of the Mongrel Mob who believed they enjoyed greater loyalty from their smaller groups. While Black Power sought a façade of respectability, placing its members in work and training schemes and nurturing its own legitimate enterprises (Walker 1990, 261–62), the Mob clumsily followed suit with several chapters registering as trusts and obtaining government funding (Winter 1998). What the public had no difficulty grasping, and academic researchers largely ignored, was that the gang presence was national. From the isolated hamlets of the far north, to the prosperous east coast towns of Gisborne and Nelson, to the southern cities of Dunedin and Christchurch, gangs erupted, fought, menaced, and went about their business, occasionally lawful, bringing fear to once tranquil neighborhoods.

Increasingly, there was a divergence of paradigms as many social work practitioners, social policy theorists, and ethnic activists clung to a vision that gangs might be redeemed while police, corrections, probation and court officials grappled with an overload of crime and offender processing. Since it was often impossible to prove well-founded suspicions of gang involvement in thefts, robberies, drug distribution, insurance fraud, rape, and other offenses, the dimensions of gang criminality would always be statistically understated. Police estimates of gang numbers might be accepted (about fifty separate gangs with 6,550 members by 1990, stabilized at around 5,000 thereafter, with perhaps another 1,000 in youth gangs). But speculation by the Police Association that 80 percent of "serious" crime was gang related would have less credibility (Newbold 2000, 222).

By the early 1990s, both public and academic debates were wearily pre-dictable. Jane Kelsey, an activist in the 1970s and now a legal academic at the University of Auckland, reminded readers of her polemic, *Rolling Back the State*, that most of the recommendations of four government inquiries into gangs, crime, and violent offending in thirteen years had been ignored. Con-ceding that violent and property crime "were genuinely on the increase," her concern nonetheless remained not so much with "genuine" public fears as with the "moral panics" she had made her own and a drift towards "a sur-veillance society." After a free-market economic revolution and the shrink-ing of both employment and welfare safety nets, Maori were structurally "a third world colonised people trapped in a first world metropolitan society."[15] Kelsey foresaw "dissent, including a more organised, historically sourced, political resistance" (Kelsey 1993, 325–26, 361, 363). She did not forecast the progressive criminalizing of the victims of the shriveled welfare system or the international criminal networking that was already accompanying eco-nomic globalization. Other writers were to endorse the relevance to New Zealand of Mertonian strain theory and of the literature that portrays free-market economies as intrinsically "crime-producing." For George Pavlich, in a chapter on crime and crime control that never mentions gangs, "official discourses" that indicate a growing problem requiring increased crime-con-trol resources tell a "deeply flawed story that will do little to eradicate the quantum of harmful behaviour" (Pavlich 2000, 142–43).

Jane and James Ritchie (1993, 142–43), who did mention gangs, shared the cynicism exhibited by Kelsey and others about government and public will-ingness to put aside prejudice and fear and construct a coherent social policy. More inclined than Kelsey to recognize that there was a tide of violence to be turned back, the Ritchies were also despondent about the lack of action: "the most active thing we do about violence is to get someone to report on it while we all look the other way." Among the pigeonholed documents was the report of the Ministerial Committee of Inquiry into the Prison System in 1988. The report had verified and quantified perennial media and prisoner support-group allegations that prisons were gang incubators. A quarter of all male prisoners and a third of females were either fully "patched" gang members or associates.[16] As the Department of Justice's submission to the inquiry put it with masterly understatement: "Gangs create considerable management problems in prisons because of their propensity for cohesive group action according to their own codes. Inter-gang violence, the recruit-ment of new gang members and intimidation of other inmates also cause considerable management problems." What could be done? Two solutions were proposed. The "most intransigent" gang members could be segregated in maximum security units. Small locally based "habilitation centres" could assist the reintegration of others who could be influenced by family and community (Department of Justice 1988b).[17]

While steps were taken in both these limited directions, Pavlich's quantum of harmful behavior appeared to be a variable insignificantly responsive to government policy of any kind. Successive administrations had vacillated between strategies of prevention, persuasion, and suppression. In the 1990s, instructed by two decades of government reports, academic sympathy, op-ed commentary, legal advice, and civil libertarian advocacy, most gang spokesmen could articulate the vocabulary of deprivation and oppression. When the leader of a Black Power faction in Wellington called the Movement was challenged about the violent robberies and assaults committed by its younger members, he was ready: "they have to eat, they have to survive" (Kayes 1995). Social statistics—an unemployment rate of 24 percent, rising to 60 percent in some areas in 1991, disproportionate numbers of one-parent families, incidents of domestic violence, and truancy—certainly gave credence to the survival theme. In her book *New Growth from Old*, Metge discussed "indications of stress on individuals and families," drawing attention to the fact that "Maori made up 42% of all convicted offenders in 1993 and almost half the prisoners received by penal institutions" (1995, 23). Her profound work on Maori families, households, communities, and groups gave insight into the world many gang recruits leave. But it left large imaginative leaps to be made, meagerly illuminated by research findings, in order to explain individual decisions over several generations to join and stay in groups that others spurn as brutally unattractive.

## Millennial Rethinking

As authorities intermittently looked overseas for understanding, a change was occurring in official language and conceptualization of gangs. By law (Section 312A of the Crimes Act), they were defined as "organised criminal enterprises." To the police and government spokesmen, they were subsumed under the rubric of "organised crime." Academics, eager to be au courant, followed suit, augmenting the torrent of official statistical compendia and police press releases with the substance of privately circulated reports. From the summary of an internal police survey, Newbold concluded that organized crime was the domain of "a fairly large number of mainly small groups operating . . . principally at a local level. Organised criminal groups are a relatively recent phenomenon and few have links with organised conspiracies overseas" (2000, 216). There was no mention of the possibility that this perception might result from the fragmentation and paucity of police intelligence resources or the poor responses to the flawed survey acknowledged by the author of the survey report (McCardle 1999).

Academic research understandably could do little independently to illuminate clandestine arrangements and dangerous liaisons. It is no secret that major outlaw motorcycle gangs have long histories in New Zealand, or that offshore Asian crime groups have also established footholds. Neither the Hells Angels presence nor that of the offshore Triads, yakuza, or Colombians can be linked directly to fluctuations in domestic economic indices. Nor does any analysis of urban development, the loss of economic sovereignty, or marginalization in the network society adequately account for their growth and expanding impact. "Sophisticated, unpretentious, well attired and polite to its neighbours, HAMC (Auckland) could be the prototype of the successful gang of the future" (Newbold 2000, 208). For Greg Newbold, the most authoritative of recent writers, the worst-case scenario was of Asian groups forming "functional alliances with large violent gangs such as the Mongrel Mob" (2000, 222–23) and thereby developing a national criminal monopoly. That such linkages could be contemplated—and there were already glimpses of developing relationships that had become obvious five years later—underlined important elements of the small-nation experience. By the end of the century, one in fifteen New Zealanders were of Asian immigrant origin (predominantly Hong Kong and Taiwanese Chinese, Malaysian, Singaporean, and Thai). International connections were commonplace. Yet a national territorial monopoly, even a substantial market presence, negotiated between a proud and highly visible indigenous gang and a larger, more powerful but obviously alien group, would demonstrate a transcendence of space and race that had yet to be achieved. Transactional networks, filaments of mutual interest, were connecting in an unbounded global economy. But international and local criminal enterprises appeared still to be constrained as much by their own prejudices, resources, and rivals as by an underequipped state and transnational law enforcement capability newly distracted by the war against terror.

To predict the future, as law enforcement agencies must, requires an understanding not only of the gangs themselves, the gang community and "processes of integration and codetermination" (Venkatesh 1997), the markets, supply chains, and distribution networks for gang products and services, but of the political, juridical, legal, and law enforcement environments that encompass them. It would be possible to define away some gangs and other organized criminal entities so as to make explanation simpler. The newer Polynesian youth gangs, territorially bounded, self-consciously emulating "Bloods" and "Crips," certainly had characteristics that set them apart from the established Maori and motorcycle gangs. It was possible to distinguish "wannabes" and predominantly "wannabe" gangs, and "New Jacks" (Eggleston 2000). But most of the entities themselves, the communities they inhabited, and the state agencies that dealt with them, recognized commonalities and relationships sufficient to make it sensible to consider them all in one analytical framework.

New Zealand certainly exhibits community dislocation, alienation, and inequalities accentuated by shifts in global economic power (UNRISD 1995). But at the beginning of the twenty-first century, most gangs (the Polynesian Islanders were an exception) stood apart not as a result of community rejection, geographical isolation, or economic exclusion but by choice. They behaved the way they did less because they were forced to by circumstance and more because they chose to do so. Forster long ago concluded that "to accept the fact that there is a criminal community with its own standards, norms, sanctions, and views of morality is a greater jump than most of us can make" (1969, 299). To accept that these are groups not to be understood merely as the victims of multiple marginality or as proto-resistance movements is the first step towards understanding the actual importance of the circumstances and environments in which they operate.

Gangs have been created and have endured both in times of national prosperity and severe adversity. If there is a causal relationship between economic conditions and gang formation or attenuation, its parameters are undetermined.[18] If some contemporary reports are to be given credence, the excessive attention of the police may have given greater impetus to early gang development than adverse social conditions (Two Detached Social Workers 1981). While it might once have been true that happier homes, more appropriate schooling, abundant job alternatives, a generous welfare safety net, and a flourishing indigenous culture might have made the emergence and growth of gangs less likely, it does not seem credible to suppose that any conceivable increase in national wealth or reduction of outcome disparities would have a significant impact on the existing major gangs.

The 1990s saw autonomous goal-oriented developments. Outlaw motorcycle gangs, ethnic gangs, and white power gangs became self-sustaining and adaptable organisms, retaining old members and recruiting new ones from their own families and sparingly from among penumbral "wannabes." Estimates of gang membership indicated that entrepreneurial organized crime groups were offering attractive job prospects in an otherwise unpromising labor market.[19] As Levitt and Venkatesh (2000) suggest, gang adherence may be economically suboptimal in the long term, but there are compensating "social/nonpecuniary benefits."

Gangs are not all confined to urban localities or by particular geographic boundaries. Although two or three New Zealand cities constitute "strategic sites," this is more a consequence of history or inheritance than of positioning in Saskia Sassen's "new geography of centrality." Police thought of most organized crime groups as independent, locally focused, but with extensive networks of affiliation (McCardle 1999). Some remained by choice in places where they were comfortable, secure against competitors, accessible to enough opportunities for group sustainability but able to draw on neighborhood support if necessary. Others, for similar reasons, relocated. Still others—Hells Angels and emerging Asian groups among them—operated with the freedom of movement characteristic of buoyant corporate enterprises. They were not so much part of a separate informal economy as they were economic actors whose point of difference was the degree to which they operated unlawfully as suppliers of goods and services, the most profitable of them illicit. The informal economy they inhabited is conceptually distinct from, but organically codependent with, the general economy. "Serious crime networks are now stretched across time and space, members inhabiting terrains indistinguishable from the local economic sphere" (Hobbs 2001, 553).

The business conduct of gangs may be, but is not always, distinguished from other enterprises by the nature of what they buy and sell. Selling drugs, whether LSD, marijuana, cocaine, or heroin, has been an evolutionary development, but the recent explosion in middle-class demand for methamphetamines has been a notable discontinuity. Gang business behavior is distinguishable by a willingness to intimidate and to do openly illegal harm to others. Some gangs choose to flaunt a rebel existence: damage, inflict pain, and kill rivals; antagonize law enforcement authorities; intimidate neighbors, police families, and witnesses; and maintain their own self-esteem by ensuring public awareness that they are "bad." Others seek anonymity, doing their business without publicity, content for it to be known that their wrath and retribution can be ferocious but not seeking to prove their staunchness by frequent and open battles with enemies. Differences in style indicate continual differentiation of appeals and motivations for involvement. Business arrangements mimic conventional business supply chain and distribution networks (*New Zealand Herald,* March 1, 2001). Paradoxically, gangs are at their most vulnerable to the extent that they seek conformity with community norms and their income depends on legitimate enterprise.

The majority of mature ethnic gangs are predominantly Maori (though proclaiming themselves to be "multicultural" organizations),[20] and their members mostly recruited from an underclass. But they are neither stranded in ghettos[21] nor integrated with their neighborhoods. Maori gang members may live in poorer neighborhoods, but as prior occupants of the rural hinterland, many with provable ties to rural kin, they have homelands to which retreat is possible.[22] Twenty years of Maori community revitalization left many gang members unmoved. "I don't think about my race or what I am" (Payne 1991, 23). It is credible that "cultural alienation may be a contributing factor" to aggregate Maori criminal behavior and that crime prevention programs that express Maori cultural values diminish risks of offending and recidivism (Doone 2000). But they have had no appreciable effect on established gangs.

"Estrangement from cultural roots" (Department of Justice 1988a) or multiple marginality (Vigil and Yun 1998) may once have been an outcome of colonial dispossession or urban migration. It may be accentuated by global developments. However, for gang members there is also an element of choice, a rejection as much as a lamented loss. Many of the young, drawn by powerful media representations, emulate what they think is African American culture (Ihaka 1993). Islander gangs, also undeniably deriving from the underclass, are largely restricted operationally to the outer suburbs of the major metropolis from which they see no escape route, either to the hinterland or to the islands from which their parents or grandparents came. Community leaders persist in offering diversion; family ties though fragile are not abandoned.

Older gangs, resilient and adaptive, have evolved modes of governance that provide for stable leadership and enable regional and nationwide cooperation. Black Power's national confederated structure has proved viable over three decades, notwithstanding several factional defections, notably the Nomads who rejected the "soft" engagement in government work schemes. The assertive independence of Mongrel Mob chapters has not precluded coordinated action. Hells Angels MC, internationally franchised, maintains awesome discipline and public relations. The continuity of roles and of personnel has given gangs advantages of corporate memory, operational efficiency, and morale over chronically underresourced law enforcement organizations.

The gang environment needs to be conceived as a structure of law and government as well as of local economy, topography, and social geography.

Gang action boundaries are set as much by a legal and policing framework that contains, prohibits, and punishes as by community engagement, hostility, or indifference. Territoriality is important for youth street gangs, but the markets to be controlled by larger gangs mirror the national and international domains of "legitimate" enterprises. Though they are the objects of ongoing surveillance, undercover penetration, and intensified sanctions, gangs continue to enjoy political access. While there is no evidence of significant political or public service corruption in New Zealand, there appears to be a tacit understanding, often strained, that gangs will be both policed and tolerated. Gangs and governments (especially Labour governments) have a mutual interest in keeping the "gang menace" off the political agenda. Recurrent "law and order" elections demonstrate the inutility of the "law and order" solutions that have so far found favor.

Conventional macro-economic and welfare policies have limited capacity to transform the social ecologies in which ethnic gangs thrive. Neighborhood regeneration strategies demand targeted, coordinated, and committed government-community partnerships. At least two generations would be needed to "break the cycle of family dysfunction, and restore or invent socialisation processes that begin to have a significant positive impact on large tracts of demoralized urban areas and jobless small towns" (C. Hazlehurst 1997; see also Chilton 1991).

Unless facing overwhelming public pressure, governments are reluctant to act against gangs when they risk violating an academic and professional consensus or lack the comfort of unimpeachable research. There are therefore real dangers when it can be said of many of a nation's social scientists that they "have lost their professional nerve in an excess of cultural and epistemological relativism" (Nash 1990, 116). Timid and co-opted scholarship reinforces current theories and models. But the influence of social science paradigms on social policy and justice system practice places responsibility on all engaged in criminological and related research to think ahead as well as explain retrospectively.

New Zealanders have often resorted to seeing their own phenomena through a succession of borrowed prisms. Taking refuge in the belief that social change in New Zealand always lagged behind American and European developments, scholars and professionals have been reactive: "we wait until we have the problem" (interview with Sgt. Bruce Horne, December 16, 1994). But a new mood is perceptible, "a dislike of relying on overseas social values and debates to inform local issues" (Bull 2001, xvii). The story of New Zealand's search for understandings about gangs and how society ought to respond to them may help in the fundamental task of discerning the universal in the unique.

## Notes

1. When New Zealanders were asked in the census of 1996, "Which ethnic group do you belong to?" a total of 523,374 answered in a way that led to their being classified as the "New Zealand Maori ethnic group." They constituted 14.5 percent of the total population of 3,681,546. Subsequent analysis revealed that one in four of those officially counted Maori in 1996 had not called themselves Maori in 1991; one in twenty self-identified Maori in 1991 no longer identified as Maori in 1996; one in ten "Maori descended" persons in 1996 had not claimed Maori ancestry five years earlier; one in twenty ceased to acknowledge the Maori identity they had previously recorded (Chapple 2000).

2. About half of non-Maori pupils left school without qualifications. In the mid-1950s, there had been only eighty-nine Maori university students. Had Maori been represented proportionately to the population aged eighteen to twenty-four there would have been twelve times as many. A decade later there were 300, with the under-representation still sevenfold (Harker 1970, 148–50). Until mid-century, educational disparities were "masked by the capacity of the tribal hinterland to absorb the failures" (Walker 1982, 79).

3. The "cultural misunderstanding" interpretation of Maori property offending has frequently been criticized as a "marked oversimplification" (O'Malley 1973, 387).

4. In data for 1974, Pomare (1980, 46) noted that for the age group of fifteen years and above, the hospital admission rate for "schizophrenia and paranoid states" was 1.6 times greater for Maori than for non-Maori. Curiously, a Maori psychiatric unit at an Auckland hospital became the focus of controversy in 1989 over the authenticity of the supposedly Maori cultural practices being employed.

5. The debate continues: "seeing Maori purely as victims of police discrimination denies their own agency and culpability" (Bull 2001, 10).

6. Howman's paper was forwarded to the Minister for Maori Affairs by the secretary of his department, who commented, "It is refreshing to find somebody who has the gang business in perspective" (Department of Maori Affairs Papers, National Archives of New Zealand).

7. It should be noted that some scholars in this period included Maori in the Polynesian category.

8. For a more generally accepted Maori view, see Mahuta (1989).

9. Police were aware of some eighty Black Power chapters by 1974 (interview with Det. Sgt. Alan McGhie, December 1994).

10. Such was the primacy of traditional personal ties over radical political influences that in 1981 discreetly clothed Headhunters gang members armed with knives provided a secret protective phalanx around the conservative Maori politician Sir

Graham Latimer, a kinsman of gang leaders, whose investiture as a knight was threatened with disruption by a radical action group (C. Hazlehurst 1995, 110).

11. Jackson's analysis was based on a combination of the criminological literature he criticized and extensive consultations. His prescriptions for reform mixed widely held views about targeted programs and a controversial call for an autonomous criminal justice system that was instantly rejected by those responsible for the existing system. Jackson rightly reiterated what most previous writers had long remarked on, the difficulty of reconciling studies based on inconsistent foundations: census definitions of Maori differed from justice system and police definitions.

12. One explanation of the paradox was the readiness of courts and diversion conferences to accept offers from gangs to provide whanau (surrogate family) support for youth offenders with incarcerated parents or otherwise inappropriate families.

13. "The brute fact which tends to be suppressed by opportunists in the Maori Renaissance is that the great majority of Maori are not only working-class and urban but they speak no Maori at all and would be surprised to be credited with the cultural ideals they are, let alone those which have some ethnographic documentation as traditional customs" (Webster 1989, 48).

14. Most of the early studies had never been published: e.g., Green (1959), Levett (1959), Jensen (1970), Rangihaka (1979).

15. In fact, as the statistics of recent Maori emigration to Australia revealed, the trap had no lock (Pool 1991, 193–94).

16. Similar proportions over the ensuing decade sit incongruously with the police estimate that their "organised crime staff commitment is 2%" (private communication).

17. It evidently did not occur to well-meaning officials that reintegration into the community might also lead to integration into local criminal groups.

18. Statistical modeling by the ministry of justice of "factors associated with the growth of recorded crime" between 1962 and 1995 ignored gangs but found that "violence and property damage increase, as business optimism increases," and "occurs 2–3 years after low GDP growth" (Triggs 1997, 17).

19. According to Detective Inspector Graham Bell, "the gang network in New Zealand [is] estimated to comprise between 25,000 and 30,000 people" (*New Zealand Herald,* March 1, 2001). The estimate was quickly repudiated as exaggerated by the police commissioner's office.

20. For Black Power, see www.blackpower.co.nz.

21. I use "ghetto" here in accordance with New Zealand usage and note that Loïc Wacquant's concept with four fundamental constituents—stigma, coercion, physical enclosure, and organizational parallelism and insulation (Wacquant 2002)—may not have as good a fit with a subordinated indigenous population as with a population of transported slave descent.

22. "Recent census data reveal that even after twenty years of rising ethnic solidarity and a sense of personal identity among many Maori, about 25% of those living

in urban areas cannot identify their *iwi* ('tribal') affiliation" (Webster 1993, 325). Not so the other 75 percent.

## References

Ausubel, David P. 1960. *The Fern and the Tiki, An American View of New Zealand: National Character, Social Attitudes and Race Relations.* Sydney: Angus and Robertson.

————. 1977. *Maori Youth: A Psychoethnological Study of Cultural Deprivation.* North Quincy, Mass.: Christopher Publishing House. (Originally published in 1961.)

Bedggood, David. 1980. *Rich and Poor in New Zealand.* Auckland: George Allen and Unwin.

Brosnan, Peter. 1984. "Age, Education, and Maori-Pakeha Income Differences." *New Zealand Economic Papers:* 49–61.

Bull, Simone Jessie. 2001. "The Land of Murder, Cannibalism, and All Kinds of Atrocious Crimes? An Overview of 'Maori Crime' from Pre-colonial Times to the Present Day." PhD diss., Victoria University of Wellington.

Butterworth, G. V. 1974. *The Maori People in the New Zealand Economy.* Department of Social Anthropology and Maori Studies, Massey University, Palmerston North.

Chapple, Simon. 2000. *Maori Socio-economic Disparity.* Paper for the Ministry of Social Policy, [Wellington], September.

Chilton, Roland. 1991. "Urban Crime Trends and Criminological Theory." *Criminal Justice Research Bulletin* 6, no. 3.

Committee on Gangs. 1981. *Report of the Committee on Gangs.* [Wellington], April.

Department of Justice. 1968. *Crime in New Zealand.* Wellington: Government Printer.

————. 1988a. *Criminal Justice in New Zealand: An Overview 1988.* Wellington.

————. 1988b. *Prisons in Change:* The Submission of the Department of Justice to the Ministerial Committee of Inquiry into the Prisons System. Wellington.

Doone, Peter. 2000. *Report on Combating and Preventing Maori Crime.* Crime Prevention Unit, Department of the Prime Minister and Cabinet, [Wellington], September 25.

Dukes, Richard L., Ruben O. Martinez, and Judith A. Stein. 1997. "Precursors and Consequences of Membership in Youth Gangs." *Youth and Society* 29, no. 2: 139–66.

Eggleston, Erin J. 2000. "New Zealand Youth Gangs: Key Findings and Recommendations from an Urban Ethnography." *Social Policy Journal of New Zealand* 14 (July): 148–63.

Fifield, June, and Anne Donnell. 1980. *Socio-economic Status, Race, and Offending in New Zealand.* Research Report No. 6, Research Unit, Joint Committee on Young Offenders, Wellington.

Fleras, Augie. 1985. "Towards 'Tu Tangata': Historical Developments and Current Trends in Maori Policy and Administration." *Political Science* 37, no. 1: 18–39.

Forster, John. 1969. "Perceptions of Social Conflict." In *Social Process in New Zealand, Readings in Sociology,* ed. John Forster, 298–307. Auckland: Longman Paul.

Forster, John, and Peter Ramsey. 1969. "Migration, Education, and Occupation: The Maori Population 1936–66." In *Social Process in New Zealand: Reading in Sociology,* ed. John Forster, 198–232. Auckland: Longman Paul.

Green, J. G. 1959. "Gang Misbehaviour in Wellington," mimeograph. Wellington: Interdepartmental Committee on Adolescent Offenders.

Greenland, Hauraki. 1991. "Maori Ethnicity as Ideology." In *Nga Take: Ethnic Relations, and Racism in Aotearoa/New Zealand,* ed. Paul Spoonley, David Pearson, and Cluny Macpherson, 90–107. Palmerston North: Dunmore Press.

Gustafson, Barry. 2000. *His Way: A Biography of Robert Muldoon.* Auckland: Auckland University Press.

Harker, R. K. 1970. "Maori Enrolment in New Zealand Universities 1956–1968." *New Zealand Journal of Educational Studies* 5, no. 2: 142–52.

Havemann, Paul, and Joan Havemann. 1995. "Retrieving the 'Decent Society': Law and Order Politics in New Zealand 1984–1993." In *Perceptions of Justice, Issues in Indigenous and Community Empowerment,* ed. Kayleen M. Hazlehurst, 217–43. Aldershot: Avebury.

Hazlehurst, Cameron. 1997. "Presentation to New Zealand Ministry of Justice Workshop." February 7.

Hazlehurst, Kayleen M. 1993. *Political Expression and Ethnicity: Statecraft and Mobilization in the Maori World.* Westport, Conn.: Praeger.

———. 1995. "Ethnicity, Ideology, and Social Drama: The Waitangi Day Incident 1981." In *The Urban Context: Ethnicity, Social Networks, and Situational Analysis,* ed. Alisdair Rogers and Steven Vertovec, 81–115. Oxford: Berg.

Hobbs, Dick. 2001. "Organisational Logic and Criminal Culture on a Shifting Terrain." *British Journal of Criminology* 41: 549–60.

Howman, J. D. 1972. "Polynesian Gangs in Auckland and Wellington." *Victoria University of Wellington Law Review* 6, no. 3: 222–42.

Ihaka, Jodi. 1993. "Why the Kids Wanna Be Black." *Mana* 3 (August/September): 10–15.

Jackson, Moana. 1988. *The Maori and the Criminal Justice System: He Whaipaanga Hou—A New Perspective, (part 2).* New Zealand Department of Justice, Wellington.

Jensen, J. 1970. "Juvenile Gangs: A Summary of Theories and Research Findings," mimeograph. Wellington: Joint Committee on Young Offenders.

Kayes, Jim. 1995. "Staunch for the Patch." *Evening Post,* November 11.

Kelsey, Jane. 1993. *Rolling Back the State: Privatisation of Power in Aotearoa/New Zealand.* Wellington: Bridget Williams Books.

———. 2002. *At the Crossroads: Three Essays.* Wellington: Bridget Williams Books.

Kelsey, Jane, and Warren Young. 1982. *The Gangs: Moral Panic as Social Control.* Wellington: Institute of Criminology, Victoria University of Wellington.

Levett, A. E. 1959. "Gangs in Auckland." unpublished report.

Levitt, Steven, and Sudhir Alladi Venkatesh. 2000. "An Economic Analysis of a Drug-selling Gang's Finances." *Quarterly Journal of Economics* (August): 755–89.

Lipson, Leslie. 1948. *The Politics of Equality.* Chicago: University of Chicago Press.

Mahuta, R. T. 1989. "Maori Wealth and Its Contribution to Maori Wellbeing." In *Social Policy and Inequality in Australia and New Zealand,* Proceedings of Joint Conference with the New Zealand Planning Council, Wellington, New Zealand November 10–11, 1988, ed. Peter Saunders and Adam Jamrozik, 105–22. SWRC Reports and Proceedings 78 (September).

McCardle, Hamish. 1999. *Organised Crime Project: Report on the Organised Crime Group Survey.* New Zealand Police, Wellington. March.

McGee, T. G. 1969. "The Social Ecology of New Zealand Cities." In *Social Process in New Zealand: Readings in Sociology,* ed. John Forster, 144–80. Auckland: Longman Paul.

Meek, John. 1992. "Gangs in New Zealand Prisons." *Australian and New Zealand Journal of Criminology* 25: 255–77.

Melvin, Kenneth. 1968. "Education." In *The Pattern of New Zealand Culture,* ed. A. L. McLeod, 98–131. Melbourne: Oxford University Press.

Metge, Joan. 1964. *A New Maori Migration, Rural and Urban Relations in Northern New Zealand.* London: Athlone Press.

———. 1976. *The Maoris of New Zealand Rautahi.* London: Routledge and Kegan Paul (originally published in 1967).

———. 1995. *New Growth from Old: The Whānau in the Modern World.* Wellington: Victoria University Press.

Miller, Harold. 1950. *New Zealand.* London: Hutchinson University Library.

Mitchell, Austin. 1968. "Politics." In *The Pattern of New Zealand Culture,* ed. A. L. McLeod, 68–97. Melbourne: Oxford University Press.

Nash, Roy. 1990. "Society and Culture in New Zealand: An Outburst for 1990." *New Zealand Sociology* 5, no. 2: 99–124.

New Zealand Planning Council. 1989. *The Economy in Transition: Restructuring in 1989.* Wellington: New Zealand Planning Council.

Newbold, Greg. 2000. *Crime in New Zealand.* Palmerston North: Dunmore Press.

O'Reilly, Denis. 1979. "Gangs: Villains or Victims? No Problem." *New Zealand Listener* (February 24): 14.

Pavlich, George. 2000. "New Zealand." In *Crime and Crime Control: A Global View,* ed. Greg Barak, 133–46. Westport, Conn.: Greenwood Press.

Payne, Bill. 1991. *Staunch: Inside the Gangs.* Auckland: Reed.

Pearson, David. 1990. *A Dream Deferred: The Origins of Ethnic Conflict in New Zealand.* Wellington: Allen and Unwin/Port Nicholson Press.

———. 1991. "Biculturalism and Multiculturalism in Comparative Perspective." In *Nga Take: Ethnic Relations and Racism in Aotearoa/New Zealand,* ed. Paul Spoonley, David Pearson, and Cluny Macpherson, 194–214. Palmerston North: Dunmore Press.

Peters, Michael, and James Marshall. 1990. "Institutional Racism and the 'Retention' of Maori Students in Northland." *New Zealand Sociology* 5, no. 1: 44–66.

Pomare, Eru W. 1980. *Maori Standards of Health: A Study of the Twenty-Year Period 1955–1975*. Auckland: Medical Research Council of New Zealand.

Pool, D. Ian. 1977. *The Maori Population of New Zealand 1769–1971*. Auckland: Auckland University Press.

Pool, Ian. 1991. *Te Iwi Maori: A New Zealand Population Past, Present, and Projected*. Auckland: Auckland University Press.

Rangihaka, R. 1979. "Maori Gangs." Officers' course dissertation, New Zealand Police College, October.

Ritchie, Jane, and James Ritchie. 1993. *Violence in New Zealand*. Wellington: Huia Press.

Rowland, D. T. 1971. "Maori Migration to Auckland." *New Zealand Geographer* 27: 21–37.

———. 1972. "Process of Maori Urbanisation." *New Zealand Geographer* 28: 1–22.

Sanchez, Lisa. 1998. "Boundaries of Legitimacy: Sex, Violence, Citizenship, and Community in a Local Sexual Economy." *Law and Social Inquiry* 22, no. 3: 543–80.

Sassen, Saskia. 1999. *Guests and Aliens*. New York: New Press.

———. 2002. "Locating Cities on Global Circuits." In *Global Networks—Linked Cities*, ed. Saskia Sassen. New York: Routledge.

Sassen-Koob, Saskia. 1989. "New York's Informal Economy." In *The Informal Economy: Studies in Advanced and Less Advanced Countries*, ed. Alejandro Portes, Manuel Castells, and Lauren A. Benton, 60–77. Baltimore: Johns Hopkins Press.

Schumacher, Mary E. 1971. *Violent Offending: A Report on Recent Trends in Violent Offending and Some Characteristics of the Violent Offender*. Wellington, Department of Justice Research Section, research series no. 2.

Schwimmer, Eric. 1968. "The Aspirations of the Contemporary Maori." In *The Maori People in the Nineteen-Sixties: A Symposium*, ed. Eric Schwimmer, 9–64. Auckland: Longman Paul.

Sinclair, Keith. 1971. "Why Are Race Relations in New Zealand Better than in South Africa, South Australia, and South Dakota?" *New Zealand Journal of History* 5 (October): 121–27.

Spoonley, Paul. 1990. "New Times, New Racism." *Sites* 20 (Autumn): 44–53.

Steadman, Karen. [1979]. *Juvenile Gang Membership: A Review of the Literature*. Advisory and Research, Department of Internal Affairs, [Wellington].

Thomas, David R. 1980. *Gang Violence in New Zealand*. Report to the New Zealand Psychological Society Council, July.

Triggs, Sue. 1997. *Interpreting Trends in Recorded Crime in New Zealand*. Wellington: Ministry of Justice.

Trlin, A. D. 1971. "Immigrants and Crime: Some Preliminary Observations." In *New Zealand Society: Contemporary Perspectives,* ed. Stephen D. Webb and John Collette, 397–406. Sydney: John Wiley and Sons.

———. 1977. "State Housing: Shelter and Welfare in Suburbia." In *Social Welfare and New Zealand Society,* ed. A. D. Trlin, 106–31. Wellington: Methuen.

Trlin, Andrew D. 1979. "Race, Ethnicity, and Society." In *The Population of New Zealand, Interdisciplinary Perspectives,* ed. R. J. Warwick Neville and C. James O'Neill, 185–212. Auckland: Longman Paul.

———. 1982. "The New Zealand Race Relations Act: Conciliators, Conciliation, and Complaints (1971–1981)." *Political Science* 34, no. 2: 170–93.

Two Detached Social Workers. 1981. "Myths about 'Gang Violence' in New Zealand: A Grass Roots View." *Alternative Criminology Journal* 4 (July): 104–12.

UNRISD (United Nations Research Institute for Social Development). 1995. *States of Disarray: The Social Effects of Globalisation.* An UNRISD report for the World Summit for Social Development, London. March.

Vellekoop, Cora. 1969. "Social Strata in New Zealand." In *Social Process in New Zealand: Readings in Sociology,* ed. John Forster, 233–71. Auckland: Longman Paul.

Vellekoop Baldock, Cora. 1977. "Occupational Choice and Social Class in New Zealand." In *Social Class in New Zealand,* ed. David Pitt. Auckland: Longman Paul.

Venkatesh, Sudhir Alladi. 1997. "The Social Organization of Street Gang Activity in an Urban Ghetto." *American Journal of Sociology* 103, no. 1: 82–112.

Vigil, James Diego, and Steve Chong Yun. 1998. "Vietnamese Youth Gangs in the Context of Multiple Marginality and the Los Angeles Youth Gang Phenomenon." In *Gangs and Youth Subcultures: International Explorations* ed. Kayleen Hazlehurst and Cameron Hazlehurst, 117–39. New Brunswick, N.J.: Transaction Publishers.

Wacquant, Loïc. 2002. "From Slavery to Mass Incarceration: Rethinking the 'Race Question' in the U.S." *New Left Review* 13 (January–February): 41–60.

Walker, Ranginui. 1978. "Black Power and Pakeha Paranoia." (*New Zealand Listener,* 6 May 1978), in Ranginui Walker, *Nga Tau Tohetohe, Years of Anger,* 216–18. Auckland: Penguin.

———. 1982. "Development from Below: Institutional Transformation in a Plural Society." In *Development Tracks: The Theory and Practice of Community Development,* ed. Ian Shirley, 69–89. Palmerston North: Dunmore Press.

———. 1990. *Ka Whawhai tonu Matou: Struggle without End.* Auckland: Penguin Books.

Webster, Steven. 1989. "Maori Studies and the Expert Definition of Maori Culture: A Critical History." *Sites* 18 (winter): 35–56.

———. 1993. "Postmodernist Theory and the Sublimation of Maori Culture." *Oceania* 63: 222–39.

Whitelaw, J. S. 1971. "Migration Patterns and Residential Selection in Auckland, New Zealand." *Australian Geographical Studies* 9: 61–76.

Winter, Pahmi. 1998. "'Pulling the Teams out of the Dark Room': The Politicisation of the Mongrel Mob." In *Gangs and Youth Subcultures: International Explorations,* ed. Kayleen Hazlehurst and Cameron Hazlehurst, 245–66. New Brunswick, N.J.: Transaction Publishers.

Yska, Redmer. 1993. *All Shook Up: The Flash Bodgie and the Rise of the New Zealand Teenager in the Fifties.* Auckland: Penguin.

# 6

# Rapid Urbanization and Migrant Indigenous Youth in San Cristóbal, Chiapas, Mexico

JAN RUS AND DIEGO VIGIL

> Gangs! Painting walls, smoking pot, drinking, committing assaults, etc., etc., they can be seen around the turn of every corner in San Cristóbal, and no human power has been able to stop them! . . . it was one thing for the city government to worry about other things and make no provision for night patrols in the past . . . but now, with armed robberies, murders, sales of contraband, prostitution, drug running, and every other kind of crime everyday occurrences . . . Gentlemen of the city council, we are waiting to hear your voice!
>
> —Editorial in *La Foja Coleta,* San Cristóbal, June 27, 2002, in response to fear that hypothetical Mayan youth gangs were responsible for the city's crimes

Once a small colonial city, San Cristóbal de Las Casas, in the central highlands of Mexico's southernmost state of Chiapas, has over the last thirty years been the recipient of a massive rural-urban migration. The reasons for this movement are not unlike those that have brought rural people into most of Latin America's cities over the last half century: too many people and too little work in the countryside versus the chance to make at least a survival wage and perhaps find a better life in the city. What makes San Cristóbal's case noteworthy, however, is that historically the city has been a defiantly *ladino* place, proud of its "Spanish" traditions and hostile to indigenous people, while almost all of the recent migrants have been Mayas from surrounding villages.[1] After nearly two generations of this movement, San Cristóbal has in effect become two cities, one Spanish-speaking and culturally, socially, and politically conservative, the other Maya, now urban in location but still tied to rural, communal ways of organizing itself, increasingly conscious of its collective "indigenous" identity, and largely opposed to the ladino society that still discriminates against it.[2]

Even in brief conversations with San Cristóbal's ladinos, it soon becomes clear that many, perhaps most, feel they have been under siege through most of this transition, that the Mayan newcomers' "pushiness" in making a place for themselves has been deeply and continuously resented. When violent street gangs (*pandillas*) began to be an issue in Mexico as a whole in the early 2000s, it did not take long—as the quotation at the head of this chapter suggests—for many of San Cristóbal's ladinos to conclude that their own feelings that their city was spinning out of control must be very like the fear of unemployed, unruly youth and increasing street crime in the much larger cities of Mexico's center and north. Never mind that most of the offenses attributed to San Cristóbal's supposed "Mayan youth gangs"—standing around in groups on street corners in the evening, playing music loudly, drinking—were not criminal. Indigenous youth *felt* dangerous, and it was not difficult to fuse the feeling of discomfort they engendered with the real increase in crime as the city has grown and become a major center of tourism with thousands of outsiders passing through every week.

This is not to say that there are not marginalized or disaffected Mayan youth in San Cristóbal; there are. Despite the relatively smooth transition to urban life of most of the tens of thousands of migrants over the last three decades, many are still struggling economically, socially, and culturally. Even among those who appear to have adapted successfully, San Cristóbal's continuing exclusiveness and the persistent barriers to indigenous people in Mexico as a whole have compelled the Mayas to maintain strong ethnically based organizations to defend themselves, reinforcing a dual urban society. Perhaps the intermittent hysteria about "Mayan youth gangs" of the last few years is unwarranted. But the integration of the Maya—and their children—into the city is still an ongoing process, incomplete and difficult to predict.

Our purpose in the following pages is to trace in broad strokes the course of this process so far, since the first rural Maya began resettling in San Cristóbal in the mid-1970s, and then to evaluate the impact of that process on migrant indigenous youth. We will begin by outlining the causes and course of the migration, looking particularly at the ways by which the newcomers have attempted to make a place for themselves in their new environment. From there we shall move on to sketch the ways the city, in turn, has worked its way through the lives of the migrants. In particular, we will concentrate on the similarities and differences across various groups of migrant families and the ways these characteristics relate to the ease or difficulty of their adaptation to the new locale.[3] Finally, we shall return to address the ways that the kinds of marginalization the Maya—and Maya youth—have faced in the city, and the kinds of groups and organizations they have formed in response, are similar—or not—to the conditions and reactions that have led to the growth of gangs in cities elsewhere.

## The Crisis of the Countryside

The last generation has been a time of unprecedented crisis for rural economies and societies not just in Mexico, but throughout the world, especially the global south. By themselves, deteriorating markets for less developed countries' and regions' agricultural products—often their *only* products—would have caused severe hardships. As international prices stagnated after the mid-1970s, however, they exacerbated a series of preexisting, linked maladies that had already made it difficult for many countries to provide for all their citizens: rapid population growth, unpayable national debts, inadequate governmental and administrative structures, and political instability. Tragically, the "solutions" to these crises offered by world financial institutions typically made conditions worse, especially for the poor. Mexico is a case in point. Following a severe financial downturn in 1982, Mexico was forced to impose neoliberal "structural readjustments" on itself before the U.S. government and the IMF (International Monetary Fund) would agree to the loans it needed to keep its economy going. Not only were public expenditures—including those for education and public health—restricted, but also many government services and public enterprises were eliminated or privatized, and national economic policy came under close international scrutiny, if not control. These austerity policies were tightened yet again at the end of the 1980s as Mexico submitted itself to a further round of "free market" reforms in order to prepare itself for partial economic union with the United States and Canada through NAFTA (the North American Free Trade Agreement). Once more the rural economy, and especially the rural, working poor, were asked to make disproportionate sacrifices in the form of cuts in price supports for agricultural products, elimination or privatization of agricultural extension and marketing services, and discontinuation of public credit for farming.[4]

In Chiapas, one of the two poorest of Mexico's thirty-one states—and one until very recently almost entirely dependent on agriculture—the squeeze on rural society caused by these policies led, famously, to the Zapatista rebellion of January 1, 1994, "by coincidence" the very day NAFTA took effect. By that time, prices for coffee, sugar, corn, and beans—Chiapas's principal products—had been in decline since the mid-1970s, with no sustained government effort to help them recover. As a result, cultivation of all of those crops had grown only slowly, well below the growth rate of the rural population over the same twenty years. The effects of this stagnation on rural workers who depended on agriculture, whether as small producers themselves or as migrant laborers on large plantations, were disastrous. Not only did agricultural employment decline even as the rural population doubled between the mid-1970s and mid-1990s—meaning that the number of country people without work grew rapidly and steadily—but pay also declined. Communities of rural workers and peasants, already accustomed to a spare existence, suddenly found themselves unable to eat from the land. Men and women with children were increasingly forced to abandon agriculture to feed their families; younger people, hoping to start families, realized they had no hope of marrying and raising children if they remained in the countryside.

To this point, the rural crisis in Chiapas sounds like that of the rest of Mexico, indeed, of much of the rest of the world. There is, however, one important difference: in much of Chiapas, especially the Central Highlands surrounding San Cristóbal, most of the rural poor are indigenous Mayas. As of 2000, the region was home to more than 300,000 Maya people who inhabited sixteen tightly organized, ethnically distinctive *municipios,* or townships, each with its own distinctive style of dress, its own dialect of Tzotzil or Tzeltal Maya, and governed by a local, exclusive, indigenous civil-religious political structure. As the economic and demographic crises burst on these communities in the 1970s, their desperate residents were increasingly forced to compete for the region's scarce resources, struggling with surrounding private landowners, neighboring communities, and even among neighbors within the same *municipio* for a share of land big enough to feed their families.

Conflict with nonindigenous landowners is perhaps the struggle most often noticed by the world beyond Chiapas, perhaps because it best fits with preconceptions about indigenous people battling powerful outsiders to preserve their way of life. Indeed, many of those who held land on the borders of indigenous communities were wealthy ranchers who occupied land expropriated from indigenous communities barely a century earlier. By the second half of the 1970s, many indigenous people in regions with such nonindigenous landholdings had begun to organize themselves across community and linguistic lines to struggle for the land, and within a few years more had begun staging sporadic invasions. The response of the landowners and state was violent repression—murder of rural leaders, raids by the army and police on indigenous settlements involved in conflicts, and destruction of crops and homes. By the mid-1980s, many parts of the state had become tense, armed camps—a situation that led finally to the Zapatista uprising (see Collier 1994; Harvey 1998; J. Rus 1995).

Meanwhile, conflict over land was not confined to fights between indigenous and nonindigenous people. Where borders between neighboring communities were not well surveyed, or where people from one community had pushed over borders and planted in the lands of another community, indigenous people also fought with each other.

Most cruel of all, however, were the struggles within communities. As the "external" sources of income available to indigenous people—migrant agricultural work, jobs on publicly financed construction projects, and land to rent for subsistence farming—declined, communities divided into factions and fought among themselves for control of "internal" resources within their own *municipios*—common lands, water, forests, or government aid granted to the community as a whole. As these factional struggles progressed, many of the contending sides, particularly the smaller or weaker ones, eventually looked for nonindigenous organizations and institutions to support them—political parties, churches, even competing agencies of the government (Cancian 1992; Collier 1994; Rus and Collier 2003). Such fights were often bitter as fights between neighbors and relatives tend to be. But none were harsher than those in which one or more of the factions found their outside support in new churches and distinguished themselves from their rivals by religion. In the case of Chamula, for instance—the largest *municipio* in the Central Highlands with almost 30,000 inhabitants in 1970 (when the indigenous population of the entire region was approximately 140,000)—the conversion of an important faction to Protestantism in the mid-1970s split the community. By 1976, several years of systematic assaults and house burnings directed against the converts' faction had culminated in the violent "expulsion" of the entire Protestant group of some 1,000 members. By 1978, the number of Chamula expelled had grown to more than 3,000, and by the 1980s the phenomenon of factional, usually religious, expulsion had spread to other *municipios* (Gossen 1989; J. Rus 2005).

The result of these multiple and overlapping crises—the decline of agriculture, the austerity that followed the national financial collapse of 1982, and the growing factional violence within communities—was an exodus from the countryside, with wave after wave of rural people forced to move.

By 2000, barely thirty years after the rural crisis began, more than a third of Chiapas's indigenous people had abandoned—or been driven out of—their original territories. Of approximately 1.5 million indigenous residents in the state, almost 250,000 now lived in new homesteader colonies in the Lacandón Jungle (the heartland of the Zapatistas), another 200,000 had migrated to Chiapas's seven principal cities and large towns, and several tens of thousands more—mostly young men—had begun to migrate around the rest of Mexico looking for work, from Cancún in the extreme southeast, to Tijuana in the far northwest.[5] From one of the most stable, rooted rural populations in Latin America, Chiapas's indigenous people had in one generation been forced to abandon home and become migrants.[6] Although all of the subsidiary migrations have much in common, our interest is the part of this movement that took as its destination San Cristóbal de Las Casas.

## Indigenous Migrants to San Cristóbal

Over the last two decades, the impact of growing up as a poor migrant in a third-world city has increasingly attracted the attention of researchers. In Mexico, where the rural poor have been moving to Mexico City and a handful of major urban areas in the country's center and north for more than fifty years, such studies have an even longer trajectory (Arizpe 1975; Lewis 1952, 1959; Lomnitz 1977). Parallel processes appear to be at work elsewhere in Latin America for almost as long.[7] While in many ways the cities of southern Mexico now appear to be following a similar course, in this region, where the rural populations are predominantly indigenous, the processes and cultural dynamics of urbanization appear to differ in important ways.[8]

San Cristóbal is a case in point. Despite its rich traditions—it was Chiapas's capital from the 1520s until 1892—the city had been left behind in the twentieth century. It was only connected by a paved road to the rest of Mexico in the 1950s, and from 1900 to 1970 its population only increased from 14,000 to 28,000.[9] Meanwhile, the indigenous population of the surrounding Central Highlands more than tripled in the same period, from barely 40,000 in 1900 to some 140,000 in 1970 (Aubry 1991). More than neighbors to the cristobalenses, these Mayan villagers were the city's principal resource. Too far off the beaten track to be a commercial hub, too high and cool at 7,200 feet above sea level to be an agricultural center, San Cristóbal's principal occupation since the last decades of the nineteenth century was contracting indigenous laborers for Chiapas's lowland plantations, provisioning them for the trip (often several hundred miles), and then selling them "city goods" in return for the wages they brought back with them to the highlands. Protective of their precarious position as exploiters of indigenous people who at the same time surrounded and outnumbered them, during most of those decades San Cristóbal's ladino inhabitants enforced exclusionary, racist barriers within the city. These made the city a privileged space for ladinos and an extremely hostile one for the indigenous. As late as 1952, for example, indigenous peoples were not allowed on San Cristóbal's streets after dark. Those who found themselves in town at sunset either had to make their way to the houses of ladino patrons or to a shelter maintained by the coffee workers' union, or risk being picked up by the police, kept in jail overnight, and then forced to perform such free labor as sweeping the streets and market in the morning. As for indigenous children, the relatively few in town on any given day in those years were either the servants or employees of ladinos, and thus under their protection, or young people who had accompanied their parents to the city's market or a government office, and who would most likely return to their rural communities by nightfall. To the extent there were any street children, they were vendors of cigarettes and candies, shoe-shiners or errand boys—all of them, at least in appearance, *ladinos* (Sánchez 1995; Sulca Báez 1997; Villa Rojas 1976).

During the mid-1970s, as agriculture began to fail and strife increased within surrounding indigenous communities, however, San Cristóbal suddenly became a refuge for indigenous migrants who had little choice but to move to the city, despite all the obstacles. It should be noted that most legal and administrative—"official"—discrimination against indigenous people had been lifted following the arrival of the federal National Indigenous Institute (INI) in 1952. What remained by the early 1970s was what local people called "custom"—on both sides—ladinos who continued to discriminate, often defiantly, expecting indigenous people to step aside for them on sidewalks, for example, or refusing to sit in pews with them at church, and indigenous people who still preferred not to stay overnight in the city. The first large group of migrants were the 1,000 Protestants expelled from Chamula in 1976. Having distinguished themselves from their Chamula traditionalist rivals by becoming Presbyterians, the *expulsados* brought a triple identity with them to the city: Mayan, Protestant, and refugee. The violent circumstances of their exile, their coherence as a Presbyterian congregation, and the fact that with the financial support of the Presbyterian Church of Mexico and the Reformed Church of the United States they were soon able to buy a piece of land on the northern edge of the city on which to resettle left San Cristóbal's ladinos little choice but to accept their immigration to the city.

Within four years, three other small Mayan Protestant *colonias* followed, all composed of people exiled from their home communities, and all notably self-reliant. By 1980, there were some 3,000 indigenous people living in the city more or less permanently (see Aramoni and Morquecho 1997; Gossen 1989; J. Rus 2005; Rus and Wasserstrom 1981; Sterk 1991).

Almost before anyone realized it, the barrier against indigenous residence in San Cristóbal had been broken. Since the economic and political conditions that were driving them out of their traditional niches remained in force, the growth of the city's indigenous population continued and then accelerated through the 1980s. By 1990, San Cristóbal had reached 90,000 inhabitants, perhaps 20,000 of them indigenous. By 2000, the overall official population was 120,000, with some estimates placing it as high as 160,000—an increase of between 460 and 570 percent in just thirty years. Of this number, approximately 60,000 were indigenous. More important to us here, of those 60,000, more than half were children under eighteen (Aubry 1991, 77; INEGI 1991, 92; INEGI 2001).

If the city in which these indigenous children found themselves had a history of being inhospitable to indigenous people, by the 1990s they—Mayan children—had probably become its most numerous single population category. Despite their numbers and their clear importance to San Cristóbal's future, however, the city into which they moved and in which they were coming of age continued to bear the marks of the castelike social divisions of the past. For one thing, indigenous people lived confined to identifiable, separate *colonias* around the edges of the city. In part, this was because land was expensive for indigenous newcomers, and it was easier to obtain a foothold as a group, collectively (more about the variety of these *colonias* below). However, it was also clear that San Cristóbal's "old" ladino inhabitants continued to think of indigenous migrants as second-class citizens and to discourage them from becoming close neighbors.[10] In myriad small ways, they made it clear on a daily basis that indigenous people who presented themselves as such via their language and clothing were not welcome in "ladino" stores, churches, or downtown public spaces.

In response to this rejection by ladinos over the last twenty years, urban Mayas have in turn developed their own parallel institutions as well as self-affirming markers of indigenous *urban* identity. If just a few decades before Mayas had to relinquish their "Indianness" to stay in San Cristóbal without being harassed, in the "new" city of indigenous migrants, signs of Mayan identity became valued as a source of solidarity and resistance and were accentuated. In the new urban communities formed by indigenous people drawn not only from different *municipios* but even different Mayan languages, for instance, the lingua franca is often not Spanish but Tzotzil-Maya, the language of the Chamulas, the original and still most numerous migrants. To participate in community politics and religion, as well as signify their solidarity with their neighbors as against Spanish-speaking ladinos, speakers of Tzeltal-, Tojolabal-, and Ch'ol-Maya learn Tzotzil, often *before* Spanish. Similarly, new, "urban" styles of dress, particularly for young women, have incorporated makeup, new hairstyles, and fashionable shoes (rural indigenous women considered it shameful to wear more than sandals) while keeping traditional *huipils* (embroidered blouses) and wrapped, sashed skirts. Moreover, such signs of a stable (at least for now) urban, indigenous identity appear to have been strengthened since the 1994 Zapatista rebellion, when indigenous people in general felt a new, pan-indigenous sense of pride on seeing an indigenous force capable of confronting the government, army—and ladinos (Kovic 1997; Peres Tzu 2002; J. Rus 1997).

## The Stages of Urbanization

Despite their appearance as an almost continuous, undifferentiated settlement around San Cristóbal's periphery, and the many characteristics that unite them, the city's indigenous *colonias* vary widely in origin, internal organization, and social and cultural cohesiveness. These factors in turn have profound effects on the lives of their inhabitants and, perhaps most of all, their children. Before discussing the *colonias* as environments in which to raise children, though, we turn first to the historical roots of the differences among them.

Since the 1970s, three migratory waves have washed over San Cristóbal. Given the speed of economic, demographic, and social structural change, the countryside that each wave left—and the city that it entered—have differed significantly from one period to another. First-wave migrants, in the second half of the 1970s, were, as we have seen, typically Protestant converts who were allowed to settle on the outskirts of San Cristóbal largely because they were viewed as refugees from religious persecution who had migrated involuntarily (Estrada 1995; Gossen 1989). San Cristóbal's ladinos seem to have been simultaneously moved by the plight of the *expulsados* and convinced their sojourn in the city would be brief—that eventually they would return to their home *municipios*. Accordingly, the view of many ladinos is that they *permitted* the *expulsados* to purchase ranches on the edges of the city to set up temporary camps; that it was a charitable, temporary—and thus revocable—solution to the refugees' plight.

Against expectations, however, these camps soon became permanent settlements. Built around a church, characterized by sharply defined borders and memberships, and governed through modified, though still recognizably "traditional" Mayan civil and religious structures (that is, civil-religious hierarchies) in which community members served voluntarily for a year at a time, such *colonias* functioned as virtual religious communes. New residents were provided with land and construction materials for their houses; earlier community members found jobs for those who followed; and, in general—although they have never stopped protesting their expulsion from their ancestral homes—members of these first colonies kept to themselves. Their orderly, religiously oriented lives and unobtrusiveness, in turn, made them almost tolerable neighbors to ladinos. Indeed, it was the commonly expressed opinion of San Cristóbal's elite at the start of the 1980s, congratulating themselves on their broad-mindedness, that *expulsados* made ideal servants because they worked hard, were polite, and impeccably honest.

Although by the end of the 1970s there were still only four indigenous *colonias* with a total population of approximately 3,000, their historical importance, again, was that for the first time since the sixteenth century Mayas had managed to move into the valley of San Cristóbal *as Indians,* without relinquishing their own languages, traditional clothing, and customary forms of family and community organization. In retrospect, many ladinos now perceive those first *colonias* to have been a kind of Trojan horse for the massive immigration that was to follow. To the migrants who came after them, these first-wave pioneers provided both a template for reorganization in the city and, in their demonstration that it was possible to be both Mayan and urban, a cushion to culture shock.

The second wave began with the economic crisis of 1982. Not only did demand for agricultural laborers contract sharply following the financial crash, but as government funds for infrastructure projects dried up, thousands of indigenous men who had been able to ride out the initial agricultural crisis and maintain their families in their home communities by migrating to distant construction sites also found themselves out of work. The intracommunal strife described earlier became especially sharp in this period (Collier 1994, 116–47). In the face of the gathering depression and instability, San Cristóbal's *colonias* of Protestant refugees suddenly appeared to rural indigenous people as islands of prosperity. Having begun with nothing six or seven years earlier, many of the original Protestant settlers had by 1982–83 moved up from menial work in the market or hod-carrying at local construction sites, to owning their own market stalls, or contracting independently for construction jobs within the *colonias*. Moreover, one of the few industries that actually grew after 1982 was tourism, creating a demand in San Cristóbal for hotel and restaurant employees and vendors of artisan products—not to mention artisans. All of this, in turn, increased yet again demand for market and construction workers (Eber and Rosenbaum 1993; O'Brien 1994; D. Rus 1990). Under these dual influences—rural deprivation and relative prosperity in the city—the indigenous population of San Cristóbal increased during the 1980s from around 3,000 to more than 20,000, and the number of mostly indigenous *colonias* on the city's outskirts from four to sixteen (Calvo Sánchez 1990, 56ff).

In addition to the different circumstances that drove them from the countryside, the second-wave migrants moved, for the most part, into *colonias* with a different origin from those of the first wave. Unlike the virtual communes of 1976–81, almost all of the post-1982 *colonias* were formed on land purchased by indigenous entrepreneurs who already lived in the city—most of them first-wave migrants. Often working with wealthy ladinos who saw the chance to unload nonproductive, relatively low-value land (pastures, swamps, rocky hillsides) for a relatively high price, such indigenous brokers contracted for 10– to 20–acre parcels, subdivided them, and then sold them to newcomers. More often than not, the buyers were pastors looking to form their own, new congregations out of the many indigenous people moving to the city (examples are the *colonias* of Getsemaní and Paraíso[11])—although another common pattern was for new, "daughter" *colonias* to begin as breakaway groups from established *colonias* and churches (Kovic 1997, 2005, 21–43; Ruiz 1996). It is noteworthy that even new migrants to the city who had *not* been Protestants before leaving their home *municipios*—and who had thus not been "expelled"—became Protestants on moving into these *colonias*. The model for urbanization included religious conversion, in part because it provided the newcomers with access to the first Protestants' work and land networks, but also in part because through the mid-1980s it was still the supposedly involuntary nature of the Protestant Mayas' move to the city that made their presence tolerable to ladinos (Sullivan 1995; Gutiérrez 1996).[12]

Finally, the latest, third wave appears to have begun with the collapse of the international coffee market in 1989 and accelerated following the Zapatista uprising of 1994. If the first wave had been led by bilingual, mostly younger people willing to change religions and run the risk of settling outside of their home communities, and the second largely of economic refugees attracted to the new residential and occupational opportunities opened by the first, this third wave seems to have consisted increasingly of simple refugees, both from economic conditions and, following 1994, from violence. The vertiginous fall of coffee prices profoundly impoverished tens of thousands of rural families that had depended on either their own small production or labor in the coffee orchards of others. Meanwhile, government support for other agricultural products was also sharply reduced. Under these circumstances, violence—land invasions, repression by gunmen hired by landowners and by the army and state police, and internecine strife within native communities themselves—remained high from the end of the 1980s on. After the 1994 uprising, however, it reached new peaks. Within the first four years after the uprising, as many as 5,000 direct refugees were driven into San Cristóbal, with perhaps another 15,000 moving to the city as their economic and social conditions worsened.[13]

Those who fled the countryside for the city during this period generally seem to have been less prepared for urban life than their predecessors. Poor, monolingual, often traumatized by violence, they moved, moreover, into a city already crowded with indigenous people with whom they had to compete for work and inhabited as well by increasingly resentful ladinos. That said, however, they also came into a space in which indigenous people had for twenty years been organizing churches, political advocacy groups, and economic unions. After January 1, 1994, the leaders of all these organizations quickly recognized that the state was eager for indigenous allies and certainly did not want to make more indigenous enemies. If there was a time to press the demands of the urban indigenous, this was it. Within that first January, indigenous peddlers who had previously found it difficult to gain spaces in San Cristóbal's municipal market expanded into the parking lots and sidewalks surrounding the market building and set up their own "liberated market." When the authorities failed to dislodge them, they took further initiatives, refusing to pay rental fees for their spaces, setting up impromptu stalls, and forming themselves into alliances with indigenous taxi drivers, *colonia* associations, and churches (Peres Tzu 2002). At the same time, all worked feverishly to enroll as many as possible of the refugees flooding into the city to strengthen their own organizations' membership.

These were the circumstances under which, in April 1994, the first indigenous invasion of vacant land occurred on the northeastern side of the city. The state, after an initial, failed attempt by the police to retake the invaded land, apparently feared that a more violent response would drive the invaders into the arms of the Zapatistas. Perhaps hoping as well that leniency would win the urban indigenous to the side of the governing party, the state essentially stood aside. When the invaders appeared to have won, more invasions followed. Since 1994, no new *colonia* has been formed that did *not* originate with an invasion. The days of indigenous people buying tracts of land for their settlements had ended (Angulo 2003, 69–77). Eventually in every case—typically, during the months preceding elections—the municipal or state government organized the "regularization" of the invasions, paying off the original ladino owners and offering the invaders legal titles in return for small monthly payments over a number of years—and their votes.[14] Of the thirty major *colonias* in existence by the end of the 1990s, nine had been formed this way. In addition to those that had been regularized, there were several dozen unrecognized, "irregular" ones, including two that were still little more than refugee camps (Betancourt 1997).

If the bulk of the third-wave migrants were refugees from economic collapse or war, and in that sense more marginal than their predecessors, they soon became part of a city much more "indigenous" than that the earlier waves had entered. In the chaos and frank extralegality that prevailed after 1994, indigenous leaders increasingly challenged San Cristóbal's old ladino society. Not only did new, more powerful indigenous organizations emerge from these confrontations, but informal and illicit economic activities also began to surface.

## Adaptation to the City

Many of the physical differences among the various migrant *colonias* follow from the history presented in the last section. By now, the oldest ones, dating from the 1970s, are virtually indistinguishable in appearance from working-class ladino neighborhoods. The latest ones, on the other hand—which may be as new as last week—often consist of little more than ragged rows of lean-tos covered with plastic sheeting or the outer bark-cuttings from lumber mills.

Beyond differences of physical appearance, however—beyond even contrasts in the levels of sophistication and prosperity of their residents—there is much that unites the *colonias* socially, economically, and politically. Especially in the first two waves, the migrants tended to move to the city not as individuals, or even nuclear families consisting of two parents and their children, but as lineages: three or four generations of family members who continued to live together and have mutual responsibilities to each other.[15] Surveys suggest that among first- and second-wave migrants, up to 90 percent of those from the *municipio* of Chamula, for instance, moved to the city with their spouses, and that male lineages including older parents and grandparents eventually reunited there within three or four years (Rus and Rus 2004). Such lineages, interlocked with those of brothers and cousins, in addition to providing a ready-made "community" in the new environment, make it possible to organize economic activities (market stalls, construction crews, artisan groups, and so forth) among related, trusted individuals. They also made it possible to care for children collectively. This, in turn, offers a clue about the relatively smooth transition of many children to the city: most, at least in the earlier waves, were still enveloped in extended families, just as in the countryside.

In addition to family structures, migrants also brought with them a common civic and political culture, and social organization within *colonias* in many ways reproduces that of Chiapas's rural indigenous communities. Religion is at the center of local life, and although the *colonias* have become more pluralistic since the 1980s, for most residents the temple, chapel, or mosque, with the mutual support it provides, is the most important institution beyond the family.[16] As in rural indigenous communities, moreover, civil and religious government are closely related. Once a *colonia* achieves recognition from the state, either singly or with neighboring *colonias,* it is incorporated into the municipal organization of the city as an *agencia municipal,* with a part-time local official named from among the residents to act as a justice of the peace and chairman of the local council. Known as *agentes municipales,* many of these men are also Protestant pastors or Catholic catechists, thus uniting religious and civil authority just as in the countryside.

Finally, the third most important official institution in the *colonias* are the public primary schools. Indeed, recognition as an official "place" typically begins with the granting of a school, and parents are avid for a school as much for the measure of security that recognition gives to the *colonia* as for the deeply felt necessity for their children to be educated. Fifty percent of all urban indigenous children under sixteen attended school in 2000, as compared to less than 25 percent in rural communities (Melel Xojobal 2000; Rus and Rus 2004). Censuses and surveys have still not distinguished the rates of school attendance for first- and second-wave migrants as opposed to those who have come to the city more recently. However, anecdotal evidence suggests that in the oldest *colonias,* particularly the Protestant ones founded in the 1970s, attendance is more than 75 percent, while for the most recent arrivals it is well below 50 percent and may approximate the rates for rural indigenous children.

Not surprisingly given the existence of close, extended families, powerful religious institutions, and customary social control, life *within* the indigenous *colonias*, particularly the older ones, is relatively safe, not only for their residents but for passersby. Crimes against persons like theft or assault are much less common than one might expect for the poorest precincts of a poor city. Indeed, for such a densely settled valley, with extremely poor people living within a mile of tourist hotels and the homes of the well-off, there are virtually no reports of personal crime by indigenous people against nonindigenous. That said, however, *extralegal* behavior—flouting of administrative, economic, and property laws, law breaking that offends ladinos—is not only widespread, but widely accepted. Examples are the land invasions by which *colonias* are formed, the sit-ins to gain footholds in the market, the tapping of power lines and water pipes to satisfy *colonia* demands, and the blockades of streets and public buildings to force the government to charge indigenous *colonias* only nominal rates for electricity and water, for instance, or to withdraw unpopular taxes and fees. All of these activities lead ladinos to feel they are living in a lawless, out-of-control environment, a belief reinforced by every ladino candidate for municipal office since 1994, all of whom have called for the reimposition of an estado de derecho ("state of law," essentially "law and order"), by military force if necessary—even as they negotiate favorable settlements with land invaders and indigenous organizers in exchange for their votes.

What all of these extralegal activities have in common is that they are made possible by the fact that *colonia* members have been represented since the 1980s by a handful of powerful umbrella *sindicatos,* or "unions." The oldest of these originated as advocacy groups for Protestant *expulsados.* Others are local branches of official, government unions that began representing indigenous migrants in the 1980s in the (vain) hope that they could co-opt them and moderate their activism. Still others, dating from the land struggles of the 1970s and 1980s, drew large numbers of urban members after 1994 when they became expressions of the indigenous empowerment movement.[17] Among the many functions of the *sindicatos* have been leading the fights for recognition of new *colonias,* for market space, and for lower utility rates. At the same time, they also compete with each other for members and power. Each group tends to represent the residents of a particular group of *colonias* and, to varying extents, to specialize in different economic activities. However, they have on occasion resorted to street fighting and even arms to settle rivalries among themselves—as, for instance, when one of the unions feels another is encroaching on its space in the market (Aramoni and Morquecho 1997;

Morquecho 1992). To indigenous migrants, the *sindicatos* have become the battering rams by which they have secured places to stay, jobs, and services in a city that has never been hospitable to them. To San Cristóbal's ladinos, on the other hand, they are "mafias," or criminal enterprises. Nothing illustrates these opposing perspectives better than attitudes to the most powerful of the *sindicatos,* the taxi and microbus owners and drivers.

At the beginning of the 1990s, San Cristóbal had some 100 taxis, the overwhelming majority, if not all, the property of ladinos. Legal operation of a taxi or microbus required a route license (*placa*), and the number of these was sharply limited by the state. One of the demands of the indigenous organizations after 1994 was that their members be given more chances to profit from transport for which indigenous people, who needed taxis to travel between their outlying *colonias* and city center, had long since become the principal customers. Although the state did, grudgingly, increase the number of *placas* to 140, it responded far too slowly, and not before indigenous entrepreneurs took matters into their own hands. Within three years after the 1994 uprising, there were 600 taxis, and by 2000 there were more than 1,100.[18] The great majority of these were operated, at least at first, without route licenses, and were thus *piratas,* or pirates, and most of the *pirata* owners were indigenous. Repeated attempts by the state police to regain control of taxi licensing during the second half of the 1990s by setting up roadblocks and seizing pirate vehicles led the indigenous *sindicatos* to mount counter roadblocks, effectively cutting the highways to San Cristóbal until the seizures stopped and impounded taxis were returned. Meanwhile, through the entire period from 1997 to the present, new *placas* were repeatedly granted in batches as political concessions to the urban migrant unions in return for their blocks of votes at election time.

Beyond organizing through the indigenous *sindicatos* to defend themselves economically, the taxi owners and drivers also organized to defend themselves physically in response to a number of well-publicized robberies and murders of taxi drivers in 1997–98.[19] Within months, every taxi had a CB radio, and it was widely claimed—and believed—that almost all were armed. A distress call by a taxi driver, even a claim that a passenger had refused to pay, would, within minutes, bring a dozen or more fellow *taxistas,* including some ladinos, who would surround the site and block all surrounding streets until the matter was resolved. This response was more certain and effective than any of the police forces available in the highlands—a fact that was quickly noted by all of the indigenous unions. By 1996, it was clear that all of the *sindicatos* were using their taxista sections as de facto police departments, defending the union's interests in market fights, for example, or sending three or four cars to summon union members involved in disputes with each other. Beyond that, however, when indigenous people were victims of crime, particularly in their own spaces, in the *colonias,* but eventually anywhere in the city, it became more common for them to stop an indigenous taxi to ask for help than to bother calling the police. In essence, by 1996–97, the *sindicatos,* with their police forces of taxis, had become the day-to-day government of the indigenous *colonias.*[20]

From the ladino point of view, this was obviously intolerable, especially because the "taxi-police," if forced to choose between ladino and indigenous disputants, virtually without exception took the side of the indigenous.[21] At the beginning of 2001, roadblocks jointly manned by the army and various state police corporations did manage to get firearms out of the hands of the "taxi-police." Even armed only with clubs and lengths of iron pipe, however, they remain a potent force for peacekeeping and dispute resolution in parts of the city where the regular municipal police do not deign—or are afraid—to go.

In addition to the extralegal activities of the unions and taxistas acknowledged by all, San Cristóbal's ladinos also insist they engage, "without remorse," in frankly illegal activities. It is claimed, for instance, that members of some of the urban *sindicatos* are involved with car-theft rings, which repaint stolen cars and either sell them in indigenous *municipios* or move them to other states; with trafficking in arms and drugs; and with transporting undocumented Central Americans across Chiapas. In the course of our interviews, credible indigenous witnesses did confirm that all of these activities go on in the city, in some cases even with the participation of union members. But none linked them to the unions per se.[22]

The differences in interviewees' attitudes about legality and illegality are a bright line demarcating the division between San Cristóbal's two societies. From a ladino perspective, looking at indigenous organizations from the outside, the assumption appears to be that anyone who would engage in tapping a power line, for example, could just as easily steal a car. Colonia residents make much finer distinctions. Most have participated in, and all have certainly benefitted from, the land and market invasions, tapping of power lines, and so on, described earlier—all, strictly speaking, illegal actions, but all accepted and approved of by virtually all indigenous migrants. "Ladino law" is considered partial and unjust, and *colonia* members who are outraged by crime against persons within their communities—and who would not approve of personal crimes against ladinos either—see nothing wrong with righting generations of exploitation and repression by turning the tables and taking advantage of ladinos when they get the chance. Attitudes about smuggling migrants, weapons, and drugs and about the theft and resale of cars also tend to be tolerant, though more complicated. Many from the *colonias* have themselves become undocumented migrants to the United States in recent years, making them identify more with Central American migrants and their smugglers than with the state. Some have also purchased contraband guns, and many who would not steal a car might nevertheless be willing to buy a stolen one. As for drugs, cases of indigenous use of narcotics are few, but there does not seem to be an automatic rejection of the idea of moving them from place to place if it is profitable. Their moral view of these activities, in other words, does not coincide with the legal view. Unlike the extralegal measures described earlier, however, which are pursued publicly by the *sindicatos,* it is widely recognized that involvement with smuggling foreigners, arms, stolen cars, and drugs can lead to prison. If there is not an automatic rejection of these activities and those engaged in them—evidenced, among other things, by the number of people who know about them without informing—neither do the numbers who participate in them appear to be great.[23]

## The Urban Environment and Indigenous Youth

In general, as we have seen, San Cristóbal's indigenous youth are growing up in close, extended families, in urban *colonias* that in many ways still exhibit the solidarity and powerful social control of rural communities, and in a citywide social, economic, and political environment in which indigenous organizations—the *sindicatos*—provide almost an alternative municipal government. As a result, many signs of exclusion that might in other circumstances be indicators of marginality, and perhaps precursors to social pathologies—residential segregation, indigenous dress, preference for native languages over the national standard Spanish, membership in new, minority religions, and, perhaps most of all, participation in various illicit activities—are actually viewed as sources of strength by most of San Cristóbal's indigenous residents. Indeed, since the 1994 rebellion, some markers of indigenous ethnicity have even been accentuated.

All of that said, there are also developments among some of the city's indigenous youth that disturb their elders. Reports of street-socialized children, alienated from the city's indigenous community and excluded from its ladino one, are still isolated but no longer unheard of. Two such groups concern us here. The first consists of the very young and very poor. Following the 1994 rebellion, there began to be stories about groups of children under ten or eleven years of age hanging around alone in the market all day. This was undoubtedly not a new phenomenon, but for the first time the numbers—several dozen—had begun to attract the attention of indigenous observers. The children described had nothing to eat and were given tortillas, vegetables, and fruit by the market sellers, who said most of their mothers were single, abandoned women forced to work on the street as peddlers or beggars. Part of the market people's charity was self-defensive because some of the children had started to steal.[24] Five years later, a nongovernmental organization found 638 children working full-time on the street themselves, most of them newcomers since 1994. These were children *on* the street, not *of* the street, in the sense that most lived with at least one parent and returned to some sort of lodging at night. But half were unsupervised during the day, and even those who stayed close to a parent were, of course, not in school (Melel Xojobal 2000).[25]

As time goes on, some of the children who have arrived in this last wave of migration may continue to find it difficult to adapt to the city. As poor as all indigenous migrants have been since the 1970s, survey data suggests that those who came after 1994—now constituting almost half of the entire indigenous population of the city—are even worse off. Sixty-five percent of these latest arrivals reported incomes of less than 260 dollars per year for families of four (including the value of subsistence corn farming).[26] Since many of these most recent migrants live in refugee camps, invaded lands that have still not been "regularized," or even regularized lands where they get their foothold by affiliating with a *sindicato,* they are among the city's most vulnerable residents. Young children would appear to be particularly at risk. Inhabiting settlements in many cases still devoid of schools and other services, with poor, often traumatized parents displaced suddenly from the countryside, they are a new challenge for a city that through its first twenty years of receiving indigenous migrants left many of the organizational and adjustment aspects of urbanization to urban indigenous organizations themselves, supported only by Protestant and Catholic churches.[27] As for the teens in this last wave of migrants, since 2000–2001 many appear to be entering the undocumented stream to the United States after only brief stays in the city (more about this alternative in a moment).

Paradoxically, the other group that appears to be becoming unsettled includes youth from the older colonies, including many of the first wave. In the early 2000s, stories began to circulate about groups of twenty and more teens meeting in the evenings at crossroads on the peripheral highway through the oldest northern *colonias*. By 2001, at least two of these congregations were being referred to in the (alarmist?) local press as *pandillas*, "gangs."[28] Both groups were described as drinking and perhaps smoking marijuana, and both were accused in the press of having participated in robberies in nearby ladino *colonias*—although never with any details. Local columnists also fretted that graffiti had appeared at various points around the city, and that here and there rap music was being played on boomboxes—all signs, they worried, that the violent gangs that had already appeared in Tapachula, on Chiapas's south coast, could be coming to the highlands. For all the alarm, however, there were no arrests to report, nor any crimes against persons that could be firmly attached to the supposed *pandillas*, nor, for that matter, anything that connected the graffiti to the very visible groups of indigenous youth. Nevertheless, the fact that the assembly points for these "gangs" were on the outskirts of three of the original, first-wave *colonias* suggests that some indigenous youth who grew up in the city, perhaps were even born there, may be feeling alienated from the religious communities of their parents as well as the ladino society that still scorns them.[29] Also worrisome to local authorities is the fact that the illicit activities of some of the *sindicato* members are, of course, also based in some of the older colonias (though more in those of the second wave than those of the first). Is there a connection between the groups of carousing youth and the very organized, clandestine activities of some of their elders? No one has yet shown that there is.

Whether any of these groups—the poor children who hang out in the market or the sets of teens who meet on the highway—will eventually coalesce into street youth cultures, much less formal "youth gangs" in the sense they are understood in Mexico's metropolitan areas or the United States is far from certain. On the one hand, there continue to be strong countervailing pressures from the solidarity and traditions of indigenous families and communities, as well as, now, from ethnically based social and political organizations. In addition, indigenous people as a whole are ever more integrated into the city. On the other hand, racism and discrimination against indigenous people are still strong in the city, and there is still great poverty in the urban *colonias*.

The situation continues to evolve rapidly, and which way it goes in coming years may depend on some of the new influences that are constantly being introduced into the mix. Some of these in recent years are listed below.

**UNDOCUMENTED WORK IN UNITED STATES.** In 1997, Chiapas was twenty-seventh of Mexico's thirty-one states in the remittances (and presumably numbers) of undocumented migrants. Since 2001, however, migration to the north has taken off, and Chiapas is now fifth, with more than 300,000 mostly young, mostly indigenous people (out of a state population of 3.5 million) in the U.S. The highlands are a major source of this movement (Rus and Rus 2004; also Balboa 2005; Banamex 2004, 151; Villafuerte 2004). Migration and its remittances are a source of advancement for indigenous people in the city, not least from the pride that comes from taking a chance and succeeding. At the same time, U.S. migration brings indigenous Chiapanecos in contact with U.S. urban fashions (about half are working in U.S. cities and suburbs and living in Spanish-speaking barrios), as well as with the smuggling rings related to their migration.

**CONTACT WITH ORGANIZATIONS IN CHIAPAS THAT PARTICIPATE IN VARIOUS SMUGGLING AND ILLICIT ACTIVITIES.** Smuggling drugs and undocumented workers across Chiapas are activities that already appear to have organized, if numerically small, urban indigenous participation. Nevertheless, such activity necessarily brings indigenous people from San Cristóbal into contact with national cartels and smuggling rings. According to our interviews, so far the indigenous side of these interactions is managed by adult "investors" who own vehicles or grow marijuana, for instance, and who depend on ethnic solidarity and ethnically based patterns of organization to manage their collaborators—factors that suggest both organizers and workers may continue to avoid being drawn into nonindigenous gangs. As far as we have been able to tell, to the extent that young people participate in the indigenous side of these activities, they do so as junior members brought in by their elders, not as members of youth gangs. That said, in the course of interviews with returned undocumented workers, one young man described working for a syndicate of smugglers in California, delivering boxes of blank forms for green cards (legal immigrant IDs), driver's licenses, and social security cards up and down the state. The patterns of organization, contacts, and "fashions" of those groups are by now certainly known in the formerly isolated Chiapas highlands.[30]

**THE PRESENCE OF NATIONAL AND TRANSNATIONAL GANGS.** Since the late 1990s, Mara Salvatrucha, a spectacularly violent Salvadoran gang with roots in Los Angeles, has operated on the Chiapas coast. By itself, the gang has little attraction for indigenous urban youth in the highlands. However, Mara's notoriety did attract a following—the *maramaniáticos,* or "Mara-maniacs"— among young, urban ladinos in the state's two biggest cities, Tapachula and Tuxtla Gutiérrez, where there are now local gangs that imitate Mara organization, dress, hand signs, and tattoos (*La Jornada,* Mexico City, March 7, 2004; see also Vigil 2002b). Perhaps these more local manifestations of Mara will act as a bridge to indigenous youth—although, given that the *maramaniáticos* are ladinos, it seems unlikely at the present time.[31]

**FINALLY, FASHION AND INTERNATIONAL YOUTH CULTURE ITSELF.** "Gangsta" fashions are available to young people internationally, including to indigenous youth in Chiapas. "Gangsta rap" and rap video are on radio and television, baggy clothing is sold in local discount stores, tattoos have suddenly appeared on some young indigenous men's arms and shoulders (and a few young women's), and such customs as "tagging" are beginning to appear in San Cristóbal.[32] Most of this in the *colonias* of San Cristóbal, as in high schools in the United States, is more an attitude and "look" than an indication of the presence of actual gangs—and this is a distinction those in the city quick to jump to conclusions should keep in mind. But at least the fashions of the youth gang, as a culture distinct both from the parents of indigenous youths and the ladino city that surrounds them, are present and beginning, tentatively, to exert their pull.

While the futures of the large, and growing, number of indigenous children on the street in San Cristóbal, or of the disaffected youth who live in what otherwise appear to be well-established, stable *colonias,* or, for that matter, of the young people who assist their older relatives in smuggling, invading land, and so on, can of course not be known, what does appear to be true is that San Cristóbal's Maya youth do not seem to exhibit the anomie as a result of culture conflict that might be expected had their families migrated individually to urban centers (compare Moore 1978, 1991; Vigil 1988b, 1993). The fact that they have come in large, coherent waves, bringing their culture, village organization, and pride with them, appears to have made them an example of what Oscar Lewis (1952) called "urbanization without breakdown." In this respect, they appear to stand in contrast to urbanized peasants in many other parts of Mexico, where researchers have found that migrants often have great difficulties in finding a place to live and work in a hostile and uninviting setting (Arizpe 1975; Lomnitz 1977; Mangin 1970).

## Who's a Deviant? Whose Rules? Some Final Thoughts

What is a gang? Do the ethnically defined *sindicatos*—unions that secure land, jobs, and services for San Cristóbal's indigenous migrants—count? Do the bands of taxi drivers affiliated with the unions? What about the shadowy, multigenerational groups of indigenous men who deal in stolen cars, drugs, weapons, and undocumented migrants? If these groups—organized along ethnic lines as Mayan people attempt to adapt to the city, and numbering from a handful of individuals in the case of the last to many thousands in the first—are all "gangs," does it stretch the meaning too far? What about the informal groups of young men, marginal in different ways, but all "alienated" by their very Mayanness from the city in which they live, who drink, take drugs, and commit petty crimes? Are they precursors to gangs, incipient gangs, or already gangs?

Migration and adaptation to urban locales is a difficult process. For the formerly rural, indigenous peoples of Chiapas, the difficulty is compounded by a variety of historically specific obstacles. While we have also identified cultural resources and adaptation strategies that seem to be leading most to a relatively steady, stable integration to San Cristóbal, we have also detected the transitional problems and responses that in themselves may well continue to divide indigenous people from their new, ladino neighbors. As we have tried to show, even in a society like that of San Cristóbal, divided historically into two ethnic groups, indigenous and ladino, neither group is uniform. Community dynamics within the indigenous side of the equation—differences in *municipios* of origin, in when and under what circumstances the migrants arrived in the city, in the kinds of family and community ties they brought with them, and in the kinds of organizations they joined after they arrived—have a great deal to do with how quickly and successfully individuals and families adapt. But the way the city receives them, the extent to which it makes a place for the newcomers, opening positive outlets for their energies, also matters.

As we have seen, some of San Cristóbal's indigenous young have become involved in groups whose activities neutral observers might describe as extralegal, even illicit. As we have also seen, however, whether these activities are "deviant" or not depends greatly on one's perspective. In our ongoing research, we intend to continue following the evolution of several of these groups, particularly those composed of "marginal" young people who do not fit the expectations of either of San Cristóbal's ethnic communities, tracing the kinds of adjustments and adaptations they make as they attempt to secure their place as adults.[33]

## Notes

We would like to thank University of California/MEXUS, the Jacobs Foundation of Billingham, Washington, and INAREMAC/San Cristóbal for their support. Thanks as well to Polly Vigil and Diane Rus, and from the Department of Anthropology, UCLA, Carlos Ramos and Gisela Hanley. Finally, our gratitude to the people of the *colonias* of the Periférico Norte.

1. Ladino is not a racial but a cultural category, meaning someone who speaks Spanish, wears national Mexican dress, and is not an indígena. Essentially, it means "nonindigenous" (see D. Rus 1998; Sulca Báez 1997).

2. Sharing the city with these two societies there is arguably a third: it is smaller (perhaps 20 percent of the total) and largely self-segregated, composed of the bureaucrats, aid workers, businesswomen and men, and laborers attracted from other parts of Mexico and abroad by San Cristóbal's emergence as a major tourist destination over the last twenty years. There may even be said to be a fourth, that of the thousands of tourists who flock to the city during the summer and Christmas high seasons. Aside from a brief description in van den Berghe (1994), there is no systematic treatment of either of these groups.

3. Our initial approach was ethnographic and ethnohistorical (e.g., Rus and Collier 2003), informed by the integrated, multidimensional considerations used by Vigil (1988a and b, 2002a) to investigate urban adaptation in immigrant communities in Southern California.

4. For the impact of these policies in Chiapas, see Collier (1994), Harvey (1998), and J. Rus (1995); for Mexico as a whole, Barry (1995) and Ochoa (2000).

5. As an indication of this movement, the population of Chiapas's four biggest cities, Tuxtla Gutiérrez, Tapachula, San Cristóbal, and Comitán collectively increased from 250,894 in 1970 to 686,244 in 1990—a twenty-year period when there was little in-migration to Chiapas from other states (INEGI 1973, 1991).

6. Among other factors that played a role in Chiapas's indigenous urbanization beginning in the 1970s are the demand for construction workers on massive infrastructure projects (Cancian 1992; van den Berghe 1994), the influence of twenty years of bilingual education (Pineda 1995), and rural electrification and the penetration of electronic media.

7. The Mayas of Chiapas are perhaps the last large indigenous population in Latin America to begin urbanizing—a process already far advanced in Central Mexico in the 1930s and 1940s, Peru in the 1950s, and Guatemala in the 1960s and 1970s (Morse and Hardoy 1992; Roberts 1995; Roberts and Lowder 1970).

8. It should be noted that the rural crisis and subsequent urbanization that have affected the region of San Cristóbal over the last twenty years have impacted all of southeastern Mexico (the states of Oaxaca, Chiapas, Tabasco, Campeche, Yucatán, and Quintana Roo), both Mexico's most indigenous region and, until the last twenty years, by far the most rural. From 1980 to 1990, three of the ten fastest growing cities

in Mexico were in the southeast; from 1990 to 2000, five of ten. In 1998, of Mexican cities with more than 100,000 inhabitants, eight of the ten poorest in terms of individual income were also in the southeast (Banamex 1998a).

9. For fuller versions of this general historical, political-economic background, see Wasserstrom (1983) and Rus, Hernández, and Mattiace (2004, 1–26).

10. For a stubborn defense of the idea that San Cristóbal should be a ladino city, see Gutiérrez (1996).

11. Ulrich Köhler describes a secular version of this process (personal communication to Rus, 2004); M. Peres Tzu, a Catholic version (interview with Rus, summer 1991).

12. Among indigenous migrants to the city, researchers have noted that a disproportionate share after 1982 appeared to be women with children, either escaping unemployed abusive husbands, or moving to the city's *colonias* following abandonment by men who had not returned from labor migrations. Anecdotally, Protestantism is often credited in the former cases with helping "tame" men's drinking and abuse and reuniting families. In any case, many of the most active, successful social, political, and economic organizations in the colonias have been women's groups (Cantón Delgado 1997; I. Castro Apreza 2003; Y. Castro Apreza 2003; Sanchiz Ochoa 2004).

13. For example, following the 1998 Acteal massacre in Chenalhó, up to 2,000 refugees came to the city from that *municipio* alone. Moksnes gives the total number of displaced persons from Chenalhó to all refuges as 10,000 out of a total population of 30,000 (Moksnes 2004).

14. Interviews with M. Peres Tzu (interview with Rus, 2000; see also Peres Tzu 2002). One study put the number of such *colonias* at over seventy at the end of the 1990s (Melel Xojobal 2000).

15. This appears to be true for those who came in through the mid-1990s as well. The situation of the latest third-wave arrivals is as yet unclear, perhaps because they have not had time to settle down and unite their families, perhaps because they fled their homes in couples or as members of single households. Eventually, however, we would expect the same pattern to hold. This description does not take into account families of single mothers, widows, and abandoned women, anecdotally more common in the city than in the countryside. Follow-up surveys are needed (see Sanchiz Ochoa 2004).

16. There are currently more than twenty different denominations among the *colonia* residents, from Roman Catholicism and Presbyterianism, which remain the two largest, through many varieties of Pentecostalism. In the last four years, Islam has also attracted urban indigenous converts, and the 300 families of mostly Tzotzil Muslims in San Cristóbal make them the largest Muslim community in Mexico.

17. Originally Protestant organizations are CRIACH (Consejo de Representantes Indígenas de los Altos de Chiapas) and OPEACH (Organización de Pueblos Evangélicos de los Altos de Chiapas). "Official" union affiliates include CROC (Confederación Revolucionaria de Obreros y Campesinos), CROM (Confederación Regional

Obrera Mexicana), and CTM (Confederación de Trabajadores Mexicanos). "Indian movement" groups are SCOPNUR (Sociedad Cooperativa Pro-Mejoramiento de Nuestra Raza) and UNAL (Unión Nacional Lombardista). This is not an exhaustive list.

18. One of the explanations for the great number of taxis is that purchasing a car is an investment within reach of many small investors (D. and J. Rus, interviews with taxistas, August 9, 1997, September 1997; *Foja Coleta,* San Cristóbal, January 23, 2001). For comparison, the number of registered trucks and cars in San Cristóbal increased from 3,500 in 1994, to 15,900 in 1999, to 17,000 in 2001 (*Foja Coleta,* January 6, 2001).

19. Rus, interviews with M. Peres Tzu, August 27, 1997, December 15 and 18, 1998.

20. It should be noted that according to D. and J. Rus's interviews, by 2001 the 1,100-plus taxis were represented by more than fifty unions and associations. The largest had more than 100 units, while some of the smaller ones, united by common *colonia* or church membership, had as few as five.

21. For example, they surround traffic accidents and force ladino drivers to pay damages before they can leave the scene. Many ladinos tell of the municipal police arriving at accident scenes, finding that the "taxi-police" had already arrived, and retreating without intervening (interviews with JPL, July 1999; PRS, August 22, 2004).

22. Smuggling of arms, drugs, and Central Americans are described in numerous newspaper reports of arrests, e.g., *Foja Coleta,* San Cristóbal, November 11, 2001, or *Cuarto Poder,* Tuxtla Gutiérrez, April 7, 1998. Also Rus, interviews with SGB, August 26, 2003; and XJ, August 2002.

23. Rus, interviews with MP, April 26, 2003; *Foja Coleta,* San Cristóbal, January 9, 2003.

24. Rus, interviews with SB, *colonia* "Patria Nueva," August 4 and 11, 1998; JPL, July 30, 1998.

25. This distinction between children "in" and "of" the street is made as well in a study of street children in Mexico City, which found that 90 percent of indigenous children on the street merely worked there; only 10 percent lived there full time. The proportion of street children to children working on the street among the nonindigenous was twice as high (Banamex 1998b).

26. Rus and Rus 2004; Melel Xojobal (2000, 43–46) reports that 37 percent of all families in the *colonias* fell below the level of "extreme poverty," defined by the World Bank as 1 dollar per person per day. Melel does not break out the data to show differences by *colonia* or by date of arrival in the city. However, comparison to our figures suggests that the latest migrants are much poorer than the urban indigenous group as a whole.

27. Several projects have arisen to ameliorate conditions for these newcomers. As of 2003, some of the more prominent were Manos Amigas de Jovel, a residential project initiated by a Catholic priest with approximately forty residents, some of

whom are runaway street children, but most are from poor families who could not afford to send them to school; Don Bosco, a residential project operated by Salesian priests close to 100 street children and/or runaways; and El Mono Pintado, a project initiated by a U.S. anthropologist to provide daytime activities for scores of children of indigenous street vendors.

28. *Foja Coleta,* San Cristóbal, June 27, 2002, and August 7, 2002; Rus, interview with MP, April 26, 2003.

29. Letter to Rus from M. Peres Tzu, May 10, 2003.

30. D. and J. Rus, interviews, summer 1998. It should be noted that several Tzotzil undocumenteds are reported by peers to have spent time in county jails in the U.S. This is another pathway to street knowledge that should be explored.

31. At the same time, if the local press was, as mentioned earlier, alarmist about "gangs" in Chiapas, since 2003 the national and international media have been frankly alarming about the gang threat to the region as a whole, with repeated stories about the "potential" ties of Mexican and Central American street gangs to "international terrorism," and parallel stories suggesting that the indigenous movements of Latin America should perhaps be treated as "terrorist organizations." The danger of U.S. police, military, and financial support for misguided repression in provincial Latin America latent in such charges should be sobering to all (see, for example, "Four Presidents Seek Help in Gang Battle: Central American Leaders say the groups pose a hemispheric threat," *Los Angeles Times,* April 2, 2005; "FBI Teams with Mexico to Probe International Gang: Effort to counter Mara Salvatrucha focuses on Chiapas State," *Los Angeles Times,* April 15, 2005; "'War on Terror' Has Latin American Indigenous People in Its Sights," *Inter Press Service,* June 6, 2005).

32. Examples of graffiti observed in areas bordering indigenous *colonias* include spray-painted "tags" by "locally famous" individuals, among them "Fiel," "Susto," and "Kaspar." Subsequent interviews by Vigil with local residents also uncovered graffiti in the same general areas by what are apparently more street-based groups, for example, "Los Jaguares," "Chicos Serpientes," "Los Asesinos," "Los Indominables," and "Banda Escuadrón." At least some of these are believed to be ladino *esquéiter* ("skater," or skateboard) groups.

33. Whether these groups become "street gangs" in the accepted sense is one of our ongoing questions. The street gang is the result of complex processes that stem from multiple levels and forces over a long period of time, the incipient phases of which do appear to exist in San Cristóbal. The phrase "multiple marginality" reflects the complexity and persistence of these forces, which include inadequate living conditions, difficult personal and family transformations, racism, and cultural repression in public institutions and settings (see Covey, Menard, and Franzese 1992; Vigil 1988a and b, 2002a; Yun and Vigil 1996, 1998).

# References

Angulo Barredo, Jorge I. 2003. "Migraciones y asentamientos de población indígenas en San Cristóbal, Un recuento y caracterización," *Anuario de Estudios Indígenas,* v. IX, Universidad Autónoma de Chiapas, pp. 63–82.

Aramoni Calderón, Dolores, and Gaspar Morquecho E. 1997. "La otra mejilla . . . pero armada: El recurso de las armas en manos de los *expulsados* de San Juan Chamula." *Anuario 1996,* Centro de Estudios Superiores de México y Centroamérica, Universidad de Ciencias y Artes de Chiapas, pp. 552–611.

Arizpe, Lourdes. 1975. *Indígenas en la ciudad de México: El caso de las "Marías."* Mexico City: SepSetentas/Secretaría de Educación Pública.

Aubry, Andrés. 1982. *Indígenas urbanos: Nuevos cinturones de miseria en San Cristóbal.* San Cristóbal, Chiapas: INAREMAC.

———. 1991. *San Cristóbal de Las Casas: Su historia urbana, demográfica y monumental, 1528 1990.* San Cristóbal, Chiapas: INAREMAC.

Balboa, Juan. 2005. "Pasa Chiapas al quinto lugar de los estados con mayor recepción." *La Jornada,* Mexico City, June 6.

Banamex (Banco Nacional de México). 1998a. *Examen de la situación económica de México* 872 (July).

———. 1998b. *Examen de la situación económica de México* 874 (September).

———. 2004. *Examen de la situación económica de México* 940 (April).

Barry, Tom. 1995. *Zapata's Revenge: Free Trade and the Farm Crisis in Mexico.* Boston: South End Press.

Betancourt Aduén, Darío. 1997. *Bases regionales en la formación de comunas rurales-urbanas en San Cristóbal LC, Chiapas.* Facultad de Ciencias Sociales, Universidad Autónoma de Chiapas, San Cristóbal, Chiapas.

Calvo Sánchez, Angelino. 1990. "Las *colonias* nuevas de migrantes y *expulsados* en San Cristóbal de Las Casas." *Anuario III,* Centro de Estudios Indígenas, Universidad Autónoma de Chiapas, pp. 55ff.

Cancian, Frank. 1992. *The Decline of Community in Zinacantán: Economy, Public Life, and Social Stratification, 1960–1987.* Stanford, Calif.: Stanford University Press.

Cantón Delgado, Manuela. 1997. "Las expulsiones indígenas en los Altos de Chiapas: Algo más que un problema de cambio religioso," *Mesoamérica* 33 (June): 147–69.

Castro Apreza, Inés. 2003. "Contemporary Women's Movements in Chiapas." In *Women of Chiapas, Making History in Times of Struggle and Hope,* ed. Christine Eber and Christine Kovic, 197–206. New York: Routledge.

Castro Apreza, Yolanda. 2003. "J'pas Joloviletik-Jolom Mayaetik-K'inal Antzetik: An Organizational Experience of Indigenous and Mestiza Women." In *Women of Chiapas,* ed. C. Eber and C. Kovic, 207–18. New York: Routledge.

Collier, George. 1994. *Basta! Land and the Zapatista Rebellion in Chiapas.* Oakland: Food First Books.

Covey, H. C., S. Menard, and R. J. Franzese. 1992. *Juvenile Gangs*. Springfield, IL: Charles C. Thomas.

Eber, Christine, and Brenda Rosenbaum. 1993. "Women Weavers in Highland Chiapas, Mexico." In *Crafts in the World Market: The Impact of Global Exchange on Middle American Artisans*, ed. June Nash, 154–80. Albany: State University of New York.

Estrada Martínez, Rosa Isabel. 1995. "El problema de las expulsiones en las comunidades indígenas de los Altos de Chiapas y los derechos humanos." Comisión Nacional de Derechos Humanos, México, D.F.

Fernández Liria, Carlos. 1993. "Enfermedad, familia y costumbre en el periférico de San Cristóbal." *Anuario 1992*, Instituto Chiapaneco de Cultura, pp. 11–56.

Garza, Anna María. 1993. "Madres frente a la muerte infantil en el periférico indígena de San Cristóbal." *Anuario 1993*, Instituto Chiapaneco de Cultura, pp. 58–69.

Gossen, Gary H. 1989. "Life, Death, and Apotheosis of a Chamula Protestant Leader." In *Ethnographic Encounters in Southern Mesoamerica*, ed. G. H. Gossen and V. R. Bricker, 217–19. Albany: State University of New York.

Gutiérrez Gutiérrez, José Antonio. 1996. *Infundios contra San Cristóbal de las Casas*. México, D.F.: Fundación Chiapaneca Colosio.

Harvey, Neil. 1998. *The Chiapas Rebellion: The Struggle for Land and Democracy*. Durham, NC: Duke University Press.

INEGI (Instituto Nacional de Estadística, Geografía e Inform tica). 1973. *IX Censo general de población y vivienda, 1970*. México, D.F: INEGI.

———. 1991. *Anuario Estadístico del Estado de Chiapas*. Gobierno del Estado de Chiapas, Tuxtla Gutiérrez/INEGI, Aguascalientes, México.

———. 1992. *XI Censo general de población y vivienda, 1990*. INEGI, Aguascalientes.

———. 2001. *Resultados preliminares del XII Censo General de Población*. INEGI, Tuxtla Gutiérrez, Chiapas, and Aguascalientes.

Kovic, Christine Marie. 1997. "Walking with One Heart: The Catholic Church and Human Rights among the Maya of Highland Chiapas, Mexico." PhD diss., City University of New York.

———. 2005. *Mayan Voices for Human Rights: Displaced Catholics in Highland Chiapas*. Austin: University of Texas Press.

Lewis, Oscar. 1952. "Urbanization without Breakdown." *Scientific Monthly*, no. 75: 31–41.

———. 1959. *Five Families: Mexican Case Studies in the Culture of Poverty*. New York: Basic Books.

Lomelí Radillo, Raul O. 1986. "Los protestantes en Chiapas, México." Working Paper, Centro de Investigaciones Humanísticas de Mesoamérica y Chiapas, Universidad Nacional Autónoma de México, San Cristóbal y México, D.F.

Lomnitz, Larissa A. de. 1977. *Cómo sobreviven los marginados*. Mexico City: Siglo Veintiuno Editores.

Mangin, W. 1970. *Peasants in Cities: The Anthropology of urbanization.* Boston: Houghton Mifflin.

Melel Xojobal. 2000. *Rumbo a la Calle: El trabajo infantil, una estrategia de sobrevivencia.* San Cristóbal, Chiapas, Mexico: Melel Xojobal.

Moksnes, Heidi. 2004. "Factionalism and Counterinsurgency in Chiapas: Contextualizing the Acteal Massacre." *European Review of Latin American and Caribbean Studies* 76 (April): 109–18.

Moore, J. W. 1978. *Homeboys.* Philadelphia: Temple University Press.

———. 1991. *Going Down to the Barrio.* Philadelphia: Temple University Press.

Morquecho, Gaspar. 1992. "Los indios en un proceso de organización." Tesis de Licenciatura en Antropología Social (undergraduate thesis in anthropology), Universidad Autónoma de Chiapas, San Cristóbal, Chiapas.

Morse, Richard M., and Jorge E. Hardoy, eds. 1992. *Rethinking the Latin American City.* Washington, D.C.: Woodrow Wilson Center Press.

O'Brien, Robin. 1994. "The Peso and the Loom: The Political Economy of Women's Work in Highland Chiapas." PhD diss., University of California–Los Angeles.

Ochoa, Enrique C. 2000. *Feeding Mexico: The Political Uses of Food Since 1910.* Lanham, MD: SR Books of Rowman and Littlefield.

Peres Tzu, Mari n. 2002. "A Tzotzil Chronicle," trans. from Tzotzil by Jan Rus. In *The Mexico Reader,* ed. Gilbert Joseph and Timothy Henderson, 655–69. Durham, NC: Duke University Press.

Pineda, Luz Olivia. 1995. "Maestros bilingües, burocracia y poder político en los Altos de Chiapas." In *Chiapas: Los rumbos de otra historia,* ed. Juan Pedro Viqueira and Mario H. Ruz, 279–300. México, D.F.: UNAM-CIESAS-CEMCA-UAG.

Roberts, Bryan. 1995. *The Making of Citizens: Cities of Peasants Revisited.* London: Arnold Publishers.

Roberts, Bryan, and Stella Lowder. 1970. *Urban Population Growth and Migration in Latin America: Two Case Studies.* Liverpool: Centre for Latin American Studies, University of Liverpool.

Ruiz Ortiz, Juana María. 1996. "Los primeros pobladores de Nich'ix, la *Colonia* de la Hormiga." In *Anuario de Estudios Indígenas VI,* Centro de Estudios Indígenas, Universidad Autónoma de Chiapas, pp. 11–24.

Rus, Diane L. 1990. "La crisis y la mujer indígena: El caso de Chamula, Chiapas." Working Paper, INAREMAC, San Cristóbal, Chiapas.

———. 1998. *Mujeres de tierra fría: Conversaciones con las coletas.* Tuxtla Gutiérrez, Chiapas: Universidad de Ciencias y Artes de Chiapas.

Rus, Diane L., and Jan Rus. 2004. "Encuestas económicas y demográficas de Ch'ul Osil, Chamula, 1974, 1987 y 1998." Paper presented to the international colloquium "Chiapas diez años después," San Cristóbal, Chiapas, August 23–27.

Rus, Jan. 1995. "Local Adaptation to Global Change: The Reordering of Native Society in Highland Chiapas, 1974–1994." *European Review of Latin American and Caribbean Studies* 58 (June): 71–90.

————. 1997. "Shared Destinies: Lineage and the Redefinition of Identity among the Urban Tzotzils of Chiapas, Mexico." Paper presented to the American Anthropological Association, Washington, D.C., November 24.

————. 2005. "The Struggle against Indigenous Caciques in Highland Chiapas, 1965–1993." In *Cacique and Caudillo in Twentieth Century Mexico,* ed. Alan Knight and Wil Pansters, 169–200. London and Washington, D.C.: Institute of Latin American Studies/Brookings Institution.

Rus, Jan, and George A. Collier. 2003. "A Generation of Crisis in the Chiapas Highlands: The Tzotzils of Chamula and Zinacantán, 1974–2000." In *Mayan Lives, Mayan Utopias,* ed. J. Rus, R. Hernández, and S. Mattiace, 33–61. Lanham, MD: Rowman and Littlefield.

Rus, Jan, R. Aída Hernández Castillo, and Shannan Mattiace. 2004. Introduction to *Mayan Lives, Mayan Utopias: The Indigenous People of Chiapas and the Zapatista Rebellion,* 1–26. Lanham, MD: Rowman and Littlefield.

Rus, Jan, and R. W. Wasserstrom. 1981. "Evangelization and Political Control in Mexico." In *Is God an American?,* ed. Søren Hvalkof and Peter Aaby, 163–72. Copenhagen, Denmark: International Work Group on Indigenous Affairs.

Sànchez Flores, Magdalena Patricia. 1995. "De la ciudad real a la ciudad escaparate." In *Chiapas: Una modernidad inconclusa,* ed. Diana Guillén, 72–113. México, D.F.: Instituto Mora.

Sanchiz Ochoa, Pilar. 2004. "Matrifocalidad en la periferia de San Cristóbal: Una vía para el desarrollo e igualdad entre las mujeres indígenas chiapanecas." *Mesoamérica* 46 (June): 173–90.

Sterk, Vern. 1991. "The Dynamics of Persecution." D.Miss. diss., Fuller Theological Seminary, Pasadena, CA.

Sulca Báez, Edgar. 1997. *Nosotros los coletos: Identidad y cambio en San Cristóbal.* Tuxtla Gutiérrez, Chiapas: Centro de Estudios Superiores de México y Centroamérica, Universidad de Ciencias y Artes de Chiapas.

Sullivan, Kathleen. 1995. "Reestructuración rural-urbana entre los indígenas Chamula de los Altos de Chiapas, México." In *La explosión de las comunidades en Chiapas,* ed. June Nash, 69–95. Copenhagen: IWGIA.

Van den Berghe, Pierre L. 1994. *The Quest for the Other.* Seattle: University of Washington Press.

Vigil, Diego. 1988a. *Barrio Gangs: Street Life and Identity in Southern California.* Austin: University of Texas Press.

————. 1988b. "Group Processes and Street Identity: Adolescent Chicano Gang Members." *Ethos* 16, no. 4: 421–45.

————. 1993. "Gangs, Social Control, and Ethnicity: Ways to Redirect Street Youth." In *Identity and Inner-City Youth: Beyond Ethnicity and Gender,* ed. Shirley B. Heath and Milbrey W. McLaughlin, 94–119. New York: Teachers College, Columbia University.

————. 2002a. "Community Dynamics and the Rise of Street Gangs." In *Latinos! Remaking America,* ed. M. Suarez-Orozco and M. M. Paez, 97–109. Berkeley: University of California Press and the David Rockefeller Center for Latin American Studies, Harvard University.

————. 2002b. *A Rainbow of Gangs: Street Cultures in the Mega-City.* Austin: University of Texas Press.

Villa Rojas, Alfonso. 1976. Introducción to *El indigenismo en acción: XXV aniversario del Centro Coordinador Tzeltal-Tzotzil, Chiapas,* ed. Aguirre Beltrán, Gonzalo, Villa Rojas, et al. México, D.F.: Instituto Nacional Indigenista.

Villafuerte, Daniel. 2004. "El campo chiapaneco a diez años del levantamiento armado." Paper presented to the international colloquium "Chiapas diez años después," San Cristóbal, Chiapas, August 23–27.

Wasserstrom, Robert W. 1983. *Class and Society in Central Chiapas.* Berkeley: University of California Press.

Yun, Steve, and Diego Vigil. 1996. "Southern California Gangs: Comparative Ethnicity and Social Control." In *Gangs in America,* 2nd ed., ed. Ron Huff, 139–56. Thousand Oaks, Calif.: Sage Publications.

————. 1998. "Vietnamese Youth Gangs in the Context of Multiple Marginality and the Los Angeles Youth Gang Phenomenon." In *Gangs and Youth Subcultures: International Explorations,* ed. K. Hazlehurst and C. Hazlehurst, 117–39. New Brunswick, N.J.: Transaction.

# PART III

# Identities of Resistance

# 7

# Female Gangs: Gender and Globalization

### JOAN W. MOORE

Gangs are responsive to changing economic and political structures. That statement is, by now, a truism, and certainly the globalization of economic and political activity is the kind of change that dramatically affects youth groups of all stripes. But when they discuss "gangs," most researchers confine themselves to males. As usual, this begs the question of gender.

Globalization has a very broad range of connotations, but for my purposes, two processes are particularly important. These are peripheralization and migration.

Peripheralization means that in developed nations, large segments of both new immigrants and the old working class increasingly function outside of the main economic life of cities. Ladders of mobility are virtually inaccessible. The gap between rich and poor increases. Long-term unemployment is not much alleviated by the creation of low-paid, dead-end jobs. An informal economy flourishes, with strong illicit components.

Working in tandem with peripheralization, migration has substantially worsened the conditions of many urban poor. Both intranational and international migration has accelerated throughout the world. In developing nations, would-be workers pour in from the countryside and, often, out again to developed economies. In developed nations, global cities experience huge increases in the numbers of foreign workers (cf. Moore 1998). Labor migration produces what has been called "a paradox . . . [that] gears together modern supranational networks and traditional, even archaic . . . forms of relationships" (Roy 2001, 21). Young people in both sending and receiving countries are affected. Families from nations like Somalia are rearing their children in modern cities like Oslo. Young gang members deported from Los Angeles are raising hell in El Salvador.

Both of these processes change the life chances of young adults—and especially of those from immigrant families. Changes occur in both receiving and sending nations. The result might be anomie, or the formation of youth movements, or it *might* be the formation of gangs. The path toward the formation of gangs seems to be encouraged by another feature of globalization: the worldwide spread of media images of American gangs, and especially those of Los Angeles. Los Angeles-style gang graffiti are scrawled on the walls of Oaxaca villages, and young Indians in Winnipeg try their best to look like the latest Hollywood version of South Central Los Angeles gangbangers.

In what follows, I will deal first with the relevance of peripheralization to the emergence of female gangs and second with immigration. Finally, because there is so much variation in the ways in which women are drawn into gang activity (and so much confusion among researchers), I have added a brief survey of some international data on the differences between membership in a female gang and female "affiliation" with a male gang. This may be seen as yet another pedantic exercise in defining what is a gang and what is not, but this distinction is one that carries a major difference.

## Globalization, Peripheralization, and American Gangs

The American experience in the last decade or so shows the linkage between labor peripheralization and the emergence of female gangs. First, there are the statistics. Even though they had existed in some cities for generations, youth gangs—female as well as male—popped up all over the United States in the mid-1980s. This, of course, happened just as industrial jobs were vanishing and, in some regions, where immigration was stepped up (cf. Vigil 2002). Even though they are less common than male gangs, female gangs show up most frequently in cities where gangs—in general—are a new phenomenon. In most such cities gangs didn't exist until the mid-1990s (Howell, Egley, and Gleason 2002; Moore and Hagedorn 2001).

Are these just dependent girlfriends of the male gang members? The changes in older, more established female gangs offer some insight into the dynamic of the relationship between labor peripheralization and female gangs. These changes are not fully understood because there are so few studies with even a hint of historical focus. However, researchers *think* that women are more likely now than in the past to be involved in drug dealing. They are also more likely to take an assertive stance toward their male gang-member associates (Brotherton 1996; Brotherton and Salazar 2002; Hamid 1996; Moore 1991; Moore and Hagedorn 2001; Taylor 1993; Venkatesh 1998). These features represent the kinds of shifts that might be associated with economic restructuring. By that I mean that, at the very least, women may be more effectively penetrating the illicit markets that expanded so rapidly as economic restructuring further marginalized inner-city populations.[1] There are also hints in our research in Los Angeles and Milwaukee that today's gang females are ruefully aware of the shallowness of the "male marriageable pool" (cf. Hagedorn 1998).[2] If women are more assertive, it seems to follow that they see males as generally rather unreliable.

Incidentally, I am not claiming that today's gang girls are autonomous, powerful superwomen: there is too much evidence of victimization for that. But I am claiming that they exert more agency than they are given credit for, and more than they did in the past, both with regard to economic activity and with regard to their familial roles. The "Molls" studied in Boston in the early 1970s (W. Miller 1973) were said to "glory in" their dependency on their male gang. That attitude is not common nowadays among gang girls (cf. J. Miller 2001). In sharp contrast, New York's Latin Queens (analyzed by Brotherton and Salazar 2002) provide an example of gang women's beginning to build a new institution.

It would be nice to be able to say that similar trends are found in female gangs in other developed nations. Unfortunately, there is virtually no literature on female gangs outside of the United States. This is partly because in Europe, at least, gangs of either gender have been seen as a recent phenomenon.[3] In England, for example, there is convincing evidence in studies since the 1970s that most young people who are defined as "problems" are not organized into American-style gangs. With some exceptions, they are, instead, bonded with each other in "loose and independent cliques of friends" who all follow some stylistic fad (Campbell and Muncer 1989, 278). But even within that subcultural framework, young working-class Englishwomen studied in the 1990s were likely to reject "the traditional roles of housework and domestic labor" that their 1970s counterparts had embraced (Burke and Sunley 1998, 49). There may be many female gangs, and many studies of them, but I could find very little. But I believe that the American experience can stand as grounds for arguing that young women in poor communities are just as deeply affected as men by labor peripheralization and almost as likely to form gangs.

## A CRISIS OF GENDER IDENTITY?

This has not always been apparent to researchers. It has been obvious that the lives of young males are strongly affected by economic shifts—simply because everyone expects boys to work. It follows that most researchers accept the notion that economic restructuring has played a major role in the upsurge of male youth gangs in the United States.

Similar connections to "youth problems" are also made by European social scientists and are linked even more specifically to young *males.* In England, for example, an increase in youth crime is associated with what has been called a "crisis of masculinity." Traditional male identities, based on work and marriage, became problematic as working-class labor became marginalized (Collier 1998, 84). Campbell (1993) worries about the viciousness of unemployed and unrestrained groups of "lads"—short-term alliances of neighborhood youth involved in serious race riots. She also refers to a crisis of masculinity (205) and, further, argues that their role models are no longer the working men around them but, rather, "globally transmitted images and ideologies of butch and brutal solutions to life's difficulties" (323). Kersten makes a parallel point for Germany, arguing that "the current underclass and former working class youth are presently—at best—booked for tertiary sector jobs, feminized work that they deeply detest and find unmanly. This fuels their hate and their aggression" (2001, 250). These arguments imply that the peripheralization of ghetto populations has social-psychological, developmental consequences—for males.

But what about young women? I do not know of anyone who has discussed economic restructuring as creating a "crisis of femininity." Is this because women are not affected by labor-market trends? Of course not. But labor-market trends are conceived as affecting women mostly by indirection. In particular, it has been argued that women are less likely to get married. Young ghetto men are less attractive as potential marriage partners because their job prospects are less promising (Wilson 1987). Certainly this happens, but we also know quite well that labor-market shifts have direct effects on young women, as well. In developed nations, they are very likely to be in the labor market side by side with their male neighbors.

This peculiar blindness to the direct effects of labor-market shifts on women may be based on the common assumption that female identity is *generally* not as contested as male identity. This assumption rests on the notion that female identity is rooted almost entirely in the family and that the family is somehow less volatile than economic institutions. This notion is deeply flawed. Even if women were not directly affected by trends in the labor force, changes in marriage patterns mean that the family as an institution is changing. When the pool of "marriageable males" shrinks, the roles of women change accordingly. Still more important, perhaps, is that the family may come to play a weaker role in the socialization of children and teenagers.[4]

In short, if there is a crisis in male identity related to economic shifts in developed nations, there is also a crisis in female identity. And if there is a crisis in gender identity among ghettoized adolescents and young adults and, further, if illicit economic opportunities open up, youth gangs might well be one outcome.

## Immigration

### THE RECEIVING COUNTRIES: MUSLIM IMMIGRANTS IN EUROPE

If peripheralization helps create a crisis in gender identity, migration has even more profound effects. Peripheralization may weaken the male's role in the family, but migration even more seriously jeopardizes intergenerational socialization in both the sending and receiving nations. Virtually every north European country has experienced large influxes of immigrants over the past several decades. Remember? Large-scale immigration was one of the preconditions for the emergence of American gangs in the early twentieth century. To an American observer, the fact that gangs—including female gangs—*have* recently appeared in Europe is not at all surprising.

Muslim immigrants to Europe, coming from many different countries, present an extreme case of disparity between immigrant and host cultures. In this discussion, I will focus on Muslim girls, who form a large component of Europe's labor migrants.

One of the very few reports of female gangs in Europe deals directly with these girls. Inger Lien studied junior high schools in Oslo, Norway (Lien 2002). Pakistani, Filipino, Somali, Vietnamese, Latin American, and ethnically mixed gangs appeared in Norway in the 1980s (Lien 2001). While most Muslim boys were highly traditional, and while the vast majority of Muslim girls (especially Pakistani) were secluded at home after school, there was a fringe of what Lien calls "hypermodern" boys—and girls. Female gangs were found in four of the schools, and in addition to the Norwegian girls, they included Somali, Moroccan, and Latin American girls. These girl gangs, like their male counterparts, were violent, carried knives, and were "willing to commit crimes." But, paradoxically, "they sought and achieved the protection of hypermodern boys."

We don't know if the Muslim girls in these gangs were rebelling against family norms or whether their families were marginal to their communities.[5] We do know that they were aggressively rejecting the traditionalist gender norms acted out by the majority of Muslim girls around them. If we view youth gangs as adolescent peer groups that compete with others in school, this is an important observation. Gary Fine (1987) contended that male adolescent peer groups permit teenagers to experiment—"in secret," that is, away from adults—with forbidden issues such as sexuality and aggressiveness. This he termed "normal deviance." It is "normal" since it applies to "imperatives of development," and it is "deviance" because even the most conventional of adolescent peer groups (like the Little Leaguers he studied) do things that violate adult expectations.

This theory is useful in understanding youth gangs (cf. Moore 1991). It places the youth gang in one of its most salient contexts—that is, other age peer groups encountered every day in school. Each crowd sets its own norms for sexuality, aggressiveness, and self-control vis-à-vis drug and alcohol use. Gangs are the rowdiest of these crowds, partly because they go further in flouting conventional norms, and partly because they revel in their reputation for doing so. For boys, participation in such groups helps establish masculine identity. Fighting and sexual assertiveness clearly announce to one's peers that one is not a mama's boy. (This may be particularly important if a boy's work prospects are indeed as feminized as Kersten and others claim.) For girls, such participation may also announce to one's peers that one is *not* bound to the circumscribed world of traditionalist Muslim domesticity and grinding poverty, but that one is nonetheless still a female, capable of asking boys for protection (cf. A. Campbell 1987). A supportive gang may be even more important for second-generation girls than for their brothers. Girls are generally expected to have a stronger role than males in maintaining the traditional culture, and girl gang members are more likely than boys to be stigmatized.

It seems glaringly obvious that second-generation Muslim girls in northern Europe would experience some kind of culture conflict, even if their communities are rigidly segregated and tightly controlled. There is some evidence to this effect. Even though most Muslim girls in Norway seemed to conform to traditionalist parental norms, several studies indicate that in England many Muslim girls were beginning to break away from traditional patterns even when they faced strong community sanctions and severe discrimination.[6] They worked, they went to university, and they wore Western clothes when away from home (Bowlby, Evans, and Mohammad 1998; Dwyer 1998). There are also hints that in the Parisian banlieux, Muslim girls were beginning to participate in the established gangs (Esterle-Hedibel 2001).

This situation changed as pan-Islamic sentiments swept Muslim communities in 2002, and as anti-immigrant, anti-Muslim sentiment hardened throughout the Western world. Algerian gangs in a Paris banlieu were described by a *New York Times* reporter as involved in a kind of nationalist hooliganism. Three gangs were said to dominate this project, and all were involved in rock throwing and anti-Semitic activities in addition to their normal work of dealing drugs (October 16, 2001, p. A4). Olivier Roy argues that a "new brand of supranational neo-fundamentalism is more a product of contemporary globalization than of the Islamic past. . . . [The immigrants] think of themselves as 'Muslims' and not as citizens of a specific country" (Roy 2001, 21). Israeli incursions into the West Bank and American saber rattling against Iraq raised the ante further. Gangs of Muslim immigrants reportedly firebombed synagogues in Marseilles, for example (*New York Times,* April 23, 2002, p. A10). The gang girls in Paris may well have been inspired by Palestinian female suicide bombers. The impetus given to Islamism may also have tightened community controls over girls who chafe at traditionalist restrictions. In 2002, a Somali immigrant woman living in the Netherlands began to receive death threats from fellow Muslims—as a "traitor"—because she had been exposing the physical and sexual abuse that Muslim women and girls had been suffering at the hands of family members (*New York Times,* November 9, 2002, p. A4). American gang researchers take note: Muslim immigrants form extremely strong communities, with very little evidence—at least, very little *overt* evidence—of the kind of "social disorganization" that characterized first-generation immigrant communities in the U.S.

### THE SENDING NATIONS: VIRTUAL GANGS AND REAL EXPORTS

If we know very little about female gangs in countries that have received substantial immigration, we know even less about countries that send immigrants. We do know that globalization seriously disrupts traditional gender roles in many of the less developed "sending" nations. Young women from traditional communities begin entering the labor force in large numbers as multinational firms shift menial, low-paying jobs from core nations to the outskirts of the capitalist system (cf. Parrado and Zenteno 2001, 458). Mexican maquiladoras, though declining recently (cf. *New York Times,* April 12, 2002), were an excellent example, serving as magnets for young women from all over Mexico.

What happens to immigrant youth has repercussions back home in the sending country. For example, when Salvadoran gang youth involved in Los Angeles riots were deported to their home communities, they quickly formed new gangs. The gangs adapted to their "new" environment and were reported to be much more violent and more criminal than the gangs they had left behind in the United States. One source "notes official estimates of 20,000 gang members in San Salvador, many of whom got their start in gang activity as immigrants to Los Angeles" (Wallace 2000, cited in Orellana et al. 2001, 584).[7] Similarly, Algerian gangs in Paris probably have some echo in Algeria.

## AMERICA'S NEIGHBORS: COME-AND-GO MIGRATION AND THE EFFECT ON THE SENDING NATION

Gang culture is directly imported to our neighbor, Mexico, which sends hundreds of thousand workers to the United States every year. However, what happens in Mexico cannot be taken as typical of all sending nations. Mexico has presented a classic case of dependent development for decades because its economy has been so intertwined with that of the United States. Rural economic crises push and urban opportunities pull people to the cities and from there, often, to the United States. In many small towns, come-and-go migration has been going on for so many years that direct pathways from home to Los Angeles have become well established.

In the process of migration, settlement, and/or return migration, traditional institutions of socialization are disrupted, formal agencies like the schools almost invariably falter, a street subculture develops, and police and media get involved. This sequence of events has been repeated over and over throughout the twentieth century (cf. Vigil 1988). Because it has been such a long-lasting process, migration from Mexico to the United States has left an interesting mix of families in Mexican communities. There are families who have never left home, sometimes living side by side with truly transnational families, who in turn live next door to families whose younger members regularly migrate to the United States without papers, just as their parents did, or next to older members whose family heads are struggling to bring their families over to the other side. There are counterparts in many Chicano barrios in the United States. Though many in the Mexican American population have no kinship or any other linkages in Mexico, many do. Back and forth visiting and temporary residence is not at all uncommon. A few teenagers become familiar with the street culture of both nations.

As a consequence, Mexican street subculture has often taken the form of American-style youth gangs—Chicano gangs, not African American, and directly transmitted from return migrants or visitors, not absorbed from TV or films. Los Angeles has had a thriving Chicano gang subculture since the 1930s, and "Los" is the acknowledged source for today's so-called "cholo" street culture of Mexico. In an earlier day, El Paso was the source for pachuco youth gangs of the 1930s and 1940s in American border cities (Laura Cummings, personal communication, 2002). Cholo youth in some communities "consider themselves to be cultural descendants of the Pachucos (or Zootsuiters) of the 1930s and 1940s. Originally a border culture, it is a hybrid tradition with demonstrable continuity in style, social organization, and language" (Cummings 1994a, 189).

Cholo youth, in gangs, are found in cities in the Mexican states bordering the United States (like Baja California, Chihuahua, and Sonora), in states like Jalisco and Michoacan that have a generations-old tradition of migration to and from the United States (Valenzuela Arce 1984), and in Mexico City (Castillo Berthier 2001; Gomez Jara 1987).[8] This sounds like cultural diffusion, but it is considerably stronger than that. Our research in Los Angeles (Moore 1978) found that, as they matured, some members of youth gangs in Los Angeles were directly involved in cross-border trafficking in drugs and other commodities (arms, stolen cars), and Valdez and Stifaneck (2002) imply the same. It seems logical that their contacts in Mexico should include some cholos, members of gangs. In short, it may not be only a matter of cultural diffusion, but also of actual economic ties, as well as come-and-go migration, that accounted for the wide spread of cholismo in Mexican cities.

And females are associated with these cholos. Castillo Berthier notes that there are Los Angeles–style female gangs in Mexico City (personal communication, 2002), although there is some question about this interpretation (Cummings, personal communication, 2002). Cummings (1994a) documents patterns of gender-segregated fighting between girls from different barrios (that is, gangs) that occurred in Chihuahua, Nogales, and Tijuana. She also documents variations in the style of fighting among these three locales that match variations in police behavior toward the gangs.

## AMERICA'S NEIGHBOR: CULTURAL DIFFUSION IN CANADA?

American movies, television, and music have disseminated an image of the street gang that is based largely on African American gangs in Los Angeles. The image has shaped the way the media represent troublesome youth groups throughout the Western world. It also probably helped shape youth gangs themselves in Europe.

There is direct evidence to that effect from our other next-door neighbor,

Canada, where youth workers in Winnipeg believe that their gangs appropriate the visible representations—clothing, signs, music, and tattoos—of the
gangs of Los Angeles as portrayed by Hollywood (Nimmo 2001). For three
generations, the city has had three major street gangs, all overwhelmingly
"Aboriginal." Community youth workers claim that at least as many females
as males are affiliated with these gangs in poor, inner-city communities and
that the females are just as criminally active as the males. Most come from
severely disrupted family backgrounds, and most are expelled from school
at an early age. Most of the girls that respondents identify as connected to
the gangs are "affiliated" loners, with some forming a named female auxil-
iary (for example, the "Sisterhood"). These named gangs have a distinct and
notable presence in Manitoba's women's prisons. Whatever their status, it *is*
clear that the females are subservient to the male gang members. Elsewhere
in Canada, five familiar characteristics of gangs were found among female as
well as male adjudicated delinquents in Montreal: a name, a specific meeting
place, a leader, distinctive signs, and initiation rituals. Girls who were members of structured gangs were significantly more likely than nonmembers,
or members of more loosely structured cliques, to be seriously delinquent
and to be involved in physical aggression (Lanctot and LeBlanc 1997).

## Gang-Affiliated Girls, Street Girls, and Gang Members: There's a Difference

There are two other issues that need to be clarified. First, how do members
of female gangs differ from girls who are "affiliated with" gangs? Second,
how do other street females differ from gang-related women? Some analysts
seem to assume that all of these statuses are interchangeable, and they are
most definitely not.

First, girls who belong to their own gang are not in the same social situation as girls who are simply "affiliated" with a male gang. One poignant
study from New Zealand and another from Australia highlight the peculiar
vulnerability of girls who are affiliated with a male gang but who are not
members of a female gang (Dennehy and Newbold 2001). The first study is
coauthored by the former wife of a biker gang member. It was based on her
observations amplified by interviews with women who had been associated
with the major national gangs in the country. (Most of these gangs are either
"ethnic," that is, Maori and Polynesian, or bikers, who are largely white and
multiethnic.) The level of battery directed by gang men toward their women,

including the author, is shocking. Hospitalization is not uncommon. While wife bashing is far from rare in New Zealand, the gang "missuses" tolerate this extreme behavior because, the authors argue, they "learn their place." They are socialized within the gang to recognize that a bashing can be triggered by trivial cues—sometimes stemming from flirtation with other gang members or, simply, by "disrespect." A woman's status in the gang depends on her man, and if he dumps her, she becomes community property. They also learn that the other women attached to the gang are not to be trusted but are, instead, constantly on the lookout for women who have designs on "their" men. The upshot is that these gang-affiliated women are socially isolated, with no "unity or sense of group identity" (Dennehy and Newbold 2001, 98). Thus the women "not only became resigned to their status, they also colluded in it, giving tacit support to male definitions and blaming female victims for any abuses they suffered, . . . Moreover the code of silence and loyalty, which is so central to gang life, also operated to prevent women talking about the abuse" (101).[9] In the Australian study, the girls affiliated with a highly patriarchal Vietnamese gang were described as "not so much a gang as a group of young women engaged in domestic service provision to criminally involved young men" (Maher 2000, 87). When they began to use heroin, their gang boyfriends first "bashed them" and then kicked them out. Most tried to survive by dealing heroin, but most wound up in prison.

Girls who are members of their own gangs are not, of course, always protected from abuse from male gang members: there is plenty of evidence to the contrary. But there is a fundamental difference between the social dynamics operating within a female gang and the social dynamics operating within a cluster of girls who are affiliated with a gang by virtue of their being a single male member's "missus."

The second question is how female gang members differ from other street girls. Several studies identify a kind of unaffiliated street girl who hangs around the gang. In New Zealand, these are the "dirty girls" or "crew shags." They are drawn to the gang and casually exploited as sexual conveniences by the male members. They have no recognized attachment to a single male, like the "missuses." In New Zealand, these girls often have serious drug and alcohol problems and work in the sex industry (Dennehy, personal communication, 2002). We found a similar vulnerability among a cluster of "wannabes," or hangers-on in Milwaukee; so did Valdez and Cepeda (1998) among the "hoodrats" in San Antonio, and so did Nimmo in Winnipeg (personal communication). In contrast to the New Zealand "missuses," girls who were members of the Milwaukee gang were respected, as were the sisters and girl-friends of the boys in the San Antonio gangs.

Most vulnerable of all are the isolated street girls, found throughout the world, usually as commercial sex workers. In the second largest city in the Philippines, OudeBreuil (1997) found clear distinctions between three types of street girls: girls in gangs that were usually affiliated with male gangs, rowdy crowds of high school girls, and sex workers under the age of eighteen. Rowdy high school girls had supportive families; gang girls had abusive or no families and were often runaways who relied on the gang for meeting basic needs. Young sex workers were often in-migrants from villages, with no female peer affiliations.

Earlier I argued that the combination of peripheralization and immigration changes the life chances of young adults and that gangs may be an occasional outcome. It is important to recognize how gangs differ from other formations. Girls who are members of gangs have mutual peer reinforcement for their feelings and behavior. It may be especially important for girls like the "hypermodern" Muslims in Norway to have the kind of support that a gang offers. It may be easier for these girls to find affirmation in a gang than it is for them to violate Muslim community norms in lonely isolation. This kind of support is absent for girls and women who are linked to the gang only by virtue of their connection to one male member. Such an attachment simply reinforces their dependency on males, often coercively. And isolated street girls are the most vulnerable of all.

## Conclusion

There is much that is familiar in the studies of female gangs outside the United States. Like their counterparts in the United States, there are hints that a female gang may serve as a refuge from an abusive family, and there are stories of abuse at the hands of male gang members. There are portraits of immigrant girls struggling to find a place in an alien culture, and portrayals of native-born women of color—Maori, Polynesian, Aboriginal—in what used to be called white settler societies. Sometimes these portrayals seem like exaggerations of the American situation. Mexican American gang girls in Los Angeles struggled with restrictive parental norms, but compared with the constraints experienced by Muslim girls, they were relatively liberated. Gang hoodrats in San Antonio were subject to abuse, but routine brutalization, as in New Zealand, was far from the norm.

But there are differences from the American pattern. Labor migration to the developed world from weak states with archaic cultures combines with the erosion of job markets to create conditions that favor the development of gangs. These include ghettoization, faltering institutions of socialization, and degraded life chances for the adolescent children of immigrants. Girls are as much affected as boys by these developments. For both, there is a crisis in gender identity. Though they may be less conspicuous and less common, where male gangs arise, girl gangs also often appear, and vulnerable gang-affiliated women also show up.

Chicago of the 1920s saw the gangs of children of Italian immigrants, but the disparity between Chicago and southern Italy, great though it seemed at the time, in no way approaches the disparity between Oslo and Somalia today. Schooling was not as important then as it is now, and school failure had less impact. Working-class jobs for males were more available, and far fewer women were in the labor force. The extreme differences between sending and receiving countries may also imply that labor-related immigration in today's global society not only has the potential for generating youth street gangs, but also for generating pan-national social movements of substantial political importance. A seemingly powerful Muslim identity transcends diverse origins in weak states and also transcends one's degraded status in Paris.[10]

Gangs may be especially useful for girls from immigrant families, as in the case of the most extreme culture clash—between Muslims and secular North Europeans. For rebellious girls, gangs have a distinct advantage over other forms of adolescent grouping, such as "affiliation" with a gang via a male, in that they provide peer support for innovative paths such girls may want to take. Furthermore, gender norms tend to be much more restrictive for immigrant girls than for boys, and joining a gang may be a much more significant act for girls. This suggestion is not confined to Muslim girls or to today's gangs: for example, a student of early pachuco (Mexican American) gangs in Tucson commented, "All in all, through their cohort activities and relation to pachuco identity itself, . . . males sought to enhance or consolidate their male identity in line with rather mainstream standards, while females sought to go beyond the imposed bound of appropriateness for their gender" (Cummings 1994b, 150).

Unfortunately, though the girls may perceive the gang as innovative, what gang membership usually offers disaffected young women is socially supported, straight-out rejection of available roles, as Campbell (1987) clearly delineated. It is extraordinarily rare for a gang to offer young women truly new avenues for development: New York's Latin Queens (as described by Brotherton and Salazar [2002]) are an outstanding exception.

Thus it is no surprise that a review of the literature on American female gangs finds two major themes. Some researchers assume that gangs "liberate" girls by providing new, often criminal identities. Others conclude that in the long run gang membership creates "social injury" for its female members (Curry 1998). The first perspective may well be that of the active gang member—a hopeful, frustrated girl who joins a gang in the hope of some kind of liberation. The second may be that of the disillusioned older member or ex-member who found the pressures of conformity to be overwhelming and, in retrospect, regrets joining. But these insights were developed in an era when gangs were relatively trivial, relatively transient features of some but not all major cities. How women will fare in a world where gangs play a more significant and more long-lasting role is an open question.

## Notes

1. We know from anecdotal evidence that there have been powerful women heroin dealers in the past, both in Los Angeles and El Paso, and autonomous female gangs. It is best not to overgeneralize about women's being shut out of all lucrative gang-related activity or as having been universally relegated to the roles of sex object for male gang members.

2. As one woman said, marriage has become "a little white girl's dream" (Jarrett 1994).

3. This perception may simply reflect a surprisingly ahistorical approach to youth groups outside the United States. American gangs have been documented for a century, and researchers are sensitive—perhaps oversensitive—to their presence.

4. The one continuing difference between males and females is that females bear children and males do not, and for most young women that does indeed have consequences.

5. In first-generation Mexican communities in Los Angeles, gang girls often came from families that were stigmatized in the neighborhood (Moore 1991).

6. A researcher studying a group of Bengali boys in London was particularly incensed at the way the local media labeled these boys as a "gang," but in a more than usually fierce diatribe against such labeling, the author of the study commented:

> Notions of "gang" identity . . . exist more as convenient fiction than reality.
> . . . The label of "the Gang" has been re-imported into Britain in its already deeply raced and gendered American formulation and used to provide a set of common-sense associations and understandings in redefining and refining "the problem" of black youth. . . . It has worked, as in the US, to impose a conservative culturalist perspective on black youth identifications, which has focused on cultural pathology at the expense of structural inequality . . . erasing the wider place of racial violence in the policing of black communities in Britain. (Alexander 2000, 167, 238)

These English/Bengali boys are reported as deeply respecting women, and as accepting the notion of arranged marriage, while their sisters stay demurely at home. No "hypermodern" Muslim girls are reported here.

7. As usual, any mention of gender is missing from this skimpy report.

8. Interestingly, in the far southern state of Chiapas, a similar but more recent process of urbanization has not produced Los Angeles-style youth gangs (Rus and Vigil this volume).

9. Many of these large, national gangs became actively involved in drug dealing, but, partly because during the 1980s they received large sums from the government to develop jobs, they also became involved in a number of legitimate businesses. In the 1990s, small adolescent street gangs emerged in Maori and Polynesian areas of cities, and several had female gangs attached to them (Dennehy and Newbold 2001, 178–89).

10. This observation is reminiscent of the shift in the behavior of some of the predatory gangs in Soweto in 1976 when students began their uprising. On a sporadic and spontaneous basis, the gangs carried out the occasional act of political confrontation and stopped targeting fellow Africans as crime victims. Some fled the township to join the African National Congress (Glaser 2000). On the American scene, it is also reminiscent of the development of the militant Brown Berets and the Young Lords of the Chicano and Puerto Rican movements of the 1970s, both of which had ties to local gangs.

## References

Alexander, Claire. 2000. *The Asian Gang.* Oxford: Berg.

Bowlby, S., S. L. Evans, and R. Mohammad. 1998. "The Workplace: Becoming a Paid Worker: Images and Identity." In *Cool Places,* ed. T. Skelton and G. Valentine, 228–48. London: Routledge.

Brotherton, David. 1996. "'Smartness,' 'Toughness,' and 'Autonomy': Drug Use in the Context of Gang Female Delinquency." *Journal of Drug Issues* 26: 261–77.

Brotherton, David, and C. Salazar. 2002. "Amor de Reina: The Pushes and Pulls of Group Membership among the New York Latin Queens." In *Alternative Perspectives on Gangs and the Community,* ed. Louis Kontos, D. Brotherton, and L. Barrios, 183–209. New York: Columbia University Press.

Burke, Roger, and Ros Sunley. 1998. "Post-Modernism and Youth Subcultures in Britain in the 1990s." In *Gangs and Youth Subcultures,* ed. Kayleen Hazlehurst and Cameron Hazlehurst, 35–66. New Brunswick, N.J.: Transaction Publishers.

Campbell, Anne. 1987. "Self-Definition by Rejection." *Social Problems* 34: 451–66.

Campbell, Anne, and Steven Muncer. 1989. "Them and Us: A Comparison of the Cultural Context of American Gangs and British Subcultures." *Deviant Behavior* 10: 271–88.

Campbell, Beatrix. 1993. *Goliath.* London: Methuen.

Castillo Berthier, Hector. 2001. "Youth, Culture, and Social Policy." Paper delivered at Strasbourg, European Youth Centre.

Collier, Richard. 1998. *Masculinities, Crime, and Criminology*. London: Sage.

Cummings, Laura. 1994a. "Fighting by the Rules: Women Street Fighters in Chihuahua, Chihuahua, Mexico." *Sex Roles* 30: 189–98.

———. 1994b. "Que Siga el Corrido: Tucson Pachucos and Their Times." PhD diss., Tucson, University of Arizona.

Curry, David. 1998. "Female Gang Involvement." *Journal of Research in Crime and Delinquency* 35: 100–118.

Dennehy, Glennis, and Greg Newbold. 2001. *The Girls in the Gang*. Auckland, N.Z.: Reed Books.

Dwyer, Claire. 1998. "Contested Identities: Challenging Dominant Representations of Young British Women." In *Cool Places*, ed. T. Skelton and G. Valentine, 50–65. London: Routledge.

Esterle-Hedibel, Maryse. 2001. "Youth Gangs in France." In *The Eurogang Paradox*, ed. M. Klein, H.-J. Kerner, C. Maxson, and E. G. M. Weitekamp, 203–7. Dordrecht, Netherlands: Kluwer.

Fine, Gary Alan. 1987. *With the Boys*. Chicago: University of Chicago Press.

Glaser, Clive. 2000. *Bo-Tsotsi: The Youth Gangs of Soweto, 1935–1976*. Portsmouth, N.H.: Heinemann.

Gomez Jara, Francisco, ed. 1987. *Las Bandas en Tiempo de Crisis*. Mexico City: Ediciones Nueva Sociologia.

Hagedorn, John. 1998. *People and Folks*. 2nd ed. Chicago: Lakeview Press.

Hamid, Ansley. 1996. "Resurgence of Drugs/Gangs/Violence in New York City." Unpublished manuscript. New York: John Jay College.

Howell, James C., Arlen Egley Jr., and Debra K. Gleason. 2002. *Modern-Day Youth Gangs*. Youth Gang Series Bulletin. Washington, D.C.: U.S. Department of Justice, Office of Justice Programs, Office of Juvenile Justice and Delinquency Prevention.

Jarrett, Robin. 1994. "Living Poor: Family Life among Single Parent African American Women." *Social Problems* 41: 30–49.

Kersten, Joachim. 2001. "Groups of Violent Young Males in Germany." In *The Eurogang Paradox*, ed. Malcolm Klein, H.-J. Kerner, C. Maxson, and E. G. M. Weitekamp, 247–52. Dordrecht, Netherlands: Kluwer.

Lanctot, Nadine, and Marc LeBlanc. 1997. "Les Adolescentes Membres des Bandes." *Criminologie* 30: 111–30.

Lien, Inger-Lise. 2001. "The Concept of Honor, Conflict, and Violent Behavior among Youths in Oslo." In *The Eurogang Paradox*, ed. Malcolm Klein, H. J. Kerner, C. Maxson, and E. G. M. Weitekamp, 165–74. Dordrecht, Netherlands: Kluwer.

———. 2002. "The Dynamics of Honor in Violence and Cultural Change." Unpublished ms. Oslo, Norway: Norwegian Institute for Urban and Regional Research.

Maher, Lisa. 2000. "Gangs: Cabra Girls (Australia)." In *Encyclopedia of Women and Crime*, ed. Nicole H. Rafter, 86–88. Phoenix, Ariz.: Oryx Press.

Mares, Dennis. 2001. "Gangstas or Lager Louts? Working-Class Street Gangs in Manchester." In *The Eurogang Paradox*, ed. Malcolm Klein, H. J. Kerner, C. Maxson, and E. G. M. Weitekamp. Dordrecht, Netherlands: Kluwer.

Miller, Jody. 2001. *One of the Guys: Girls, Gangs, and Gender*. New York: Oxford University Press.

Miller, Walter. 1973. "The Molls." *Society* 11: 32–33.

Moore, Joan. 1978. *Homeboys*. Philadelphia: Temple University Press.

———. 1991. *Going Down to the Barrio*. Philadelphia: Temple University Press.

———. 1998. "Understanding Street Gangs." In *Cross-Cultural Perspectives on Youth and Violence*, ed. Meredith Watts, 65–78. Stamford, Conn. JAI Press.

Moore, Joan, and John Hagedorn. 2001. *Female Gangs: A Focus on Research*. Washington, D.C.: U.S. Department of Justice, Office of Justice Programs, Office of Juvenile Justice and Delinquency Prevention.

Nimmo, Melanie. 2001. *The "Invisible" Gang Members: A Report on Female Gang Association in Winnipeg*. Ottawa, Canada: Canadian Centre for Policy Alternatives.

Orellana, Marjorie, Barrie Thorne, Anna Chee, and Wan Shun Eva Lam. 2001. "Transnational Childhoods: The Participation of Children in Processes of Family Migration." *Social Problems* 48: 572–92.

OudeBreuil, Brenda. 1997. "Girls Just Wanna Have Fun: Buntogs in Davao-City the Philippines." Utrecht, Netherlands: University of Utrecht.

Parrado, Emilio, and Rene Zenteno. 2001. "Economic Restructuring, Financial Crises, and Women's Work in Mexico." *Social Problems* 48: 456–78.

Roy, Olivier. 2001. "Neo-Fundamentalism." *Items and Issues* 2: 21.

Taylor, Carl. 1993. *Girls, Gangs, Women, and Drugs*. East Lansing: Michigan State University.

Valdez, Avelardo, and Alice Cepeda. 1998. "Homegirls, Chicks, and Kicking It: Females Associated with Mexican American Gangs." Unpublished paper. San Antonio: University of Texas.

Valdez, Avelardo, and S. J. Stifaneck. 2002. "Getting High and Getting By: Dimensions of Drug Selling and Dealing among Mexican American Male Gang Members in South Texas." Unpublished paper. Houston, Tex.: University of Houston.

Valenzuela Arce, Jose Manuel. 1984. "A La Brava Ese: Cholo y Que." Tijuana, Mexico: Centro de Estudios Fronterizos del Norte de Mexico.

Venkatesh, Sudhir. 1998. "Gender and Outlaw Capitalism." *Signs* 23: 683–709.

Vigil, James Diego. 1988. *Barrio Gangs*. Austin: University of Texas Press.

———. 2002. *A Rainbow of Gangs*. Austin: University of Texas Press.

Wallace, Scott. 2000. "You Must Go Home Again: Deported Gangbangers Take Over El Salvador." *Harpers Magazine* (August): 47–56.

Wilson, William J. 1987. *The Truly Disadvantaged*. Chicago: University of Chicago Press.

# 8

# Youth Groupings, Identity, and the Political Context: On the Significance of Extremist Youth Groupings in Unified Germany

## JOACHIM KERSTEN

In previous work I have concentrated on the phenomenology of youth groupings, cliques, and juvenile gangs in a comparative perspective and with a focus on gender aspects (Kersten 1993a, 1993b, 1998, 2000a, 2000b, 2002a, 2002b). While this has remained a priority in my research, teaching university courses abroad during the last ten years (Melbourne and Tokyo 1991–92, Sydney 1998, Chicago 1999–2001) has taught me something about the significance of neo-Nazi and skinhead groupings for the contemporary image of unified Germany. Two years ago after a fireside, an informal lecture, at a Northwestern University student residence, I was asked by a student whether I thought it was safe for her to change planes (to Islamabad) at Frankfurt airport. She thought that skinhead or neo-Nazi groups might attack her because, being a Muslim woman, she wears a head scarf. Non-Germans, particularly family members of people who had to flee from Nazi Germany, have an image of omnipresent Nazi attacks originating from street-corner groups. Although this image grows from media coverage of individual events of hate crimes that occurred in unified Germany after 1990, it is, additionally, connected to a deeper fear of a German capacity for brutality and violence. In 1991, a picture showing German skinheads, their faces expressing hate and anger, as they threatened people of Asian origin in a train compartment went around the newspapers of the world. I saw it on the front page of a Tokyo newspaper, and I was shocked and embarrassed.

Since unification, German and international media have used the image of Nazi skinheads as a reminder, an indicator of the country's atrocious past.

Although right-wing youth groupings are a marginal feature in the gamut of contemporary German youth styles and subcultures, probably comprising not more than 1 percent of the population (Wetzstein, Erbeldinger, and Eckert 2002), their image is a powerful representation of an aspect of Germany's political identity. Accordingly, one thing I will try to do is to describe the scope of youth participation in present German right-wing extremism. The discussion also deals with the position of right-wing youth groupings in the network of right-wing associations and political parties: the wider organizational context of Germany's extreme right. Furthermore, I am interested in the image of skinheads and right-wing groupings as a symbol for national identity. How can a minuscule proportion of youths displaying nationalistic symbols ("proud to be German") become a symbol of the whole nation? As an analogy, quite a number of Germans who have not visited the United States and cities like New York, Chicago, or Los Angeles believe that street gangs of black or Latino youths roam the streets and rob tourists at random. For them, U.S. cities go with an image of ubiquitous gang criminality. To investigate the political heritage and the *quality* of images of gangs or youth groupings and their long-term political significance can be a meaningful exercise of de-demonization of youth and crime phenomena.

Over the last decade, countless waves of quantitative research, mostly surveys of German secondary school students, have indicated a varying degree of identification with extremist issues, xenophobia, and anti-Semitic attitudes. Similar to right-wing voting preferences, such survey data tell us next to nothing about the origin, the significance, and the dynamics of the problem. For a deeper understanding of the problem, it is necessary to differentiate between *attitudes, organizations,* and *displays* of extremist behavior: who takes part in which activities and at which times. What is the criminological nature of right-wing violence? Can we discriminate different focal concerns in the diverse groupings and organizations that form the right-wing network? What were the historical developments in Germany's eastern and western part that led to the unexpected visibility of a nationalistic and parochial lifestyle after unification? Finally, what are the reactions of state and society, and are they likely to come to grips with the problem?

## The Criminological Perspective

The total right-wing extremist membership is estimated at 51,400 persons (Office for the Protection of the Constitution 2001), which amounts to 0.06 percent of Germany's population. Nearly ten thousand German right-wing extremists have violent orientations or propagate direct violence against "others." Skinheads represent 85 percent of violence-prone right-wing extremists, and about 5,000 of those live in the former East. They are the force behind what is termed the "hegemonic status of the extreme right" (*alltagskulturelle Dominanz der Rechten*): a local but very visible dominant position of right-wing emblems, attitudes, and opinions in everyday life culture.

It is a criminological rule that police statistics should be handled with suspicion (Holzberger 2001, 28ff; Rammelsberger 2002). In the absence of German victim survey data, little is known about the size of unreported racist crime and intimidation. In Germany, where police and the criminal justice system have traditionally been accused of turning a blind eye to the violence of right-wing extremists (while hunting down leftists), counting has become more accurate given the attention right-wing violence and propaganda have gained in this country.

In the year 2000, according to official data presented by the Office for the Protection of the Constitution (Bundesverfassungsschutz 2001), there were about 16,000 right-wing criminal offenses out of which nearly 1,000 or 6.3 percent were registered as violent crimes. Approximately 3,500 were of a xenophobic nature. Two-thirds of the offenses were Propagandastraftaten, literally propaganda offenses, a term that relates to displays of prohibited Nazi emblems (swastika, SS signs, Hitlergruss, that is, raised arm and so forth). More than three hundred offenses were reported threats/intimidation of a criminal quality. Estimates of the total number of hate crime homicide victims in the twelve years since unification differ between 38 (criminal justice system data) and 117 according to German media. In the year 2000, hands-on criminal violence included two homicides. One victim was a migrant from Mozambique, the other a homeless person. In the same year, there were fifteen counts of attempted homicide; nearly nine hundred cases of assault, out of which twenty-nine were anti-Semitic (2001, 18); fifty-six cases of desecration of Jewish cemeteries (2001, 30); forty-one cases of arson, and seven cases of detonating explosives. Half of the criminal violence was committed in the former East. This means the eastern states are definitely overrepresented in hate crime activity because the New Länder constitute just above 20 percent of the total German population. Furthermore, the East German regions have comparatively low proportions of migrant population (between 1.2 percent and 2.5 percent). Cities like Hamburg or Stuttgart have 15 percent to 20 percent migrant residents and their families. The prevalence of right-wing phenomena including violent orientations and actual offenses is dramatically higher in the region that used to be the East German state GDR (German

Democratic Republic). Additionally, in the East and among young people, anti-Semitic attitudes have become more pronounced (Bundesamt für Verfassungsschutz 2002, 4).

Most frequently, right-wing crimes, that is, xenophobic or racist assaults and anti-Semitic acts, have been carried out by groups of young males. The most obvious common denominator for male-dominated youth groups is their "action." Activities that cause harm to others or damage to public property can be understood as an "accomplishment of gender" in the terms of Robert W. Connell (1995) and James Messerschmidt (1993). This is as much true for groups of right-wing youths as it is for multiethnic cliques of young males from migrant family backgrounds. It is the behavior nearly exclusively of young males toward a situational claim of hegemonic masculinity, that is, displays of territorial protection or the protection of "native" females, of German or ethnic pride and honor. This can be combined with displays of risk behavior, an aggressive "front" frequently involving assaults on "others." Connell's book *Masculinities* provides a number of illustrations for the meaning of "front" and displays of risk-seeking behavior for young males. Young men, although representatives of the dominant sex, can take little advantage of the "dividend of patriarchy." They frequently lack the resources to become marriageable or even a "family man." They have no regular income and very little when it comes to status. So they are left with their aggressive idea of "honor" and "pride" and their displays of risk seeking, for example, confrontations staged in public with peer or even neighborhood audiences. A down-and-out status is transformed into that of a rebellious hero, a man who earns respect and is feared because of his "front" and his "action."

Such displays of risk seeking could be described as "protest masculinity" (Alfred Adler). Becoming a good boy by being a bad boy was, according to Talcott Parsons, once the destiny of working-class boys. With the demise of the working class and working-class culture, the factory no longer guarantees a venue for learning of masculine discipline. The factory scenario that formed the lifeworld of white lower-class males has almost disappeared. The culture of rewards after a hard day's work in the mill has remained: a culture of beer, mateship, and football coupled with misogyny, homo- and xenophobia. For many skinheads, including those "not interested in politics," the working-class mythology of the nineteenth and early twentieth century is still alive but just the pub version without the class discipline of the mill. The latter has been replaced by displays of authoritarianism and nationalism, partly in a rebellious form. In particular, young men from East Germany, the former state socialist system ("workers' paradise"), are presently destined for at best tertiary-sector jobs. This is work with a feminine image, which these young men deeply detest and find unmanly, and which fuels their hate and their aggression. Their belief in violence as the most formidable means of protection, fighting, and honor, is not completely outdated. It makes sense in their lifeworlds as it obviously does among world leaders in their wars against international terrorism and "rogue" governments.

## The Political Impact

Since German unification, outbreaks of hate crimes perpetrated by groups of youths have been interpreted as the reemergence of Germany's ugly fascist and militaristic face. This has raised fears about the country's political stability. While a neutral stance allows for a less pessimistic assessment of unified Germany's political state of affairs (Turner 1999), the debate inside the country has been anything but self-assured. The 1992 pogroms of Hoyerswerda and Rostock-Lichtenhagen (East Germany) followed by fire bomb attacks on buildings housing German citizens of Turkish origin in the cities of Solingen and Moelln (West Germany) have confronted Germans and their neighbors in Europe and overseas with Germany's history of racist violence. In the early 1990s, hate crimes associated with displays of right-wing extremism have been met with different responses. Police and the criminal justice system of the New Länder have been accused of underestimating the danger and also that they have treated the perpetrators too mildly. Meanwhile Germans in the West organized candlelight marches, and since 1993 the federal government, then still in Bonn, poured millions of deutschmarks into an Anti-Aggression Youth Program that was meant to curb violence and xenophobic "action." At the turn of the millennium, most experts agree that neither the candlelight processions of the "Good Germans" nor the social work programs dealing with youth groupings, mainly in the former East but also in the old Länder, have managed to eradicate occasional extremist violence and hate crimes. Some argue that social work projects have actually been instrumental in creating networks of extremists like right-wing "groups of comrades" (*Kameradschaften*) and other subcultural groupings in the New Länder. While most researchers and critics agree on the very limited territorial scope of "ethnically cleansed regions" (National befreite Zonen), the mere existence and the communication of the concept as such is difficult to stomach for most citizens of unified Germany. Right-wing skinheads, neo-Nazis, and other symbols of the fascist past are rarely conceived as an ugly but *only partial* reality of Germany's political life and culture as would certainly be the case with British or Belgian racists, Polish, Czech, or other Eastern European Nazi skins. In unified Germany however, symbols of the fascist past still function as a "marker" of a German Nazi master status: Germany's past remains the antithesis of civilized society and the idea of its potential reemergence feeds the fear and the disgust of civilized people in Germany and elsewhere.

On each and every occasion, members of Germany's "National Resistance Movement" (Nationale Widerstandsbewegung) have succeeded in organizing protest demonstrations (roughly fifty times per year), there is nationwide evening news coverage of young men with skinhead or Nazi clothing, Doc Martens boots and black pilot blousons. They are shown marching through the streets, their faces full of hate and screaming their favorite slogans: "Wir sind der nationale Widerstand" ("We are the national resistance") or "Ausländer raus!" ("Foreigners out!"). Generally, media use skinheads and young

*Figure 8.1.* Total Right-Wing Membership Estimate: 50,900 in 144 Organizations (OPC)

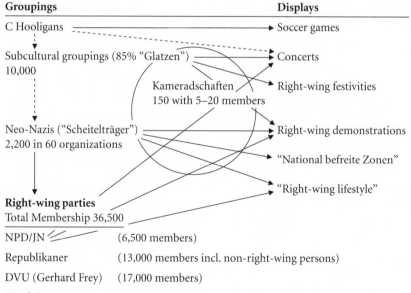

**Groupings**            **Displays**

C Hooligans → Soccer games

Subcultural groupings (85% "Glatzen") → Concerts
10,000

Kameradschaften → Right-wing festivities
150 with 5–20 members

Neo-Nazis ("Scheitelträger") → Right-wing demonstrations
2,200 in 60 organizations

"National befreite Zonen"

"Right-wing lifestyle"

**Right-wing parties**
Total Membership 36,500

NPD/JN     (6,500 members)

Republikaner     (13,000 members incl. non-right-wing persons)

DVU (Gerhard Frey)     (17,000 members)

**Focal Concerns**

"Action": Hools, Skins

Visibility: R-W Parties, Skins, Neo-Nazi/Kameradschaften

Territory: Neo-Nazi/Kameradschaften, "Nationalgesinnte" youth groupings

Organization: R-W Parties, Neo-Nazis

neo-Nazis as a marker for the right-wing movement. Since the early 1990s, national and international media coverage uses a specific clothing style, particularly boots and shaved heads to signify the rise of Germany's right-wing problem. The image has become consensus-based in that it locates the roots of extremism not at all in the societal mainstream but in an extremely identifiable subculture.

Right-wing skinhead groups are a problem for society and the criminal justice system, but they constitute neither the origin nor the organizational core of Germany's new xenophobia, racism, and anti-Semitism. The chart in figure 8.1 is split into "groupings" and "displays" to indicate the differences and the similarities between subcultural groupings, party organizations, and the less organized associations of groups of comrades (*Kameradschaften*) somewhere in between. In order to explain the related violence, a third dimension needs to be added which would include the *situational factors,* circumstances that are often instrumental for outbreaks of violence. The situational aspects will be dealt with in the case studies of recent xenophobic violence at the end of this essay. In the chart, the groupings are vertically ordered into a hierarchy of their political significance, and in a less systematic fashion, the same applies to the vertical order of the "display" column. The further down the chart, the more serious is the impact.

## Soccer Hooligans

Right-wing affiliation can be observed with some of Germany's more violence-prone soccer fans. On the whole, they are not interested in politics. However, violent groupings on the political right and soccer have frequently formed a nexus in German politics. Big-money soccer games and soccer club loyalty can be understood as the smallest common denominators of groupings with a nationalistic orientation. One of the more infamous songs by the former skinhead band Böhse Onkelz (misspelled Mean Uncles) was called "Türken raus!" ("Turks Out"). This song was frequently chanted in German soccer arenas. The game of soccer is certainly not the cause for racism, nationalism, and masculinist hysteria, but it serves as a perfect public stage for such sentiments while the actors remain anonymous in the mass of screaming and shouting fans. In a marked contrast to American or Australian football or rugby, soccer has an extremely territorial logic without the scoring possibilities of other ball games. It is penetration (of the enemy's goal) or nothing. Soccer, more than other ball games, resembles and goes along well with nationalistic warfare, and therefore, at least in the European context, frequently serves as a scenario for the amplification of regionalism, nationalism, and racism. While most skinheads are attracted to soccer, only some hooligans flock to right-wing rock concerts. The Federal Republic's C-hooligans ("C" being a criminal justice marker for soccer fans who are registered for multiple assaults) number about 3,000.

## Subcultural Groupings

Other subcultural groupings that are definitely right wing have an estimated ten thousand members, 85 percent of which are right-wing skinheads. At least for the New Länder, the traditional claim of youth and subculture theorists that the skinhead cult is basically "apolitical" (not interested in politics) or outspokenly nonpolitical is misleading. The majority of East Germany's Glatzen (bald heads) may not be politically organized, but they are definitely nationalgesinnt (nationalistically minded) and willing to carry this sentiment to the streets and to protest demonstrations. West German skinhead affiliations can be more heterogeneous. "Left of the 'Oi'" faction skins ("Oi" is the war cry of skinheads during concerts and get-togethers), there is a minority component of SHARP skinheads (Skinheads against Racist Prejudice), or even Redskins who, instead of the rightists' affection for Hitler and Hess, want to keep the memory of Joseph Stalin alive. The minuscule SHARP faction, Redskins, and Gayskins are by far no match for the postunification proliferation of Nazi skins or "boneheads" as they are called by the non-Nazis.

Skinheads are soccer fans but even more interested in right-wing rock concerts or festivities, most prominently "Rudolf Hess days," Hitler's birthday parties, or BBQs at summer solstice, which is believed to be a traditional Germanic custom. Nationalgesinnte skinheads join right-wing demonstrations, mainly organized by the NPD (National Democratic Party of Germany).

## Kameradschaften

Skinheads also join Kameradschaften, the loosely knit regional right-wing amalgamations of neo-Nazis: NPD/JN (Junge Nationaldemokraten, that is, Youth Organization of NPD) members, Nationalgesinnte, and otherwise dissatisfied young males. The latest federal estimate counted 150 of these associations in the whole of Germany, with five to twenty members each. Neo-Nazi membership is estimated at 2,200 in sixty organizations, and while many of them become members of the NPD/JN they also join the right-wing fraternities of Kameradschaften. The latter, skinheads and other extremists, communicate via electronic channels, cell phones, and the Internet. Their main incentive is visibility at protest marches, for example, the demonstrations against Wehrmachtsausstellung (exhibition of documents about the war crimes of the Hitler Army) when about 5,000 of them paraded through Munich, the former capital of the Nazi movement (Hauptstadt der Bewegung).

Kameradschaften perceive themselves as the base of the National Resistance Movement. In principle, their organizational setup is quite similar to that of the Leninist revolutionary cells in Tsarist Russia and during the civil war. These right-wing cells in Germany are the authors of calls for ethnic cleansing (National befreite Zonen), although the term was coined by the rightist intelligentsia, namely Nationaldemokratischer Hochschulbund, the student organization of NPD. While in terms of regional distribution and latitude such "zones" are rare and minuscule—very often just a street corner or a children's playground—this right-wing idea has gotten widespread attention. As is the case with a number of extremist phenomena, media reporting and publicized academic disapproval have helped to spread the term through the entire republic. The more the rhetoric of East German politicians and criminal justice representatives has denied the existence of such ethnic cleansing, the more "Good Germans" feel obliged to publicly proclaim their sincere worries about this virtually nonexistent problem. The term "National befreite Zone" has become the linguistic equivalent of the visual image of the violent right-wing skinhead. Both constructs, the "zones" and the skinheads, have little value for an actual analysis of present right-wing strategy and activities. Nonetheless, they rarely fail to serve as a device for the mental hygiene of morally outraged Germans.

While the "zones" are hard to find, a "right-wing lifestyle," that is, a professed belief in parochialism and open celebrations of nationalism and xenophobia, are much more visible aspects of the present German situation, particularly in the former GDR. Postwar developments in both parts of Germany have led to the emergence of right-wing sentiments and have fostered a respective lifestyle.

### Right-Wing Parties (NPD, Republikaner, DVU)

The total right-wing party membership amounts to 37,000, out of which most persons belong to Gerhard Frey's German People's Union (Deutsche Volksunion, or DVU). Frey is a wealthy Munich-based publisher (with family ties to the well-known Bavarian fashion outfitter Loden-Frey) of right-wing books and journals, most prominently of the oldest extremist and anti-Semitic weekly *National- und Soldatenzeitung,* a prominent mouthpiece of revisionism and the most acerbic nationalistic and xenophobic journalism in Germany. Despite its financial strength, DVU is basically a one-man enterprise. The main strength of DVU is professional campaigning that appeals to populist and xenophobic sentiments. While during federal elections none of the three right-wing extremist parties have scored much above the 1–2 percent margin, these parties have scored occasional successes during Länder parliament elections, the DVU particularly in Sachsen-Anhalt where they managed to receive 13 percent of the votes. However, after the election's spectacular outcome, DVU had no local party representatives that could be presented to the media. Dr. Frey had to be called in Munich to decide about policy and personnel.

While Frey and his DVU have been identified with an openly racist and anti-Semitic agenda, the Republikaner party is a more moderate vehicle of the right-wing movement. Not all members foster extremist views. Many Republikaner members and voters are a segment of political protest, dissatisfied with the mainstream parties, migration politics, and unemployment, analogous to Jörg Haider's Freedom Party in Austria. But in addition to populist sentiments, there are segments of more explicit extremism as well. Accordingly, members of the Republikaner cannot serve as public servants in Germany, for example, as members of the police force. NPD, although the smallest membership of all German parties on the extreme right, is perceived as the most significant threat to German democracy. Between the 1960s and the 1980s, NPD served as an organization for old and middle-aged Nazis. In the 1990s, the party has succeeded in attracting a new clientele that is not only much younger but also much more willing to use violence than the old Nazi network. The new party platform includes ecological and anti-globalism/-capitalism issues, as well as a less explicit racism (rather a theory of cultural apartheid) and a definite rejection of the politics of European unification. After serving a prison sentence of nearly twenty years, Horst Mahler, a lawyer and former Red Army faction terrorist trained in a Palestine camp, presents himself as the anchorman of right-wing intellectualism. NPD chairman Udo Voigt, a former army officer, remains the spokesman for the proletarian NPD electorate and the party's skinhead and young neo-Nazi supporters. NPD has definitely stressed the "street-fighting" component of its long-term strategy, and this is exactly the feature of NPD that has attracted young people, skinheads, and neo-Nazis to this organization. During such "street campaigns," NPD supporters and youths have had extremely violent clashes with antifascist protesters and also with riot police. Since the German Ministry of Interior Affairs has taken legal action against the German division of "Blood and Honour," a UK-based racist and anti-Semitic skinhead music agency founded by Ian Stuart Donaldson, right-wing rock music festivals that used to be organized by Blood and Honour are now put together by NPD/JN organizations. As music, much more than rhetoric or printed material, carries extremist sentiments and fosters "Gemeinschaftsgefühl," the very much sought-after feeling of common belonging, the NPD's new musical efforts are seen as an obvious recruitment vehicle.

## Focal Concerns of Right-Wing Groupings/Political Parties

Hooligans and skinheads are action-oriented young males with a masculinist orientation towards risk-taking behavior. Skinheads express few strategic goals and a superficial ideology of ethnic or racial superiority. Visibility, particularly media representation, is a common aim of extremist parties, skinheads, and neo-Nazi Kameradschaften as well. The latter together with youths leaning towards nationalistic orientations make efforts to claim territory similar to U.S. street gangs and minority neighborhood cliques in most postindustrial societies. Only the Nazis, the extremists, and their parties share a concern toward organizational structures.

## The Failure of Mainstream Theorizing

There have been numerous attempts to explain the reemergence of right-wing extremism after unification and the East German skinhead and hate crime problem. Theories have fluctuated between traditional macro and micro approaches. Most prominent among the macro is desintegration (in English, "disintegration") theory, which sees globalization and the forces of modernity in a critical neo-Marxist light. Although the "desintegration" concept is somewhat similar to the "disorganization" theory, its adherents are probably not aware of this heritage. "Bielefeld School" theory (not to be confused with Bielefeld University historians around H.-U. Wehler) consists of a vulgarized Marxist vein of blaming unemployment and globalization as a causal factor for youth violence. Bielefeld research was about the only study that had been published on the subject (based on primarily anecdotal material) just before unification and in its immediate aftermath. To the astonishment of some sociologists and criminologists, the 900–page volume of the first Bielefeld study of right-wing extremism (Bielefelder Rechtsextremismus Studie) did not even bother to mention gender as a factor. While the theory has been proven inaccurate from a number of angles and in a series of empirical studies, the so-called desintegration theory has remained the most frequently quoted explanatory model when youth violence in general and more specifically right-wing youth violence are under scrutiny (for a critique, see Liell 2002). In the meantime, researchers have started to use more complex causal models.

Among micro explanations, a vulgarized version of Horkheimer and Adorno's conceptual framework of the "Authoritarian Personality" has been used to specifically explain the East German side of the problem. The authoritarian structure of East German society, early childhood separation of children from their mothers, and in its latest version "potty training" methods served as an explanatory vehicle (with a very limited range). "Potty theory" (GDR children were allegedly forced to collective potty sessions in child care) goes back to Columbia University's cultural anthropology research in the 1940s that attempted to explain Japanese violence during the Pacific War and in U.S. prisoner of war camps. Ruth Benedict took an immediate dislike to the mixture of cultural theory and crude psychoanalysis promoted by her student Margaret Mead and British researcher Geoffrey Gorer. After the end of the war, empirical studies failed to prove that Japanese babies were exposed to premature toilet training, but ever since Margaret Mead's invention of "potty theory" has been used to explain a collective brutality in an "us" versus "them" dichotomy (Geertz 1988).

The most dramatic problems of the micro/macro approaches in the "desintegration" and "authoritarian personality" paradigms is their practical uselessness, their failure to differentiate, and their gender blindness. Authoritarian attitudes, violent, xenophobic, right-wing extremist orientations, and support for violence on the one hand are different, particularly in their consequences for victims, from actual acts of hands-on violence, arson, or pogrom-like riots. Both theories fail to account for situational factors, context, and very obvious gender orientations in what has become visible as Germany's postunification hate crimes against people of different color of skin or ethnic background, but also against homosexuals, homeless, or challenged persons.

## What Ought to Be Considered When We Look at the East German Youth Violence Problem

Anti-Semitism and xenophobia are related orientations of dissatisfied citizens. Nationalism and German patriotism have always been linked to chauvinism, xenophobia, racism, and anti-Semitism. The idea of the German nation and German national pride ("Ich bin stolz Deutscher zu sein!") reappeared after 1989 and spread from a subcultural right-wing margin into the mainstream. An increased revisionism, rhetoric of denial, and historical falsification ("denial boom") have spread from rightist intellectuals into the current of a wider rightist system of beliefs. There are decisive differences in East-West anti-Semitic attitudes. The GDR fostered an ideology of antifascism that eradicated (or suppressed) dissenting prejudices and worldviews. The reference points of GDR society were antifascism, resistance to the Nazis, and the idea of a socialist new start after the war. Jews and the Holocaust had no significance in GDR historiography of the Nazi past, and at least from the late 1960s onwards the GDR antifascist habitus never gained any of the characteristics of laying to rest the ghosts of the past (Vergangenheitsbewältigung) that occurred in West Germany.

*Table 8.1.* Right-Wing Elements in Postwar Germany

|  | West FRG | East GDR | Political Climate |
|---|---|---|---|
| 1950s and 1960s | *Anticommunism/re-Nazification* (reintegration of Nazis into elites), followed by '68 rebellion (antitotalitarianism?); victim status  (divided, threatened by USSR & GDR communism) | *State-socialist Stalinist dictatorship;* official antifascist ideology defined by "freedom from guilt"; at the same time victim status (lost the war, reparations, no freedom, violent repression of '53 rebellion and opposition movements) | Authoritarianism  Divided nation |
| 1970s and 1980s | *Democratic welfare state (pluralistic?)*; 1970–80s widespread anti-Nazi education;  marginal right-wing groupings/skinheads and secondary anti-Semitism(?); successful and "good" West Germans as identity but continuation of victim status because of divided Germany; ambivalence about status as migration society (pluralism) | *Split psychosocial economy* in the 1980s; growing skepticism and hooliganism among GDR youths; formation of subcultural soccer, punk, and skinhead groupings; increased victimization through wall, border, Stasi secret police; prevalence of "public private sphere" (Kupferberg); climate of institutionalized parochialism | "Private public sphere" in the East  "Good Germans" in the West |
| Post-1990 | End of victim-status; no longer divided from brothers/sisters; reemergence of right-wing youth and organizations; reemergence of the burden of the past: Historikerstreit; Goldhagen, Wehrmachtsausstellung, Nationalstolz Debatte | Continued victimization because of second-class-citizen status; colonialism of the West; loss of "GDR" culture and social networks; visibility of Nationalgesinnte youth groupings and right-wing lifestyle; nationalism/ parochialism (?) | Crises of postwar identity; expectations of new (fear of old) German national identity; increased ambivalence about status as migration society |

Bergmann (1997) terms the GDR attitude (in relation to the Holocaust) "freedom from guilt." His is a helpful metaphor to explain why the outbreak of anti-Semitism and xenophobic hate crimes occurred after unification and also why the targets of hate seemed so arbitrary. In West Germany until the late 1960s, postwar de-Nazification was followed by wholesale re-Nazification of the judiciary, the police and health service, and, most prominently, academia. Only after the student rebellion of the late 1960s and the resulting changes in the public mind, did Auschwitz become a topic of education, politics, and a forming West German identity.

Right-wing ideology transfer from the West to the East increased perceived legitimacy for violence and tolerance in East Germany, and this transfer of legitimacy for orientations and actions was fed through the German asylum debate (Asyldebatte) with media campaigns including respected media like *Der Spiegel* in the early and mid 1990s. There was an obvious hate crime activist transfer during "Rudolf Hess" days, Hitler's birthday parties, and demonstrations against Wehrmachtsausstellung.

At the time of transition and in the absence of formal and informal social control mechanisms, agencies, and routines, existing taboos in the GDR (anti-Semitism as part of fascism, for example) were no longer enforced. Anomie resulting from the social control chaos coincided with a gender specific crisis of hegemony (political elite, police, army) and a high level of perceived threat (loss of jobs, competition with West Germans, migrants). A peak of secondary anti-Semitism (in the absence of Jewish people) substituted "others" as the objects of hate and dehumanization. Ausländer ("foreigner," often referring to people of Turkish origin, or in East Germany, people of African or Asian background) became the functional equivalent of what traditionally used to be the Jew.

## Subcultural/Lifestyle Factors Reconsidered: The Hate of Skinheads (Glatzenhass)

It has been pointed out by Watts and others that skinheads can be best understood as a mediated subculture of "anti-authoritarian authoritarianism." At the same time, they serve as an irresistible symbol of rebellion. Nazi skinheads are the antithesis of what served as the good postwar (and postunification) German identity. As an example of the "semi-isolation of other specialized symbolic environments" (Watts 1997, 162), extremist subcultures gain visibility in musical culture and everyday lifestyle. However, skinhead style romanticizes and promotes violence. The popularity of skinhead style (Watts has termed this the "romantic rebel image") serves as a means of general identification among youths who have claimed victim status for themselves that legitimizes aggression and dehumanization of "others." While the style as such is perceived as basically apolitical and more closely related to rebellion and self-assertion than to explicit political content, which explains the leniency of the immediate post-1990 criminal justice reactions, the result of skinhead xenophobia and hate crimes for postunification Germany can hardly be termed apolitical.

Skinhead popularity (and resentment) is a mediated effect, and the main motor of identification with a right-wing lifestyle remains imitation, not a rational discourse. Among skinheads, the leitmotif is an identification with an idea of an "Aryan" masculinist working-class culture of the past. It has been observed that stylistic epiphenomena tend not to result directly from structural factors. Although the disappearance of the material basis of a white working men's cult is a structural factor, structural factors like unemployment do not determine whether right-wing lifestyle elements become acceptable or even attractive. Identification with aggressive skinhead style and masculinist attitudes (posturing, symbolic violence, actual fights) are associated with an acceptance of violent means. This in turn makes such youths and their Kameradschaften a "natural ally" of ideological groups on the extreme right (Watts 1997, 154). The fact remains: skinheads are not an organizational phenomenon.

The predominant characteristics of a political climate that engenders a right-wing lifestyle in Germany today can be identified as resentment, a diffuse sense of threat, and hostility. This is also true for ghetto youth groups and gangs and would provide an ample fundament for comparative research. In Germany, for obvious historical reasons all of these sentiments are more prevalent in the former East, but with unemployment at an all-time peak and an unsolved migration problem, similar feelings can be measured in the West. However, in both parts of Germany and in a marked difference to 1933, there is no coherent ideology. Parties on the extreme right serve as symbolic reference groups but not as a primary form of extremist association. The primary forms of association at present are neo-Nazi and skinhead Kameradschaften with high mobility and a high potential for mobilization (through Internet, mobile phones, and so forth). The most likely offenders are male youths aged under twenty-one with a very limited association with the right-wing scene or parties, and not gangs of adult unemployed SA troopers like in the late 1920s. Manifest violent behavior is greatly dependent on situational circumstances, but it is spreading and radicalized within a subpopulation. In other words, political racism in unified Germany is put into action by rebellious elements of a marginal part of the youth culture. In this climate, the political parties have gained symbolic impact, and they have changed their agenda and content compared to the 1960s through 1980s. The politico-cultural environment has to be understood as the demand side of the opportunity structure; aggressive youth styles represent the supply side of the outbreak of fascist-like xenophobic violence.

## Situational Factors

A qualitative study in 2001 (Mackert 2001) looked at reported cases of right-wing (xenophobic/anti-Semitic) hate crimes in the city of Karlsruhe in the southwest of Germany using prosecutors' files. There were fifteen cases out of which eight constituted offenses of aggravated assault. Nine cases could be classified as xenophobic acts. However, in a significant number of cases, situational factors initiated the outbreak of hands-on violence. Four of the cases could be classified as everyday-life conflicts. Initially, the altercation did not start as a xenophobic act but (as in most public conflicts between young males) over honor and territory. However, since the victim was an Ausländer (person of non-German ethnic background), the offense fell under the category fremdenfeindliche Straftaten (xenophobic offenses). Two-thirds of all cases had more than one offender. Again, as in many cases of violence taking place between young males, group dynamics are an essential factor. Only four cases had a single offender. In summary, spontaneous and group-related factors have to be taken into account as well as the fact that many such incidents take place in public. As such these acts are displays of territoriality and masculinity. The altercations occur in the evening or at night. Alcohol functions as the principal stimulator in most cases; in less than one-third, alcohol plays no role. In a marked difference to the criminological "routine" of interpersonal violence, only one case revealed a previous victim-offender relationship. Usually in crime incidents, violence occurs between people who know each other. Nearly all these altercations originated as verbal conflicts. The escalation into hands-on violence fed on situational circumstances and group dynamics. The initial starting point was trivial or resulted from "en passant" provocation. Eighteen of twenty-two offenders had been registered previously by police. Skinheads as offenders are not only the most aggressive actors; they are also most likely to be multiple offenders. Furthermore, in cases where skinheads are involved as perpetrators, lack of empathy with the victims and lack of regret for their wrongdoing is regularly observed.

The findings from this small sample confirm the need for qualitative analysis of hate crimes committed by young persons in groups. Situational factors, affective factors, and group dynamics have to be investigated more thoroughly to understand this particular type of group/gang violence.

## Outlook

The problem with public, media, and state reactions after 1990 was that there was far too little differentiation. Some criminal justice practitioners saw youth violence, even when directed against minority members or asylum seekers, as a routine feature of juvenile crime and no specific reason to change their traditionally lenient sentencing practice (in comparison to punitive U.S. sentencing). Others, particularly leftist academics, saw Nazi skinheads and hate crimes committed by young rightists as an intolerable attack on what they have defined as the postwar German identity. They tended to insist on harsh reactions by the criminal justice system.

During the last decade, state reactions have become much less lenient. As a result, juvenile prisons in the former GDR are crowded and have occasionally turned into right-wing cadre institutions. It is difficult to prove that harsher sentencing has resulted in less hate crimes being committed.

There is some empirical data to use in policy formation, however. Given the relatively small numbers of hands-on crimes, any causal effects are difficult to prove. Effects that have been demonstrated by research into right-wing criminality were obvious copy-cat crimes after spectacular acts, particularly arson and riots. This was at least indirectly a result of media presentation. Information about the crimes of the Nazis and the suffering of the victims of the Holocaust seems to achieve very little in terms of curbing xenophobic and anti-Semitic acts among group offenders and skinheads.

Because of the country's particular sensitivity about Germany's history and the German guilt issue, the provocative potential of any racist and anti-Semitic symbolism is extremely high and therefore, very attractive for sub-cultural expression. The skinhead lifestyle is confrontational and risk seeking. Violent group action is the most desirable proof of masculinist rebellion, and Nazi emblems remain an ultimate provocation in Germany. There are other indicators that there is not a strong political motivation to skinhead behavior.

Xenophobia and to some extent also hate crimes committed by groups of young males originate more often than not from situational factors. A self-proclaimed victim status, a masculinist orientation, and routines of high alcohol consumption combined with territorial, situational, or "honor" issues are the best proven causes for violent altercations with foreigners or minority members as victims. This was demonstrated above and shown in similar research carried out with much larger samples (for example, Cornel 1999). To prevent such situations from escalating to violence, criminal justice or police are not suitable agencies for addressing the issues. Nonspecific youth work programs designed as antiaggression projects did not result in long-term improvement.

In a smaller number of German Länder, undercover police officers have infiltrated right-wing groupings and Nazi skinhead subcultures. In some cases this may have prevented crime, but on the whole such criminal justice measures are more effective when directed against the organized part of the right-wing network. With subcultural groupings of young males, surveillance is much more difficult to establish.

Exit programs that originated in the Scandinavian countries and that had some success in getting young Nazis out their groups have shown some success in Germany. Such programs have helped particularly to get high-ranking members out of their groups. This could be one reason for the present reduction of right-wing hate crimes.

The most promising activities are community-based networks in cities or regions affected by visible right-wing subcultures that help to restore the self-esteem of citizens and youngsters alike.

## References

Bergmann, Werner. 1997. "Antisemitism and Xenophobia in Germany since Unification." In *Antisemitism and Xenophobia in Germany after Unification,* ed. H. Kurthen, W. Bergmann, and R. Erb, 3–20. New York: Oxford University Press.

Bundesamt für Verfassungsschutz. 2002. *Entwicklungen im Rechtsextremismus—Die Bedeutung des Antisemitismus im aktuellen deutschen Rechtsextremismus.* Cologne: Bundesamt für Verfassungsschutz.

Bundesministerium des Inneren. 2001. *Verfassungsschutzbericht 2000.* Berlin: BMI.

Burke, R., and R. Sunley. 1998. "Post-modernism and Youth Subcultures in Britain in the 1990s." In *Gangs and Youth Subcultures,* ed. Kayleen and Cameron Hazlehurst, 35–65. New Brunswick, N.J.: Transaction.

Connell, Robert W. 1995. *Masculinities.* Cambridge: Polity Press.

Cornel, Heinz. 1999. *Schwere Gewaltkriminalität durch junge Täter in Brandenburg* (research report). Potsdam/Berlin: Camino.

Craig, Gordon A. 1999. *Politics and Culture in Modern Germany.* Palo Alto, Calif.: Society for the Promotion of Science and Scholarship.

Deutsche Shell, ed. 2002. *Jugend 2002–14. Shell Jugendstudie.* Frankfurt am Main: Fischer.

Erb, Rainer. 1997. "Public Responses to Antisemitism and Right-Wing Extremism." In *Antisemitism and Xenophobia in Germany after Unification,* ed. H. Kurthen, W. Bergmann, and R. Erb, 211–23. New York: Oxford University Press.

Farin, Klaus. 2001. *Generation kick.de —Jugendsubkulturen heute.* München: Beck.

Farin, Klaus, ed. 1997. *Die Skins—Mythos und Realität.* Berlin: Ch. Links.

Findeisen, H.-V., and J. Kersten. 1999. *Der Kick und die Ehre—Vom Sinn jugendlicher Gewalt.* München: Kunstmann.

Geertz, Clifford. 1988. *Works and Lives: The Anthropologist as Author.* Cambridge: Polity Press.

Gensicke, Thomas. 2002. "Individualität und Sicherheit in neuer Synthese? Wertorientierung und gesellschaftliche Aktivität." In *Jugend 2002—14. Shell Jugendstudie,* ed. Deutsche Shell, 139–212. Frankfurt: Fischer.

Grunenberg, Antonia. 2001. *Die Lust an der Schuld: Von der Macht der Vergangenheit über die Gegenwart.* Berlin: Rowohlt.

Hazlehurst, Kayleen, and C. Hazlehurst, eds. 1998. *Gangs and Youth Subcultures: International Explorations.* New Brunswick, N.J.: Transaction.

Holzberger, Mark. 2001. "'Offenbarungseid der Polizeistatistiker': Registrierung rechtsextremistischer Straftaten," *Bürgerrechte & Polizei/CILIP* 68, no. 1: 26–35.

Hurrelmann, Klaus, Ruth Linssen, Mathias Albert, and Holger Quellenberg. 2002. "Eine Generation von Egotaktikern? Ergebnisse der bisherigen Jugendforschung." In *Jugend 2002—14. Shell Jugendstudie,* ed. Deutsche Shell, 31–51. Frankfurt: Fischer.

Jarausch, Konrad H., ed. 1997. *After Unity: Reconfiguring German Identities.* Providence, RI: Berghahn Books.

Kaplan, Jeffrey. 1995. "Right-Wing Violence in North America." In *Terror from the Extreme Right,* ed. Tore Bjorgo, 44–95. London: Frank Cass.

Kaplan, Jeffrey, and L. Weinberg. 1998. *The Emergence of a Euro-American Radical Right.* New Brunswick, N.J.: Rutgers University Press.

Kersten, Joachim. 1993a. "Kulturvergleichende Betrachtungen zum Thema: Jugend und Gewalt." *Rechtsradikale Gewalt im vereinigten Deutschland,* ed. Hans-Uwe Otto and Roland Merten, 227–36. Bonn: Bundeszentrale für politische Bildung.

———. 1993b. "Street Youths, *Bosozoku,* and *Yakuza:* Subculture Formation and Societal Reactions in Japan." *Crime and Delinquency* 39, no. 3: 277–95.

———. 1998. "German Youth Subcultures: History, Typology, and Gender Orientation." *Gangs and Youth Subcultures: International Explorations,* ed. K. and C. Hazlehurst. New Brunswick, N.J.: Transaction.

———. 2000a. "Groups of Violent Young Males in Germany." In *The Eurogang Paradox: Street Gangs and Youth Groups in the U.S. and Europe,* ed. Malcolm W. Klein, Hans-Jürgen Kerner, Cheryl L. Maxson, and Elmar G. M. Weitekamp, 247–55. Dordrecht, Netherlands: Kluwer.

———. 2000b. "Rechte Gewalt in Deutschland: 'Dieser Waggon ist nur für Weiße.'" *Psychologie Heute* (October): 46–54.

———. 2002a. "Jugendgewalt und Bilder von Männlichkeiten." In *Jugendgewalt ist männlich—Gewaltbereitschaft von Mädchen und Jungen,* ed. Detlef Gause and Heike Schlottau, 36–52. Hamburg: EBV.

———. 2002b. "Jugendgewalt und Gesellschaft." *Aus Politik und Zeitgeschichte* b44 (November): 14–20. http://www.bpb.de/publikationen/41XNIY,0,0,Jugendgewalt_und_Gesellschaft.html.

Kupferberg, Feiwel. 1999. *The Breakup of Communism in East Germany and Eastern Europe.* New York: St. Martin's Press.

Kurthen, Herrmann. 1997. "Antisemitism and Xenophobia in United Germany: How the Burden of the Past Affects the Present." In *Antisemitism and Xenophobia in Germany after Unification,* ed. H. Kurthen, W. Bergmann, and R. Erb, 21–38. New York: Oxford University Press.

Kurthen, Herrmann, W. Bergmann, and R. Erb, eds. 1997. *Antisemitism and Xenophobia in Germany after Unification.* New York: Oxford University Press.

Liell, Christoph. 2002. "Gewalt in modernen Gesellschaften—zwischen Ausblendung und Dramatisoerung." *Aus Politik und Zeitgeschichte* b44 (November): 6–13. http://www.bpb.de/publikationen/41XNIY,0,0,Jugendgewalt_und_Gesellschaft.html.

Mackert, Thomas. 2001. "Fremdenfeindliche Gewalttaten—Sekundäranalyse." Diplomarbeit zur Erlangung des Grades eines Diplom-Verwaltungswirts. Villingen-Schwenningen: University of Applied Police Sciences.

Maier, Charles S. 1997. *Dissolution: The Crisis of Communism and the End of East Germany.* Princeton, N.J.: Princeton University Press.

McCarthy, Barry. 1994. "Warrior Values: A Socio-Historical Survey." In *Male Violence,* ed. J. Archer, 105–20. London: Routledge.

Merkl, Peter. 1995. "Radical Right Parties in Europe and Anti-foreign Violence: A Comparative Essay." In *Terror from the Extreme Right,* ed. Tore Bjorgo, 96–118. London: Frank Cass.

Merkl, Peter H., ed. 1999. *The Federal Republic of Germany at Fifty: The End of a Century of Turmoil.* New York: New York University Press.

Messerschmidt, James W. 1993. *Masculinities and Crime: Critique and Reconceptualization of Theory.* Lanham, Md.: Rowman and Littlefield.

Parkes, Stuart. 1997. *Understanding Contemporary Germany.* Routledge: London.

Rammelsberger, Annette. 2002. "Anzeichen der Beruhigung bei Neonazis." *Süddeutsche Zeitung* (October 25): 6.

Schoenbaum, David, and E. Pond. 1996. *The German Question and Other German Questions.* New York: St. Martin's Press.

Schubarth, Wilfried. 1997. "Xenophobia among East German Youth." In *Antisemitism and Xenophobia in Germany after Unification,* ed. H. Kurthen, W. Bergmann, and R. Erb, 143–58. New York: Oxford University Press.

Sprinzak, Ehud. 1995. "Right-Wing Terrorism in a Comparative Perspective: The

Case of Split Legitimization." In *Terror from the Extreme Right,* ed. Tore Bjorgo, 17–43. London: Frank Cass.

Turner, Henry Ashby, Jr. 1999. "Germany's Past after Fifty Years of Democracy." In *The Federal Republic of Germany at Fifty,* ed. Peter H. Merkl, 27–32. New York: New York University Press.

Watts, Meredith W. 1997. *Xenophobia in United Germany.* New York: St. Martin's Press.

Wetzel, Juliane. 1997. "Antisemitism among Right-Wing Extremist Groups: Organisations and Parties in Postunification Germany." In *Antisemitism and Xenophobia in Germany after Unification,* ed. H. Kurthen, W. Bergmann, and R. Erb, 159–73. New York: Oxford University Press.

Wetzstein, Thomas, Patricia Erbeldinger, and Roland Eckert. 2002. "Jugendliche in Cliquen." *Neue Kriminalpolitik* 14, no. 4: 147–51.

# 9

# Gangs and Spirituality of Liberation

## LUIS BARRIOS

New religious movements have emerged . . . One approach suggests
that the new religions develop in response to crises in the world economic order and that the type of religious movement varies according
to the location of adherents relative to the bases of economic power.
Another possible interpretation views new movements (in modern
Western societies, at least) as responses to the disintegrating old
bases of moral or political order.

—Meredith B. McGuire, *Religion: The Social Context*


Among the working class, however, which includes many Hispanics
caught in dead-end jobs with little hope of upward mobility, there may
well be a much stronger ethnic identity. These Hispanics take great
pride in their ethnic and religious traditions.

—Wade C. Roof and Christel Manning, "Cultural Conflicts and Identity"


Youth are joining us now not because they want to have a clique and
somebody to defend them, now they got a voice to be heard and
that's what we represent in New York City. A strong Latino voice that
is not muzzled by these sell-out politicians that are Latinos and Black
Americans that sold out the community for years. The Latin Kings
wants to be something that stays in the community,
for the people, by the people, with the people.

—King Tone, Supreme Crown


Within any experience of rejection, exploitation, criminalization,
oppression, or exclusion, and injustices such as racism, ethnocentrism, sexism, xenophobia, heterosexism, or classism, individuals or groups on the
journey to liberation unveil their resistance to the dominant group in different forms and styles. History is full of stories about oppression and exploita-

tion where people's creativity and imagination are underdeveloped in their struggle to change a social reality. In my own historical memory, I can recall three examples: the resistance and struggle for the liberation of the Vietnamese people during the U.S.-Vietnam War, the nationalist self-determination movement of the Cuban revolution against the inhumane and illegal economic and political blockade by the U.S. government, and the Puerto Rican anticolonial and national movement of liberation that has endured for more than a century and continues to organize against the United States.

In this introduction, I want to establish that there is no such thing as complete subordination of the oppressed or complete domination by the oppressor. Maduro states that "any social group on its way to becoming a dominated group adopts a strategy of resistance to dominance—independently of its consciousness and will. For their part, the dominant classes, even in the apparently most stable phase of consolidation of their hegemony, never attain to an absolute control over the collective life. There always remains a certain resistance on the part of the dominated—even if only in the form of silence, confusion, non-cooperation, hysteria, or purely destructive terror" (1982, 75). Our biggest challenge is to discover, from a critical perspective, how a particular group put into practice their forms and/or styles of resistance to the dominant forces. To understand this phenomenon we need to implement a liberating methodology in which we "promote the values of self determination and human diversity" (Fox and Prilleltensky 1997, 34) of those who we want to understand. In other words, we need to find a way to learn from "them."

In this chapter, I will discuss how Latinos and Latinas make use of spirituality of liberation to deconstruct, construct, and reconstruct their collective identity. More specifically, I will discuss how a particular "street gang," the Almighty Latin King/Queen Nation (ALKQN) in New York City, in the process of becoming a social movement, used this spirituality of liberation as a psycho-social force to search for and preserve their collective identity at the same time that they struggled to resist forces of oppression, rejection, and marginalization.

It should be clear that my approach to the issue of "gangs" is not in the mainstream but rather emerges from an orientation that I call critical self-reflection. This perspective is informed not only by my training as a social scientist but by my practice and experience as an Episcopal priest exposed to liberation theology. My biography helps to explain my interest in this neglected area of street life and the sources of analytical inspiration outside of the legitimate knowledge found in most criminological texts. However, before proceeding with this discussion, several issues deserve clarification.

In this discussion I wish to clarify an understanding of our contemporary society as one that is shaped by the ideology and the structures of globalization, neoliberalism, corporate capitalism, imperialism, and militarism. It is a society where spirituality has been both misappropriated and misinterpreted by most of our religious organizations and leaders. I agree with Paloutzian, who states,

> because of religious motivation, both conservative and revolutionary events have occurred. This is true in both the personal and social sense. Religion may represent a profound revolution in the life of the individual. It may also motivate people toward social revolution—social revolution either in the sense of effecting change in some facet of society such as church function, health care, or race relations; or in the sense of changing the entire social structure. On the other hand, religious motivation can stimulate people to maintain the status quo and hold onto existing forms and consequently resist change. In either case, religious influences on behavior can be potent. (1996, 3)

First, it is common for the terms *religion* and *spirituality* to be used interchangeably by people most of the time. Some people believe that to be spiritual you need to be a religious person, an approach to spirituality with which I have serious difficulties. It is my understanding that spirituality is not unique to religion or to those who believe in God, but rather it an intrinsic component of all human beings whether they believe in God or not (Barrios 1998, 2000, 2004). However, in this chapter I claim that for some people, or groups like the ALKQN—a group that maintains that they are a religion—spirituality becomes a form of religious motivation. This forces us to face the reality that spirituality, either for oppression or liberation, always has political and social dimensions. Two basic questions arise: what do they mean by spirituality, and is this spirituality maintaining or changing the existing sociopolitical and economic disorder?

Because a spirituality of oppression is shaped by the ideology of submission, obedience, and steadiness, it creates in people and/or groups a "false consciousness" about our social, political, and economic reality. In the process of resisting and deconstructing this false reality, a spirituality of liberation functions as a force raising consciousness, organizing and then mobilizing people to fight and change those injustices that they are facing. For this reason, there is always a need to build the course of action of repoliticizing and resocialicizing our spirituality in a way that the experience empowers us to see the outcome of liberation.[1]

Second, a spirituality of liberation, as a religious motivation with its social and political dimensions, has been consciously or unconsciously ignored, misjudged, and/or underestimated, by "gang" researchers. In *The Almighty Latin King and Queen Nation,* Brotherton and Barrios (2004) claim that the ALKQN resistance activities in New York City need to be analyzed from a social movement perspective. For years the ALKQN have claimed that "Kingism is a religion." We need to ask how people come together and create organizations or movements that, instead of adopting a passive or neutral attitude similar to a spirituality of oppression, oppose and resist any injustice in ways similar to a spirituality of liberation (Barrios 1998, 2000, 2004; Casaldáliga and Vigil 1994). In trying to answer the question of how religion becomes a force for social movement activism, Mirola states that "early sociological research on religion and social change typically argued either that religion was a conservative force for social change order or, in light of the civil rights protests on the 1950s and 1960s, that religion was a force for social change" (2001, 399–400). Mirola continues, "Only in the last two decades have scholars shifted away from an 'either/or' approach to the relationship between religion and social change. Instead, a 'both/and' has emerged that sees religion's potential to both mobilize social activism and resist social change." The question that emerges in this new approach, according to Mirola, is "what conditions shape the likelihood that any particular religious tradition will generate activism or maintain the status quo?" To ask this question of gangs recognizes that spirituality is a critical aspect of gang life and without its analysis we cannot understand how marginalized, oppressed, excluded, and/or colonized members of gangs can preserve their personal and collective identities.

As an example of the foregoing, I will explore how the ALKQN through different forms and styles of resistance manifest their spirituality of liberation. They have constructed these beliefs in their *realidad humana* (human reality) as a moral authority that in some way becomes the foundation to their belief that interactions between the oppressed and the oppressors make freedom and justice more sensible than freedom and law.

## The Methodology

The data for this article derives from ethnographic research that the Street Organization Project[2] at John Jay College of Criminal Justice has been conducting in New York City with the ALKQN for the last five years. One of the major findings is that during 1995–1999, the ALKQN, under the leadership of King Tone, went through a social, cultural, political, and spiritual transformation. They moved away from being a street gang to being a street political organization, defined as "a group formed largely by youth and adults of a marginalized social class which aims to provide its members with a resistant identity, an opportunity to be individually and collectively empowered, a voice to speak back to the dominant culture, a refuge from the stresses and strains of barrio or ghetto life and a spiritual enclave within which its sacred rituals can be generated and practiced" (Brotherton and Barrios 2004).

In a critical qualitative inquiry, and following what Fox and Prilleltensky state, first I "seek not to manipulate 'subjects' but to hear the voice of 'participants' who join our search for knowledge and justice." Then I "amplify the voice of participant's interview, as a way to promote the values of self determination and human diversity, through dialogue with participants about the meaning of the data, foster collaboration and democratic participation" (1997, 34). In addition, we chose to hire a leading member of the group to consult with us throughout the project's duration. In practical terms, this ensured several goals: the continuity of the project, the permanent and mutually understood presence of a "gatekeeper," the provision of a cultural broker to help us interpret unfamiliar meaning systems, and the project's ethical integrity with the targeted community. To this end, we hired the leader of the ALKQN, Antonio Fernández, who worked as a part-time paid research assistant during six months from July 1998 (when he was under house arrest) until just prior to his incarceration in January 1999. In addition to Fernández, several other Kings and Queens, among them King H., King M., Queen D., and Queen N. helped in the recruitment of respondents from both the adult and youth sections of the group. Further, both Fernández and King H. consistently responded to our analyses of the data, offering their own interpretations while also suggesting new research areas.

Using a snowball strategy to recruit participants, the project yielded sixty-seven individual life-history interviews covering a range of the group's membership, that is, males and females, young and old between the ages of fourteen and forty-five, long-standing members and new recruits, members in the leadership and those in the rank-and-file. In addition, several leading members who were at the heart of the changes in the organization were interviewed multiple times throughout the research period. Further, we interviewed a wide variety of "outsiders," that is, those who had interacted with the group in different capacities, for example, non-group family members, members of the clergy, leaders of nonprofit community groups, defense lawyers, public high school teachers and administrators, correctional officers, journalists, former members of the city's gang task force, and film-makers. Unfortunately, no active members of law enforcement agreed to be interviewed and neither did any members of the specialized gang unit with the city's correctional department.

Regarding the sample that was used for this research allow me to highlight the following information.[3] The vast majority of Kings and Queens, accord-ing to descriptions of their own economic well-being as youths, were from the lower or lowest socioeconomic groups. In terms of ethnicity, eighteen respondents, that is, just over 25 percent of the total sample, were born outside of the United States with equal numbers (seven) born in Puerto Rico or the Dominican Republic. The category "other" included Latin American coun-tries such as México, Ecuador, and Guatemala. The parents of these first- and second-generation children were born mostly outside the U.S. mainland, with thirty-seven born in Puerto Rico and ten born in the Dominican Republic.

In terms of their educational qualifications, as might be expected with respondents from backgrounds of little economic and cultural capital, schooling was a mixed blessing and for many, especially the males, it was difficult to stay through the twelfth grade for a variety of reasons. Perhaps counterintuitively, a two-parent family was the dominant type for most of the sample, although a one-parent family, some kind of guardianship, or a group home was the experience for 40 percent of the respondents. The size of the families for most respondents was quite modest, with most respon-dents reporting only one or two siblings in their household, while twelve respondents stated that they came from relatively large families with four or more children.

Of the Kings who answered questions on their criminal histories (one could argue that the eight who refused to answer were protecting their past), the majority said that they had been arrested at least once compared to a minority of the Queens who declared the same. This accords with other studies of street subcultures and gangs, where the vast majority of male respondents have entered the criminal justice system at least once while females have generally been able to remain without a criminal record.

## Acting Out Spiritual Opposition to Oppression

I argue in this essay that in their way of resisting oppression and marginal-ization, groups come together and build creative strategies—this includes organizations—for liberation, which the dominant culture has a tendency to criminalize. The use of a spirituality of liberation is one of the resistance strategies that not only preserve the identities of these groups but also empower them to continue their liberation struggle. Groups like the ALKQN raise class and cultural, political, and religious consciousness through the use of agency, cohesion, sacred collectivity, religious imagery, and liberating rituals. They shape their own spirituality of liberation to understand and change the oppressive ideologies and the institutions that attempt to dehumanize, objectify, and criminalize them. In order to understand the global perspective of their liberation struggle, it is important that we comprehend what the ALKQN means by Kingism/Queenism and its relationship to liberation theology and spirituality of liberation. In the discussion that follows, I will describe more specifically the meaning of these concepts and show the parallels between Kingism/Queenism and liberation theology and spirituality of liberation.

## Where Is the Gang Literature?

For a complete discussion of gang literature from a social movement perspective, I refer you to chapter two in Brotherton and Barrios (2004). However, let me highlight here that in recent years, a minority of researchers have attempted to explore the resistance aspects of gang development with studies of the Chicano inmate community in Los Angeles (Moore et al. 1978), the black "underclass" in Milwaukee (Hagedorn 1988), the street nations (Conquergood 1993, 1997) and drug-based community gangs of Chicago (Venkatesh 2000), and the emergence of communitarian street organizations in New York City (Brotherton 1999).[4] And while all these studies show the existence of innovative social, political, and economic praxes employed by gangs not only to fill glaring voids in their communities' resources but to respond to changes in the more macro dimensions of society (Hagedorn 2002), there is a great deal still to be written about the gang and its connection to organized youth resistance that extends beyond the narrow foci of crime and deviance. In particular, little if anything has been written about this resistance from a spiritual perspective. Consequently, with such a limited frame of reference to guide us in the gang literature, it is time to turn to other fruitful avenues of analysis to be able to consider this chronically overlooked element of the gang phenomenon.

## Parallels between Kingism/Queenism and Liberation Theology

> Self-identity refers to each person's biographical arrangement of meaning
> and interpretations that form a somewhat coherent sense of "Who am I."
> Often the question "Who am I?" is answered in terms of "This is where I
> belong" . . . Another major source of identity is based on the individual's
> sense of belonging to a distinctive group—tribe, nation, ethnic group.
>
> —Meredith B. McGuire, *Religion: The Social Context*

### WHAT IS KINGISM/QUEENISM?

The spirituality of liberation places great emphasis in what is believed, and our study of Kingism/Queenism help us to understand the ALKQN's beliefs, doctrine, and/or creed. In one of our life history interviews, King Felix told us,

> I didn't need the Nation, what I needed to do—what I needed the Nation to do for me was to help me change my life. You know, to get out of this negative way of thinking and get into something more positive, you know get into my culture. And that's where I really—I learned—everything I know now was in prison, you know, just being in prison, and being a king, it helped me completely. It helped me learn my culture, it helped me be a man, it helped me accept reality, you know and it also helped me get out of my drug addiction. Completely out of it. And to this day I've been home for what? About ten months now, and I gotta thank—I thank the Nation for that because if it wasn't for the Nation, I'd probably be right back in jail. (King Felix, field note March 22, 1997)

In the ALKQN traditions, Kingism/Queenism is a path to identity in which Kingism/Queenism is a spiritual syncretism that develops and preserves the collective identity of the ALKQN. King Roman explains, "Kingism is something that came out of the [ALKQN] Bible. That's how we created the Latin Kings—out of Kingism" (King Roman interview October 5, 1998).

In the ALKQN Bible, and this includes the Manifesto, the Constitution, and the rituals that they practice, we often see that there are no differences between religion and spirituality, and that the group sees both concepts as synonymous.[5] For example, in the New York Bible it states:

> Kingism as a religion, as a belief, as a way of giving our blessings to the Almighty and as a way of showing love and respect to ourselves as a Latino Nation did not take form or was revealed to us until 1960, at the State Ville Correctional Center in Chicago to King Crazy Dino . . . So with members from 5 different Latin King Tribes incarcerated there at State Ville the task of

putting down our religion was revealed to King Dino. Our means of giving worship and blessing to the Almighty Latin Kings shall be known as Kingism . . . Kingism should be the glue that hold us together, the faith that is unshakable, so we give to those that came before us and showed us the righteous path to the Almighty seeing eyes.

In this tradition of the ALKQN, we see that the organization itself is the religion and Kingism/Queenism is the doctrine. However, in the notion that Kingism/Queenism is "the glue that hold us together," we also see the degree to which Kingism/Queenism can be interpreted as a religion, as a doctrine, or as a spirituality, and how it becomes the philosophical and emotional means by which the group is able to combat, with very few resources, the dominant culture's denigrating categories.

This collective identity construction in Kingism/Queenism through the medium of spirituality not only changes the way they (the members) see themselves (by redefining who they are), but it reaffirms their own culture as part of the collective identity process. For example, to be called a King or a Queen is the antithesis of being called poor and being treated as culturally invisible. Similarly, instead of feeling inferior because of one's designation in a white-dominated society as a "minority," one now feels specially selected because he or she to join the group must "have a cultural heritage of Latin decent. This very simply means that you must have direct blood relation to some one of Latin origin" (ALKQN Bible, 10).

These aspects of Kingism/Queenism through which the ALKQN organizes itself and shares its meaning system with religious beliefs, religious rituals, religious experiences, and religious communities also provides a form of status distinction and divine kinship that help to justify and solidify group cohesion. "The new King recognizes that the time for revolution is at hand. Yes revolution, a revolution of the mind, and the revolution of knowledge. A revolution that will bring freedom to the enslaved, to all Third World people as we together sing and praise with joy what time it is—it is Nation time! Time for all oppressed people of the world to unite."

In the above, taken from the ALKQN's Bible, we see how the notion of Kingism/Queenism has close similarities with liberation theology in Latin America in that it claims that there is an experience of liberating faith and hope for the oppressed (see Alves 1975; Barrios 2000; Betto 1994; Boff 1978; Croatto 1987; Gutiérrez 1972). This brings us to the next part of the analysis, which is a discussion of what I mean by sacred collectivity, religious imagery, and liberating rituals in the spirituality of the ALKQN.

## WHAT ARE THE PARALLELS?

It is clear that Kingism/Queenism departs from the theological principles of a fundamentalist Christian faith, which requires those who need salvation to accept Jesus as their personal savior. Instead they search for a community faith praxis that brings liberation from all kind of injustices that keep humanity under oppression. In addition, those searching for liberation are constantly asking questions about rights. They do not ask, what, when, how, or why religion talks to my *realidad humana;* they ask, what, when, how, or why my *realidad humana* talks to religion. In other words, my *realidad humana* is not in a passive interaction because it has something to say.

Another facet in Kingism/Queenism is how their *realidad humana* has some kind of global interdependence with the *realidad humana* of others. In the process of raising political and class consciousness, a precondition of organizing and mobilizing people to change their *realidad humana,* it is necessary to teach some kind of "global responsibility" (Küng 2001) by helping people to learn how to make "global interdependence." Take, for example, youth violence and the approach of "violence reduction" where most of the time we end up blaming the victims. Van Soest states that "violence, in particular, is a pervasive problem of critical importance. From the teenager in Los Angeles or El Salvador to the mother in Washington, DC, or the Sudan to the infant in New York City or India, violence affects million of people worldwide. Like other social problems, violence cannot be solved without acknowledging and understanding the complexities of global interdependence" (1997, vx). To this interdependence, I will add the need to understand and acknowledge the interconnections and interrelations with other realities like poverty, drugs, prisons, and so on.[6] Of course, we also need to identify oppressive ideologies such as racism, male chauvinism, heterosexism, homophobia, ethnocentrism, xenophobia, Cristocentrism, and scapegoating of youth. In other words, and this is a strong foundation in Kingism/Queenism, our *realidad humana* is always connected to our *solidaridad humana* (human solidarity). In both Kingism/Queenism and liberation theology[7] in the *solidaridad humana,* they promote some kind of social ethic in which people need to feel someone else suffering pain, oppression, exclusion, and lack of freedom.

This is the reason why the description of a spirituality of liberation makes a better framework to this subversive praxis. This is also the reason why it is possible to identify strong parallels between liberation theology in Latin America, a "self-consciousness movement" that according to Gustavo Gutiérrez started in 1968.[8] In this movement, Leonardo Boff and Clodovis Boff claim that "as a faith reflection on the praxis of liberation, the theology of liberation is the thinking of the faith under the formality of a leaven of historical transformation—as the salt of the earth and the light of the world, as the theological virtue of charity exercised in the area of the social" (1986, 83). These social and political dimensions of spirituality are rescued by both, liberation theology and Kingism/Queenism, in their praxis. In other words, both reflect seriously how as social agents we can use our spirituality in the transformation of this world.

Another parallel between liberation theology and Kingism/Queenism is the process of *declericalization*, so that it ceases to constitute the monopoly of specialists and moves more into a course of action that empowers lay people (Boff and Boff 1986). The social movements of faith communities in Latin America reflect parallels with the universals meeting that the ALKQN celebrate. The methods of doing theology that both movements develop are also similar: *the doing of theology from a starting point in practice* (Boff and Boff 1986). This is why during ALKQN meetings, they reflect on those issues that are responsible for their oppression. More important, they celebrate in community the capacity that they have to change these oppressive realities into liberation experiences.[9]

Similar to liberation theology, the writings in Kingism/Queenism are a reflection of their own struggles and resistances, in other words, some kind of praxis, that produces the theory that is relevant to them. This is why when they write they do it from their own experiences, from the bottom to the top.

Let us not forget two things. One is what Vigil reminds us regarding Mexicans in particular, and Latinos/as in general, in the United States: "many families and their children experience acute poverty and limited social mobility opportunities in these barrios, and thus, over time, there developed an underclass with its own set of problems. It is from among these children that the youth most intensely involved in the gangs tends to come" (1995, 127). The other is that when they use writing as a means of resistance, they are also documenting their own experiences and struggles within their own realities. For this reason, in order to understand what they are writing, we need to comprehend these realities, their realities. Hagedorn and Macon describe these realities by saying that "gangs have always formed from powerless minorities and have often become part of the political struggle of their own ethnic group to achieve equality" (1995, 135). Let us not forget that not only do they want us to learn about them but, more importantly, to learn from them.

The most radical, in my opinion, of Latin American theologians, José Porfirio Miranda,[10] also brings a great reflection of parallels that I want to take into consideration before ending this concise theological discussion. In his book *Being and the Messiah: The Message of St. John*, Miranda stated that "the defining characteristic of the God of the Bible is the fact that he cannot be known or loved directly; rather to love God and to know him means to love one's neighbor and do to one's neighbor justice" (1977, 137). Here again we can contemplate the dialectical praxis of the spirit and the material, faith and life, not from an antagonistic view but from a complementary approach. In other words, Kingism/Queenism and liberation theology are constantly asking the question; can we comprehend God out of our *realidad humana*? The only way to do this is by accepting what both Kingism/Queenism and liberation theology are rejecting: a colonialist spirituality.

Let me close this section with the following question: are there other influences in the ALKQN than liberation theology? My answer is yes. For future research, I want to explore how two religious traditions, Judaism and Yoruba,[11] make contributions to their resistance heritage. In addition, the group has been influenced by contact with the Young Lords Party, the Black Panthers Party, and some of the leaders of the Socialist Party in New York City. My own function as a spiritual advisor to some of the leaders like King Tone and King Héctor and my direct participation in their monthly meetings at our church has also had an impact that should be detailed.

## Parallels between Spirituality of Liberation and Kingism/Queenism

> Only when alternative religious beliefs about God's will, social relations, and change emerged from the theologies of liberation—constructed by religious activists living among the poor in developing countries—did oppressed groups begin to reject the religions that kept them in their place.
>
> —William A. Mirola, "Introduction to Social Movement and Religion"

### WHAT IS A SPIRITUALITY OF LIBERATION?

We need to understand that spirituality is not a credo, a doctrine, a dogma, or a way of knowing.[12] Spirituality is a way of living, in which I demonstrate how I relate to other people and the remainder of creation. In other words, spirituality is about doing, not saying. The primary source of spirituality is our *realidad humana*. This human reality manifests itself in a specific time and space and never in a vacuum.[13] Thus, when we talk about our *realidad*, we are talking about our social, political, and economic reality, the meaning of being a Latino or Latina person in this racist society, or the meaning of being a woman in this society of male supremacy. This *realidad humana* is the one in which everything human is supposed to be familiar to our spirituality. This brings us to what we have said before, that all human beings have spirituality, be they already religious people or not. Spirituality is a human *reencuentro* (reencountering) with the creation of God that cannot be limited to the practice of religion. This interpretation of spirituality allows people who do not believe in God to be able to manifest their spirituality.

Can spirituality be developed in an apolitical way? My answer is no. Spirituality always has a political and a social dimension. What we then need to identify is what kind of political or social approach the spirituality that I am manifesting is using. This is why it is possible that we give spirituality to people so they do not think, do not question, and of course, take things the way they were given because this is God's will. Let us not forget that the ruling class has their own spirituality with political and social dimensions that respond to their interests or their social reality. It is here that spirituality also becomes an opiate. Following this line of thought, one can identify at least two types of spirituality: spirituality of oppression and spirituality of liberation. The first is reflected in individuals who are subjected, whether voluntary or involuntary, to processes of oppression, and in the oppressor. In both we see how *espiritualismo* (spiritualism) works to take away our sacred responsibility with all that it has created, which is the *solidaridad humana* (human solidarity).[14]

The second kind of spirituality, the spirituality of liberation, is the exact opposite and refers to a constant resistance to all processes of oppression and thereby protecting God's creation. Following this second manifestation of spirituality, I argue that if we want to practice a spirituality of liberation, we need to deideologize our *espiritualismo* in the search for a quality of life that demonstrates respect for our diversities; searches for an equal distribution of God's creation; reaches a compromise of our actions for the elimination of whatever, or whoever, oppresses, colonizes, excludes, or coerces people for participating equally in that creation; and celebrates people's liberation in all its magnitude (for example, social, political, sexual, religious, economic, and psychological arenas). In other words, more than just a contemplation of life or a philosophy of knowledge, spirituality is a life performance that reconnects me with those responsibilities that I have to my neighbors and myself. Spirituality of liberation rescues the interdependence that exists between the personal and the communal.

How do we understand this conception of deideologizing? Montero claims, "Deideologization is closely linked to the notion of consciousness raising . . . Everyone has consciousness. The purpose of this work is to create awareness about life conditions, about causes and effects, and to promote change and empowerment. The process of change begins with placing people, through their own actions and efforts, in control of their immediate environment. Action and reflection are carried out in order to transform passivity into activity, and apathy into commitment, decision making and the transformation of everyday life" (1997, 242).

For those of us who believe in God, the best way to reconcile this *reencuentro* (reencountering) and responsibility with the creation is to define our Higher Power, or God, as Justice. It is in the manifestation or praxis that we *reencontramos a Dios* (reencounter God). Spirituality, therefore, from a liberation perspective, is about expressing with actions our concern for the creation of God. It is the way we manifest with actions our personal and collective responsibilities. The more human we are, or the more we are connected to the *realidad humana,* then the more responsible we are with our *solidaridad humana.* As a result, the more human we are, the more spiritual we become.

According to Díaz-Stevens, "Latinos find a way to define themselves as an ethnic group; in Latin América, on the other hand, popular religiosity is the vehicle for a town or region to affirm itself" (1996). In other words, in her understanding, spirituality plays different roles for Latinas and Latinos in their country of origin than in the United States. She distinguishes between popular religiosity and what she identifies as communitarian spirituality. For her, popular religiosity illustrates restrictions that are territorial or class-based, and provides a means for authentication of the community itself. She thinks that the Latino popular religiosity practiced in the United States is more a communitarian spirituality, which not only creates but also reaffirms communal attachment between social classes in a particular community. This will bring a path for a group to define itself as an ethnic group.

My concern with this approach is that it implies that the manifestation or expression of spirituality is only related to religiosity and the search for ethnic identity. I believe that this kind of search is only one path but not the path. When we bring to the discussion the liberation of people in all spheres (political, economic, social, cultural, sexual, religious, and so forth), we are claiming that our spirituality has to be dialectical. In other words, a dialectical spirituality appears in the presence of injustice with the intention of eliminating these injustices with the implementation of justice. In our particular reality in the United States, this dialectical process of our spirituality also needs to be anticapitalist. However, going back to Díaz-Stevens's (1996) approach, we need to amplify the conceptualization by recognizing that ethnocentrism in the United States is not the injustice that we need to fight. It is only one injustice that can be added to the list of classism, sexism, heterosexism, racism, ageism, xenophobia, and so on. This is why the search for power, for identity, and for respect are also factors that build up the social agenda of street groups such as the ALKQN, and these injustices must be part of the critical analysis of their resistance. For a specific example I look at my experience working with other street organizations, such as the *Asociación Ñeta*. For this group, a major issue is that Puerto Rico continues to be a colony of the United States; another injustice that can be defined as political terrorism, it inspires them also to search for national identity: the decolonization and freedom of their country, Puerto Rico.

### WHAT ARE THE PARALLELS?

But what is the function of spirituality? Let us keep in mind that functional descriptions deal with explanations that help us to understand spirituality in terms of what it does. One of the biggest issues any organized group has to face is how to keep people together. In his solution to this problem, a spiritual leader of the ALKQN claimed, "The new King recognizes that the day of resurrection is here. A time for the appearance of a new manifestation of truth. The rising of the dead means the spiritual awakening of those who have been sleeping in the graveyard of ignorance. The day of the oppressor must now be judged by the oppressed" (The King's Manifesto, p. 10). From a radical position, Kingism/Queenism recognizes that there is a need for the resurrection of those who are metaphorically dead. This spiritual, not physical, death in front of oppression and exclusion keep them in a state of silence and calmness. This is what they mean by the spiritual awakening of those who are sleeping in the graveyard of ignorance. "Spirituality is the basic foundation that generates the energy and magnetism that binds the Kings and Queens together" (interview with Héctor Torres, June 30, 2000).

In his eyes, the key to maintaining a high level of internal solidarity in the ALKQN was through practicing a form of spirituality out of which a collective identity and praxis could be constructed. King Tone, the Inca of the ALKQN, also describes the role of spirituality and links it to a new way of being:

And the movement took on. And I started, you know, putting in religion. I started using King's lessons and using the Bible as a concordant. So everything I learned in Kingism I would match a story from the Bible, I would preach it to the kids and break it down in knowledge and it started working on them. They started getting a sense of spirituality; they got a sense of belonging. They got a sense that I didn't want them, like the pastor, to be Jesus. I just wanted them to try and walk like he did.

In King Tone's interpretation of spirituality, people are brought face to face with their own reality and encouraged to take responsibility for their own lives. Spirituality, then, in ALKQN terms, is linked to the notion of agency. This is very close to my own interpretation and to my own praxis. It is this process of action by which we change, transform, and convert injustice into justice, and spirituality is the process of thinking about the world in order to change it. Consequently, spirituality should not be used to distance ourselves from our personal or community relationships and obligations, for example, through isolating ourselves in monasteries, convents, temples, synagogues, churches, or mosques, even though I find these places helpful to rediscover and to define our responsibility. Rather, spirituality is a way to bring us closer to the world. Queen Helen, below, articulated this position when she was asked to explain how and why she came into the ALKQN:

But my ex husband—he mainly got involved first. Don't ask me how, but he just did it came home and said, this is great! They have so many things about the people that we could help each other and help the poor, and, you know, all this and all that, so I was like, "Hmmm." I'm not gonna lie—at first, I thought it was a gang, yeah. I did, 'cuz I wasn't familiar with any activities of gang members, but you know, out here, you know how it is in the street. But as I go along he kept bringin' me the papers and kept tellin' me—you know, papers that had things to do and activities and rallies and—I was like, "That sounds great. That sounds great. I think I should join. Why not? Why not help our people? Nobody else is gonna do it for us, right?" (Field note, October 25, 1997)

In Queen Helen's description of her entry into the ALKQN, I see a perfect example of someone discovering her spirituality where spirituality has a principal function to destroy social sin. Some of the social sins that are constantly challenging our spirituality are the lack of food, the lack of medical and educational services, the lack of jobs and housing, violence against women, police brutality, discrimination against undocumented immigrants, racism, classism, heterosexism, and homophobia. These are the physical, cultural, and ideological structures that exist to systematically ensure that the exploitation of human beings continues as a fundamental characteristic of our society.

In contrast, liberation spirituality first awakens our consciousness to recognize our *realidad humana*, for example, our conditions of subjugation, and then it empowers us to change that reality by encouraging us to be utopian. In other words, it implores us to struggle for a different society despite the mundane everyday rituals of oppression, and it justifies both a spirit and a spirituality of resistance and transformation that is captured by Maduro: "No class society is a society of pure dominance. Dominance is exercised over individuals and groups who dispose of only a bare minimum of power over any means of production, over distribution of even their own labor and over the division of the end products of their labor. But these individuals and groups, though generally unarmed, are never altogether inert. Faced with dominance, the dominated always, somehow offer resistance" (1982, 75).

Before closing this discussion, let me also clarify two other issues. One is that in the ALKQN traditions, which includes its bible, constitutions, and other documents, religion and spirituality are used interchangeably, giving the impression that they are synonymous. For the purpose of this article I will follow the same approach. Second, I am not claiming that this spirituality of resistance is unique to Latinos or Latinas, or more specifically to the ALKQN. Rather, I believe that in every group's search for identity there is a presence and manifestation of spirituality of liberation, and we need to learn how to identify, interpret, and appreciate this reality from a critical perspective. However, ALKQN does bring a unique, specific, distinctive culture and a particular historical and sociopolitical reality to New York City. This context produces them and, as for any oppressed group in the search for liberation, a unique way of resistance.

Before I close, let me clarify that when people or groups are manifesting a spirituality of oppression, this is when in the route for deideologization it is necessary to repoliticize and resocialize to build the foundation for personal and/or group liberation. Again, I argue that spirituality of liberation is not an abstract set of inner beliefs or a pathway into self-reflection but a means to understand the multiple ways people (not just others but ourselves) fight back against the ruling class and their oppressive institutions that have a way of making people invisible, marginalized, and excluded. Because spirituality of liberation emerges from our *realidad humana,* we can say that it is also the product of culture, which means that in some way, and to avoid cultural colonialism, there is a need to reculturize. In the analysis of Kingism/Queenism, this is a significant social phenomenon that I like to identify as the latinization of the spirituality of resistance.

## Conclusion

> I love being a Queen. It gives me hope, it makes me proud to say that I've got family that I know I can always count on and no matter what happens in my life I know they'll always be there for me and they may not physically be there, but I know them spiritually and I know they will be there. You know, I've been in gangs, I've been in other nations, I've been in a lot of things, and I've never felt so at home as I have when I joined the Queens.
> —Queen Justice (Field note, June 20, 1998)

> A civilization can founder as readily in the face of moral and spiritual bankruptcy as it can through financial bankruptcy.
> —Martin Luther King Jr., *Where Do We Go from Here: Chaos or Community?*

Through their spirituality of liberation, the ALKQN resisted the dominant culture's attempts to dehumanize, objectify, psychopathologize, and criminalize them. As a group they not only organized to resist the dominant class, but through deideologizing spirituality, they moved closer to liberation by destroying their colonial consciousness.

In their quest for identity, the ALKQN's religious collectivity also developed in relation to their own needs, becoming what can be called a *"popular cultural religion."* In time, with their own beliefs and practices, they also became a challenge to the official or mainstream religions.

This spirituality is not unique to Latinos or Latinas, or to the ALKQN; rather, I believe that in every group's search for identity there is a presence and manifestation of resistance—again there is no such thing as complete domination or subordination—to those who oppress, marginalize, and exclude them. It is here that we identify a spirituality of liberation. We simply need to learn how to identify, interpret, and appreciate this resistance from a critical perspective.

What has happened to the ALKQN now: are they still political? Are they still spiritual? I have to answer the two questions with a big yes. However, again, the real question needs to be what kind of politics or spirituality they are practicing at this moment. From a political perspective, they do not exhibit the same kind of social activism that put them in the category of social movement during our research. In informal conversations with some of the leaders, it is clear that the idea is there, but they are lacking the leadership that can organize, educate, and mobilize them in a political agenda where they get involved as an organization in projects like the peace movement, the Vieques liberation movement, or the movement against police brutality—to mention only three experiences. From a spiritual perspective, they are practicing at this moment what I identify as a spirituality of oppression, becoming more and more fundamentalist and/or traditionalist in their approaches and interpretations that they give to their social realities.

I believe that there is a dialectical process where the oppressive circumstances also produce the contradictions for liberation, and because there is no such thing as complete domination, there is a strategy of resistance in the ALKQN. They are a sleeping giant waiting for a right moment to wake up.

## Notes

1. Repoliticizing and socialicizing is the process by which we bring back the political and social dimensions that lead us to liberation from all kind of injustices: economic, social, political, sexual, gender, race, ethnicity, etc.

2. This research project was created by Dr. David Brotherton, from the sociology department of the John Jay College of Criminal Justice of the City University of New York, and me.

3. For more details and elaboration of the research participants, see Brotherton and Barrios, *The Almighty Latin King and Queen Nation,* chapter 1 (2004).

4. This is not a complete list. However, my point is that we cannot forget that there is always a prophetic resistance from scholars who continue raising their voices and activism, rejecting any type of intimidation or submission to self-censorship. These scholars believe that in a serious critical analysis of social problems, it is necessary to understand class struggle in order to understand the roots of human realities—this of course include "gangs" or street organizations—and how it is that capitalist globalization, global corporate interests, globalized authoritarianism, the social construction of false knowledge, male supremacy, white supremacy, heterosexism, and adultarchy—an ideology that promotes the privileges of adults—produce local oppression and how the resistance to this oppression and marginalization is organized by the oppressed. And, of course, we also need to acknowledge and understand how the ruling class makes efforts to eradicate any dissidence.

5. It is not clear when they started using the Queenism concept; however, this is another way of recognizing the presence of females in the Nation.

6. Due to the fact that "street violence," "interpersonal violence," or "intergroup violence" are some of the most highlighted topics in the "gang" literature, it is very important that, in order to avoid any myopic conceptualization, we have a clear understanding that we cannot understand interpersonal or group violence without a clear understanding of institutional, structural, and cultural violence. Most of what the government with its law enforcement agents and what academic research with its

narrow-minded analysis is telling us in discussing personal and/or group violence is not describing the problem but a symptom. This is the reason why we need to understand the different forms of violence and how they are interdependent, interrelated, and interconnected. If not, we are going to continue blaming the victims.

7. As a point of clarification, liberation theology is a global movement in the search for human liberation. This movement is not unique or an isolated Latin American movement; on the contrary, it is a global movement also found in Western Europe (Bria 1985; Casalis 1985), Eastern Europe and Canada (Arbour 1985), Asia (Rayan 1985), United States (Barrios 2000; Cone 1984, 1985; Elizondo 1983; Gottwald 1983), and South Africa (Goba 1985), to mention some places. In this global liberation movement, at the same time that they promote service to wholeness of life, they struggle against religious poverty (Rayan 1985), economic injustices (de Santa Ana 1985), male chauvinism (Ruether 1985), racism (Cone 1985), inculturation of the Gospel (Mveng 1985), Cristocentrism (Driver 1981), colonialism and political terrorism (Barrios 2004), and heterosexism and homophobia (Edwards 1984), to mention some of the issues.

8. During this time, Gustavo Gutiérrez started writing his book *Teología de la liberación,* and it was published in the English language under the title *A Liberation Theology* in 1976.

9. In addition, in Juan Luis Segundo's book *The Liberation of Theology,* he explains the use of methodology by liberation theology the following way: "The continuing change in our interpretation of the Bible, which is dictated by the continuing change in our present-day reality, both individual and societal . . . The circular nature of this interpretation stems from the fact that each new reality obliges us to interpret the word of God afresh, to change reality accordingly, and then to go back and reinterpret the word of God again and so on" (1976, 8). This what he identifies as "the hermeneutic circle."

10. In 1974, José Porfirio Miranda also published the book *Marx and the Bible: A Critique of the Philosophy of Oppression* (Maryknoll, N.Y.: Orbis Books).

11. This is an African religion that some people in the Caribbean call *Santería.*

12. A complete discussion of this topic is elaborated in Barrios (2000, 2004).

13. As a point of clarification, sometimes people literally translate the English word "experience" as *"experiencia"* in Spanish, and this is not correct. In Spanish, the term *"experiencia"* is much closer to the concept of, in English, reality, i.e., *la realidad.*

14. I define *espiritualismo* as a centralized worship, or consecration, to our persona. In a spirituality of liberation, we always begin with the persona and then we move to the community, in this order. This is the reason why without the *solidaridad humana,* we can not move beyond the personal.

## References

Alves, Rubem. 1975. *A Theology of Human Hope.* St. Meinrad, IN: Abbey Press.

Arbour, F. 1985. "Canada: The Inter-church Committee on Human Rights." In *Doing*

*Theology in a Divided World*, ed. Virginia Fabella and Sergio Torres, 45–50. Maryknoll, N.Y.: Orbis.

Barrios, Luis. 1998. "Santa María as a Liberating Zone: A Community Church in the Search of Restorative Justice." *Humanity and Society* 22, no. 1: 55–78.

———. 2000. *Josconiando: Dimensiones sociales y políticas de la espiritualidad.* Santo Domingo, Dominican Republic: Editorial Aguiar, S.A.

———. 2003. "The Almighty Latin Kings Queens Nation and the Spirituality of Resistance: Agency, Social Cohesion, and Liberating Rituals in the Making of a Street Organization." In *Gangs and Society: Alternative Perspectives,* ed. Louis Kontos, David Brotherton, and Luis Barrios. New York: Columbia University Press.

———. 2004. *Pitirreando: De la desesperanza a la esperanza.* San Juan, Puerto Rico: Editorial Edil.

Betto, Frei. 1994. *Fidel y la religión: Conversaciones con Frei Betto.* La Habana, Cuba: Editorial SI-MAR, S.A.

Boff, Leonardo. 1978. *Pasión de Cristo, pasión de muerte: Hechos interpretaciones y significado, ayer y hoy.* Madrid, Spain: La Editorial Vizcaína.

Boff, Leonardo, and Clodovis Boff. 1986. *Liberation Theology: From Confrontation to Dialogue.* New York: Harper Row.

Bria, I. 1985. "An East European, Orthodox Perspective." In *Doing Theology in a Divided World,* ed. Virginia Fabella and Sergio Torres, 212–15. Maryknoll, N.Y.: Orbis.

Brotherton, David C. 1999. "The Old Heads Tell Their Stories." *Free Inquiry in Creative Sociology* 2, no. 1: 1–15.

Brotherton, David, and Luis Barrios. 2004. *The Almighty Latin King and Queen Nation: Street Politics and the Transformation of a New York City Gang.* New York: Columbia University Press.

Casaldáliga, Pedro, and José M. Vigil. 1994. *The Spirituality of Liberation.* New York: Hyperion Books.

Casalis, G. 1985. "Methodology for a West European Theology of Liberation." In *Doing Theology in a Divided World,* ed. Virginia Fabella and Sergio Torres, 106–23. Maryknoll, N.Y.: Orbis.

Cone, James. H. 1984. *For My People: Black Theology and the Black Church.* Maryknoll, N.Y.: Orbis Books.

———. 1985. "Black Theology: Its Origin, Methodology, and Relationship to Third World Theologies." In *Doing Theology in a Divided World,* ed. Virginia Fabella and Sergio Torres, 93–105. Maryknoll, N.Y.: Orbis.

Conquergood, Dwight. 1993. "Homeboys and Hoods: Gang Communication and Cultural Space." In *Group Communication in Context: Studies of Natural Groups,* ed. Larry Frey, 23–55. Hillsdale, N.J.: Lawrence Erlbaum.

———. 1997. "Street Literacy." In *Handbook of Research on Teaching Literacy through the Communicative and Visual Arts,* ed. James Flood, Shirley Brice Heath, and Diane Lapp, 354–75. New York: Simon and Schuster.

Croatto, Severino. 1987. *Biblical Hermeneutic: Toward a Theory of Reading as the Production of Meaning.* Maryknoll, N.Y.: Orbis.

De Santa Ana, J. 1985. "The Perspective of Economic Analysis." In *Doing Theology in a Divided World,* ed. Virginia Fabella and Sergio Torres. Maryknoll, N.Y.: Orbis.

Díaz-Stevens, Ana. M. 1996. "Latino Popular Religiosity and Communitarian Spirituality," Program for the Analysis of Religion among Latinos (PARAL). Occasional Paper no. 4. September: 1, 2. Talk at the Graduate Center, City University of New York.

Driver, Tom F. 1981. *Christ in a Changing World: Toward an Ethical Christology.* New York: Crossroad.

Edwards, George R. 1984. *Gay/Lesbian Liberation: A Biblical Perspective.* Cleveland, Ohio: Pilgrim Press.

Elizondo, Virgilio. 1983. *Galilean Journey: The Mexican-American Promise.* Maryknoll, N.Y.: Orbis Books.

Fox, Dennis, and Isaac Prilleltensky, eds. 1997. *Critical Psychology: An Introduction.* Thousand Oaks, Calif.: Sage.

Goba, B. 1985. "A Black South Africa Perspective." In *Doing Theology in a Divided World,* ed. Virginia Fabella and Sergio Torres, 53–58. Maryknoll, N.Y.: Orbis.

Gottwald, Norman K., ed. 1983. *The Bible and Liberation: Political and Social Hermeneutics.* Maryknoll, N.Y.: Orbis.

Gutiérrez, Gustavo. 1972. *Teología de la liberación.* Salamanca, Spain: Ediciones Sígueme.

Hagedorn, John 1988. *People and Folks.* Lake View Press.

———. 2002. "Gangs and the Informal." In *Gangs in America,* 3rd ed., ed. C. Ron Huff, 101–20. Thousand Oaks, Calif.: Sage.

Hagedorn, John, and Perry Macon. 1995. "What Happened to the Beer That Made Milwaukee Famous?" In *The Modern Gang Reader,* ed. Malcolm W. Klein, Cheryl L. Maxson, and Jody Miller, 132–38. Los Angeles: Roxbury.

King, Martin Luther, Jr. 1967. *Where Do We Go from Here: Chaos or Community?* New York: Harper and Row.

Küng, Hans. 2001. *Global Responsibility: In Search of a New World Ethic.* Eugene, Ore.: Wipf and Stock.

Maduro, Otto. 1982. *Religion and Social Conflicts.* Maryknoll, N.Y.: Orbis Books.

McGuire, Meredith B. 1997. *Religion: The Social Context.* 4th ed. Belmont, Calif.: Wadsworth.

Miranda, José P. 1977. *Being and the Messiah: The Message of St. John.* Maryknoll, N.Y.: Orbis.

Mirola, William A. 2001. "Introduction to Social Movement and Religion." In *Sociology of Religion: A Reader,* ed. Susanne C. Monahan, William A. Mirola, and Michael O. Emerson, 399–403. Upper Saddle River, N.J.: Prentice Hall.

Montero, Maritza. 1997. "Political Psychology: A Critical Perspective." In *Critical*

*Psychology: An Introduction,* ed. Dennis Fox and Isaac Prilleltensky, 233–44. Thousand Oaks, Calif.: Sage.

Moore, Joan, with Robert García, Carlos García, Luis Cerda, and Frank Valencia. 1978. *Homeboys: Gangs, Drugs, and Prison in the Barrios of Los Angeles.* Philadelphia: Temple University Press.

Mveng, E. 1985. "A Cultural Perspective." In *Doing Theology in a Divided World* ed. Virginia Fabella and Sergio Torres, 72–75. Maryknoll, N.Y.: Orbis Books.

Paloutzian, Raymond F. 1996. *Invitation to the Psychology of Religion,* 2nd ed. Boston: Allyn and Bacon.

Rayan, S. 1985. "Reconceiving Theology in the Asian Context." In *Doing Theology in a Divided World,* ed. Virginia Fabella and Sergio Torres, 124–42. Maryknoll, N.Y.: Orbis Books.

Roof, Wade C., and Christel Manning. 2001. "Cultural Conflicts and Identity: Second-Generation Hispanic Catholics in the United States." In *Sociology of Religion: A Reader,* ed. Susanne C. Monahan, William A. Mirola, and Michael O. Emerson, 89–95. Upper Saddle River, N.J.: Prentice Hall.

Ruether, R. R. 1985. "A Feminist Perspective." In *Doing Theology in a Divided World,* ed. Virginia Fabella and Sergio Torres, 65–71. Maryknoll, N.Y.: Orbis Books.

Segundo, Juan Luis. 1976. *The Liberation of Theology,* trans. John Drury. Maryknoll, N.Y.: Orbis.

Van Soest, Dorothy. 1997. *The Global Crisis of Violence: Common Problems, Universal Causes, Shared Solutions.* Washington, D.C.: National Association of Social Workers Press.

Venkatesh, Sudhir Alladi. 2000. *American Project: The Rise and Fall of an American Ghetto.* Boston: Harvard University Press.

Vigil, James D. 1995. "Barrio Gangs: Street Life and Identity in Southern California." In *The Modern Gang Reader,* ed. Malcolm W. Klein, Cheryl L. Maxson, and Jody Miller, 125–31. Los Angeles: Roxbury.

# PART IV

# Response to Neoliberalism

# 10

# Toward the Gang
# as a Social Movement

## DAVID C. BROTHERTON

A number of interrelated issues have long been occupying my thinking about street gangs in relationship to the field of political and social action.
For almost a decade, I have been pursuing the question of whether members
of street gangs can perform as politicized subjects and begin a process of
consciencization (Freire 1969), that is, the process of consciousness development as social actors engage the overt and covert structures of power that
keep them in a state of subjugation. If the process does occur, what form
will it take and how will it allow them (the gangs) to resist both objective
and subjective forces of marginalization that lie at the root of their subcultural genesis? In short, can gang members transform the gang and become
the progenitors of a street-based social movement, or are they doomed to
reproduce their own oppressed location? Although such questions have not
been asked frequently in gang studies, it seems reasonable to expect that in
the current period of late- or postmodernity, when many new social movements have entered the public sphere, gangs also might be open to qualitative change. Like these other movements, gangs must operate within the
constraints and possibilities of an intensifying global system of exploitation
and sociocultural exchange (Burawoy 2000; Harvey 2000; Sassen 1998), and
amid the ever deepening crisis of the penal-welfare state (Garland 2001).
Thus, in our (that is, my, Luis Barrios's, and various colleagues' at the Street
Organization Project at John Jay College of Criminal Justice) research carried out with New York City street gangs/street organizations, it is the twin
issues of social and political agency that have been our major foci.

What I would like to do in this brief discussion of one of the most overlooked areas of gang research is to first outline what I have found to be the primary themes surrounding the gang-politics nexus over the last century in the criminological literature. Following this, I will suggest other literatures that provide insightful guidance in this area and enable us to make the conceptual leap into constructs and paradigms to complete our analysis. Finally, I will give an overview and short description of selected aspects from our research that emphasize the social movement aspects of the Almighty Latin King and Queen Nation (ALKQN), whose transitional stage between a gang and a social movement we have termed a "street organization" (Brotherton and Barrios 2004).

## The Criminological Literature on Gangs and Politics

In the bulk of the criminological literature, there are few takers of the view that gangs can be politically reformed to become vehicles of grassroots opposition to the status quo. Rather, the overwhelming consensus is that the semi- or lumpen proletarian gang does not make for a sociocultural milieu from which class-conscious actors can emerge, nor does the urban outlaw life produce too many primitive rebels (Hobsbawm 1959). While most of the findings run counter to the notion of the gang as a putative social movement, there have recently been some modifications, with the gang cast as a community resource in specific "hyper-ghettoized" (Wacquant 2002) contexts. Altogether, there are five themes that run through the gang-politics discussion in the U.S. literature: (1) gangs as goon squads, (2) gangs as inherently conservative entities, (3) supergangs and radical rhetoric, (4) underclass gangs and the implosion effect, and (5) postindustrial gangs filling a political economic void.

Thrasher's (1927) classic work on the process of street gang development set in early-twentieth-century Chicago found gangs to be intricately connected to machine politics and often used as pliant tools of corrupt, powerful players of the city's spoils system. Such gangs could be involved early on in urban athletics' clubs, where the political boss of a district first begins to develop his attachments to and influence over the youths. Later on, many gang members take advantage of the local opportunity structure and become part of the political boss's padded municipal payrolls, providing a key link between crime and big city politics. Finally, as election time rolls around, gang members could be used as goon squads hired to perform criminal acts against political competitors that could be plausibly denied by the true conspirators.

By the 1950s, with many studies focusing on the autonomous and semi-autonomous nature of the lower-class gang subculture (see Cloward and Ohlin 1960; Cohen 1955; Miller 1958), more attention was paid to the conflicting class value systems embedded in American daily life but obscured by the hegemonic notion of the American Dream (Merton 1949). Nevertheless, despite what could be construed as attempts by gangs to politically reject or at least live independently of the dominant culture's social and economic imperatives, few theorists regarded such lifestyles as significantly progressive; if anything, the politics of gang members were quite mainstream if not reactionary. This notion of gangs belonging to the right of the political spectrum, even while harboring a range of ideological "penetrations" (Willis 1977), is essentially an argument that the "false consciousness" of gang members triumphs over their objective race and class locations (see Campbell 1984; Katz 1988), "magically" preparing them to relive the subordinate fates of their parents.

By the 1970s, however, the gang was being transformed by major social, political, cultural, and economic upheavals in what was being described as the "mass society" (Shils 1971). In Jacobs's study (1977) of an Illinois prison, in which he traces the institution's shifting location from "the periphery to the center," he encountered a new form of prisoner self-organization that he called the supergang (for example, the Vice Lords, Gangster Disciples, Black Stone Rangers, Latin Kings, and so forth). Such gangs appropriated a nationalist radical rhetoric from discursive systems rampant in the counterculture of the time, but they only did so as a form of "justificatory vocabulary." Jacobs concluded that the supergangs could not mount a truly oppositional threat to institutional power structures due to the socially and intellectually constraining nature of the status system in which they were embedded. For all their rhetoric and their more sophisticated level of organizing, the supergang could not produce a leadership that would act on behalf of a greater cause, place their neighborhood above their membership, or be motivated by an idealism and alternative societal vision that he called "transcendent values," all of which were primary properties of a genuine social movement.

If the 1960s and 1970s could not produce ongoing radical gang movements, what political era could? By the 1980s, as the social and cultural pendulum swung further to the right with the political class of Reagan deepening the stratification and fragmentation of the country, the notion of the underclass became a favored explanation of rising gang membership. Joan Moore wrote that gang members were "a kind of lumpen proletariat, a stratum of men and women who simply cycle around and around with little if any chance to climb out of the realities of their decayed and defeated neighborhoods" (Moore 1991, 6).

In other words, the underclass gang, socially and culturally isolated from most mainstream community structures (Decker and Van Winkle 1996), ends up as Jacobs had predicted. For all their "opposition" to the "system" and their embrace of an oppositional value system to bourgeois, "straight" morality, the gang could not envision itself acting in behalf of broader community interests. Moreover, the underclass gang could also be conceived in more damaging political terms and, rather than coexisting with other community institutions, may be the site of implosion, turning its alienation from the power structure in on itself and on the community (Hagedorn 1988).

With the end of the millennium approaching and the country ensconced in a postindustrial, information age, another view gained momentum that saw gangs as political players in urban neighborhoods socially and economically left behind by the combined and uneven development of late capitalism. In this reading of gangs and politics, the gang is seen as filling a low-level political and economic void, perhaps protecting a community from the abuse of the state, mediating in street justice disputes, and dispensing certain services and favors in the absence of any meaningful state presence or legitimate economic capital accumulation (Jankowski 1991; Spergel 1995; Venkatesh 2000). However, Jankowksi concludes, such gangs because of their quid pro quo relations with the community cannot transcend their consensual norms; therefore, they (the gangs) cannot play a role in the political vanguard.

## Turning toward a New Literature: Gangs and the Politics of Performance, Resistance, Reflexivity, and Identity

As French sociologist Alain Touraine suggests, one of the most important questions that a sociologist can ask is how do people who are not generally considered the makers of "history" become movement actors in the postindustrial epoch? We argue that the ALKQN, in its incarnation during the 1996–1999 period, provides a perfect case study through which to pursue this interrogation.

Nevertheless, as we excavate these movement "possibilities," it is clear that the gang literature alone cannot adequately guide our inquiry or our analysis. For the most part, the tendency in the research is still to treat gangs and gang members as socially deviant phenomena, reacting rationally but ultimately pathologically to impossible structural constraints and giving rise to individual and collective strategies to resolve everyday issues of powerlessness, discrimination, exclusion, and alienation. Over time these repertoires of adaptation, all of which are historically situated, become embedded in the cultural and subcultural traditions and folkways of families, neighborhoods, and (nowadays) geo-social spaces whose borders are difficult to define. Nonetheless, for all the humanistic and empathetic attention gangs have received, the criminological imagination still has difficulty broaching the possibility that gangs can produce a pro-social transformation. Consequently, the relationship between politics and the street gang has been occluded, although where it has merited attention, the consensus has been that gang members remain somewhere on the continuum between apolitical and overwhelmingly conservative.

Therefore, to appreciate the dynamics of the ALKQN's intensely radical development, we have turned primarily to the literature in cultural and social movements studies, particularly focusing on resistances among traditionally oppressed and subaltern classes. In this endeavor, we have found the work of research theorists such as Conquergood, McAdam, Morris, Castells, and Touraine to be especially enlightening.

## CONQUERGOOD AND THE STREET PERFORMANCE OF THE CHICAGO LATIN KINGS

Conquergood's long-term in situ documentation of neighborhood Latin Kings in Chicago has produced a number of highly innovative cultural interpretations of the customs, rituals, and symbolic universes of gang members (Conquergood 1990, 1992, 1994, 1997). Borrowing from the British school of cultural resistance studies, the labeling theories of Becker, and the interdisciplinary discourses of performance studies (for example, Bakhtin 1981; Clifford 1988; Geertz 1983; Rosaldo 1989; Trinh 1989; and Turner 1986), Conquergood alerts us to the actively produced and reproduced worlds of gangs. For him, gang members are not to be viewed as adapting fatalistically, pathologically, or even innovatively to their environment but rather as consciously making their culture in between the structures and crevices of an imposed bourgeois social order. As Conquergood phrases it, "The homeboys are keenly aware of class difference in communication style, and are critical of what they take to be the tepid, distant, interpersonal mode of the middle class. . . . Against a dominant world that displaces, stifles, and erases identity, the homeboys create, through their communications practices, a hood: a subterranean space of life-sustaining warmth, intimacy, and protection" (1994, 47).

Conquergood's work stands in direct contrast to most gang studies, not least because he requires us (the author, the observer, the listener) to unearth the hidden and the opaque and to question our own taken-for-granted expert positionality. In advocating that we go beyond "rhetorical reflexivity," that is, the wide-ranging critique of traditional ethnographic empiricism and positivism engendered by poststructuralist and postmodernist writers, Conquergood asks researchers to more honestly situate themselves and their respondents in their texts.

Thus Conquergood calls upon the research community to go beyond seeing gang members as other than the mechanistic "other" but rather as cultural agents who function dialectically both as subjects and objects in their own social sphere as well as in the gaze of the researcher. In table 10.1, I summarize some of these conceptual differences between Conquergood's approach and those of mainstream criminology across the analytical categories of (1) social agency, (2) processes of cultural construction, (3) presumed character of society, and (4) perceived relations between the gang and the community.

For all the profundity of Conquergood's epistemological approach and his richly layered analyses, Conquergood can only accomplish theoretically that which his empirical data allow him to reveal. And while the decade-long focus of his neighborhood studies, the Latin Kings in Chicago, has produced an impressive and hitherto unexplored range of symbolic and linguistic treatises, his subjects did not exhibit the level of political development we have witnessed with the same group in the New York City area. Therefore, it is to the studies of collective behavior and social movements that we turn for further illumination.

### RESISTANCE AND SOCIAL MOVEMENTS

As I have argued, the question of politics in the gang literature has been largely tangential to the central discourse on crime throughout the last century. Oddly enough, an analogous critique could also be leveled at the social movement literature in terms of understanding or even appreciating the presence of indigenous politics and organizations of subaltern or lower classes.

Both McAdam's and Morris's studies of the black civil rights movement during the 1960s represented a sharp break from the early social-psychological models of collective behavior and from the power elite orientations of resource mobilization theorists. McAdam's and Morris's sociohistorically grounded studies of the evolution of the protest movement among the Southern poor led them to make the following correctives to the dominant frameworks in social movement discourse:

*Table 10.1.* Comparison between Conquergood's Approach to Gangs and That of Orthodox Criminology across Four Analytical Categories

| | (I)<br>Social Agency | (II)<br>Cultural Processes | (III)<br>Character of Society | (IV)<br>Gang-Community Relations |
|---|---|---|---|---|
| Conquergood | • Active<br>• Purposive<br>• Resistant<br>• Empowering<br>• Spatially transformative | • Symbolically-appropriating, rational self-articulating<br>• Learned in interactions with juveniles and adults<br>• Regenerative | • Capitalist mode of production<br>• Class- and race-based hierarchies<br>• Coercive apparatuses of bourgeois state | • Organically emergent<br>• Contradictory |
| Orthodox Criminology | • Adaptive<br>• Reproducing itself pathologically | • Learned criminal deviance<br>• Cultures and subcultures of poverty<br>• Apart lower-class cultural milieu | • Non-defined, modern<br>• Industrial<br>• Disorganized<br>• Rapidly changing<br>• Naturally poverty-producing<br>• Transhistorical | • Strained with mainstream<br>• Reflective of community pathologies<br>• Fundamentally anomic |

1. Oppositional movements to the status quo are not irrational responses by alienated individuals but reflect a rational necessity given the constantly unresolved social problems based in systems of unequal power and distribution.

2. Movement actors and leaders do not suddenly arrive on the historical scene but rather are nurtured over time and emerge out of a long drawn-out process of collective resistance traditions, including charismatic leadership traditions and multiple movement centers (see Morris 1984).

3. Many of the resources for social movements do not come from the coffers of generous outsider benefactors but from the development of a network impetus and the already existing indigenous organizations that create social and cultural resources to meet the demands of the situation.

For McAdam (1982) and Morris (1984), movement members were essentially political actors who saw themselves struggling against and potentially transcending contemporary historical power lines. This precondition of social movement genesis McAdam calls "cognitive liberation," and it is one of the most crucial factors behind a movement's success, even though it is difficult to measure. For Morris, in turn, what is critical for movement building and movement sustainability is the intervention of indigenously trained social activists who are able to "read" accurately the possibilities in politically fertile social conditions.

### REFLEXIVITY AND THE WORK OF TOURAINE

Earlier in the paper with reference to Conquergood, I stated that reflexivity in the research act was of critical importance in gang studies. Equally important is an understanding of reflexivity that focuses on the fluctuating relationship between a movement and its community and its own set of actions. If we are to get closer to the lifeworlds of movement actors, then it is imperative to develop an understanding of this terrain, or what Touraine calls a sociology of action.

Touraine's theory of social movements is probably the most developed reflexively based analysis in the literature. Despite the reactionary winds of the postindustrial age, he continues to argue that social movements are the key to social change. Such movements contain what he calls "class actors," members of movements who are "fighting for control of historicity, that is, control of the great cultural orientations by which a society's environmental relationships are normatively organized" (1988, 26).

For Touraine, and McAdam, there always exists a dynamic reflexivity between a social movement and its allied community that serves to generate and to regenerate a movement's momentum and at the same time helps shape and influence its agenda. Touraine also considers two other aspects of the reflexive process: (1) the roles that social movements play not only in promoting and generating social change itself but in revealing the underlying structures of the formal institutions with which social movements are in conflict, and (2) the culture that is created by the social movement, which in turn generates more social action.

Touraine's approach is extremely insightful when we come to study movements that arise from seemingly atypical sociopolitical forces such as gangs. Specifically, his work helps us to understand how collectivized social actors struggle for alternative visions of a society or, at least, of certain aspects of its culture, despite facing overwhelming opposition from society's elites. We gain further insight into the reverse dynamics of oppression, that is, those developmental processes of an oppositional movement that occur because of an increase in oppression rather than being thwarted by it.

## IDENTITY IN LATE MODERNITY

The fourth analytical theme to be drawn from the discussion on gangs and politics is the crucial importance of identity as it is constructed by marginalized movement populations in the late- or postmodern period. While this concept is exhaustively discussed and rehearsed in a plethora of works on new social movements that emerged in the latter part of the last century (see Melucci 1996 for a summary), for now I want to focus on one theorist, Castells, whose work is critical for an understanding of social movements in highly marginalized locales.

In Castells' work *The Power of Identity* (1997), the author applies the theories of Touraine to the information age and within a highly eclectic theoretical framework explains the emergence of myriad resistance movements—which have been notable not for their commitment to structural change but to acquiring their own social and cultural spaces—within the shifting boundaries of the globalized and decentered nation-state. But what is identity in the social movement context? For Castells, it is a process of meaning construction both for individuals and for collectivities by which certain "sources of meaning" (1997, 6) are prioritized over others and eventually internalized.

Castells sees three different types of identity that all have to be factored into social movement development. These he calls legitimizing, resistance, and project identities (1997, 8), and it is the interplay between these identities that largely underscores the complexity of the social movement process.

While the first identity obviously refers to the condition of domination, in a Gramscian sense, the other two are strictly associated with oppositional movement development. It is to the concept of resistance identity that Castells attaches most weight given the postmodern context, not least because it reveals the process by which individuals and their respective affiliations both come to believe in certain self-representations and act upon them accordingly.

## From Gangs to the Analysis of the Street Organization

What I am arguing is that the second literature provides us with limitless possibilities to study the phenomena of politicized gangs and gang members that, based on our experience in New York, are increasingly coming to the fore within old and new gang subcultures. This, of course, is not to say that the gang literature should be dismissed, but rather it must be rethought and extended, which is a primary reason for this conference. At the more general theoretical level, this rethinking has been practiced by Burawoy in his two ethnographic research compilations (1991, 2000) produced by the method he calls extended case study analysis. Based on the tensions between these two literatures, however, and the empirical data that interconnects them, how do we proceed?

The first problem to be faced is what to do with the concept of the street gang? Our answer to devise an alternative social construct that better accords with our observations, which we have called a "street organization." Table 10.2 compares the characteristic properties of the two phenomena.

The second problem is how do we devise a schematic that will allow a deeper, more grounded analysis of the phenomenon and at the same time extend our theoretical horizons qua the gangs-politics conundrum? Our answer has been to take a page from Touraine's own tripartite construct of the postindustrial social movement, which he divided into the following separate "principles": identity, opposition, and totality.

Therefore, integrating concepts from research on gangs, performance studies, and the social movements literature, we have arrived at the following analytical model of the politicized gang or street organization. In the final part of this paper, this model will be operationalized with reference to research findings highlighting social movement qualities of a group that

*Table 10.2.* A Comparison of Street Organizations and Gangs

|  | Street Organizations | Gangs |
|---|---|---|
| Period | 1996–99 | 1985–95 |
| Structure | Vertical with increasing level of decentralization | Vertical with limited level of local autonomy |
| Territory | Extraterritorial | Situationally territorial |
| Ideology | Communitarian/utopian/ spiritual | Street survivalism/ entrepreneurial/cultish |
| Education | Pro-school rhetorically and in practice | Anti-school in practice but rhetorically pro-school |
| Delinquency | Although some individuals do engage in delinquency, this is not sanctioned by the group | Rhetorically anti-delinquent but high tolerance in practice |
| Conflict management | Mostly negotiation & mediation in inter- and intragroup conflicts with physical solutions as a last resort | Negotiation and mediation used but confrontational & retributional solutions to inter- and intragroup conflict are common |
| Attire | Beads & colors often situationally displayed | Colors & artifacts of conspicuous consumption universally displayed |
| Integration | High solidarity maintained through moral and political group pressure | Loyalty maintained through physical threats and group pressure |
| Duration | Long-term commitment; exiting and entering the group through signed mutual consent | Long-term commitment; entering through mutual consent; exiting more difficult and may include physical penalties |
| Communication | Local and general meetings; newsletters; face-to-face meetings | Local, general, & face-to-face meetings but many decisions made through secret missives |

would normally be outside the purview of a gang analysis (see Brotherton and Barrios 2004; Kontos, Brotherton, and Barrios 2003).

## Gangs as Street Organizations on the Streets of New York

The research project came about through a relationship that had developed between my colleague, Father Luis Barrios, and the ALKQN in the summer of 1996. Essentially, the group's leadership had decided to reach out and ask for his help to secure a safe space to hold the group's monthly general membership meetings and to seek social and spiritual support for the group's move from a gang to a communitarian movement of the barrio. The context of the rendezvous is worthy of comment.

*Figure 10.1.* Definitional Model

The year, 1996, was midway through the term of Mayor Rudy Giuliani, arguably the most authoritarian populist city leader New York has had during the last century. A great deal of his political legitimacy was based on his successful efforts to bring down the crime rate, rein in the "excesses" of New York's public and civic culture (that is, curtail its spending on welfare and related services, diminish its progressive tax rates, and contain its residents' irreverent hedonism and urban expressionism), and improve or at least safeguard the city's investment and lifestyle climate for his influential financial and real estate backers. On the other side of the social control spectrum were positioned the quintessential "folk devils" of the moment, the ALKQN. Labeled by the tabloid press as a vicious lower-class Puerto Rican and Dominican street gang now present in all five boroughs, a number of the group had done their best to live up to their name. At the time, the biggest trial in town was the federal prosecution of King Blood, the founder of the ALKQN, plus thirty-five other leaders all charged under the Racketeering Influence and Corrupt Organizations Act of 1970. Blood was specifically being charged with ordering eleven assassinations of group members from his jail cell. The explosive imagery of the superdeviant versus the supercop could not have been better scripted and shows the enormous task the group faced in trying to reinvent itself before the public. Nonetheless, the lived reality of the communities from whence the ALKQN came also contains currency in processes of resistance.

According to the New York Current Population Survey for 1996, the life chances for most Puerto Ricans and Dominicans were extremely grim. Regarding income and schooling, 43.6 percent of Puerto Ricans and 45.7 percent of Dominicans lived below the poverty line; 53.6 percent of adult Puerto Ricans (that is, over twenty-five years of age) had no high school diploma and 19 percent no high school at all; among adult Dominicans 54.7

percent had no diploma and only 4 percent had completed college. Regarding the family, only 27.3 percent of Puerto Rican children had both parents present; 84.2 percent of them qualified for free school lunch and 75 percent had no health insurance. For Dominicans, more than 50 percent of the children lived in single-parent homes, a 10-percent increase in less than seven years. The starkness of the statistics continued through other categories, providing an appalling picture of social and economic misery for any population in a modern industrial democracy. Not only was the socioeconomic status of both groups light-years behind that of whites, but it was even significantly below that of African-Americans, the group that was usually referred to as the benchmark of poverty in the city.

After observing and participating in several revivalist-type rallies/meetings with attendances numbering between 600 and 700 Kings and 50 to 100 Queens, Reverend Barrios asked if I might like to collaborate on a project that would document the process of transformation he had been witnessing. Within a year of our initial contact, we received a grant to study the formal and informal educational roles that the group was playing in the lives of its members. This support enabled us to carry out sustained ethnographic research that included participatory and nonparticipatory observations of the group's social and organizational practices in street, neighborhood, college, work, court, and prison settings; multiple life-history interviews with forty-two males and twenty-eight females; archival collections of the group's wide-ranging texts; and long-term correspondences with member-inmates. After three years in the field, 1996–1999, the following is a partial summary of what we found, focusing on the social movement ascendancy of the group.

## SUBCULTURAL TRADITIONS

Of course the group's origins in the Chicago Motherland were enormously influential, with the texts and rituals mimicking their Midwest counterparts in a range of ways. The founding documents of King Blood, replete with his diatribes on dignity, righteousness, the tactics of war, and self-esteem were held as sacred by many if not all of the members. There were other traditions that also permeated the group that had very different origins and constituted what I have called indigenous empowerment models of the subcultural tradition.

## INDIGENOUS EMPOWERMENT MODELS

With a new leadership, more or less, in control of the organization after federal raids and a bloody internal power struggle had left the organization leaderless in the early 1990s, and with the emphasis on improving the self-image of the group, two of the immediate tasks that lay ahead were to develop indigenous models of self-organization (Morris 1984; Oberschall 1973) that historically resided in the members' own communities, would demonstrate to the public the new status of the group, and would be self-reinforcing once in place.

This feat of drawing on the community's "mentalities," or the members' "structures of feeling" (Williams 1977) was not without its problems, however. There was no shortage of members who preferred to restrict their oppositional behavior to delinquency and resentment rather than purposive social action (see Tarrow 1992, 180). Despite the interests of some hard-core members who clung tenaciously to their old gang lifestyles, many others made good-faith efforts to elevate the organization from a street subculture to an antiestablishment community force.

Table 10.3 delineates the major models of "collective action" (Tarrow 1992) that influenced both the philosophy and the practices of the new Latin Kings and Queens during the 1996–1999 period. These models of community resistance and self-organization and -empowerment complemented each other and constituted powerful frames of reference for the group to reconfigure and reimagine itself during its transitional phase.

## LEVEL OF ORGANIZATION

While the group was still very hierarchical and looked in many ways like the vertical gangs described by Jankowski (1991), there were other aspects of its organizational development that were bound to the group's new democratic trajectory. In short, we found that the group was reaching for a level of organizational sophistication and dedication among its membership that finds few parallels in the history of street gang subcultures. But the reform path the group was treading was very different from its prior development, and

*Table 10.3.* Empowerment Models Used in the ALKQN's Reform Phase

| Radical Political Models | Spiritual Models | Self-Help Models | Other Models |
|---|---|---|---|
| Black Panthers | Judaism | Alcoholics Anonymous | Orthodox Jewish community |
| Young Lords | Christianism | Alternatives to Violence | black civil rights movement |
| Puerto Rican Socialist Party | (Roman Catholics and Protestants) Africanism (Yorubas/Santeria and Paleros) | program | |

*Table 10.4.* Comparative Organizational Characteristics of the ALKQN Pre- and Postreform

| Before Reform (prior to 1996) | Reform and Postreform (1996–99) |
|---|---|
| Death penalty enforced | Death penalty abolished |
| Initiation could include physical violence | Initiation through prayer and probation |
| Forbidden to talk to "outsiders" about the group's business, especially the media | "Outsiders" welcome to inquire about the group and many interviews given to the media |
| Physical intimidation used to control members | Physical threats ended against members |
| Few formal rights of representation for members accused of wrongdoing | The notion of a "fair hearing" incorporated into trials |
| Females largely subordinate to males | Efforts made to reduce gendered power hierarchies |
| Little emphasis on developing youth sections | Great emphasis on developing a disciplined and committed youth cadre |
| Limited engagement in political and community matters | High level of engagement in city and community politics |
| Little emphasis on educational attainment among members | Great emphasis on both educational and occupational attainments among members |
| Tolerance and discrete promotion of illicit activities, e.g., drug dealing through the group | Rhetorical and demonstrative intolerance of illicit activities by group members |

it might not have lasted too much longer if the series of structural changes described below did not take place.

## MEMBERSHIP

The membership of the ALKQN was both similar to and unlike most gangs described in the literature. In age, there was a substantial membership between fifteen and nineteen years old who appeared to represent the bulk of the new recruits. However, there were also many members in their twenties and thirties who often filled the leadership positions, providing the kind of organizational experience and emotional stability that the group needed. Educationally, the members also ranged both in terms of their positive and negative experiences of schooling and their attainment of credentials, but all agreed with the group's conviction that education was the key to bettering both their own life chances and that of the community. Involvement with the criminal justice system also ranged widely, with many older members who, having served time in state and/or federal penitentiaries, were on a quest to convince the Nation's youth that "crime doesn't pay," while others had little direct experience of the "system" and wanted to keep it that way. And finally, the twin concepts of family background and social class also varied, with some members recounting horribly deformed and abusive familial relationships in the depths of urban poverty, while others told of their very mainstream two-parent upbringing and remembered few instances of hardship during their formative years.

This diversity of the members was a basic ingredient of the organization's dynamism and ensured that issues such as the group's identity, its social agenda, its politics, and its structuring were kept at the fore of the efforts to reform and pursue the goals of social movement building. At the same time, we should not lose sight of the commonalities among members. They were all Latino/a, primarily Puerto Rican and Dominican, and they had all experienced some form of marginalization that they attributed to the white-dominated system of economic, political, and cultural power. Further, they were all from working-class backgrounds, the sons and daughters of primarily blue-collar workers who, perhaps a generation before, would have been rural peasants. Finally, they were the result of a fairly recent process of social and geographical displacement, their parents having migrated for economic reasons to the United States, leaving their children to figure out their cultural place in the world.

## IDENTITY

The struggle for a group identity was critical to the process of transition. This, of course, is obvious in the public sphere where the group had to neutralize the messages of the dominant ideology that constantly used the group as an example of internal subversion, both political and criminal. But more importantly, the group had to know who and what it was. It had to have a coherent sense of itself in order to proceed with any momentum toward the construction of an identity built in opposition to the mainstream. One area that we have focused on is the group's interpretation of spirituality, a subject that is rarely present in the gang literature. In a recent paper by Father Barrios, he describes this aspect of the organization as follows:

> fundamental experiences of spirituality. . . . . is a path to identity in which, Kingism/Queenism (the group's ideology) is a spiritual syncretism that develops and preserves both the collective identity of the ALKQN and of the individual member through action. What that action consists of is very important. It is the learning of one's culture, the active reciprocity of friends and comrades, and the development of self-esteem. Therefore, the agency and practice of Kingism/Queenism's spirituality is concrete and functions almost like a form of self-organized therapy for the poor and marginalized. (Barrios 2003)

## GOALS VERSUS ACTS

For the most part, the group was seriously engaged in trying to become something new and distinct as far as street subcultures were concerned but something traditional when it came to the history of social movements. These contradictions of the organization subjected the group to an empirical test of its social movement credentials. In other words, in order for the group to be defined as a street organization with social movement properties, the group's political and oppositional actions had to significantly outweigh the importance of its criminally deviant actions. We found the group consumed with the following goals: (1) shifting the group to a radical political position, (2) empowering the Queens, (3) taking up the challenge of acquiring a quality education, and (4) ending the group's violent traditions.

In Touraine's language, the group was functioning as if it were the continuator and "mutator" (Touraine 1988) of a radical and even revolutionary history, unafraid to turn to outsiders for advice and support to develop this history. Did this mean, however, that the group was progressing without stumbling over the many contradictions contained in its own gang history? Quite the contrary, the organization openly conceded that it could not transform itself overnight and that its links to Chicago, to the prison system, and to the street both compelled it to make and constrained it from making the kind of radical changes that a bona fide social movement required before it could proudly declare its new identity was firmly in place.

### PERCEIVED ADVERSARIES

The group's members had many different adversaries who they envisioned and identified. These foes were both social actors and institutional forces that had a hand in preventing the group from making as much progress as it desired. Some of these oppositional forces were predictable, since they belong to the network of social control apparatuses whose raison d'etre is to fight such deviants as the ALKQN. But the ALKQN to some extent understood this characteristic of the current system of political economy and did their best to keep their energies focused on the major players who were determining both their present and their future. We found that the three major political opponents that fueled the group's ire and that heavily influenced its organizational strategies were the institution of law enforcement, the mayor, and the media. Another rival street gang, the Bloods, came a distant fourth, which indicated to us that the group had come a long way from its localized gang mentality of three or more years earlier.

There were also some internal adversaries, such as drug dealers, "fakes," "ghost tribes," and "snitches," but such forces actually operated in the less-patrolled border areas of the group, that is, in sociocultural spaces inhabited by ex- or disgruntled members or in the secret networks of state-sponsored surveillance teams where conspiracies are hatched, intelligence is gathered, and self-survival is being negotiated. It is striking that the group's strategy for dealing with its enemies was not reactive and at no time did the group engage in a tit-for-tat conflict spiral either with the other street groups or with the police. Quite the contrary, its reaction to attack was reserved and reasoned, and when it had analyzed the identities of the perpetrators, it mobilized to protect itself, neutralize the assault, and strike back in its own time.

## Commentary

Two interrelated questions that have frequently been asked in relationship to the above findings are to what extent is the ALKQN phenomenon in New York City unique and under what conditions did the group's reform emerge. In the following, I will briefly respond to these inquiries, offering some explanations and qualifications for what we have witnessed.

I would agree that there are few reports from other large gang cities such as Chicago or Los Angeles suggesting that groups like the ALKQN are undergoing similar radical transformations, even though we may occasionally read of efforts to politically mobilize certain gang memberships. At the same time, however, the qualitative development of the ALKQN was not entirely unique in New York City. During the same time period, there were reform efforts among street groups such as the Asociacion Neta and Zulu Nation, although neither group made the same institutional headway as the ALKQN. What was present in the case of the ALKQN that perhaps has been absent in other gangs and their sociocultural milieux?

In our case study of the ALKQN (Brotherton and Barrios 2004), we have pointed to the critical importance of at least three converging factors: (1) the internal and external presence of street-savvy and community-based intellectuals; (2) the unintentional consequences of local, state, and national repressive police and criminal justice practices; and (3) the changed class and motivational nature of the membership. Very briefly, each of these factors receive more explanation below.

External, street-related, radical intellectuals not only had strategic ties to the group during the early period of reform, but they were consistently on hand to provide advice, training, and network support during the entire period of the group's volatile transitional phase. These external change agents connected to and enabled internal forces of the group to embrace a more intellectual course, paving the way to a culture of self-criticism, debate, and transparency. The influence of intellectual social agents has been critical in nearly all social movements, as many other case studies have shown. However, the relationship between intellectuals and gangs has rarely been studied.

The systematic police assault on the group over a number of years had the unintentional consequence of compelling the organization to seek a new leadership and a new identity instead of the intended consequence of the leaderless gang collapsing. This occurred at a time when the membership was being greatly affected by reactionary local and national policies with regard to welfare and criminal justice. Such state policies succeed in politicizing almost any attempt at organizing from below.

As news of reform in the organization spread, the group appeared to attract to its ranks a new kind of member: many capable young street organizers from Latino working-class backgrounds who wanted to challenge the status quo and reject received notions of ethnic pluralism. Such youth had grown up during the crack epidemic and were keen to regain the social spaces of their neighborhoods, develop a positive sense of self, and embrace an activist agenda in relation to the resolution of everyday social problems. The ALKQN gave them both an individual and collective identity that satisfied their internal quests.

## Conclusion

The need to move outside the box of criminological gang discourse, to embrace other literatures that tackle not only the issues of domination and adaption but transformation, is extremely important. We have been caught for too long in a Durkheimian time warp with our gaze focused on positioned notions of order and disorder at the expense of appreciating the often masked, contradictory, and fluid expressions of resilience and transcendence. The new period of heightened globalism and decentered capitalism has transformed all social actors in ways that are often difficult to comprehend. Time/space compression has required us do things more quickly and with less reflection than we would like; however, it has also allowed us to rub shoulders both physically and symbolically with those we would not normally encounter in our segregated social spheres. Certain gangs have taken advantage of this new era of possibility, seeing in the borders that formerly kept them in quarantine barriers that should be dismantled. I argue that this increased sense of political volition from below opened the doors for gang members to reflexively embrace the community in a way that was unthinkable just a few years ago.

Five years on from our original encounter, the group has been battered and bruised by its interaction with the state, and, at first glance, it might appear that the repressive tactics of law enforcement, so characteristic of the 1960s government-led war against radicalism, have had their intended effect. The key leaders have been removed, the group has been flooded with informants, and a demoralized membership has allowed some of the most destructive, antipolitical elements to come to the fore. Reduced to a shell of its former political self and organizationally fractured across New York's cityscape, it is hard to imagine when or if the group will politically reemerge. Yet, despite this somber assessment, there is room for spiritual optimism.

If we remember that globalization both aggregates and unhinges established power relations, then we must always be prepared to recognize new and sometimes unexpected processes of collective resistance. Whether it is the grassroots movements of Latin America, effectively challenging the diktats of neoliberal elites or the more subterranean movements of the New York street, the globalized social scientist has to appreciate agency in all its forms, interconnectedness, and historicity. It is in this context that Queen N., a leader of the ALKQN from the suburbs of Long Island, enters my office on a recent weekday to announce the following:

> It's true, we were very demoralized by what happened to us at the end of the nineties. But you should know that many of us never left the organization. We just became less visible, you know, keeping to ourselves, meeting at the weekends and trying to live by our lessons. But we never forgot what we had been through or where we had come from. Those days [of reform] were the most important of our lives. The speeches, the rallies, the big meetings, all of those people who came to listen to us . . . you can't just go back . . . You knew you had to keep going forward, but how? So, for a while, we were very confused, but we stuck at it. Eventually it became clear; one of the most important lessons was there was more need for the Nation now than ever! I have fifty Queens in my tribe and we cover all ages and all races. I just wanted to let you know that we're here and we're not going anywhere. (Queen N., November 24, 2003)

## References

Bakhtin, Mikhail. 1981. *The Dialogic Imagination*, ed. M. Holquist. Austin: University of Texas Press.

Barrios, Luis. 2003. "Spirituality and Resistance in the Latin Kings and Queens." In *Alternative Perspectives on Gangs and the Community,* ed. Louis Kontos, David Brotherton, and Luis Barrios. New York: Columbia University Press.

Brotherton, David, and Luis Barrios. 2004. *Between Black and Gold: The Street Politics of the Almighty Latin King and Queen Nation.* New York: Columbia University Press.

Burawoy, Michael. 1991. *Ethnography Unbound.* Berkeley: University of Berkeley Press.

————. 2000. *Global Ethnography: Forces, Connections, and Imaginations in a Postmodern World.* Berkeley: University of California Press.

Castells, Manuel. 1997. *The Power of Identity.* New York: Blackwell.

Campbell, Anne. 1984. *Girls in the Gang.* 1st ed. London: Blackwell.

Clifford, James. 1988. *The Predicament of Culture: Twentieth-Century Ethnography, Literature, and Art.* Cambridge, Mass.: Harvard University Press.

Cloward, Richard A., and Lloyd Ohlin. 1960. *Delinquency and Opportunity.* New York: Free Press.

Cohen, Albert. 1955. *Delinquent Boys.* New York: Free Press.

Conquergood, Dwight. 1992. "On Reppin' and Rhetoric: Gang Representations." Paper presented at the Philosophy and Rhetoric of Inquiry Seminar, University of Iowa.

————. 1994. "Homeboys and Hoods: Gang Communication and Cultural Space." In *Group Communication in Context: Studies of Natural Groups,* ed. Larry Frey, 23–55. Hillsdale, N.J.: Lawrence Erlbaum.

————. 1997. "Street Literacy." In *Handbook of Research on Teaching Literacy through the Communicative and Visual Arts,* ed. James Flood, Shirley Brice Heath, and Diane Lapp, 354–75. New York: Simon and Schuster.

Conquergood, Dwight, and T. Siegel, producers and directors. 1990. *The Heart Broken in Half* (videotape). New York: Filmmakers Library.

Decker, Scott H., and Barrik Van Winkle. 1996. *Life in the Gang.* Cambridge: Cambridge University Press.

Freire, Paulo. 1969. *Pedagogy of the Oppressed.* New York: Seabury Press.

Garland, David. 2001. *The Culture of Control: Crime and Social Order in Contemporary Society.* Chicago: University of Chicago Press.

Geertz, Clifford. 1983. *Local Knowledge: Further Essays in Interpretative Anthropology.* New York: Basic Books.

Hagedorn, John. 1988. *People and Folks.* Chicago: Lake View Press.

Harvey, David. 2000. *Spaces of Hope.* Berkeley: University of California Press.

Hobsbawm, Eric. 1959. *Primitive Rebels.* London: W. W. Norton.

Jacobs, James B. 1977. *Stateville: The Penitentiary in Mass Society.* Chicago: University of Chicago Press.

Jankowski, Martin. S. 1991. *Islands in the Street: Gangs in American Urban Society.* Berkeley: University of California Press.

Katz, Jack. 1988. *Seductions of Crime: Moral and Sensual Attractions in Doing Evil.* New York: Basic Books.

Kontos, Louis, David Brotherton, and Luis Barrios, eds. 2003. *Gangs and Society: Alternative Perspectives.* New York: Columbia University Press.

McAdam, Doug. 1982. *Political Process and the Development of Black Insurgency 1930– 1970.* Chicago: University of Chicago Press.

Melucci, Alberto. 1996. *Challenging Codes: Collective Action in the Information Age.* New York: Cambridge University Press.

Merton, Robert. 1949. *Social Theory and Social Structure.* Glencoe, Ill.: Free Press.

Miller, W. 1958. "Lower-Class Culture as a Generating Milieu of Gang Delinquency." *Journal of Social Issues* 14: 5–19.

Moore, Joan. 1991. *Going Down to the Barrio: Homeboys and Homegirls in Change.* Philadelphia: Temple University Press.

Morris, Aldon, D. 1984. *The Origins of the Civil Rights Movement.* New York: Free Press.

Oberschall, Anthony. 1973. *Social Conflict and Social Movements.* Englewood Cliffs, N.J.: Prentice-Hall.

Rosaldo, Renato. 1989. *Culture and Truth: The Remaking of Social Analysis.* Boston: Beacon.

Sassen, Saskia. 1998. *Globalization and Its Discontents.* New York: New Press.

Spergel, I. 1995. *The Youth Gang Problem: A Community Approach.* New York: Oxford University Press.

Tarrow, Sidney. 1992. "Mentalities, Political Cultures, and Collective Action Frames: Constructing Meanings through Action." In *Frontiers in Social Movement Theory,* ed. Aldon D. Morris and Carold McClurg Mueller, 174–202. Newhaven, Conn.: Yale University Press.

Thrasher, Frederick. 1927. *The Gang: A Study of 1,313 Gangs in Chicago.* Chicago: University of Chicago Press.

Touraine, Alain. 1971. *Post-Industrial Society.* New York: Random House.

———. 1988. *Return of the Actor.* Minnesota: University of Minnesota Press.

Trinh, Minh-ha. 1989. *Women Native Other.* Bloomington: Indiana University Press.

Turner, Victor. 1977. *The Ritual Process: Structure and Anti-Structure.* Ithaca: Cornell University.

Venkatesh, Sudhir A. 2000. *American Project: The Rise and Fall of an American Ghetto.* Cambridge, Mass.: Harvard University Press.

Wacquant, Loic. 2002. "Deadly Symbiosis." *Boston Review* (May 1): 1–25.

Williams, Raymond. 1977. *Marxism and Literature.* Oxford: Oxford University Press.

Willis, Paul. 1977. *Learning to Labor: How Working Class Kids Get Working Class Jobs.* Westmead, UK: Saxon House.

# 11

# Americanization, the Third Way, and the Racialization of Youth Crime and Disorder

## JOHN PITTS

Throughout the postwar period, the United States has been a shaping influence upon the economy, culture, and politics of the United Kingdom, and this has fostered the belief that what happens in the United States today is destined to happen in the UK tomorrow. It is a belief that has, with increasing frequency through the 1980s and 1990s, led UK governments to adopt "American-style" modes of analysis, problem definition, and "solutions." One effect of this has been that, sometimes, UK governments have anticipated, or reacted to, problems that did not actually exist.

This "Americanization" of British political life moved up a gear after 1979 as, inspired by the Reagan-Bush neoliberal experiment, the Conservative administrations of Margaret Thatcher and John Major strove to "free" the UK's economy and "reform" its welfare state. With the election, in 1997, of a "modernizing" *New Labour* government, the transatlantic relationship intensified, culminating in the construction, by New Labour premier Tony Blair and President Bill Clinton, of a *Third Way* for Anglo-American politics that promised continuity in the sphere of economics and reform in the areas of social welfare and criminal justice.

New Labour was eager to embrace the assumptions about the changing nature of economic life, the role of government, and the future of the welfare state in a globalizing economy that had become the common sense of mainstream U.S. politics by the early 1990s. It also adopted the Clinton administration's electoral strategy, which strove to win over traditional Republican supporters by making the issues of fiscal prudence, the family, welfare reform, and law and order their own and never to allow themselves to be outflanked on the political right. As Gore Vidal has observed:

> Clinton has learned to play the dull reactive media like the virtuoso he is, and Dole, if not God, can't think what to do about him. No matter what new betise the Right come up with, Clinton has got there at least a day early and has made their issue his. Currently everyone hates (when not raping or corrupting on the Internet) teenagers. What is to be done about these layabouts? This is a crucial Republican-family-values issue, the result of all that money, practically none in fact, thrown at the poor, who, by nature are lawless, drugged, sexy, violent. But before the doleful could get around to the death penalty for pubescent vagrants, Clinton struck. Curfews for teenagers he proclaimed . . . All Dole could gasp was "Character," "Integrity." Or whatever. (1998, 151)

Indeed, it was only three days after their first meeting in January 1993 that Tony Blair first voiced the now-famous Clintonism, "tough on crime, tough on the causes of crime" (King and Wickham-Jones 1999).

## Crime as Electoral Cement

The centrality of crime to the reconfigured, Anglo-American, center-left project derives from a particularly hard-nosed analysis of the imperatives of modern political life. This analysis holds that economic globalization, because it triggers widespread deindustrialization, precipitates a sharp decline in the size of the industrial working class, thus diminishing the power of the trade unions, a key traditional constituency. Meanwhile, a growing underclass of the urban poor is excluded, or excludes itself, from the political process altogether. As a result, modern "center-left" parties must build a new political constituency. It follows that, because it is the more prosperous sections of the "working" and "middle" classes that remain politically engaged, it is in the suburbs, the small towns, and the gentrified urban enclaves that elections will be won and lost. This new constituency of the center is, the argument runs, "postpolitical," in that it has rejected both right- and left-wing dogmatism (Giddens 1998), preferring governments that administer the state in accordance with the dictates of common sense, administrative and technical competence, and value for money. This is, moreover, a constituency that, next to job security, is most concerned about the threat of criminal victimization posed by an expanding "underclass," possessed of a distinctive antisocial culture, who dwell in the "unemployed ghettos" of the inner city.

## The Left and the Right Hands of the State

David Garland has observed that the advent of the politics of the third way marks the demise of the "solidarity project" (Garland 2001), marking a further step towards what Jock Young (1999) has described as the "exclusive society." In this new politics, earlier social democratic accounts of the relationship between the individual and society and the citizen and the state are inverted. Cultural change becomes a prerequisite of structural change and the responsibility of the state to its citizens is de-emphasized in favor of the duties owed by citizens to the state. Thus, Pierre Bourdieu (1998) argues, the "left hand of the state," which once assumed responsibility for creating the social, educational, and economic conditions for effective citizenship, is stilled, while the "right hand of the state," which acts to impose order and discipline and contain or expel those unable to meet their civic and economic obligations, is given free reign. Moreover, the zest with which this latter activity is undertaken appears to be in an inverse relation with the modern state's capacity to intervene in economic life, as Slavoj Zizeck observes:

> Contemporary politics is constrained by an unacknowledged impossibility. Tony Blair and Bill Clinton make minor changes to the style and presentation of public life but leave unanswered broader questions of how society should be governed . . . genuine political action is virtually impossible now because capitalism has won the ideological war and nobody is seriously questioning its values or rules. But just like post-modern culture persuades itself that it lives in an age of freedom so politicians mask their limitations with a facade of energetic political activity. (2000, 39)

And so, increasing emphasis is placed upon the control of deviant lifestyles, low-level crime, and the "incivilities" that, it is claimed, the newly constructed center-left constituencies find most offensive and most threatening to their quality of life and freedom of action (Pitts 2001).

This is, as Peter Mair (2000) has argued, a strategy that aims to remove the politics of party from the governing process by appealing directly to "the people" who count electorally, via focus groups, opinion polls, and informal contact between senior government ministers and "ordinary people." However, in what Ulrich Beck (1992) has described as "the risk society," it is the anxieties, rather than the ideals, of electors and those who wish to be elected by them that drive this "politics of good governance." As a result, in a socially and culturally heterogeneous and economically polarized world, in which those who make a difference electorally are disproportionately older, more prosperous, and white, it is their perceived anxieties that shape the political agenda.

## Color Blindness

New Labour had learned from Clinton that to win, it needed to secure the ephemeral loyalties of traditionally conservative voters, for whom tales of an ungrateful and vindictive underclass had a particular resonance, while retaining the support of the remnants of the party's traditional working class as well as its liberal intellectual constituencies. In consequence, *New Labour* plumped for a paradoxical account of events that, with William Julius Wilson (1987), located the origins of social inequality, poverty, and crime in an inequitable social structure but, with Charles Murray (1984), prescribed interventions that targeted the values, attitudes, and behavior of the poor and crime prone. The American term "underclass" was side-stepped in favor of the more recognizably European term "social exclusion." But this served to obscure the fact that the "culturalist" accounts of the "underclass" that underpinned New Labour's social and criminal justice policies were predicated upon theories that had, in the United States in the 1980s, provided the cornerstone upon which a racialized account of the link between crime and poverty was constructed (Herrnstein and Murray 1994; Murray 1984; Wilson and Herrnstein 1985). Indeed, in the hands of these commentators, the term "underclass" came to be employed as a scarcely coded reference to the purported deficiencies of ethnic minorities.

Whereas Margaret Thatcher had routinely exploited fears of "cultural swamping" and "black street crime" in the run-up to the 1979 general election and after, *New Labour* assiduously avoided discussion of any link between immigration, race, and crime, referring only to the need to extend equality of opportunity to all citizens and protect ethnic minorities from racist victimization. Indeed, *New Labour* made much of the fact that the 1997 election had brought unprecedented numbers of black and Asian MPs into the UK parliament, most of them on the Labour benches, presenting itself as a multicultural, rainbow alliance of reasonable people. Even though New Labour's proposed policies on crime and welfare were destined to bear disproportionately upon them, no reference was made to the fact that a large minority of the newly discovered UK underclass that was to be the object of their social and criminal justice policies would not be white.

## Penal Populism

In the sphere of criminal justice, the politics of the third way has perpetu-ated the populist criminal justice policies ushered in by Ronald Reagan and Margaret Thatcher (Garland 2001). Now, both policy ends and policy means are designed to accord with the dictates of a usually retributive "common sense." In the United States in the 1980s, this led to an unprecedented increase in incarceration in general and in the confinement of African American and Hispanic young people more specifically. The centrality of "youth crime" to New Labour's political project is evidenced by the fact that its first major piece of legislation, the Crime and Disorder Act (1998), hit the statute books in record time. The broad contours of this legislation are easily described. It involves the induction of a new, younger population into the youth jus-tice system via preemptive civil measures that target "incivilities," minor public nuisance offenses such as rowdyism, insulting or threatening behav-ior toward neighbors, and minor property damage or graffiti, perpetrated by younger children and the inadequacies of their parents. Informalism is abandoned in favor of earlier, preemptive, formal intervention by the police via reprimands and final warnings. Diversion from custody into "integrative alternatives" gives way to community penalties, which may be imposed on a maximum of two occasions. After this, an expanded range of semi-indeter-minate custodial penalties may apply. The age at which such sentences may be imposed has been lowered from fifteen to twelve and in some cases ten years old. The Crime and Disorder Act (1998) epitomized the New Labour project. Its account of the problem attested to the Party's commonsense hard-headedness. Its commitment to "evidence-based" solutions demonstrated its adherence to the thoroughly modern precepts of scientific rationality, while the new administrative arrangements were presented as the very model of economy, efficiency, and effectiveness.

The impact of the 1998 act was both predictable and predicted (Pitts 2000). Once the act was implemented, the numbers of children and young people consigned to secure and penal institutions began to climb even more steeply than under New Labour's hard-line Conservative predecessors, and the time they served in these institutions increased. The architects of this new youth justice system, constructed with an eye to problems purportedly presented by an "underclass" rather than the problems inherent in justice systems, paid scant attention to the possibility that preemptive formal intervention might initiate new system careers: the new system has had the effect of drawing a larger number of younger, less problematic children and young people into the system. The numbers of ten- to seventeen-year-olds inducted into the youth justice system have risen by approximately 25 percent since New Labour came to power (Pitts 2001) while the number of those placed under probation (sixteen and older) has doubled (Robinson 2002). As in the Unites States, as the numbers have risen the proportion of black and Asian inmates has also grown. This is doubly ironic when we recognize that in the UK crime rates have been falling steadily since 1994.

Whereas in an earlier period, rising penal populations had been represented as shameful on the part of the authorities because they were both wasteful and inhumane, now this leap in the incarceration of children and young people has been celebrated as a political achievement (Currie 1985; Simon 2000). But was the UK really facing an American-style crime problem?

## Race Crime and Justice

The rhetoric surrounding its launch suggested that the 1998 Crime and Disorder Act would enable robust early intervention with the progeny of a U.S.-style, welfare-dependent underclass in order to transform their antisocial values and correct their offending behavior. Yet there was simply no reliable empirical evidence that such families existed (Barry and Hallett 1998; Dean and Taylor-Gooby 1992). Similarly, the implication that the UK was facing a U.S.-style youth crime wave may have been an effective electoral pitch but it was entirely speculative. In fact, although between 1981 and 1994 crime in the UK had risen by 111 percent, from 1994, recorded crime in general had been falling steadily. It was true that violent crime had continued to rise, but this increase was accounted for in large part by brawls involving drunken white adults in the rapidly expanding, deregulated, city-center, nighttime "leisure ghettoes" that developed in most UK towns and cities in the late 1980s.

## Deindustrialization, Neighborhood Destabilization, and the Redistribution of Victimization

It was true, however, that by 1997 the UK was facing a serious problem of youth crime and victimization of a very different order. The contours of this problem were shaped, in large part, by the seismic changes in the UK economy following the international oil crises of 1974 and the rapid globalization of economic life, compounded by the UK's own neoliberal experiment, rather than a social epidemic blown eastwards from the United States. Ironically, in their efforts to emulate U.S.-style market deregulation and welfare reform, UK governments in the 1980s and 1990s succeeded in reproducing some of the conditions that had earlier fostered huge increases in youth crime in the United States (Hagedorn 1998).

From the late 1970s, the oil crisis, the globalization of economic life, and market deregulation triggered widespread deindustrialization in the UK. In the 1980s, 21 percent of the UK's industrial base was lost. This gave rise to unprecedented levels of unemployment in general and male youth unemployment in particular. Within this demographic, second- and third-generation non-white migrants were hardest hit. Between 1981 and 1991, the number of workers earning half the national average wage or less, the Council of Europe poverty line, rose from 900,000 to 2,400,000. In the same period, those earning over twice the national average wage rose from 1,800,000 to 3,100,000. This marked a reversal of the postwar tendency towards a narrowing of the income divide.

As the 1980s progressed, the state steadily relinquished its role as provider of public housing by curtailing the right of local authorities to spend housing revenue on house building and by progressive reductions in the central government's financial contribution to local government. Existing housing stock was sold en bloc to the private sector, nongovernmental housing corporations, or individual tenants. The remaining housing stock, normally the least marketable, was retained to enable local authorities to discharge their legal responsibilities to homeless families. Predictably, these developments presaged a "secession of the successful" from public housing and an influx of poorer, younger, often single-parent families. Between 1984 and 1994, annual residential mobility in public housing increased from 4 to 7 percent of households. Whereas in the 1980s and 1990s, 40 percent of heads of households in public housing were aged sixty-five or over, in the subsequent decade 75 percent of newly formed households entering public housing were headed by someone aged between sixteen and twenty-nine. The policy changes had a disproportionate impact upon ethnic minorities. In 1995, 40 percent of African-Caribbeans and 59 percent of Pakistanis and Bangladeshis in the UK were located in the poorest fifth of the population. In London, by the mid-1990s, up to 70 percent of the residents on the poorest public housing estates were from ethnic minorities (Pitts 2001). As the 1990s progressed, their ranks were swelled by refugees from Eritrea, Ethiopia, the former Yugoslavia, and Nigeria. As a result, between 1981 and 1991 the average household income of families in "social" housing fell below the official poverty line, from 79 percent to 45 percent of the national average. By 1995, over 50 percent of families in public housing had no breadwinner. By 1997, 20 percent of UK children lived in such neighborhoods (Dean 1997). Taken together, these developments precipitated an unprecedented degree of racial and class segregation.

## The Redistribution of Crime and Victimization

An analysis of British Crime Survey data for the period from 1981 to 1992 reveals not only a substantial increase in the volume of victimization but marked changes in its nature and geographical distribution (Hope 1994). These data suggest both an intensification and a concentration of youth crime and victimization in areas of acute deprivation.

The British Crime Survey divides neighborhoods into ten deciles on the basis of the intensity of the criminal victimization. By 1992, the chances of a resident in the lowest crime neighborhoods ever being assaulted had fallen to a point where it was barely measurable. Residents in the highest crime neighborhoods, by contrast, now risked being assaulted twice a year. This polarization of risk is made clearer when we recognize that by 1992, residents in the highest crime neighborhoods experienced twice the rate of property crime and four times the rate of personal crime as those in the next worst category. Unsurprisingly, the highest rates of victimization were occurring in neighborhoods with high levels of social housing. These findings point to a significant redistribution of victimization towards the poorest and most vulnerable over the intervening ten years. "In parallel with the regional restructuring of the British economy during the 1980s, the inequality in crime risk grew amongst local communities, especially those in less advantaged northern regions of England; . . . local studies at the end of the 1980s registered large increases in crime victimisation over a relatively short period" (Pitts and Hope 1998, 38).

In the areas of highest victimization, young people were most heavily represented as both victims and perpetrators. Here, the crime was implosive and symmetrical, perpetrated by and against local residents. It was repetitive—the same people tended to be victimized again and again—and their victimization was more likely to be violent, although seldom fatal. These were the neighborhoods in which racist violence and interracial street fighting were most likely to occur. The protestations of white protagonists notwithstanding, such violence was most frequently initiated by them (Campbell 1993; Pitts and Smith 1995; Porteous 1998; Power and Tunstall 1997).

## The Local Effects of Global Change

In this and subsequent sections, we will trace the fortunes of several groups of Bangladeshi young people through these turbulent times. These young people were the subjects of research on interracial violence undertaken by the present author and his colleagues from the mid-1990s (Pitts and Smith 1995; Porteous 1998; Marlow and Pitts 1999; Pitts 2001). From the 1970s, the docks in London's East End began to shed labor in anticipation of the opening of a new, "hi-tech," international container port downriver at Tilbury in Essex. This presaged the departure of a substantial segment of the economically active population of the area. As a result, family incomes shrank and long-established relationships of kinship and friendship were eroded as the accommodation vacated by high-earning white dock workers was occupied by a rapidly growing population of low-paid Bangladeshi pieceworkers employed in the expanding local garment industry, and younger, poorer, often socially disadvantaged or previously homeless white tenants.

By the 1980s, the garment industry was also shedding labor in the face of competition from Asian manufacturers. Meanwhile the construction of a vast new city, Docklands, had commenced on the site of the now defunct London docks. But its construction generated neither reasonably paid work nor much-needed homes for local residents. Docklands represented an ambitious attempt by the Thatcher government to position London as the premiere European financial services center in a rapidly globalizing financial market, in opposition to the main contender, Frankfurt. The high prices of apartments in Docklands reflected this aspiration, as did the elaborate private security arrangements instituted by the Docklands Development Corporation and private property developers, which were generally seen by local residents as a means of keeping them out. Meanwhile the working-class neighborhoods around Docklands became, in effect, an extension of the Docklands construction site as roads and railways were rerouted and inconvenient houses, shops, and small businesses bulldozed. As Docklands was being transformed from a space into a place, adjacent working-class neighborhoods were being transformed from places into spaces.

Older white residents on the Brunel Estate, a public housing project in the heart of the London docks, expressed grave concern about these developments when they were interviewed in the early 1990s. They were particularly angry with local Labour politicians and councillors, who they described as "middle-class," because they had failed to do anything about employment, housing, and the disruption caused by the Docklands development. They also accused them of being "do-gooders" who put the interests of "newcomers" (Bangladeshis) ahead of those of "local people" (the white working-class community). These white people felt that their worsening spatial, social, and economic predicament was compounded by what they saw as their abandonment by a new-style Labour Party that was repudiating its "natural" constituency in the poorest parts of the city and disclaiming its roots in the working-class movement.

At around this time, a neofascist British National Party (BNP) councillor was elected from the neighborhood. In common with other far-right political parties in Europe, hostility to non-white in-comers constitutes only part of the BNP's political platform. (The BNP would of course object that none of its policies are racist because it is only demanding equal rights for neglected white citizens in the areas of housing and employment; it is also vehemently anticapitalist.) Thus, in this traditionally Labour-voting, working-class neighborhood, the BNP was able to present itself as the true inheritor of local working-class radicalism. The BNP candidate pointed to the damage wrought to working-class communities and the lives of working-class people by immigration, crime, and the desecration of the old neighborhoods by the voracious demands of international capital (the Docklands development). All this, the BNP maintained, had been achieved with the collusion of an effete and indifferent metropolitan ruling class that was, even now, colonizing the Labour Party. However overstated, this is the rhetoric that enables parties of the radical right to seize the political terrain vacated by the "modernizing" social democratic parties. This appeal to the fundamental tenets of parliamentary socialism worked in East London in 1995 and a BNP candidate was elected. It worked again in several northern English cities a decade later, as well as in Austria, France, and Holland. As Slavoj Zizeck observes, "Participation by the far Right in government is not punishment for 'sectarianism' or a failure to come to terms with 'postmodern conditions.' It is the price the Left pays for renouncing any radical political project, and accepting market capitalism as the only game in town" (2000, 45).

## Interracial Youth Violence

The rise of the BNP in East London in the mid-1990s was accompanied by an intensification of the interracial youth violence, which had been evident in the neighborhood since the mid-1970s. What started out as attacks by white youths on Asian families in the neighborhood in the late 1970s had developed, by the mid-1980s, into episodes of inter-group violence. This transformation began in the early 1980s when some, now locally revered, older Bangladeshi adolescents and young men mounted a fierce and protracted "fight-back" against the young white people from the Brunel Estate who had taken to "marching" through Diamond Street, an area of Bangladeshi settlement, throwing missiles at the apartments and houses and abusing or assaulting any Asian residents unfortunate enough to be on the streets. From this point onwards, the Brunel Estate became a byword for radical white protagonists and Diamond Street, fifty meters away across a railway footbridge, a safe haven for Bangladeshis. The "frontline" of the Brunel Estate was marked out by spray-painted acronyms. "BNP" (British National Party) and "NF" (National Front) are neofascist political parties with links to Protestant para-military groups in Northern Ireland. "Column 88" is a loosely affiliated and avowedly violent neofascist youth group. "MFC" (Millwall Football Club) is claimed by some of its supporters to be the most violent and actively racist in British football (soccer), an audacious but probably accurate claim. Although none of the white protagonists in the interracial violence in the area were, as far as we could ascertain, "paid-up" members of any of these neofascist organizations, they appeared to derive a spurious sense of legitimacy and support from the fact of their existence. Thus they were able to portray their local struggles as part of a broader mission to defend a beleaguered white working class.

## The Racialization of Schooling

On their arrival in Walford in the 1970s, Bangladeshi children were enrolled at local schools that, as luck would have it, were mostly located on the Brunel Estate. As a result, the children and their parents were forced to run a gauntlet of abuse, and occasional attack, as they moved between home and school. From the mid-1980s, however, this began to change as older Bangladeshi adolescents and young adults, some of whom had spearheaded the "fight-back," took to "patrolling" these dangerous places when children were going to and from school. Moreover, by the late 1980s, the Bangladeshi presence in many local schools topped 50 percent (today 80 percent of the students at the community school serving the Brunel Estate and Diamond Street are Bangladeshi), and their sheer numerical superiority meant that violence in and around the schools abated. Schools with a substantial majority of Asian students tended to have far lower levels of interpersonal violence and higher levels of academic attainment than those with predominantly white students or equal numbers of Asian and white students. Whatever other reasons Asian parents may have had for sending their children to predominantly Asian schools, an ever-present threat of violence in other schools and the promise of higher grades were probably among the more compelling.

These radical demographic shifts in neighborhood schools precipitated "flight" among white school-age children and adolescents. This took three major forms. White school students from the estate would enroll in schools outside the area at age eleven, when they transferred from primary to secondary school. They were sometimes transferred later by the education authorities if they were officially excluded from school for perpetrating a "racial incident," a not-infrequent occurrence. And they would also sometimes transfer voluntarily if they were, or claimed to have been, the victims of a "racial incident." Almost all of these youngsters relocated to two secondary schools outside of the neighborhood. These were predominantly white schools to which other local white children had already fled. Sidney Burnell School, about two kilometers north of the Brunel Estate/Diamond Street, was one of the recipients of these disgruntled migrants. This was very bad news indeed for Sidney Burnell's Bangladeshi students, who constituted only 11.8 percent of the school roll.

## Interracial Violence and the School

The capacity of Sidney Burnell School to deal with this influx was undermined by the transience of the neighborhoods it served and the peculiar, racialized, nature of local schooling. Between years 7 (eleven years old) and 11 (fifteen years), 50 percent of the school roll turned over. The diversity of this student body was very wide. In 1999, Sidney Burnell had 1,043 students: 85 nationalities were represented on the school roll with 44 percent of students describing themselves as white British. "Black" students (African-British, African-Caribbean, Eritrean, Ethiopian, African) comprised 17.4 percent and South Asians 17 percent of the school roll. The largest non-white "minority" was Bangladeshi comprising 11.8 percent of the school roll. In 1999, as a result of conflicts in Nigeria, Ethiopia, Eritrea, and the Balkans, 17 percent of the school's students had refugee status, and many of these were "unaccompanied" minors in the care of an older brother, sister, or cousin. The long-term trend in the neighborhood had been the replacement of more prosperous residents with less prosperous ones, and this was also reflected in the school rolls: by 1997 over 50 percent of the students qualified for free school meals, the key indicator of social deprivation.

Because poverty and transience tend to generate educational disadvantage and erode the capacity of adults to offer consistent parenting, 43 percent of the students attending the school had been assessed as having special educational needs, twice the borough average.

A further consequence of student transience was that the school carried a high level of vacancies and was under constant pressure from the local education authority to absorb students excluded from other schools. Beyond the destabilizing effect on existing peer groups and the "pecking order" of this steady influx of new students is, as we have noted, the fact that many of them brought additional academic and behavioral problems with them.

Unsurprisingly, levels of violence in general and interracial group violence in the school and in the neighborhood were extremely high. Between September 1996 and April 1997, 41 percent of the year 11 students were assaulted, often with weapons, with 30 percent of these assaults occurring in the vicinity of the school or on the way home in the hour or so following the end of the school day (Porteous 1998). Levels of victimization were clearly shaped by race, with 46 percent of Bangladeshi respondents against only 16 percent of white respondents reporting persistent abuse and harassment in school. This echoes the findings of earlier studies (Pitts and Smith 1995; Porteous 1998). This level of violence added impetus to the attempts by Bangladeshi parents to transfer their children to predominantly Bangladeshi schools.

## An Escalation of Violence

By the late 1990s, a pattern of conflict had emerged in and around Sidney Burnell school and the other local "white-flight" school, in which small-scale interracial conflicts would sometimes escalate, in a matter of hours, into large-scale conflict between groups of white and Bangladeshi youths and young adults. This was made possible by widespread, albeit often illicit, mobile phone ownership among school students. That there were so many older adolescents and young adults available to engage in this conflict is due to unemployment that had hit young people in Diamond Street and the Brunel Estate particularly hard, and the flexible working practices of the "informal economy" and the government "training schemes" in which many of them were nominally enrolled. By this point in time, "Diamond Street" had floated free of its geographical roots, coming instead to represent a loosely knit, defensive/aggressive local network of children, adolescents, and young adults. Thus it was not uncommon for non-Bangladeshi, Asian young people, sometimes living many miles from the Estate, to claim some affiliation with it as a kind of mantra against victimization. By the late 1990s, these confrontations were fairly commonplace in towns and cities with substantial numbers of poor Bangladeshi and white families living in close proximity (Webster 1995).

## The Northern Riots

New Labour was reelected in June 2001. However, its preelection claims that it was "meeting its targets in the areas of crime and social exclusion" were thrown into doubt by large-scale violent confrontations between Muslim and white young people in the north of England in the preceding months that marked longer-running antagonisms similar to those that had occurred between whites and Bangladeshis in the East End of London. On April 17, 2001, an Asian wedding in Bradford erupted into interracial street fighting in which three pubs and a pharmacy were wrecked and eight cars set on fire. The conflict was, according to some Muslim commentators, the result of a racist attack by members of the BNP, which has a regional office on a neighboring estate. On May 3, 2001, the home secretary, Jack Straw, banned a proposed National Front March in Oldham, forty miles away, in protest at the alleged creation by Asian youths of "no-go" areas for whites. In Oldham on May 27, an estimated 500 Asian youths marched to protest violent BNP incursions into their neighborhoods and the failure of the police to protect them.

However, the ensuing political debate of these incidents was immediately, and erroneously, subsumed within a longer-running argument between the government and its Conservative opposition and the right-wing press, which hinged on the latter's assertion that the government was "soft" on migrants and asylum seekers. The emergent conventional wisdom had it that more migrants and asylum seekers would provoke more violent interracial incidents of the type seen in Bradford. The facts that between 1995 and 1999, 80 percent of migrants to the UK were from the developed world and that the overwhelming majority were white, that the non-white protagonists in these disturbances were, in fact, second- and third-generation British Asians rather than asylum seekers, and that the white protagonists were supporters of the neofascist BNP (BNP) were lost in the heat of battle.

On June 25, 2001, there were further incidents in Burnley when, following a hammer attack by three white men on an Asian taxi driver, 200 Asian youths were involved in pitched battles with National Front supporters. Subsequently in Bradford on July 8, a thousand Asian youth battled with members of the BNP and subsequently with police on the streets. Disclaiming responsibility for the disturbances, Steve Smith, the BNP's deputy regional organizer, rejected claims that his party was responsible for the unrest and blamed the undemocratic policies of Westminster politicians, saying, "This unrest is a direct consequence of enforced multiculturalism." Like Jean-Marie Le Pen in France and his predecessors in the East End of London, Smith was at pains to link the issues of immigration and crime and present the BNP as a party of "law and order." Over one hundred Asian young men had been arrested as a result of confrontations with the police following the disturbances and were being held on remand in northern jails. Later, passing judgment on four of them, Judge David Boulton revealed a disarming impartiality. "Judge Boulton said although some of the defendants had played minor roles, it was the combination that fuelled a large scale disturbance. 'To some extent, all are responsible for everything. It is wrong and misleading to look at what any one person did in isolation'" (*Burnley Today,* November 8, 2002, p. 2).

## The Third Way Revisited

In June 2002, Tony Blair and his senior ministers and advisers met Bill Clinton to discuss how the by now faltering third way might be revived. Philip Gould, the prime minister's senior strategic adviser, and the man credited with being the architect of the New Labour project, observed that the party risked losing "angry young working class men who felt disengaged from politics and abandoned by politicians. They regard themselves as very British, not European, resent rises in crime and are hostile to asylum seekers . . . they are in the mood for radical change." He produced opinion-poll and focus-group data that demonstrated "a real possibility of a surge in support among the working class for popular nationalism based on fears about crime and immigration" (*Sunday Times,* June 16, 2002, p. 9).

Introducing *Violent Community Disorders in Bradford, Burnley, and Oldham* (Cantle Report 2002), commissioned by the government, Home Secretary David Blunkett enjoined the Asian community to integrate with its white neighbors and condemned "certain cultural practices, like enforced marriages," which Muslim commentators also routinely condemn, saying that they "have no place in contemporary Britain." He spoke positively of U.S.-style nationality and language tests and the notion of the "melting pot." The Cantle Report echoed the findings of an earlier report into the Burnley disturbances by Lord Herman Ouseley, a Labour peer and former chair of the government's Commission for Racial Equality. Ouseley had bemoaned the development of "communities which were fragmenting along racial, cultural and faith lines" as a result of segregation in schools, a gang culture, drugs, white flight, political correctness, and weak political leadership. The Cantle Report took this argument the next logical step by asserting that disorders were the inevitable result of deteriorating relations among "an underclass of relatively poor white people and visible ethnic minorities, *many of whom* feel that their needs are neglected because they regard minority ethnic communities as being prioritized for more favourable public assistance" (2002, 42).

In the future, the report recommended, the needs of the socially excluded white community should be given equal priority with the needs of black and Asian minorities; we may yet look back to this moment as the point at which poor whites on the social margins became a British "ethnic minority." The Commission for Racial Equality promptly announced new initiatives to address the plight of socially excluded white minorities.

The fact that, throughout the UK, racial segregation in education had developed as a defensive strategy on the part of Asian communities subject to racial harassment and racist violence did not feature in the report. Nor did the fact that these disturbances were almost certainly orchestrated by the BNP. Neither was there a recognition that the problems experienced by both the white and Asian communities were, in large part, a product of deindustrialization exacerbated by the economic policies of a series of noninterventionist neoliberal governments, market deregulation, and the erosion of workers' rights through trade union reforms, housing "reforms," reductions in state benefits, and the rollback of state services. As Rana Kabbani has observed, "When I visited the North of England for the first time to study its impoverished Muslims, dumped like so much industrial waste once their jobs had disappeared, I was equally struck by the unedifying sight of 'poor white trash,' the dispossessed and the listless of the inner city and the suburb. They were cut out from Britain's modern-day map as ruthlessly as most British Asians and Blacks had been" (*Guardian,* June 17, 2002, p. 18). Moreover, the Cantle Report contained neither an explicit condemnation of the violence instigated by the BNP nor a proposal to strengthen the law, or its enforcement, in order to prevent future occurrences. The possibility that Asian citizens might have something to fear from a newly confident radical right wing if their painstakingly constructed defenses against victimization were pulled down by an assimilationist government was also ignored.

The Cantle Report and the government's subsequent utterances were viewed by an increasingly confident radical right wing as a vindication of their "rights for whites" stance, thus offering considerable comfort to young white people, like those in the Brunel Estate, who identified with neofascist political parties. But it generated enormous anxiety among many Asian young people, like those in Diamond Street who, in addition to feeling unvalued and unwelcome, came to believe that they stood alone and unsupported by their government in the face of the right-wing threat.

## Doing the Right Thing

These developments signalled a significant shift away from New Labour's earlier implicit multiculturalism towards a new assimilationist posture that resonated with the key demands of the radical right. In an article entitled "The Far Right Is the Enemy," the home secretary felt the need to respond to those who had criticized his apparent repudiation of multiculturalism and his implicit support for the "rights for whites" lobby and argued that unless center-left parties acted firmly on immigration and race relations, electoral support for the far right would grow. "The real battle for the left must be against the far right and against racism, not between ourselves. In Britain, the BNP is preparing for next month's local elections with relish, sensing that it can exploit problems with illegal immigration and asylum pressures in ways that have been successful elsewhere. It is a vital challenge for all mainstream parties to ensure legitimate debates about asylum, immigration, race and community relations are separated from divisive, inflammatory exploitation of fears which the fascists seize on" (Guardian, April 11, 2002, p. 21). Shortly after in a parliamentary debate, he justified the construction of new, rural "Accommodation Centres" for refugees and asylum seekers as a way of preventing local schools from being "swamped."

Within a few months, a "chain of equivalence" (Mercer 1990) in which "Youth," "Race," "Crime," and "Immigration" came to be used interchangeably in political and media discourse had emerged as a new "common sense" (Gramsci 1971), albeit one that would have been unthinkable a year previously. The rhetoric of multiculturalism was eclipsed by a new assimilationist discourse in which the Asian community, frequently conflated with asylum seekers and refugees, stood accused of being a de facto "underclass," placing an undue burden on state resources, perpetrating violent disorder, and courting victimization by its rejection of the values and practices of the sociocultural mainstream. As Peter Hain, a founding member of the 1970s *Anti-Nazi League*, minister for Europe, and acknowledged mouthpiece for the more radical thoughts of Prime Minister Blair, subsequently observed, "They (Muslims) are welcome here. But there is a tendency amongst a minority to isolate themselves and that leaves them vulnerable to either exploitation by

Osama bin Laden-type extremists and fanatics on the one hand, or targeting by racists and Nazis on the other" (*Guardian,* May 13, 2002, p. 1).

## Conclusion

In third-way politics, "the big idea is that there is no big idea." It is a post-ideological political project which seeks power in order to deliver a "partyless democracy" (Mair 2000) that is "beyond left and right." It aims to provide forms of managerially competent good governance that accord with the wishes of "the people" inferred from focus groups and opinion polls rather than the representations of necessarily partisan politicians. Thus constituted, argues Slavoj Zizeck, the third way represents "social democracy purged of its minimal subversive sting, extinguishing even the faintest memory of anti-capitalism and class struggle" (2000, 40).

In 2002 the postmodern politics of the third way was confronted with a decidedly premodern political threat. The disturbances in the northern cities, September 11 and its aftermath, and the asylum seekers' debate in 2002 breathed new life into both "respectable" and "disreputable" elements on the political right. This confronted New Labour with a choice: to stand firm, defend cultural diversity and tolerance, and try to inject some rationality and a sense of proportion into the debate, or attempt to retain the political initiative by beating the radical right at its own game.

Above all else, *New Labour* is a vehicle for the acquisition and retention of political power. As we have noted, like Clinton's Democrats, New Labour believes that the key to electoral success consists of always dominating the media agenda and never allowing itself to be outflanked on the political right. Thus, true to that other fundamental tenet of the third way—"what counts is what works"—New Labour strategists concluded that what would work this time was a swerve to the political right and the junking of multiculturalism. And, although it was destined to give comfort to racists large and small and compound the fears of Britain's black and Asian citizens and reinforce their growing sense of disaffiliation from the cultural and political mainstream, they did.

## References

Barry, Monica, and Christine Hallett. 1998. *Social Exclusion and Social Work.* Lyme Regis, UK: Russell House Publishing.

Beck, Ulrich. 1992. *Risk Society: Towards a New Modernity.* London: Sage.

Bourdieu, Pierre. 1998. *Acts of Resistance: Against the New Myths of Our Time.* Cambridge: Polity Press.

Campbell, Beatrix. 1993. *Goliath, Britain's Dangerous Places.* London: Methuen.

Cantle Report. 2002. *Violent Community Disorders in Bradford, Burnley and Oldham.* London: Home Office.

Currie, Elliott. 1985. *Confronting Crime: An American Challenge.* London: Pantheon.

Dean, Hartley, and Peter Taylor-Gooby. 1992. *Dependency Culture.* London: Harvester Wheatsheaf.

Dean, Malcolm. 1997. "Tipping the Balance." *Search,* No. 27 (Spring): 7–10.

Garland, David. 2001. *The Culture of Control.* Oxford: Oxford University Press.

Giddens, Anthony. 1998. *The Third Way: The Renewal of Social Democracy.* Cambridge: Polity Press.

Gramsci, Antonio. 1971. *The Prison Notebooks.* London: Lawrence and Wishart.

Hagan, John. 1993. "The Social Embeddedness of Crime and Unemployment." *Criminology* 31: 455–91.

Hagedorn, John. 1998. *People and Folks: Crime and the Underclass in a Rustbelt City.* Chicago: Lakeview Press.

Herrnstein, Robert, and Charles Murray. 1994. *The Bell Curve.* New York: Free Press.

Hope, Timothy. 1994. "Communities Crime and Inequality in England and Wales." Paper presented to the 1994 Cropwood Round Table Conference Preventing Crime and Disorder, September 14–15, Cambridge.

Hutton, Will. 1995. *The State We're In.* London: Jonathan Cape.

King, D., and M. Wickham-Jones. 1999. "Bridging the Atlantic: The Democratic (Party) Origins of Welfare to Work." In *New Labour New Welfare State: The Third Way in British Social Policy,* ed. M. Powell. Bristol: Policy Press.

Mair, Peter. 2000. "Partyless Democracy." *New Left Review* 2 (March/June): 21–35.

Marlow, Alan, and John Pitts. 1999. "Remember the Alamo: Action Research and Crime Prevention in a High Crime Neighbourhood." *International Criminal Justice Review* 9: 69–87.

Mercer, David. 1990. "Welcome to the Jungle: Identity and Diversity in Postmodern Politics." In *Identity, Community, Culture, Difference,* ed. Malcolm Rutherford. Basingstoke, UK: Macmillan.

Murray, Charles. 1984. *Losing Ground: American Social Policy 1950–1980.* London: Basic Books.

Pitts, John. 2000. "The New Youth Justice and the Politics of Electoral Anxiety." In *The New Youth Justice,* ed. Barry Goldson, 1–13. Lyme Regis, UK: Russell House Publishing.

———. 2001. *The New Politics of Youth Crime: Discipline or Solidarity.* Lyme Regis, UK: Palgrave.

Pitts, John, and Timothy Hope. 1998. "The Local Politics of Inclusion: The State and Community Safety." *Social Policy and Administration* 31, no. 5: 37–58.

Pitts, John, and Philip Smith. 1995. *Preventing School Bullying.* London: Home Office.

Porteous, David. 1998. "Young People's Experience of Crime and Violence: Findings from a Survey of School Students." In *Planning Safer Communities,* ed. Alan Marlow and John Pitts, 130–39. Lyme Regis, UK: Russell House Publishing.

Powell, Michael. 1999. "Bridging the Atlantic: The Democratic (Party) Origins of Welfare to Work." In *New Labour, New Welfare State: The Third Way in British Social Policy,* ed. Michael Powell. Cambridge: Policy Press.

Power, Ann, and Tessa Tunstall. 1997. *Dangerous Disorder: Riots and Violent Disturbances in Thirteen Areas of Britain 1991–1992.* York, UK: Joseph Rowntree Foundation.

Robinson, Gerald. 2002. "Exploring Risk Management in Probation Practice: Contemporary Developments in England and Wales." *Punishment and Society* 4, no. 1 (January): 17–23.

Simon, Jonathan. 2000. "From the Big House to the Warehouse: Re-thinking Prisons and State Government in the Twentieth Century." *Punishment and Society* 2, no. 2 (April): 213–34.

Vidal, Gore. 1998. *The Virgin Islands.* Harmondsworth: Penguin.

Webster, Colin. 1995. *Racial Attacks in Northern England: Qualitative Aspects of the Keighley Crime Survey.* Paper delivered to the British Sociological Society Annual Conference, April, University of Leicester.

Wilson, James Q., and Richard Herrnstein. 1985. *Crime and Human Nature.* New York: Simon and Schuster.

Wilson, W. J. 1987. *The Truly Disadvantaged: The Inner City, the Underclass and Public Policy.* Chicago: University of Chicago Press.

Young, Jock. 1999. *The Exclusive Society.* London: Sage.

Zizeck, Slavoj. 2000. "Why We All Love to Hate Haider." *New Left Review* 2 (March/April): 37–45.

**PART V**

# Conclusion

# 12

# Gangs in Late Modernity

### JOHN M. HAGEDORN

Since the demise of the Soviet Union and the 1991 defeat of Iraq, warfare between states has been largely supplanted by conflict with and among networks of armed young men (Hobsbawm 1997, 2000). These violent groups and networks include some radical fundamentalist Islamic sects; various white survivalists; Catholic and Protestant militias in Northern Ireland; communal Hindu and Moslem gangs in India; secular revolutionaries like the Zapatistas and other guerrillas in dozens of countries; terrorist cells like Al Qaeda; warlords in the Balkans and Somalia; "tribal" rivals, as in Rwanda and Burundi; and criminal syndicates in Colombia, Nigeria, Russia and elsewhere. The United States' replacement of the cold war by a war on terror is the political recognition of today's central importance of "new wars" (Kaldor 2002) waged by armed networks.

This essay asks what may be a dangerous question: Might some U.S. gangs resemble fundamentalist, nationalist, and criminal networks more than they do Thrasher's adolescent peer groups? The furor over Jose Padilla, the Al Qaeda militant who had been a Chicago gang member, led some to simplistically equate gangs with terrorists. On the other hand, empirical studies indicate that while most U.S. gangs are little more than wild adolescent peer groups, some have long been institutionalized, particularly in large cities. I argue that these gangs have important similarities to other third world groups of armed young men and understanding these characteristics can help define "gangs" more precisely.

I begin by comparing the theoretical assumptions of mid- and late modernity and applying them to the study of gangs. A discussion of the way we think about gangs is important because some of the characteristics we thought were anomalies in industrial era gangs have proven to be enduring. I then explore similarities between contemporary gangs and other groups of armed young men in their search for identity, types of organization, and the use of the informal economy. Then, refocusing the discussion to the particular nature of *gangs* internationally, I compare "street organizations" in Chicago and Soweto, South Africa. In conclusion, this argument makes it possible to more clearly define "what is a gang" and create a typology describing variation between gangs in late modernity.

## Modernity, Social Theory, and Gangs

The concept of "modernity" is not much used in academic discourse on gangs. The study of gangs has been sheltered from the stormy debates on postmodernism in other disciplines. Advances in urban political economy, critical theory, and the organizational literature have thus had negligible impact on gang scholars who work in the dominant "social disorganization" tradition. On the other hand, globalization studies have made general analyses of crime and violence with scant fieldwork among the very poor or their organizations.

Anthony Giddens has opposed the concept of "late modernity" to the postmodern notion that we are living in a wholly new era. Rather than situate social life in a poststructuralist world of signs, symbols, and texts, Giddens argues that globalization means "no one can opt out of the transformations brought about by modernity" (1991, 22). Giddens, like Jürgen Habermas (1984), places social theory in the service of the completion of the modern project.

Alain Touraine (1995) describes the modern project as a balance between rationalization and the freedom of the Subject. In his most recent work, Touraine (2000) discusses the differences between early, mid-, and late modernity. He argues that early modernity, or the Age of Enlightenment, was dominated by the principle of man-made order replacing traditional hierarchy; mid-modernity by the tensions between progress on the one hand and class struggle and national liberation on the other; and late modernity by the conflict between the Scylla of unfettered markets and the Charybdis of communal identity.

The Chicago School approach to gangs is a good example of mid-modernist thinking. Ruth Kornhauser, whose work codified the social disorganization perspective, saw social theory as explaining the transition between the dying traditions of the old world and social institutions of the new. "Culture in the modern world," she said, "is everywhere at bay" (1978, 1). The central problem was to assimilate the immigrant carriers of traditional cultures into a new, industrial society (for example, Thomas and Znaniecki 1918–1920/1996). Modernization was a solution to social disorganization and class struggle.

For Kornhauser, as for Park and Thrasher, social disorganization was "interstitial" and temporary, as urbanization and ethnic succession assimilated immigrant groups into an "American" identity. The Chicagoans were historically "progressive" in that they believed rational methods by the state and what is now called the "collective efficacy" of communities would accompany modernization, combat discrimination, and vastly reduce poverty.

Gang researchers in this tradition, notably James F. Short Jr. (1964), Irving Spergel (1964), and Malcolm Klein (1971), focused their studies on the social disorganization of poor neighborhoods and the corresponding "group process" of adolescents. My own initial study of gangs, *People and Folks* (1988), was also a successor to these studies. I found that 1980s Milwaukee gangs began as corner groups. However, I argued, deindustrialization was altering the "maturing out" process and the postindustrial era was creating new forms.

## Late Modernity and Social Thought

Social thought in late modernity questions many of the assumptions and conclusions of mid-modernist thinking. Today we can no longer assume, as did Kornhauser, that culture is in decline. Rather, we are studying its resurgence as traditional religious and communal identities rage against a homogenizing globalization (for example, Castells 1997). Neither can we assume that non-racial, universalist identities are inevitable. The Chicago School's ecological paradigm deracialized the study of gangs. However, even the briefest look at the ghetto and their gangs today questions that assumption (for example, Wacquant 2001, this volume).

Rather than gangs being a transitional form, what has been transitory has been the industrial economy. The mid-modernist notion that the informal economic sector would come under the control of strong national industrial economies proved inaccurate (for example, Portes, Castells, and Benton 1989). A close relationship of gangs to various informal economies had been seen as an exception, while in fact it may be the rule.

Some conditions are new. For example, in the global era the power of markets has weakened the nation-state, which has privatized or cut back many central functions. Castells (1998) has looked at the emergence of a powerful global criminal network as one aspect of the incapacity of nation states to control all aspects of the economy and society. The monopoly on the use of violence, which Weber (1946) saw as an essential characteristic of the state, has thus been eroded and an era of the "informalization of violence" (Keohane 2002) is upon us. The proliferation of groups and networks of armed young men thus may be a normal feature of late modernity.

## Identity, Organizations, and Economics

How are gangs similar to other kinds of groups of armed young men? And are some kinds of gangs today a new, "postindustrial" form, or are they more familiar?

### GANGS, RACE, AND IDENTITY

One major similarity between gangs and other groups of armed young men is a racialized identity. Normal science gang research, under the sway of the nonracial Chicago School, has not spent much time on this issue, since "territoriality trumps ethnicity" (Adamson 1998). However, as we have seen, matters are not quite so simple.

There has been an enormous scholarship on the centrality of race that questions Wilson's (1978) Chicago School–based concept of its "declining significance" (for example, Massey and Denton 1993). History has lent ample support to Du Bois's claim that the color line has been the central problem of the twentieth century. The economist notions that "race" will decline as an identity with modernization, as the Chicagoans believed, are far from uncontested. On the other hand, the idea that "race" is a product of modernity, of the racial division of the world between colonizers and colonized, has gained credibility (for example, Winant 2001).

The obvious fact that most gangs today are non-white reflects racial divisions that contrast to the assimilationist conclusions of the Chicago School. Little time needs to be spent documenting the predominance of non-white gangs in the United States. Walter Miller, as far back as his 1975 surveys of law enforcement, made that claim. What needs to be emphasized is that while in the United States white ethnic gangs largely disappeared in the "race relations cycle," non-white gangs did not.

Segregation and racial oppression have reinforced a racialized identity of oppressed people. Anyone familiar with black and Latino gangs cannot fail to note their strong sense of identity with their racial groups. But a *racialized* identity is not the only one held by gang members. In order to understand the "power of identity" today, a brief discussion of the work of Manual Castells is necessary.

Castells (1997, 8–10) points out that in the network society, there are three forms of identity: *legitimizing identities,* which reinforce the authority of dominant institutions; *resistance identities,* which are defensively adopted by devalued actors who generate communal values; and *project identities,* which challenge the existing order by positing a new Subject. In a shrinking and insecure world of flows of capital and information, millions retreat into essentialism. Castells sees resistance identities as the basis of social movements of all types, as well as a refuge for the oppressed. For example, he points out that Islamic fundamentalisms "proceed as a reaction against unreachable modernization, the evil consequences of globalization, and the collapse of the post-colonial nationalist project" (1997, 19).

This retreat into identity is exemplified by "gangsta rap" music videos as an expression of what Castells calls an "end of millennium" ghetto culture "made out of affliction, rage, and individual reaction against collective exclusion." Castells goes on to observe that this new culture incorporates the ever-present reality of prison and drug sales as the "shop-floor" of the criminal economy and "gang-based social organization" (1997, 57).

U.S. gang culture is also a celebration of violent masculinity, the use of force to settle disputes, and the toleration of nihilistic rage by the outcast and alienated (see West 1993). Internationally, as well as in the United States, and despite understudied female gang involvement (Chesney-Lind and Hagedorn 1999), gangs mostly represent a culture of armed young men. Los Angeles gang member General Robert Lee concisely makes this point: "I felt I was a soldier for the hood" (Jah and Shah Keyah 1995, 121).

But gang identity is more complex than rage and retreat into masculinist economics of survival and communalism (see Kelley 1997). Gang members are male and female, fathers and mothers; they hold conventional jobs and go to college. Like all of us, gang members inhabit multiple social worlds and identities. "It is not just that collective identities and ways of life are created," Calhoun says, "but that they are internally contested, that their boundaries are porous and overlapping, and that people live in more than one at the same time" (1995, 47). For example, immigrant gangs, like Jamaican posses in the United States, simultaneously hold both gangster and Jamaican nationalist identities. In this era, Giroux adds, "Identities merge and shift rather than becoming more uniform and stable" (1996, 32). One can be a gang member, a father, a student, a breadwinner, American, Mexican, and a Catholic all at once.

A variety of cultural identities, particularly religious ones, also appeal to gang members, just as they do to the "Arab Street" or the Catholic and Protestant militias in Northern Ireland. Gangs in Chicago and New York have religious principles embedded in their constitutions and documents. A strong Islamic current runs through all Chicago African American gangs, particularly the Conservative Vice Lord Nation, and Louis Farrakhan has been deeply involved with outreach to gangs in LA and Chicago. The Almighty Latin King and Queen Nation promotes a spiritual doctrine of "Kingism," and the "Nation" itself is seen by many of its members as a religion (Barrios this volume). Crips cofounder Jimel Barnes exemplifies this outlook: "I'm a very spiritual and personal individual" (Jah and Shah Keyah 1995, 151).

Now it is easy to dismiss such claims as hypocrisy, opportunism, or conversion in the face of prison. But among the oppressed worldwide, religiosity is especially influential. Castells narrowly defines African American ghetto culture as one of "rage" and omits discussion of the lure of Islam to gang members and other outcast members of urban ghettos. Our Milwaukee and Chicago fieldwork has also found that "Promise Seekers" and street-corner Pentecostal churches recruit heavily from current and former gang members, particularly Latinos. Many of these religious groupings are influenced by traditional concepts of male dominance, easing the transition of males from hypermasculine gangs.

The coexistence of "gangster," political, and religious identities are all examples of shrinking a global world into a more controllable essentialist "defensive identity" (Castells 1997). Where else but the ghetto has the promise of modernity been more sorely broken and is the need for certainty greater (Bauman 1995)? Religion and spirituality are part of the U.S. gang experience, and, like in the Middle East, India, and Northern Ireland, often closely tied to violence.

Indeed, in an earlier time, Malcolm X represented both sides of the hustler and religious world and used his religion to unite the African American struggle with the third world. More recently, Monster Kody, famed Crip leader, explained his metamorphosis into Sanyika Shakur (1993). What attracted Kody to Islam in prison was that, unlike Christianity, which believed "that religion was synonymous with passivity" (1993, 214), Islam was a religion of fighters against racial oppression. "Islam," Kody said, "is a way of life, just like banging" (1993, 220). His autobiography documents his personal struggle over identity in a way that reveals the close connections between nationalist, religious, and gang identities. In a soliloquy, he asks, "Who is Monster Kody? . . . I am Monster Kody . . . a person, a young man, a black man . . . Anything else? . . No, not that I know of . . . What is Monster Kody? A Crip, an Eight Tray, a Rollin' Sixty killer . . . a black man . . . Black man, black man, BLACK MAN" (1993, 225–26).

In late modernity, racialized "resistance identities" are a key locus of power for the oppressed, including gangs.

## GANGS AND ORGANIZATIONS

Gangs have classically (Klein 1971; Moore 1998; Short 1996; Thrasher 1927) been defined by referring to urbanization and related group processes. In mid-modernist thought, gangs are fundamentally interstitial, adolescent groupings in the process of going out of existence, residues of the irrationalities of modernization. International studies (for example, Hazlehurst and Hazlehurst 1998; Klein et al. 2001; several chapters in this volume) confirm the proliferation of this kind of grouping of wild youth or gangs in every corner of the globe.

However, it is important to note that big city gangs in the United States define themselves as "organizations," not gangs. This can be dismissed as rhetoric, but we should be mindful of Castells's (1997) advice to accept the self-definition of groups (see also Klein 1971; Moore 1998). Gangs in Chicago, for example, have written constitutions and formalized structures, as do the Latin Kings in New York City. The Crips and Bloods of Los Angeles developed a far-reaching political and economic agenda after the Rodney King riots (Jah and Shah Keyah 1995) and were part of a national "gang truce" movement. Such gangs are mainly products of the ghettos and provide their members and communities a wide range of social, economic, and symbolic functions.

But is this a "new development" of deindustrialization, as many—including the author—have claimed? Chicago's major gangs have persisted now for over fifty years, East LA's barrio gangs for even longer. The Crips and the Bloods have been around since the 1960s, and many gangs in smaller cities are now going on their third decade. In China, Triads have been around for centuries (Booth 1999) and the Mafia had its origins in the secret societies of nineteenth-century Sicily, Naples, and Calabria (Ianni 1972). In the United States, the Mafia has persisted now for a hundred years with New York City divided into "families" (for example, Mass 1968) and Chicago's Outfit (Russo 2001) has maintained social and political influence.

Clearly there are now and always have been what Taylor (1989) calls "scavenger" gangs, and such peer groups certainly predominate in terms of sheer numbers. But alongside these "interstitial" gangs, there have always been powerful institutionalized gangs.

In the United States, the Irish made up the first major urban gangs, beginning in New York City. What Monkkonen (2001) calls "voting gangs" were Irish young adults used by politicians to advance their electoral interests with intimidation and violence (see Haskins 1974). These "voting gangs" were embraced by the machine in Chicago but with one twist: in the form of "social athletic clubs" they were also crucial to the stabilization of Irish neighborhoods like Bridgeport, which were adjacent to the overcrowded Black Belt. Irish gangs were the key actors in Chicago's 1919 race riot (Chicago Commission on Race Relations 1922) and continued for decades to resist integration (Hirsch 1983).

In both New York City and Chicago, the pay-off for gang support for politicians was patronage, often a job on the police force. For members of gangs of the dominant ethnicity, "maturing out" of the youth gang meant being taken care of by the state and often careers as policemen that could be little more than a continuation of their gang background.

This pattern of gang involvement with politics is internationally familiar. In India, the nationalist parties, particularly BJP and Shiv Sena, mobilize gangs and *mitra mandals*, or male "friends' clubs" both for electoral purposes and to incite anti-Moslem violence (Heuze 1995; Varshney 2002). Gang violence has prompted observers to compare Mumbai (Bombay) and Chicago (Sharma 1995). Chinese Triads had corrupt ties with the Kuomintang (Booth 1999) and Berlin skinheads are tied to neo-Nazi parties and promote a nationalist politics of racism (Kersten, this volume). Jamaican posses began as armed groups attached to political parties (Gunst 1995) and have continued to link drugs, violence, and politics (Gray 1997). Other politicians have used irregular thugs along with official police and military forces. Haiti's Duvaliers used their Tontons Macoutes to terrorize their enemies and maintain themselves in power, and "chime" or gang violence has continued even after Aristide's return to power (Human Rights Watch 2002; James 2002).

Milosevic's Serbian gangs were used as a surrogate for his army to carry out ethnic cleansing (Zimmermann 1999) and paramilitary violence surged in "failed states" like Yugoslavia (Held 2002). In Northern Ireland, British army general Sir Frank Kitson called the Ulster Defense Forces "counter-gangs" and deployed them against the IRA (McKeown 2001). This kind of institutionalized gang often holds what Castells calls a "legitimizing identity" and supports existing authority against the oppressed. "Decommissioning" or disarming official and unofficial groups of armed young men has proved to be essential to the peace process in Lebanon, Northern Ireland, and South Africa (Schulze 2001).

In the last decades, institutionalized gangs composed of oppressed ethnic and religious groups have become more numerous. New York City's Latin Kings and Nëtas proclaim a politics of liberation (Brotherton this volume) and Chicago gangs continue to play ward politics ("Rey" 2002). Maori gangs participated in nationalist protest in New Zealand (Hazlehurst this volume). Some gangs control vast areas of cities and become alternative governments, like those in the favelas of Rio de Janiero (Jones 2002). Repression and incarceration link gangs in ghetto streets with gangs behind prison bars and stabilize both (see Venkatesh 2000; Wacquant 2001).

To conclude, institutionalized U.S. gangs consider themselves organizations and resemble other kinds of organizations of the very poor across the globe. As Castells argues, ghettos in U.S. cities are part of a new "fourth world" and share essential characteristics with socially excluded areas like sub-Saharan Africa, vast sectors of the Middle East and South Asia, and Latin America. While in earlier times, gangs institutionalized mainly within dominant or rising ethnic groups, in late modernity gangs of oppressed groups have institutionalized as well.

U.S. gangs share one other characteristic of organizations of the socially excluded: reliance on the underground economy.

## GANGS AND THE INFORMAL ECONOMY

For the past two decades, members of many U.S. gangs have been financially supported by the sale of drugs. The organization of the drug trade has become a central organizing principle for institutionalized gangs (for example, Fagan 1996; Hagedorn 1998; Taylor 1989).

As noted above, a principle characteristic of the current era is the persistence of the informal economy and its functional role globally. Rather than modernization bringing the hope of prosperity to the fourth world, millions are excluded from the mainstream and have looked for alternative ways of survival. Gangs now provide not only brotherhood for young men but also an entry-level job and a fleeting, but alluring, promise of fabulous wealth.

This has long been one of the prime functions of organized gangs. Prohibition saw the unification of Italian neighborhood gangs into Capone's mob and later the stabilization of what is known as the "Outfit" (Landesco 1968 [1929]; Russo 2001). The rackets were ready to provide entry-level employment for men, particularly those who did not have an aversion to violence. The Triads have controlled drug dealing, trafficking in women and children, and gambling all over South Asia for decades. In the last two decades, gangs across the globe have found drugs to be their most profitable business.

Many studies have documented the extent of the underground economy in urban ghettos. My Milwaukee "small business surveys" (Hagedorn 2001), for example, found in two poor neighborhoods one in ten young black and Latino men employed in drug sales, numbers that are consistent with other studies (for example, Venkatesh and Leavitt 2000). Carl Taylor (1989) described "corporate" gangs in Detroit that dominated the heroin markets. The control of drug markets by Chicago's Vice Lords, Black Gangster Disciples, and Latin Kings, and LA's Crips and Bloods is well known. The drug economy in the United States, the U.S. Office on Drug Control estimates, brings in more than $60 billion annually, much by gangs.

The role of the underground economy in the persistence of organizations of the socially excluded is not restricted to U.S. gangs. The cartels in Colombia provide both jobs for workers and cash for farmers in the absence of licit alternatives. Sendero Luminoso in Peru and FARC in Colombia began as Maoist revolutionary groups, but as Maoism collapsed worldwide, these and other guerrillas adapted and found financial support in the production of drugs (de Soto 1990). Immigrant gangs use cross-border connections to facilitate the flows of illegal goods (Castells 1998). The informal economy is estimated in many Latin American countries at about half of GNP, and that figure usually excludes the production and export of cocaine (Jimenez 1989). Studies of gangs in Jamaica (Gunst 1995), Sao Paolo (Caldiera 2000), and along the Mexican border (personal communication with Avelardo Valdez 1997) demonstrate the central role of drugs in maintaining gang organization.

The breakup of the Soviet Union has pushed young men into informal economic enterprises and the Russian mafiya. The World Bank has found that one quarter of all young men in Albania now work in the drug economy (La Cava and Nanetti 2001). Some nationalist groups, like the IRA, have responded to desperate economic conditions by controlling the informal economy (Jamieson and Grounds 2002). Shiv Sena in Mumbai (Bombay) combined *hinduvata* or appeals to Hindu nationalism with its base among *dada,* youthful subproletarian thugs in the underground economy (Heuze 1995; Lele 1995).

It is alleged by many sources (for example, Laqueur 1999) that Al Qaeda and other terrorist groups used the export of opium poppies and other drugs to finance their operations. "Al Qaeda," Jack Goldstone remarks in his National Research Council essay on September 11, "is like gangs in U.S. central cities or social protest movements throughout the world" (2002, 151). Lack of opportunity everywhere creates conditions, he adds, where "a career as an international terrorist"—or, a gang member—becomes "more attractive than menial labor or poverty." The line demarcating criminal enterprises, some nationalist, fundamentalist, and political groups, terrorists, and gangs has become increasingly permeable.

To conclude, what is new in the global era is not the racialization or institutionalization of gangs. Contrary to mid-modernist assumptions, these have always been gang characteristics. In late modernity, however, gangs resemble other organizations of the socially excluded through a shared racial or religious identity, institutionalization within oppressed groups, and reliance on an underground economy that has arisen from the charred promises of modernity.

## Defining Gangs: A Comparison of Chicago and Soweto

So far the analysis has focused on how U.S. gangs resemble other organizations of the socially excluded. However, if race and identity, violence and organization, and the underground economy are central to defining organizations of armed young men, can we distinguish *gangs* from this broader grouping? In this light, it is instructive to compare the history of black gangs in Chicago and Soweto.

### THE ORIGINS OF SOWETO AND CHICAGO GANGS

While immigrant gangs were the focus of Frederic Thrasher, the most salient factor influencing Chicago and Soweto gangs turned out to be segregation of black people. Thrasher and Park's assimilationist perspective worked fine for Irish, Polish, and Italians and their gangs but had little relevance for African Americans. In both Chicago and Soweto, gangs were shaped by racist regimes and persisted for decades.

In Chicago, early black gangs were "defensive" formations, organized against the onslaught of Irish and other white ethnic gangs (Hirsch 1983; Perkins 2002). In Johannesburg townships that would later be called "Soweto," the "tsotsi" of the early decades of the twentieth century modeled themselves after American gangs of the cinema (Glaser 2000; Mandela 1995). They battled with other territorial gangs (Mathabene 1986), and many were seen as "protectors" of their communities, committing crimes only against whites (see also Paton 1948; Pinnock 1984; "Earlier Manifestation" 1998). "It was scarcely acknowledged," Glaser says, "that a powerful, largely apolitical, gang culture dominated the world of township youth from the 1930s to the early 1970s" (2000, 2).

In the early decades of the twentieth century, Soweto and Chicago black gangs were both segregated in all-black densely packed neighborhoods. As in all poor communities, youth hung out on streets just as Thrasher described the play group to delinquent group process. Criminal opportunity structures existed in the absence of legitimate opportunities, but the gangs in both cities failed to institutionalize and came and went as wild delinquent groups (Perkins 2002; Shaw 1999).

Soweto gangs raged at the pass laws that restricted their movement, and Chicago's gangs fought against the Irish and other white ethnic gangs that blocked their "invasion" into white areas. Both sets of black gangs held special antipathy for the police, and white legal authority was seen as illegitimate. The ferocity of segregation and oppression, however, depoliticized both black communities. During decades of accommodation, black gangs were mainly street socialized and apolitical warnings of juvenile rebellion and discontent.

### SEGREGATION AND APARTHEID: RELOCATION AND GENTRIFICATION

If race characterizes both Chicago and Soweto gangs, so does space. Rather than invasion and succession,[1] or modernization integrating a black community into mainstream society, segregation and apartheid kept black people in both cities at the bottom of the ladder. Spatial segregation created the conditions for the institutionalization of black gangs.

In both Soweto and Chicago, the conscious segregation of black people within small, cramped, urban areas was a defining characteristic of their experience, not a self-segregation into "natural areas" (Burgess 1925/1961; Zorbaugh 1926/1961). Black people were allowed into the workforce only when wartime industrial economies in both cities had labor shortages. But in their communities, unlike any for other ethnic group, residential mobility was barred by violence and legal means. In Chicago, restrictive covenants and other legal ploys maintained segregation, while in South Africa, by the end of the 1940s apartheid was the law of the land.

Both urban systems required the periodic redivision of space and a resulting relocation of black residents. In Chicago, the bombings and mob action of white gangs were gradually superseded by the erection of walls made of highways, housing projects, and universities. Hirsch's *Making of the Second Ghetto* (1983) details the rationale behind the placement of the Dan Ryan Expressway between Mayor Daley's Irish Bridgeport and the Black Belt and its subsequent reinforcement by the eighteen towers of the Robert Taylor Homes.

Soweto was an African township by law, force, and custom in much the same way as Chicago's Bronzeville was. But as Johannesburg and Chicago grew, black populations eventually got in the way of whites' mobility. The politics of relocation and gentrification have dominated the experience of both black communities and their gangs for decades.

By the 1960s, industrial expansion brought waves of Africans into the southwestern townships around Johannesburg, which took the shorthand name "Soweto." These new urban settlements soon became the heartland of gang culture (Glaser 2000). Control of criminality and gangs by white authorities seldom went beyond periodic police raids.

Sophiatown, an African township outside of Johannesburg, was the home of both nationalist political leaders and notorious tsotsi, gangs named "Americans" and "Berliners," influenced by the U.S. movies (Glaser 2000; Mandela 1995). In the 1950s, the Western Areas Removal Acts forcefully reset-tled Africans from areas desired by whites. These actions mobilized political opposition from the African National Congress and tsotsi alike. Don Pin-nock (1994) graphically describes a similar relocation in the Cape Flats. The postapartheid government has continued evictions and relocations and has met much resistance (Desai 2002).

South Africa's initial relocation policies began in the 1950s and 1960s, at the same time as Chicago's first urban renewal projects. In the last two decades, however, Chicago would pursue an even more aggressive policy of black relocation through the tearing down of housing projects and gentrification. These policies maintained segregation but displaced African Americans from land desired by white "homesteaders" (J. Smith 1998). Gangs were displaced from their housing projects and neighborhoods and their relocation spurred conflict. In both Chicago and Soweto, the result of relocation was continued segregation, not social or economic integration, and violence.

## POLITICS AND IDENTITY

The 1960s saw gangs in both Soweto and Chicago adopt a racialized iden-tity and become attracted to black liberation movements. In Chicago, some African American gangs became politicized (Williams 2002) and some were drawn into mass demonstrations and militant action. In both cities, authori-ties feared unity between the grassroots gangs and the more middle-class black formal organizations—it is alleged that the killing of Black Panther leader Fred Hampton was inspired by that fear (Perkins 2002). Both Martin Luther King and Nelson Mandela saw the gangs as "raw material" (Cohen and Taylor 2000; Mandela 1995, 222) to be recruited and won over. The gangs, for their part, resented the recruitment efforts of the liberation organizations and saw themselves, in a way, as rivals. In both cities, as the movement raged, the gangs eagerly joined street protests. But as the struggle progressed, gangs in both cities retreated into a more apolitical prioritizing of economics.

The violent repression of black people in Chicago in the late 1960s and Soweto in 1976 moved the gangs away from the liberation organizations and mainstream politics. In Chicago, the civil rights movement resulted in gains for the black middle class, but conditions for the "underclass" deteriorated (Wilson 1978). Mayor Richard J. Daley's "war on gangs" succeeded in moving the leadership of all the gangs into the prisons, where they implicitly concluded that participation in the civil rights movement had gained them nothing.

Upon release, the gang leadership quickly consolidated around the creation of illicit economic enterprises and a "new concept" of organization based on the most alienated of Chicago's very poor black and Latino communities. Politically, opportunism held sway as the El Rukns even worked for Mayor Jane Byrne, the opponent of black mayoral candidate Harold Washington while the Black Gangster Disciples organized in support of various other local candidates (Spergel 1995).

In Soweto, the upsurge in the liberation struggle attracted the gangs to mass action and the politics of the more militant Pan Africanist Congress rather than Mandela's more gradualist ANC. The Soweto uprising was based in the raised consciousness of school kids (Glaser 2000), but the protests were enthusiastically joined by the out-of-school tsotsis and youth gangs. At the same time, there were reports of South African police using tsotsis as armed thugs against the liberation struggle (Shaw 1999; "Earlier Manifestation" 1998). Prison gangs also have a long tradition in South Africa, with the entrance of street gangs in the 1970s and 1980s upsetting established inmate organization similar to Jacobs's (1977) description of Chicago gangs in Stateville (Schurink 1986).

In the final struggle for liberation, groups of militant youth, the "comrades," played a central role in the mass uprisings. Glaser (2000, 188) points out the similarities between the masculine, political, and violent "comrade" and gang culture. But as the "comrades" gained in influence, Glaser argues, the gangs subsided, similar to youth reactions to the rivalry between the Black Panther Party and the gangs in Chicago (Black 2000). Some gangs, like the Hard Livings Gang in Cape Town, continue to combine criminality and politics (Sullivan 2001).

However, after liberation, like in postindustrial Chicago, "material conditions had not improved" (Glaser 2000, 189) for those on the street, and may have worsened. Gang activity surged, both in "jackrolling"—a familiar Chicago School term that in South Africa meant "murder and rape"—and gang drug sales. Following the U.S. model, South Africa has adopted neoliberal policies and stepped up evictions, shut off water and electricity to the "poors," and privatized many basic services (Desai 2002). Glaser concludes his book with a description of Soweto that also captures Chicago today: "The pull of gang life is more forceful than ever in the ghettos, offering young men a tangible route to material wealth, excitement, and local prestige" (2000, 190).

Gangs in Soweto and Chicago thus are both the same and different than other organizations of the socially excluded. On the one hand, like other networks of armed young men, the gangs developed racialized identities through the struggle against oppression, they are armed and have persisted in areas of social exclusion for decades, and they are deeply tied to the underground economy. On the other hand, both Chicago and Soweto gangs began as unsupervised territorial peer groups. In both cities, some gangs then institutionalized within segregated ghettos or townships and adapted to changing environmental conditions.

## A Formal Definition and Typology of Gangs

A gang is not a political party, a religion, a terrorist cell, nor a revolutionary organization, though in some conditions, as we have seen, gangs can be any of these. So how can we define gangs today? From the analysis above, I conclude that

> Gangs are organizations of the socially excluded. While gangs begin as unsupervised adolescent peer groups and most remain so, some institutionalize in barrios, favelas, ghettos, and prisons. Often these institutionalized gangs become business enterprises within the informal economy and a few are linked to international criminal cartels. Most gangs share a racialized or ethnic identity and a media-diffused oppositional culture. Gangs have variable ties to conventional institutions and, in given conditions, assume social, economic, political, cultural, religious, or military roles.

We can supplement this definition with a diagram that categorizes gangs across dimensions of organization and ethnicity.

What are the advantages of this typology over Cloward and Ohlin's (1960) subcultures, Klein's (1995) organizational categories, or Taylor's (1989) evolutionary types? The key difference is the stress on ethnicity and institutionalization rather than ecological or race-neutral organizational characteristics. The typology differentiates those gangs that persist from those who do not,

*Table 12.1.*

|  | Type | Ethnicity |
|---|---|---|
|  | Dominant Group or Ethnicity | Oppressed Group or Ethnicity |
| Interstitial | Industrial-era U.S. ethnic gangs; most European male & female gangs and all unsupervised peer groups of dominant ethnicities | Most black, Latino, & Asian male & female U.S. gangs; German Turkish, British Bangladeshi, & New Zealand Maori gangs; most Third World gangs |
| Institutional | U.S. "Voting Gangs"; Triads in Asia; Hindu mandals in India; U.S. mafia and Russian mafiya; Japanese Yakuza; Colombian & Nigerian cartels | Chicago and LA "super-gangs"; NYC Latin Kings; U.S. Tongs; some South African Black, Colored, and Indian gangs; many prison gangs |

and those gangs that are members of oppressed groups ("resistance identities") or were shaped by racial oppression, as in South Africa, from those who are used by elites to oppress others ("legitimizing identities"). Like all ideal typologies, specific gangs may fit into more than one category and there will be change over time. These categories, however, have salience for gangs globally in late modernity but also are a useful way to make sense of gangs in earlier times.

This typology also extends an old argument (Hagedorn 1988) of the need to reframe the gang problem outside the criminal justice matrix. To see most gangs as interstitial is to say that most gang members still are unsupervised groups of juveniles. But to say that other gangs are institutional means that they must have at least a degree of legitimacy to survive.

To say institutional gangs are similar to other organizations of the socially excluded demands a political and social treatment of these institutions as well as a criminal justice response where warranted. It sees gangs in the context of the third world response to the insecurities of globalization. To define some gangs as institutionalized is to understand them not simplistically as organized crime but as social constructions that cognitively organize reality for their members and environment (see Jenness and Grattet 2001). "Banging," as Monster Kody said, "is a way of life." Such institutions, Selznick explained long ago, are not an "expendable tool" (1957, 5) that can easily be smashed or jailed away. Law enforcement has discovered this reality in their unsuccessful decades-long wars to eradicate gangs.

Gangs, both institutionalized and interstitial, have perhaps a million members in the United States, are well armed, have oppositional identities, and possess wealth from various informal ventures. These are powerful forces within our cities and they have variable links to similar forces worldwide. While public policy can continue to wage war by stereotyping gangs as no more than groups of criminal drug dealers or terrorists, such one-sided policies have not met much success.

Gangs, in short, are social actors, and we might be well-advised to revisit Robert Park's view of the city as the "medium for the emergence of free men" (Sennett 1969, 16). A review of Park's writings would point social theory back to the city and its organizations, including gangs. Park studied social organization from the standpoint of the social ecology of the city, not from the interests of institutions of social control. While the viewpoint expressed here is institutional and ethnic, not ecological, it shares Park's sociological concern with the spaces of the city, where, as Zygmunt Bauman laments, "not togetherness but avoidance and separation have become the major survival strategies in the contemporary megalopolis" (1998, 48).

I will conclude with the risky argument that the recognition of gangs as social actors is a necessary condition for democracy in the United States. This places gangs and the socially excluded within the modern project, rather than being seen as merely the dregs of the earth. It insists we hold gangs to the norms of democracy and advocates disarmament while opposing racism and underdevelopment. At the same time, in the absence of formal opportunities, we must be prepared to avert our eyes to certain informal economic activities.

The devastating conditions in our central cities and policies of repression not only assure the persistence of institutionalized gangs but increase the likelihood that more gangs will institutionalize and adopt more hostile and violent identities. Europe, too, has to choose whether to follow neoliberal U.S. policies or seek an alternative to the "tyranny of the market" (Bourdieu 1998). Gangs are fundamentally products of social exclusion, like other social movements and groups of armed young men. They are unlikely to be destroyed as long as ghettos and conditions of extreme poverty continue.

I believe simplistically equating gangs with terrorists and refusing to treat them as social actors can bring neither peace, justice, nor security. As Touraine (2000) puts it, the persistence of different social actors and conflicting identities demands we make greater efforts to assure we can all live peacefully together.

## Note

1. Robert Park, in his discussion of ethnic succession, surprisingly compares Chicago to South Africa and cites the replacement of the "Bantu" by the Boers as an "obvious and impressive example" of succession (1936, 173).

## References

Adamson, Christopher. 1998. "Tribute, Turf, Honor, and the American Street Gang." *Theoretical Criminology* 2: 57–84.

Bauman, Zygmunt. 1995. "The Left as the Counterculture of Modernity." In *Social Movements: Critiques, Concepts, Case Studies,* ed. Stanford Lynman, 356–70. New York: New York University Press.

———. 1998. *Globalization: The Human Consequences.* New York: Columbia University Press.

Black, Timuel. 2000. "The History of African American Gangs in Chicago." Address to the Undergraduate Research Forum, University of Chicago. http://gangresearch.net/ChicagoGangs/gangsandghetto/TimuelBlackx.html (accessed February 1, 2006).

Booth, Martin. 1999. *The Dragon Syndicates: The Global Phenomenon of the Triads.* New York: Carroll and Graf.

Bourdieu, Pierre. 1998. *Acts of Resistance: Against the Tyranny of the Market.* New York: New Press.

Burgess, Ernest W. 1925/1961. "The Growth of the City: Introduction to a Research Project." In *Studies in Human Ecology,* ed. George A. Theodorson, 37–44. Evanston, IL: Row, Peterson.

Caldiera, Teresa P. 2000. *City of Walls: Crime, Segregation, and Citizenship in São Paulo.* Berkeley: University of California.

Calhoun, Craig. 1995. *Critical Social Theory.* Oxford: Blackwell.

Castells, Manuel. 1996. *The Information Age: Economy, Society, and Culture.* Vol. 1: *The Rise of The Network Society.* Malden, Mass.: Blackwell.

———. 1997. *The Information Age: Economy, Society, and Culture.* Vol. 2: *The Power of Identity.* Malden, Mass.: Blackwell.

———. 1998. *The Information Age: Economy, Society, and Culture.* Vol. 3: *End of Millennium.* Malden, Mass.: Blackwell.

Chesney-Lind, Meda, and John M. Hagedorn, eds. 1999. *Female Gangs in America: Essays on Girls, Gangs, and Gender.* Chicago: Lakeview Press.

Chicago Commission on Race Relations. 1922. "The Negro in Chicago." Chicago: Chicago Commission on Race Relations.

Cloward, Richard, and Lloyd Ohlin. 1960. *Delinquency and Opportunity.* Glencoe, IL: Free Press.

Cohen, Adam, and Elizabeth Taylor. 2000. *American Pharaoh: Mayor Richard J. Daley—His Battle for Chicago and the Nation.* Boston: Little Brown.

Davidson, Basil. 1992. *The Black Man's Burden: Africa and the Curse of the Nation-State.* New York: Times Books.

Davis, Mike. 1990. *City of Quartz.* New York: Vintage.

De Soto, Hernando. 1990. *The Other Path: The Invisible Revolution in the Third World.* New York: Harper and Row.

Desai, Ashwin. 2002. *We Are the Poors: Community Struggles in Post-Apartheid South Africa.* New York: Monthly Review Press.

DiMaggio, Paul J., and Walter W. Powell. 1983. "The Iron Cage Revisited: Institutional Isomorphism and Collective Rationality in Organizational Fields." *American Sociological Review* 48: 147–60.

Douglas, Susan J. 1995. *Where the Girls Are: Growing Up Female with the Mass Media.* New York: Times Books.

"Earlier Manifestation of Organised Criminal Groups." 1998. Originally published in Monograph 28, Organized Crime in South Africa. http://www.iss.co.za/Pubs/Monographs/No.28/CriminalGroups.html.

Fagan, Jeffrey. 1996. "Gangs, Drugs, and Neighborhood Change." In *Gangs in America,* 2nd, ed., ed. C. Ronald Huff, 39–74. Thousand Oaks, Calif.: Sage.

Giddens, Anthony. 1991. *Modernity and Identity.* Stanford, Calif.: Stanford University Press.

Giroux, Henry A. 1996. *Fugitive Cultures: Race, Violence, and Youth.* New York: Routledge.

Glaser, Clive. 2000. *Bo-Tsotsi: The Youth Gangs of Soweto, 1935–1976.* Portsmouth, NH: Heinemann.

Goldstone, Jack A. 2002. "States, Terrorists, and the Clash of Civilizations." In *Understanding September 11,* ed. Craig Calhoun, Paul Price, and Ashley Timmer, 139–58. New York: New Press.

Gray, Obika. 1997. "Power and Identity among the Urban Poor of Jamaica." In *Globalization and Survival in the Black Diaspora,* ed. Charles Green, 199–226. Albany: State University of New York Press.

Gunst, Laurie. 1995. *Born Fi' Dead: A Journey through the Jamaican Posse Underworld.* New York: Henry Holt.

Habermas, Jürgen. 1984. *The Theory of Communicative Action: Reason and the Rationalization of Society,* vol. 1. Boston: Beacon Press.

Hagedorn, John M. 1988. *People and Folks: Gangs, Crime, and the Underclass in a Rustbelt City.* Chicago: Lakeview Press.

———. 1998. "Post-Industrial Gang Violence." In *Youth Violence,* ed. Michael Tonry and Mark H. Moore, 457–511. Chicago: University of Chicago.

———. 2001. "Gangs and the Informal Economy." In *Gangs in America,* ed. Ron Huff, 101–20. Beverly Hills: Sage.

Haskins, James. 1974. *Street Gangs: Yesterday and Today.* New York: Hastings House.

Hazlehurst, Kayleen, and Cameron Hazlehurst, eds. 1998. *Gangs and Youth Subcultures: International Explorations.* New Brunswick, N.J.: Transaction.

Held, David. 2002. "Violence, Law, Justice in a Global Age." In *Understanding September 11,* ed. Craig Calhoun, Paul Price, and Ashley Timmer, 92–105. New York: New Press.

Heuze, Gerard. 1995. "Cultural Populism: The Appeal of the Shiv Sena." In *Bombay: Metaphor for Modern India,* ed. Sujata Patel and Alice Thorner, 213–47. New Delhi: Oxford University Press.

Hirsch, Arnold R. 1983. *Making the Second Ghetto: Race and Housing in Chicago 1940–1960.* Cambridge: Cambridge University Press.

Hobsbawm, Eric. 1997. *The Age of Extremes: A History of the World, 1914–1991.* New York: Vintage.

———. 2000. *On the Edge of the New Century.* New York: New Press.

Human Rights Watch. 2002. "Haiti." http://www.hrw.org/wr2k2/americas7.html.

Ianni, Fracisa J. 1972. *Family Business: Kinship and Social Control in Organized Crime.* New York: Russell Sage.

Jacobs, James. 1977. *Stateville.* Chicago. University of Chicago.

Jah, Yusuf, and Sister Shah Keyah, eds. 1995. *Uprising: Crips and Bloods Tell the Story of America's Youth in the Crossfire.* New York: Scribner.

James, C. 2002. "The Raboteau Revolt: Aristide's Political Machine." *Z* 15: 35–39.

Jamieson, Ruth, and Adrian Grounds. 2002. "No Sense of an Ending: The Effects of Long-Term Imprisonment amongst Republican Prisoners and Their Families." Monaghan, Ireland: Ex-prisoners Assistance Committee (EXPAC).

Jenness, Valerie, and Ryken Grattet. 2001. *Making Hate a Crime: From Social Movement to Law Enforcement.* New York: Russell Sage.

Jimenez, Jose Blanes. 1989. "Cocaine, Informality, and the Urban Economy in La Paz, Bolivia." In *The Informal Economy: Studies in Advanced and Less Developed Countries,* ed. Alejandro Portes, Manuel Castells, and Lauren A. Benton, 135–49. Baltimore: Johns Hopkins Press.

Jones, Patrice M. 2002. "Rio Crime Bolder, More Violent." *Chicago Tribune,* June 27.

Kaldor, Mary. 2002. "Beyond Militarism, Arms Races, and Arms Control." In *Understanding September 11,* ed. Craig Calhoun, Paul Price, and Ashley Timmer, 159–76. New York: New Press.

Kelley, Robin D. G. 1997. *Yo' mama's disfunktional.* Boston: Beacon Press.

Keohane, Robert O. 2002. "The Globalization of Informal Violence, Theories of World Politics, and the 'Liberalism of Fear.'" In *Understanding September 11,* ed. Craig Calhoun, Paul Price, and Ashley Timmer, 77–91. New York: New Press.

Klein, Malcolm W. 1971. *Street Gangs and Street Workers.* Englewood Cliffs, N.J.: Prentice Hall.

———. 1995. *The American Street Gang: Its Nature, Prevalence, and Control.* New York: Oxford University Press.

Klein, Malcolm, Hans-Jurgen Kerner, Cheryl L. Maxsen, and Elmar G. M. Weitekamp, eds. 2001. *The Eurogang Paradox: Street Gangs and Youth Groups in the U.S. and Europe.* Dordrecht, Netherlands: Kluwer.

Kornhauser, Ruth Rosner. 1978. *Social Sources of Delinquency: An Appraisal of Analytic Models.* Chicago: University of Chicago.

La Cava, Gloria, and Rafaella Y. Nanetti. 2001. *Albania: Fight the Vulnerability Gap.* Washington, D.C.: World Bank.

Landesco, John. 1968 [1929]. *Organized Crime in Chicago.* Chicago: University of Chicago Press.

Laqueur, Walter. 1999. *The New Terrorism: Fanaticism and the Arms of Mass Destruction.* New York: Oxford University Press.

Lele, Jayant. 1995. "Saffronization of the Shiv Sena: The Political Economy of City, State, and Nation." In *Bombay: Metaphor for Modern India,* ed. Sujata Patel and Alice Thorner, 185–212. New Delhi: Oxford University Press.

Maas, Peter. 1968. *The Valachi Papers.* New York: Bantam Books.

Mandela, Nelson. 1995. *Long Walk to Freedom.* Boston: Little, Brown.

Massey, Douglas S., and Nancy A. Denton. 1993. *American Apartheid: Segregation and the Making of the Underclass.* Boston: Harvard University Press.

Mathabene, Mark. 1986. *Kaffir Boy.* New York: Macmillan.

McKeown, Laurence. 2001. *Out of Time: Irish Republican Prisoners: Long Kesh 1972–2000.* Dublin: Beyond the Pale.

Miller, Walter. 1975. "Violence by Youth Gangs and Youth Groups as a Crime Problem in Major American Cities." Washington, D.C.: U.S. Department of Justice.

Monkkonen, Eric H. 2001. *Murder in New York City.* Berkeley: University of California Press.

Moore, Joan W. 1998. "Understanding Youth Street Gangs: Economic Restructuring and the Urban Underclass." In *Cross-Cultural Perspectives on Youth and Violence,* ed. Meredith Watts, 65–78. Stamford, Conn.: JAI Press.

Nightengale, Carl Husemoller. 1994. *The Edge: A History of Poor Black Children and Their American Dreams.* New York: Basic Books.

Park, Robert E. 1936. "Succession: An Ecological Concept." *American Sociological Review* 1, no. 2: 117–79.

———. 1969. "Human Migration and the Marginal Man." In *Classic Essays on the Culture of Cities,* ed. Richard Sennett. Englewood Cliffs, N.J.: Prentice-Hall.

Paton, Alan. 1948. *Cry, The Beloved Country.* New York: Simon and Schuster.

Perkins, Eugene Euseni. 2002. "Talk to the Chicago Gang History Project." http://www.uic.edu/orgs/ganghistory/perksins.html.

Perry, David A. 2001. "Contested Cities/Sovereign Engagement: Creating New Vision and Sustainable Policy through Comparative Collaboration Research: A Project Outline." Chicago: Great Cities Institute.

Pinnock, Don. 1984. *The Brotherhoods: Street Gangs and State Control in Cape Town.* Cape Town: David Philip.

Portes, Alejandro, Manuel Castells, and Lauren A. Benton, eds. 1989. *The Informal Economy: Studies in Advanced and Less Advanced Countries.* Baltimore: Johns Hopkins Press.

"Rey." 2002. Chicago Gang History Project. http://www.uic.edu.orgs/kbc/latinkings/latinking.html.

Russo, Gus. 2001. *The Outfit: The Role of Chicago's Underworld in the Shaping of Modern America.* New York: Bloomsbury.

Sassen, Saskia. 1991. *The Global City: New York, London, Tokyo.* Princeton, N.J.: Princeton University Press.

Schulze, Kirsten E. 2001. "Taking the Gun Out of Politics: Conflict Transformation in Northern Ireland and Lebanon." In *Northern Ireland and the Divided World: The Northern Ireland Conflict and the Good Friday Agreement in Comparative Perspective,* ed. John McGarry, 253–75. Oxford: Oxford University Press.

Schurink, Willem J. 1986. "Number Gangs in South African Prisons: An Organizational Perspective." Paper presented at the Association for Sociology in Southern Africa. Durban.

Selznick, Philip. 1957. *Leadership in Administration: A Sociological Interpretation.* Berkeley: University of California.

Sennett, Richard. 1969. Introduction to *Classic Essays on the Culture of Cities,* ed. Richard Sennett. Englewood Cliffs, N.J.: Prentice-Hall.

———. 1990. The Conscience of the Eye: The Design of Social Life of Cities. New York: W. W. Norton.

Shakur, Sanyika. 1993. *Monster: The Autobiography of a Gang Member.* New York: Penguin Books.

Sharma, Kalpana. 1995. "Chronicle of a Riot Foretold." In *Bombay: Metaphor for Modern India,* ed. Sujata Patel and Alice Thorner, 268–86. New Delhi: Oxford University Press.

Shaw, Mark. 1999. "The Development and Control of Organized Crime in Post-Apartheid South Africa." In *Organized Crime: Uncertainties and Dilemmas,* ed. Stanley Einstein and Menachem Amir, 97–118. Chicago: Office of International Criminal Justice.

Short, James F. 1964. "Adult-Adolescent Relations and Gang Delinquency." Pacific Sociological Review 7: 59–65.

———. 1996. "Forward: Diversity and Change in U.S. Gangs." In *Gangs in America,* 2nd ed., ed. C. Ronald Huff. vii–xviii. Thousand Oaks, Calif.: Sage.

Short, James F., and Fred L. Strodtbeck. 1965. *Group Process and Gang Delinquency.* Chicago: University of Chicago.

Smith, Janet L. 1998. "Cleaning Up Public Housing by Sweeping Out the Poor." *Habitat International* 23: 49–62.

Smith, Neil. 1996. *The New Urban Frontier: Gentrification and the Revanchist State.* London: Routledge.

Smyth, Marie, and Marie-Therese Fay, eds. 2000. *Personal Accounts from Northern Ireland's Troubles: Public Conflict, Private Loss.* London: Pluto Press.

Spergel, Irving A. 1964. *Racketville Slumtown Haulberg.* Chicago: University of Chicago.

———. 1995. *The Youth Gang Problem: A Community Approach.* Oxford: Oxford University Press.

Sullivan, John P. 2001. "Gangs, Hooligans, and Anarchists: The Vanguard of Netwar in the Streets." In *Networks and Netwars,* ed. John Arquilla, and David Ronfeld, 99–128. Santa Monica, Calif.: Rand National Defense Research Institute.

Taylor, Carl. 1989. *Dangerous Society.* East Lansing: Michigan State University Press.

Thomas, W. I., and Eli Znaniecki. 1918–1920/1996. *The Polish Peasant.* Urbana: University of Illinois.

Thrasher, Frederic. 1927. *The Gang.* Chicago: University of Chicago.

Touraine, Alain. 1995. *Critique of Modernity.* Oxford: Blackwell.

———. 2000. *Can We Live Together? Equality and Difference.* Stanford, Calif.: Stanford University Press.

Varshney, Ashutosh. 2002. *Ethnic Conflict and Civic Life: Hindus and Muslims in India.* New Haven, Conn.: Yale University Press.

Venkatesh, Sudhit Alladi. 2000. *American Project: The Rise and Fall of a Modern Ghetto.* Cambridge, Mass.: Harvard University Press.

Venkatesh, Sudhir Alladi, and Steven D. Leavitt. 2000. "'Are We a Family or a Business?' History and Disjuncture in the Urban American Street Gang." Theory and Society 29: 427–62.

Wacquant, Loic. 2001. "The New 'Peculiar Institution': On the Prison as Surrogate Ghetto." *Theoretical Criminology* 4: 377–89.

Weber, Max. 1946. "Science as a Vocation." In *From Max Weber: Essays in Sociology,* ed. Hans Gerth and C. Wright Mill. New York: Oxford University Press.

West, Cornel. 1993. *Race Matters.* New York: Vintage.

Williams, Lance. 2002. Talk to the Chicago Gang History Project. Chicago. http://www.uic.edu/orgs/ganghistory/rangers/lance.html.

Wilson, William Julius. 1978. *The Declining Significance of Race.* Chicago: University of Chicago.

———. 1987. *The Truly Disadvantaged.* Chicago: University of Chicago.

Winant, Howard. 2001. *The World Is a Ghetto: Race and Democracy since World War II.* New York: Basic Books.

Wirth, Louis. 1928/1956. *The Ghetto.* Chicago: University of Chicago.

Young, Jock. 1998. *The Exclusive Society.* London: Sage.

Zimmermann, Warren. 1999. *Origins of a Catastrophe.* New York: Times Books.

Zorbaugh, Harvey W. 1926/1961. "The Natural Areas of the City." In *Studies in Human Ecology,* ed. George A. Theodorson, 45–49. Evanston, Ill.: University of Chicago.

# 13

# The Challenges of Gangs in Global Contexts

JAMES F. SHORT JR.

When John Hagedorn first approached me about participating in a conference on gangs in global contexts, he gave me the option of writing a paper on the subject or providing a summary and critique of the other papers. Left unspoken was his assumption that I would speak to the challenges to traditional criminology posed by the conference papers. For reasons beyond my control, I was unable to take part in the conference. John graciously gave me the option of writing a foreword to the conference volume or preparing a chapter consistent with the earlier mission.

John sent me the papers as they were sent to him and followed this with copies of his commentaries and recommendations for revision. Joan Moore also generously sent me her detailed notes, taken during the conference. Although it was agreed that I would receive final revisions of chapters, as well, urgencies of publication required that my response be written before that process could be completed. I received revisions of most chapters and was able to revise, albeit hurriedly. As a result, in some cases this chapter may be unfairly critical. I hope it is nevertheless appreciative, for that is what I intend it to be.

All of these materials made for interesting reading, and they do, indeed, challenge much criminological thinking and research. I could not resist the opportunity to prepare a more fulsome response than would have been possible in a brief foreword, hence, this chapter.[1] I want first to address issues that cut across chapters rather than addressing serially the parts into which the book is organized, then to discuss briefly challenges that apply more broadly to criminology and the social and behavioral sciences.

It is clear from reading the individual chapters—even more so from initial drafts and other materials that were made available to me—that participants found the conference theme troublesome. One of those themes was that economic, political, and social happenings throughout the world influence forms of association of young people in virtually all societies. Recognizing that such influences vary a great deal in different places and spaces, the charge to participants was to document their extent and nature, and their relation to historical circumstances, degrees of modernity, and other life conditions. Because some of these influences are quite direct while others are not, relating globalization to particular institutions and forms of association is a complex and difficult task. It is only fair to note that participants in the conference recognize that their offerings are exploratory and provide only a crude sampling of such influences.

The influence of globalization on the various forms of association that are loosely termed gangs is especially difficult, in part because a rich body of new research and theory regarding gangs has recently emerged that documents rapid and continuing change in many places (see Coughlin and Venkatesh 2003; Decker and Weersman 2006; Huff 2002; Klein et al. 2001; Short and Hughes 2006; SSRC 2005; Vigil 2003). Surveys reveal greater prevalence and diversity among gangs today than in the past. Other studies document new insights regarding economic, neighborhood, and school contexts of gang behavior and the meaning of gang association (see Short 2002). As chapters in this timely volume demonstrate, global developments are implicated in many of these variations and changes.

## Challenges of and to the Conference Theme

It is not surprising that the conference theme proved difficult. Even the meaning of gangs and globalization remains controversial, and the conference and this volume are truly pioneering in relating them to one another. Both theoretical constructs are ambiguous, despite—perhaps because of—large research literatures, about gangs over nearly a century, more recently for globalization.

Although some of the conference participants are careful to identify global phenomena they find of special interest, several do not, perhaps because the topic has not been prominent in their previous work. Whatever the reason, failure to be more explicit complicates assessment and response.

## GANGS: DEFINITIONS AND OTHER CONTROVERSIES

Debates concerning the definition and the nature of gangs and interpretations based on differing approaches to their study continue, despite—again, perhaps because of—a recent resurgence of scholarly interest. One such controversy concerns whether a "gang" definition should include law breaking or a "criminal orientation." Law enforcement officials include law breaking in their definition of gangs—control of crime is, after all, an element in their job descriptions. Many scholars follow this definition, in part because doing so facilitates the use of data gathered by law enforcement agencies and reported by them (for example, the National Youth Gang Survey; see Howell, Moore, and Egley 2002; Klein 1995). Others argue that including law breaking in the definition creates a circular argument. Definitions cannot explain, and if we want to understand gang delinquent/criminal behavior, such behavior must not be part of the definition. The counter to this argument is that including law breaking in the definition does not preclude study of why and under what conditions gangs commit crimes—indeed, that is the focus of most gang theory and research. More importantly, however, including crime in the definition deflects attention from circumstances and processes that are associated with gang *formation* and *behaviors other than the commission of criminal or delinquent acts* (see Short 1997, 1998). Drawing upon Loïc Wacquant's discussion of "pernicious premises in the study of the American ghetto" in this volume, focusing narrowly on crime risks *exoticizing* gangs and gang members. Viewed historically, the extent and nature of a youth, or street, gang's involvement in criminal behavior is only one aspect of gang life and may, at any particular time, be a relatively minor aspect.

This point is especially important in view of the expanded purview of gangs set forth by editor Hagedorn and others in this volume. Criminal behavior, as well as the resistance identities and the "essentialism" of race and ethnicity stressed by Hagedorn, clearly are derivative of circumstances and processes that influence identities based on relationships with community institutions, agents, and agencies, constraints and opportunities that are embedded in historically specific circumstances, as well as certain global developments stressed especially by Saskia Sassen.

Anthropologist Mark Fleisher contributes to this debate using network analysis methods that rarely have been applied to gangs.[2] By questioning gang members about their friends and other social relationships, Fleisher identifies "ego gang networks" comprising "the total set of social relations of a gang member" (Fleisher 2002, 203). His study of female gangs in an impoverished neighborhood in Champaign, Illinois, finds that ego gang networks are socially flexible and typically include members of other gangs and non-gang members, as well as members of one's own gang. Indeed, he reports, "(*no) ego*" even "*knew* all members of her gang" (210; emphasis added to original). Unfortunately, this is but a single study of local female gangs in a particular place and time, and similar studies have not been made of male or mostly male gangs. Other data are supportive, however. My own brief contacts with former Chicago gang bangers suggest that even as gangs have become institutionalized as participants in illicit enterprise in some communities (see Hagedorn 2002a, b and herein; Portes, Castells, and Benton 1989; Venkatesh 1996; Venkatesh and Leavitt 2000), in other communities gangs may become, like Fleisher's young women, more like the voluntary associations and special interest groups that play such important roles in mainstream society.[3]

Authors here do not provide precise or formal definitions of gangs, although several of them have done so in other writings. Moore's classic *Homeboys* (1978), for example, emphasizes the "quasi-institutional" character of gangs in East Los Angeles Chicano communities, arguing that they should not be regarded "as a specialized juvenile phenomenon whose main feature is the production of delinquent acts" (36). Hagedorn (1998) describes four patterns of gang formation among the Milwaukee gangs he studied, none of which involved a specifically criminal orientation of the groups. John Pitts (herein) attributes conflict among peer groups (he does not call them gangs) in East London and Walford largely to demographic and structural economic changes that subjected those who were most vulnerable to violence (especially young Asian families), by virtue of being housed in close proximity to those most likely to victimize them. Delinquent or criminal behavior—let alone a criminal orientation—had little to do with the basis for their coming together. Importantly, however, some of the changes noted by Pitts were the result of widespread conflicts in African countries and the Balkans—a dramatic aspect of international migration (see also Sassen 2002–2003 and in this volume). Moore, Cameron Hazlehurst, and Joachim Kersten also direct attention to the effects of international migration.

Most of the foregoing chapters focus on youth groups that are, or have been, involved in delinquent and/or criminal behavior. Such behavior clearly was important to the gang that has become the Almighty Latin King and Queens Nation (ALKQN) prior to the group's transformation into a "street organization" and was a source of tension during the period of transition. It is unclear whether the ALKQN should now be regarded as a gang, a religious group, or—as Brotherton would have it—a budding social movement. Documentation and theoretical development of these hypotheses are hard to come by.

Definitions are important, if for no other reason than, absent clear definitions, it is not clear what is being talked about, analyzed, or related to globalization. To the extent that the transformations of gangs about which Hagedorn writes are real, gangs clearly are not the "play groups" that Thrasher and others have portrayed. It seems likely, however, that some of his referenced groups were never play groups. Some may have been socialized from childhood into existing cultural patterns of participation in informal economies that were well integrated with "legitimate" social, political, and economic institutions, as sometimes has been the case at various times and places (see references in Hagedorn chapter; also Chin 1986; Ianni 1973; Abadinsky 1985). Some may, from early childhood, identify themselves, their peers, and their communities as victims of oppression, as Hagedorn and others argue is increasingly the case. Clearly, growing up in territories claimed by the Vice Lord Nation or the many offshoots of Crips and Bloods in Chicago or in the barrios of Los Angeles is different today than was the case only a few years ago (see Short 1996), let alone half a century or more in the past.[4] Although some of these changes are well documented, their impact on gangs and other youth groups has received scant scholarly attention. Still less attention has been devoted to the changing nature of *youth groups in general,* and definitive research on how globalization has influenced them is virtually nonexistent. Given the rapidity of social change, definitive research may never be possible *except* at specific times and in specific places.

Because they are so at variance with mainstream scholarship concerning gangs, it is especially important that the changes observed by Hagedorn be well established empirically. One of the most documented characteristics of juvenile offending is that it takes place in small groups. However, solo offending becomes more common following adolescence, "at the very time that most offenders are leaving crime behind," as Mark Warr notes (Warr 2002, 33; see also Reiss 1986; Reiss and Farrington 1991). Hagedorn's and others' concerns with offending center more on participation in informal, often illicit, economies than on ordinary crime; and with a variety of forms of "resistance," some of which are also illicit; and they extend much beyond adolescence. Both documentation of and theoretical accounting for such changes present major challenges, not only to traditional criminology but as well to those who see their roots in political and economic changes on a global scale.

The principal scholarly interests of conference participants and other authors, herein, are both varied and distinguished. Moore, Hagedorn, and Diego Vigil each have devoted much of their scholarly lives to studying gangs. Hazlehurst is coeditor of an important book on the international scope of youth cultures and gangs (Hazlehurst and Hazlehurst 1998). Vigil's coauthor, Jan Rus, has written papers on recent changes in Chiapas, Mexico, the site of the research reported in this volume. Pitts, here and elsewhere, focuses on political, economic, and community forces that isolate some categories of citizens, including children, making them the object of discrimination, derision, and violence. Kersten has contributed to an earlier survey of gangs in Europe and elsewhere (see Klein et al. 2001). Brotherton and Barrios focus on the same "gang" in New York City, but with somewhat different theoretical and empirical interests—social movements for Brotherton, spiritual and theological matters for Barrios.[5] Gangs are not the primary research interests of Jock Young, Sassen, or Wacquant, but their previous work is relevant to both gangs and global change. Among traditional gang scholars, Hagedorn alone has devoted much attention to globalization. Differences such as these yield distinctly different perspectives on gangs and other youth groups as contributors struggle with the conference theme.

## GLOBALIZATION CONTROVERSIES

Globalization is at least as controversial a theoretical construct as "the gang." Mauro Guillen (2001b) documents the explosive growth of globalization literature, where definitions again abound. Most scholars converge on notions of information flow and networking among economic, political, and social organizations and institutions on a global scale, leading to varying degrees of mutual influence and interdependence. Some focus entirely on economic processes but disagree as to which processes are most important. Others emphasize increasing technological scale and information flows. Sociologists Martin Albrow, Roland Robertson, and Guillen emphasize *mutual influence and awareness* as well as information flow (Guillen 2001a, b). However, "one of the persistent problems afflicting the study of globalization is that it is far from a uniform, irreversible, and inexorable trend. Rather globalization is a fragmented, incomplete, discontinuous, contingent, and in many ways contradictory and puzzling process" (Guillen 2001b, 238).

Sometimes bitter and polemic controversy concerning the aims and effects of globalization is as widespread as debate over definitions and substance. A recent Social Science Research Council newsletter features "four different views of what has been at stake in recent conflicts over globalization"

(SSRC 2001, 1). The late, great Pierre Bourdieu leads off the symposium, arguing that *"unification profits the dominant"* by liberating the economically powerful from the political constraints of states (SSRC 2001, 1). Economist Jagdish Bhagwati counters that economic globalization, when properly managed, is both economically and socially benign. Political scientist Donatella della Porta and sociologist Sidney Tarrow note that excessively violent police behavior results when police responses to recent antiglobalization protests depart from experience-based procedures that are associated with peaceful protests, concluding that "criminalization of social movements contributes to [their] radicalization and polarization"[6] (SSRC 2001, 11). Anthropologist and activist David Graeber joins Hagedorn, Pitts, and Young in this volume, taking issue with neoliberalism and its antidemocratic tendencies. Based on his experience with direct-action organizations such as People's Global Action, Ya Basta!, and the Direct Action Network, he argues "if one takes globalization to mean the effacement of borders and the free movement of people, possessions and ideas, then it's pretty clear that not only is the movement a product of globalization, but that most of the groups involved in it—particularly the most radical ones—are in fact far more supportive of globalization in general than [are] supporters of the International Monetary Fund or World Trade Organization"[7] (SSRC 2001, 12)

Guillen's (2001b) review focuses on "five key debates" about the nature of the phenomenon, two of which are especially salient to this volume: (1) Does globalization produce convergence? and (2) Is a global culture in the making? Arguments advanced by Hagedorn and others, herein, that global influences on urban spaces create walls of exclusion and segregation and promote a homogeneous, globalizing culture remain controversial among globalization scholars. Presumably, however, all would agree with political scientist Robert Keohane's observation (following the terrorist attacks of September 11, 2001): "As in the past, not all aspects of globalization go together."[8]

Although authors in this book do not formally define globalization, they differ as to precisely what they regard as important, and for some neither the meaning nor the relevance of globalization is clear. Moreover, which aspects of globalization are related in what ways to what sorts of gangs, their prevalence, organization, purposes, and behavior is largely ignored in these chapters.

## Globalization and Gangs

Hagedorn, Moore, Hazlehurst, and Sassen struggle most straightforwardly with the main conference theme.

Moore focuses on processes that are widely recognized as important aspects or results of globalization: international migration and "peripheralization"; that is, "large segments of . . . in-migrants and of the old working class have become increasingly peripheral to the main economic life of cities in developed nations." Moore hypothesizes that these developments create a crisis in female identity among some young women who migrate from less developed countries to western democracies, in much the same vein as Kersten's portrayal of young males in Germany. Her review of the scant scholarly literature on female gangs and reports of journalists finds that some young women among Somali, Moroccan, and Latin American migrants to Norway formed gangs that, "like their male counterparts, were violent, carried knives, and were 'willing to commit crimes,'" suggesting that traditional gender and religious roles were being resisted.

Sassen notes that the demographic transition in global cities[9] localizes the politics of claim making concerning, for example, "the rights of the homeless, immigrants, queers and gays—and of contestation—against gentrification, against police abuse." To the extent that such rights challenge traditional gender and religious roles, however, resistance might well conflict with "essentialist" and religious fundamentalist and nationalist claims that are associated with much contemporary armed conflict and terrorism (Juergensmeyer 2002).[10] Similarly, the resistance identity of the ALKQN—including spiritual qualities (Barrios and Brotherton herein)—seems most attuned to their ethnic and collective identity and to demeaning relationships with law enforcement and other official agencies—common themes in other chapters as well (Hagedorn, Hazlehurst, Kersten, Pitts, Sassen, Rus and Vigil).

Conceptual and empirical problems are compounded when ambiguous themes and subthemes are linked together. The linkage of globalization and resistance ideology among youth gangs is an important hypothesis, but little hard evidence is presented in this volume. The resistance theme is especially prominent in the Hagedorn, Brotherton, and Barrios chapters. The latter describe resistance primarily in relation to repression and to the self-fulfilling imagery and treatment experienced by group members, rather than to features of globalization. Brotherton's depiction of the ALKQN as a "politicized gang or street organization" is instructive and is perhaps a step toward a meaningful typology of youth groups beyond the current chaos in the gang literature. Although demonstration of the political consciousness and spirituality among ALKQN members requires more systematic analysis if it is to be sustained, there is evidence of the importance of religion and spirituality among other groups of "armed young men," as Hagedorn notes.[11] Brotherton also stresses the contrast between ALKQN the street organization and traditional gangs. It is especially important that the *staying power* of street organizations that evolve from gangs be well documented and theoretically understood in both organizational and social movement terms. My reading of the gang literature—admittedly traditional and scholarly—is that organizations based on street gangs generally have proven to be ephemeral and ineffective. Moreover, although all manner of violence continues to be committed in the name of religion, the *connection between* traditional, or "transitional gangs" in this respect remains elusive. The ALKQN, their Chicago progenitors the Latin Kings (Conquergood 1994, 1997), and other "institutional" gangs may prove to be a "fourth way," in Castell's terms, but that has yet to be demonstrated. Barrios's candid closing assessment may be prescient: politically, "they do not exhibit the same kind of social activism that gave them the category of social movement during our research. . . . From a spiritual perspective, they are practicing at this moment what I identify as a spirituality of oppression, becoming more and more fundamentalist and/or traditionalist in their approaches and interpretations that they give to their social realities."

Historically, as Hagedorn notes in chapter 1 of this volume, the organizational success of youth gangs has been limited largely to their affiliation with other, well-established organizations such as political machines and organized crime. It may be the case that a necessary condition for "street organizations" such as the ALKQN to be sustained and effective beyond localized interests and over the long run is to reach out organizationally in common cause with other groups and organizations. Participation in social movements and social movement organizations offer possible avenues for such an evolution.

The social movement literature is only one of many that have been neglected by criminologists, and this volume is at least a step in the right direction. Ample evidence of the strength of nationalism and religious fundamentalism—both embedded in ethnic identities—is found in many parts of the globe. Certainly both may influence the manner in which particular groups of young people come together and organize, and the purposes they pursue. Other suggestive theoretical linkages are found in literature concerning organized crime and nongovernmental organizations (NGOs) and in Sassen's chapter herein (see also Sassen 1991, 2002–2003).[12]

Sassen emphasizes that cities concentrate diversity and that urban space is enabling of street-level political activity beyond traditional, exploitative, formal political systems. Like Castells (2000), she also argues that the Internet can facilitate cross-border networking among localized interests.

Although aspects of globalization are identified in these pages as important to the formation of gangs and other types of youth groups, sorting out which types of youth groups are affected in what ways is a daunting task. Networking surely has major potential, along with the effects of *international migration* (see, in addition to chapters, herein, Tonry 1997), the *emergence of informal economies* in many parts of the world (Castells 1998; Portes and Sassen-Koob 1987; Portes, Castells, and Benton 1989), the importance of *economic restructuring* and the *redistribution of industrial jobs and labor force competition between racial and ethnic groups;* and often counterproductive *political and law enforcement reactions* to massive changes such as these—the latter being developments upon which all of these authors appear to agree.

These forces have specific and varied impacts in local communities (Hagedorn 1998, 2002a, b; Hazlehurst and Rus and Vigil herein) but they reflect global and national political and economic policies, as well (Hagedorn, Kersten, Moore, Pitts, Sassen, Wacquant, and Young herein). Venkatesh in Chicago (1996; see also Coughlin and Venkatesh 2003) and Hagedorn in Milwaukee find that some gangs are "consciously constructed as organizations" that "play an active social, political, and economic role within their communities," in large part by means of their participation in informal and illicit economies that often involve licit businesses where customers may obtain illicit goods and services such as drugs and prostitution (Hagedorn 2002a, 119; Hazlehurst herein). Mutually exploitative symbiotic relationships such as these have a long history, but Hagedorn and Sassen argue that the new urban economy of globalization has massively distorted the operation of markets, resulting in "new dynamics of inequality" (Sassen herein). Similarly, while large numbers of young people in highly urban areas have been oriented to peer cultures at least since the emergence of youth cultures following World War II (Coleman et al. 1974), they argue that the extent and the intensity of youth culture involvement have increased and in many cases have come to supplant orientation to the worlds of work and adulthood.

These are challenging ideas. There is ample evidence in these chapters and elsewhere of the pull of youth cultures among young people in many parts of the world and of its commercial exploitation (see, for example, Anderson 1999; Sullivan 1989). Likewise, informal economies have a long history in many countries, and much evidence suggests that integration of informal and formal labor markets has increased in recent decades (Castells 2000; Portes, Castells, and Benton 1989). Similarly, as conventional economic activity has been transformed by global developments, organized crime has made headway across national borders in many parts of the world. Alexander

Salagaev's (2001) chronicle of the "Evolution of Delinquent Gangs in Russia" traces the effects of changing social and economic conditions in that country on youth groups, from traditional gangs to "organized criminal gangs" (see also, in that volume, Hagedorn 2001).

The trends noted are important, but compelling documentation of their extent and their nature has yet to be established. Among these authors, Hazlehurst most clearly identifies ethnicity with variation among gangs in style of operation, relationship with local communities, and motivation. Although he acknowledges the presence in New Zealand of economic and ethnic inequalities, community dislocations, and other changes associated with globalization, he argues that most gangs in that nation "stand apart" "less because they are forced to by circumstance and more because they choose to do so."[13] Hazlehurst implies gang *agency* of a quite different type than the *resistance* theme emphasized by others in this volume. Although the argument lacks full theoretical and empirical development, Hazlehurst's fascinating chronicle of New Zealand, stressing choice and "understanding the actual importance of the circumstances and environments" in which gangs exist, is a challenge to the ideological imputations of some authors.

Pitts and Kersten herein make the case that ethnic identity and nationalist reactions are importantly related to group violence in England and in Germany, respectively.[14] Kersten notes, however, that, unlike the Nazi emergence in Germany during the 1930s, right-wing networks of neo-Nazi and skinhead Kameradschaften in modern Germany generally lack a coherent ideology, and that violent behavior that is associated with these phenomena is largely dependent on situational circumstances, such as public conflicts between young males over honor and territory. In this sense, the "gangs" described by Pitts, Kersten, Moore, and Hazlehurst seem rather more like the "traditional" gangs of the 1950s and early 1960s that were studied in Chicago (Short and Strodtbeck 1965/1974), Los Angeles (Klein 1971; Moore 1978) and elsewhere (Jankowski 1991; Miller 1980; Miller, Geertz, and Cutter 1961; Thornberry et al. 2003) than the "postmodern" gangs hypothesized by Hagedorn (herein, 1998, 2002a, b) and spoken to by Portes et al. (1989) and others.[15]

Summarizing, contributors to this volume vary in the extent to which they are comfortable with the network society and global cities themes developed by Castells (1998), Sassen (1991), and others. It is clear, however, that global phenomena such as international migration, economic restructuring, redistribution of industrial jobs and labor-force competition between racial and ethnic groups, the proliferation of informal economies, and political and law enforcement reactions to all of these developments present new contexts within which youth groups form, organize, and adapt. The several types of research and theorizing here represented are a sampling of what is or may be happening in this regard. As these researchers are very much aware, however, much more will be required if the full implications of globalization for the individual and collective behavior of young people can be understood.

## Methods and Theories

In spite of Hagedorn's heroic efforts, variation among these chapters in their methodological and theoretical approaches to the conference themes contributes both to its lack of coherence and unevenness. Rus and Vigil's ethnographically based field studies of the nature of Mayan adaptation to changing conditions in Chiapas, Mexico, is of quite a different order than the theoretical exegeses on the impact of globalization on gangs with respect to such traditional sociological topics as social ecology, race, class, and political economy (Hagedorn), gender (Kersten; Moore) and ethnicity (Hazlehurst). The even broader strokes offered by Young (on social exclusion and insecurities related to structural economic changes), Pitts (on British neoliberal policies, many of them mimicking the United States, with respect to race/ethnicity and crime), Sassen (on global impacts on cities), and Wacquant (his critique of premises underlying ghetto studies in the U.S.) are important sociologically—and certainly for understanding youth groups. The impact of these developments on youth in general, individually and collectively—and on gangs and other youth groups—is a topic as broad as it is important; and it is certainly important. The social movement perspective of Brotherton and the spiritual interpretations of Barrios likewise cry out for additional documentation, especially over time. Indeed, every essay in this volume sets forth provocative ideas worthy of further, more systematic, investigation.

John Hagedorn et al.—and I, certainly, among them—struggle with issues such as these, theoretically and empirically. Relevant data are limited—a condition endemic to our disciplines. Hagedorn clearly recognizes the continued existence of gangs as essentially unsupervised youth groups, but how they relate to institutionalized gangs and the conditions and processes that result in institutionalization remain unspecified and undocumented.[16] His reference to "traditional" gangs as "mostly concerned with economic survival" and disillusioned with politics, for example, is inconsistent with much previous work. Neither of these characteristics was primary among most of Thrasher's traditional gangs. Nor were they, prior to the emergence of "super gangs" and gang "nations" during the 1960s, characteristic of the gangs that were studied in Chicago (Short and Moland 1976; Short and Strodtbeck 1965/1974), Boston (Miller 1958; 1976), or Los Angeles (Klein 1971, 1995), or in most countries in Europe (Klein et al. 2001). White ethnic gangs may be less common than in the past as a result of assimilation, but white gangs continue to be common throughout much of the United States (Howell, Moore, and Egley 2002), and for the most part they appear to be traditional unsupervised groups.

John Hagedorn is to be congratulated for thinking "outside the box" of traditional criminology and for highlighting vast differences among youth groups that are called gangs. He clearly intends his "interstitial/institutional" typology to be more than simply another typology of gangs. Many such typologies have been suggested, but none have been sufficiently broad or sufficiently theoretically informed to encompass the variety of gang adaptations that have been identified here and elsewhere. Pointing to institutionalization is a promising beginning, but it is clear, as well, that continuity has existed, and very likely continues to exist, among gangs that are essentially unsupervised youth groups and little else. The challenge of the vast amount of empirical variation among youth groups, and their relationships with older groups, requires careful documentation, and theoretical elaboration is daunting to say the least. As I have argued elsewhere (Short 1997, 1998), what is urgently needed is a theoretically informed typology of youth groups. Implied typologies appear in several of these chapters, but like my own (mea culpa), they fall short of the goal.

I turn, finally and briefly, to some challenges that the conference and this volume pose to criminology and to the social and behavioral sciences in general.

## Challenges to Criminology and the Social and Behavioral Sciences

Despite the persistent efforts of many scholars and international organizations, traditional criminology continues largely to be culturally and socially bound to particular nation states—especially among most criminologists in the U.S. We tend to be quite ethnocentric in this regard. This book is a welcome addition toward much needed corrective efforts.

Too often, criminologists are so narrowly focused on crime, criminal law, and crime control that we neglect relevant research from mainstream disciplines. The authors here represented cannot be faulted in this regard. Note, however, that much of the implied criticism of criminology and gang research in these chapters is equally appropriate for social scientists who have not yet caught on to the relevant literature, as well as for popular journalistic accounts and public (mis)understandings. Most of these authors draw upon research, for documentation and/or critical reference, by quite mainstream scholars as well as critical theorists (for example, Robert K. Merton, William J. Wilson, Paul DiMaggio, Walter Powell, and others).

It is, of course, fair game to criticize oversimplified portrayals of the complex realities that characterize one's subject matter, as Young and Wacquant do in criticizing too-simple portrayals of societal differences, to cite two examples among these chapters. Yet the heuristic value of typological constructs and oversimplified comparisons must be recognized. Elijah Anderson's contrast between "decent" versus "street" values among young people and their parents at "ground zero," for example, is not meant to encompass the full complexity of life in the Philadelphia ghetto. But it does poignantly capture the dilemmas faced both by parents, as they socialize and seek to protect their children from the influences and the threats inherent in the "code of the street," and children, as they meet the often conflicting expectations and requirements of family, school, work, and other conventional institutions and those of the street.[17]

We have failed to keep up with the rapidity of social change and its myriad and varied effects throughout the world. How, where, and under what conditions specific aspects of globalization result in convergence in institutional forms and substance, in community life, and in personal and group identity are important questions begging for careful and systematic study. Sassen, Castells, and many others have alerted us to vast changes such as those that are encompassed by globalization.

Too often, we focus narrowly on social control of crime and gangs rather than on what James Q. Wilson somewhat derisively termed "root causes" of crime (Wilson 1975). If all who struggle with globalization issues are correct—and I believe they are—it is imperative that we address the implications of these phenomena for our disciplines.

Rightly or wrongly, criminology often has been identified with the status quo. The always-delicate balance between criticism and appreciation of the societies that make our work possible is never easy to maintain. This applies as well to all of the social and behavioral sciences. It must be noted, however, that many mainstream social scientists are as critical of the contemporary political and economic policies of "neoliberal" states as are these authors (see, for example, Stiglitz 2002; W. Wilson 1987, 1996).

## Religious Nationalism and the Impact of September 11

Few among these authors allude to the terrorist attacks of September 11, 2001, yet those events and events subsequent to them are of critical importance to understanding young people today and for the foreseeable future. Although state-induced violence and terrorism have been staples of many conflicts throughout the globe for centuries (Tilly 1995), the events of September 11 focused the attention of the United States and other world powers on defense against terrorism as never before. In what now seems prescient, Castells—writing on the transformation of *time* in information/network society—argues that the "transformation of war ushers in new forms of violent conflict, terrorism being foremost among them" (2000, 491). Among contributors to this volume, in response to an invitation from the Social Science Research Council (SSRC), Sassen discussed her early thoughts regarding the challenges to social scientists that were and are posed by the events of September 11. She argues that these events underline "the fact of place-specific understandings" as well as "the need for global governance" (Sassen 2002, 106)—the latter a theme voiced as well by David Held and Robert Keohane in the SSRC volumes (Calhoun et al. 2002). Sassen notes especially the social costs associated with growing debt among developing nations: among them, increasing poverty, despair, trafficking in licit and illicit workers, and increasing restrictions on immigration and civil rights (Sassen 2002, 114). "Place-specific" understandings are emphasized also by Keohane, who notes that September 11 illustrates "starkly how our assumptions about security are conceived in terms of increasingly obsolescent views of geographical space" and that "the globalization of informal violence can be analyzed by exploring patterns of asymmetrical interdependence and their implications for power"[18] (Keohane 2002, 78).

Historically, youth groups such as gangs have often been the perpetrators of informal violence, although not on the scale addressed by contributors to the SSRC volumes. Hagedorn's challenge regarding global influences on gangs, implying gang identities with and participation in larger-scale violence, surely is important. He notes Jack Goldstone's observation that "Al Qaeda is like gangs in U.S. inner cities or social protest movements throughout the world" (2002, 151). Following September 11, tactics such as "attacks, harassment, and vandalism" and drive-by shootings—familiar traditional gang behaviors—were directed against Muslims and presumed Muslims and their property, as "reported in all parts of the United State and throughout Europe" (Modood 2002, 193).

In the United States, traditional (and historical) gangs have been described in terms of their isolation from affairs beyond their particular neighborhoods, preoccupied with "turf" and gang identity, or as locally politically conservative. The emergence of supergangs and nations changed this characterization for some gangs, but even gangs that adopt supergang and nation names typically retain a distinctively local identity. Seldom have supergangs engaged in political identity or action, and those that have done so have experienced little success. This, too, may be changing. Certainly, the developments highlighted in these pages have affected, and will continue to affect, gangs and other youth groups in many ways, more perhaps, in other countries than in the U.S.; and some may be transformed into "groups of armed young men," as Hagedorn hypothesizes. In recognition of this problem, the Social Science Research Council, with support from the Harry Frank Guggenheim Foundation, convened a workshop in Pretoria, South Africa, involving field workers and scholars from many countries. The workshop focused "on the development of better understandings of the contexts in which youth create, instigate, and are inducted into organized forms of violence, especially the situations that enable these organizations to flourish and evolve" (SSRC 2005, 25; see also Short and Hughes 2006). John Hagedorn participated in this workshop. Other contributors to the SSRC volumes emphasize that the appeal of terrorism beyond the small groups of religious extremists that have long embraced violence is very much dependent upon both state and local responses to terrorist acts (see, for example, Hefner 2002; Juergensmeyer 2002). Sadly, the imagery of war, the concomitant curtailment of civil rights, and the preemptive war against Iraq that have been the hallmarks of the U.S. response to the events of September 11 seem to have enhanced the appeal of terrorism to young people whose hopes of a better life are blocked by the continued failure of modern and more affluent states to address the issues highlighted by Sassen, Hagedorn, Moore, and others. Moreover, as Tariq Modood notes:

> The murder and terrorization of civilians as part of a political program . . . occurs regularly in a number of places in the world, sometimes executed, or at least supported, by Western states. The perception of these victim populations is often that they matter less than Westerners who are victims. *This deep sense that the West exercises double standards is a source of grievance, hate, and terrorism; it is perhaps the most important lesson of September 11, not the division of the world into rival civilizations, civilized and uncivilized, good and evil.* This perception has to be addressed seriously if there is to be dialogue

across countries, faiths, and cultures, and foreign and security policies need to reviewed in the light of the understanding that is achieved. Our security in the West, no less than that of any other part of the world, depends upon, to adapt a phrase, being tough on terrorism and tough on the causes of terrorism.[19] (2002, 193; emphasis added)

Said Amir Arjomand brings this point closer to the concerns of this book when he urges that the West, and the U.S. in particular, requires "a systematic cultural policy for supporting Islamic modernist elements in the Middle East and the Western diaspora instead of pushing them into the arms of Islamic terrorists. *The Islamic terrorists win if their worldview appears as the only plausible one to alienated Muslim youth, and jihad as the sole path to heroism"* (2002, 176; emphasis added).[20]

## Final Thoughts

Perhaps ironically, in view of the global emphasis of the conference and this volume, the importance of both *local contexts*—their histories, cultures, and social structures—and of *personal identities* run strongly through all of these chapters. What happens globally is always experienced locally and personally, with all of the background historical, cultural, and social nuances that are implied in notions of community and personality. Yet, global developments often set conditions for what happens locally and for what is possible, and, as Sassen notes herein the increased social and spatial polarization that accompanies global concentration of wealth and power in cities may enhance the political and economic capacity of disadvantaged people. Sadly, those capacities may also be stifled, crushed, co-opted, or otherwise diverted by these same forces, as so often has happened in the past.

Contemporary societies are increasingly faced with seemingly intransigent problems—technological, environmental, economic, political, and cultural— all *social* in the most fundamental sense. Some of these—technological and environmental especially—inevitably place us all in "the same boat," the advantaged and the disadvantaged alike. Control of terrorism—like management of common-pool resources (see National Research Council 2002; Ostrom, Gardner, and Walker 1994)—appears to be such a problem. Surely no one can be assured of refuge from its threat. Despite current trends toward increasing polarization, the hope—but certainly not the promise—is that the ubiquity and the universality of such problems may provide the basis for attacking these problems as a matter of common cause.[21]

Understanding—and helping others to understand—such changes and their challenges surely is a necessary condition for dealing with them intelligently and humanely. Whether doing so will be sufficient to the task may be the most important challenge to scholarship concerning youth today.

Young people are, willy-nilly, inheritors as well as shapers of whatever reality is to occur. In today's rapidly changing world, even the most careful scholars struggle to keep up with the literature in their special fields; even more so in the broader disciplines of which their specialties are a part. All fields have a surfeit of information and research findings that are of uneven and often difficult-to-evaluate quality. We can hope for more and better research concerning the arguments advanced and the questions posed in this pioneering book.

## Notes

1. For my earlier views concerning the political implications of street gangs and youth in general in the U.S. and elsewhere, see Short 1980 and references therein.

2. The most extensive use of network analysis to study youth groups and criminal/delinquent behavior is found in Sarnecki 2001; see also Sarnecki and Pettersson 2001.

3. Some of my contacts occurred in conjunction with a visit with John Hagedorn and his colleagues at the University of Illinois, Chicago, in the fall of 2001. Study of South Central Los Angeles's "Hoovers" was facilitated by Steven Cureton's contacts with former members of the Hoovers and other gangs who were students at WSU and another nearby university (Cureton was a graduate student at Washington State University at the time; personal communication; see also Cureton 2002 and forthcoming).

4. Some of these changes are reflected in the successive editions of Huff's edited *Gangs in America* (GIA) volumes (Huff 1990, 1996, 2002). Although cross-cultural and comparative research is stressed by some contributors to these volumes, only two of the chapters report data from gangs outside the United States, and no chapter mentions globalization (see Klein 2002; Vigil and Yun 2002).

5. Brotherton and Barrios acknowledge that they are explicitly motivated as much by activist as by scholarly interests. Although this raises the unavoidable question of how these sometimes conflicting interests are reflected in their analyses, several years of field observation of and working with ALKQN have yielded much valuable data.

6. Note the similarity to ideas presented in the Hagedorn and Brotherton chapters in this volume. For a recent study of factors associated with policing of social movement protests, see Earl, Soule, and McCarthy 2003.

7. Like globalization, the meaning of neoliberalism is controversial. Clearly it differs in different nations and cultural contexts.

8. See Keohane's discussion of "The Globalization of Informal Violence, Theories of World Politics, and 'The Liberalism of Fear'" (Keohane 2002, 79).

9. As Sassen notes in her chapter herein, similar demographic transitions are taking place in many cities, as the "network society" enables decentralization of many economic functions (Castells 2000).

10. Mark Juergensmeyer is director of global and international studies and professor of sociology and religious studies at the University of California, Santa Barbara. "It is not so much that religion has become politicized," he argues, "but that politics have become religionized. Worldly struggles have been lifted into the high proscenium of sacred battle" (Juergensmeyer 2002, 29).

11. In his forthcoming book, Steven R. Cureton also stresses the religious and spiritual nature of Hoover Gangsta Crips.

12. NGOs were especially prominent in promoting human rights concerns throughout the world following World War II. They were instrumental in securing international condemnation and legal prohibitions against genocide and war crimes through lobbying the United Nations and individual governments (see Korey 1998; Guttman 1999). They have since become active, and often effective, in other international affairs such as environmental, AIDS, and international refugee concerns. The effectiveness of NGOs in confronting such global problems clearly is related to their ability to function on a global scale, in large measure by mobilizing kindred organizations.

13. Newer Polynesian youth gangs are an exception, Hazlehurst notes, in that they are "territorially bounded" and emulate Bloods and Crips.

14. Either directly or indirectly, ethnic identity is an important factor in nearly all of these chapters. An exception is Hazlehurst's discussion of New Zealand's Maori, among whom identity, including tribal identity, appears to be less strong than it once was.

15. Here, also, New Zealand's organized crime and motorcycle gangs appear to be an exception.

16. I will pass this opportunity to critique John's appreciative critique of the Chicago School except to note that he is in good company, along with many practitioners of Chicago-style sociology. The great advantage of Chicago-style sociology is that it has been largely self-correcting—and hardly "de-racialized"—as evidenced by the contributions of William Julius Wilson—whose later work (1987, 1996) emphasizes the importance of race—Elijah Anderson (1999), Robert Sampson and his colleagues (Sampson, Raudenbush, and Earls 1997; Sampson, Morenoff, and Earls 1999), Robert Bursik (Bursik 1989, 2001; Bursik and Grasmick 1995), Gerald Suttles (1968, 1990), and Short and Strodtbeck (1965/1974) among others.

17. Note, also, that Young's chapter, although critical of portrayals of modern society that too often employ binary analyses, builds upon these in developing his own—sometimes binary (e.g., on page 18; his analogy of the "bulimic society" is essentially binary). Douglas Massey and others have advanced somewhat similar analyses (Massey 1996). Wacquant's devastating critique of premises guiding social

scientists' studies of the American ghetto nevertheless relies in part on such mainstream urban ethnographers as Gerald Suttles and Elijah Anderson. His critique, therefore, is not so much of gang researchers, or even criminologists, as it is directed toward broader audiences.

18. Keohane defines "informal violence" as "violence by non-state actors, capitalizing on secrecy and surprise to inflict great harm with small material capabilities" (2002, 79).

19. Tariq Modood is professor of sociology, politics, and public policy, and director of the Centre for the Study of Ethnicity and Citizenship at the University of Bristol, UK.

20. Said Amir Arjomand, born in Iran, is a sociologist at the State University of New York at Stony Brook.

21. For a discussion of this issue as it relates to such technological problems as disposal of high-level nuclear waste, see Short 2001.

## References

Abadinsky, Howard. 1985. *Organized Crime.* 2nd ed. Chicago: Nelson-Hall.

Albrow, M. 1997. *The Global Age.* Stanford, Calif.: Stanford University Press.

Anderson, Elijah. 1999. *Code of the Street: Decency, Violence, and the Moral Life of the Inner City.* New York: W. W. Norton.

Bhagwati, Jagdish. 2001. "Why Globalization Is Good." *Social Science Research Council Items and Issues* 2, no. 3–4 (Winter): 7–8.

Bourdieu, Pierre. 2001. "Uniting to Better Dominate." *Social Science Research Council Items and Issues* 2, no. 3–4 (Winter): 1–6.

Bursik, Robert J., Jr. 1989. "Political Decision Making and Ecological Models of Delinquency: Conflict and Consensus." In *Theoretical Integration in the Study of Deviance and Crime: Problems and Prospects,* ed. S. F. Messner, M. D. Krohn, and A. E. Liska, 105–17. Albany: State University of New York Press.

———. 2002. "The Systemic Model of Gang Behavior: A Reconsideration." In *Gangs in America III,* ed. C. Ronald Huff, 71–81. Thousand Oaks, Calif.: Sage.

Bursik, Robert J., Jr., and Harold Grasmick. 1993. *Neighborhoods and Crime: The Dimensions of Effective Community Control.* Lexington, Mass.: Lexington Books.

Calhoun, Craig, Paul Price, and Ashley Timmer, eds. 2002. *Understanding September 11.* New York: Social Science Research Council.

Castells, Manuel. 1998. *The Information Age: Economy, Society, and Culture.* Vol. 3: *End of the Millennium.* Oxford, UK: Blackwell.

———. 2000. *The Information Age: The Rise of the Network Society.* Vol. 1: *The Rise of the Network Society.* 2nd ed. Oxford, UK: Blackwell.

Chin, Ko-lin. 1986. "Chinese Triad Societies, Tongs, Organized Crime, and Street Gangs in Asia and the United States." Ph.D. diss., University of Pennsylvania.

Coleman, James S., Robert H. Bremner, Burton R. Clark, John B. Davis, Dorothy H.

Eichorn, Zvi Griliches, Joseph F. Kett, Norman B. Ryder, Zahava Blum Doering, and John M. Mays. 1974. *Youth: Transition to Adulthood.* Report of the Panel of the President's Science Advisory Committee. Chicago: University of Chicago Press.

Conquergood, Dwight. 1994. "Homeboys and Hoods: Gang Communication and Cultural Space." In *Group Communication in Context: Studies of Natural Groups,* ed. L. Frey, 23–55. Hillsdale, N.J.: Lawrence Erlbaum.

———. 1997. "Street Literacy." In *Handbook of Research on Teaching Literacy through the Communicative and Visual Arts,* ed. J. Flood, S. B. Heath and D. Lapp. New York: Simon and Schuster.

Coughlin, Brenda, and Sudhir Alladi Venkatesh. 2003. "The Urban Street Gang after 1970." *Annual Review of Sociology* 29: 41–64.

Cureton, Steven R. Forthcoming. *Hoover Gangsta Crips.* Carbondale: Southern Illinois University Press.

———. 2002. "I'll Ride for You, Gangsta." In *Gangs in America III,* ed. C. Ronald Huff, 83–100. Thousand Oaks, Calif.: Sage.

Decker, Scott H., and Frank Weersman, eds. 2006. *European Street Gangs and Troublesome Youth Groups.* Walnut Creek, Calif.: AltaMira.

Della Porta, Donatella, and Sidney Tarrow. 2001. "After Genoa and New York: The Antiglobal Movement, the Police, and Terrorism." *Social Science Research Council Items and Issues* 2, no. 3–4 (Winter): 9–11.

Deutscher, Irwin. 2002. "Gazing at the Disciplinary Bellybutton: A Review Essay on *Liberation Sociology*." *Contemporary Sociology* 31, no. 4: 379–82.

Earl, Jennifer, Sarah A. Soule, and John D. McCarthy. 2003. "'Protest under Fire?' Explaining the Policing of Protest." *American Sociological Review* 68: 581–606.

Feagin, Joe R., and Vera Hernan. 2001. *Liberation Sociology.* Boulder, Colo.: Westview.

Fleisher, Mark S. 2002. "Doing Field Research on Diverse Gangs: Interpreting Youth Gangs as Social Networks." In *Gangs in America III,* ed. C. Ronald Huff. Thousand Oaks, Calif.: Sage.

Goldstone, Jack A. 2002. "States, Terrorists, and the Clash of Civilizations." In *Understanding September 11,* ed. Craig Calhoun, Paul Price, and Ashley Timmer, 139–58. Social Science Research Council.

Graeber, David. 2001. "The Globalization Movement: Some Points of Clarification." *Social Science Research Council Items and Issues* 2, no. 3–4 (Winter): 12–14.

Guillen, Mauro F. 2001a. "Is Globalization Civilizing, Destructive, or Feeble? A Critique of Five Key Debates in the Social Science Literature." *Annual Review of Sociology* 27: 235–60.

———. 2001b. *The Limits of Convergence: Globalization and Organizational Change in Argentina, South Korea, and Spain.* Princeton, N.J.: Princeton University Press.

Guttman, Roy. 1999. "Bringing Genocide to Justice." *Washington Spectator* 25, no. 5 (March 1): 1–3.

Hagedorn, John M. 1998. "Gang Violence in the Postindustrial Era." In *Crime and*

*Justice: A Review of Research.* Vol. 24, *Youth Violence,* ed. Michael Tonry and Mark H. Moore. Chicago: University of Chicago Press.

———. 2002a. "Gangs and the Informal Economy." In *Gangs in America III,* ed. C. Ronald Huff, 101–20. Thousand Oaks, Calif.: Sage.

———. 2002b. "Globalization, Gangs, and Collaborative Research." In *The Eurogang Paradox: Street Gangs and Youth Groups in the U.S. and Europe,* ed. Malcolm W. Klein, Hans-Jurgen Kerner, Cheryl L. Maxson, and Elmar G. M. Weitekamp, 41–58. Dordrecht, Netherlands: Kluwer.

Hagedorn, John M., with Perry Macon. 1988. *People and Folks: Gangs, Crime, and the Underclass in a Rustbelt City.* Chicago: Lake View Press (2nd ed., 1998).

Hazlehurst, Kayleen, and Cameron Hazlehurst, eds. 1998. *Gangs and Youth Subcultures: International Explorations.* New Brunswick, N.J.: Transaction Press.

Hefner, Robert W. 2002. "The Struggle for the Soul of Islam." In *Understanding September 11,* ed. Craig Calhoun, Paul Price, and Ashley Timmer, 41–52. New York: Social Science Research Council.

Held, David 2002. "Violence, Law, and Justice in a Global Age." In *Understanding September 11,* ed. Craig Calhoun, Paul Price, and Ashley Timmer, 92–105. New York: Social Science Research Council.

Howell, James C., John P. Moore, and Arlen Egley Jr. 2002. "The Changing Boundaries of Youth Gangs." In *Gangs in America III,* ed. C. Ronald Huff 3–18. Thousand Oaks, Calif.: Sage.

Huff, C. Ronald, ed. 1990. *Gangs in America.* Newberry Park, Calif.: Sage.

———. 1996. *Gangs in America.* 2nd ed. Thousand Oaks, Calif.: Sage.

———. 2002. *Gangs in America III.* Thousand Oaks, Calif.: Sage.

Ianni, Francis A. J., with Elizabeth Reuss-Ianni. 1973. *A Family Business: Kinship and Social Control in Organized Crime.* New York: Russell Sage Foundation.

Jankowski, Martin Sanchez. 1991. *Island in the Street: Gangs and American Urban Society.* Berkeley: University of California Press.

Juergensmeyer, Mark. 2002. "Religious Terror and Global War." In *Understanding September 11,* ed. Craig Calhoun, Paul Price, and Ashley Timmer, 27–40. New York: Social Science Research Council.

Keohane, Robert O. 2002. "The Globalization of Informal Violence, Theories of World Politics, and 'The Liberalism of Fear.'" In *Understanding September 11,* ed. Craig Calhoun, Paul Price, and Ashley Timmer, 77–91. New York: Social Science Research Council.

Kersten, Joachim. 2001. "Groups of Violent Young Males in Germany." In *The Eurogang Paradox: Street Gangs and Youth Groups in the U.S. and Europe,* ed. Malcolm W. Klein, Hans-Jurgen Kerner, Cheryl L. Maxson, and Elmar G. M. Weitekamp, 247–55. Dordrecht, Netherlands: Kluwer.

Klein, Malcolm W. 1971. *Street Gangs and Street Workers.* Englewood Cliffs, N.J.: Prentice-Hall.

———. 1995. *The American Street Gang: Its Nature, Prevalence, and Control.* New York: Oxford University Press.

———. 2002. "Street Gangs: A Cross-National Perspective," in *Gangs in America III,* ed. C. Ronald Huff. Thousand Oaks, Calif.: Sage.

Klein, Malcolm W., Hans-Jurgen Kerner, Cheryl L. Maxson, and Elmar G. M. Weitekamp, eds. 2001. *The Eurogang Paradox: Street Gangs and Youth Groups in the U.S. and Europe.* Dordrecht, Netherlands: Kluwer.

Korey, William. 1998. *NGOs and the Universal Declaration of Human Rights.* New York: St. Martin's Press.

Massey, Douglas. 1996. "The Age of Extremes: Concentrated Affluence and Poverty in the Twenty-first Century." *Demography* (November): 395–412.

Miller, Walter B. 1958. "Lower-Class Culture as a Generating Milieu of Gang Delinquency." *Journal of Social Issues* 14: 5–19.

———. 1980. "Gangs, Groups, and Serious Youth Crime." In *Critical Issues in Juvenile Delinquency,* ed. D. Schichor and D. Kelley, 115–38. Lexington, Mass.: D. C. Heath.

Miller, Walter B., Hildred Geertz, and Henry S. G. Cutter. 1961. "Aggression in a Boys' Street-Corner Group." *Psychiatry* 24: 283–98.

Modood, Tariq. 2002. "Muslims and the Politics of Multiculturalism in Britain." In *Critical Views of September 11: Analysis From Around the World,* ed. Eric Hershberg and Kevin W. Moore, 193–208. New York: Social Science Research Council.

Moore, Joan W., with Robert Garcia, Carlos Garcia, Luis Cerda, and Frank Valencia. 1978. *Homeboys: Gangs, Drugs, and Prison in the Barrios of Los Angeles.* Philadelphia: Temple University Press.

National Research Council. 2002. *The Drama of the Commons.* Committee on the Human Dimensions of Global Change, ed. E. Ostrom, T. Dietz, N. Dolsak, P. C. Stern, S. Stovich, and E. U. Weber. Division of Behavioral and Social Sciences and Education. Washington, D.C.: National Academy Press.

Ostrom, Elinor, R. Gardner, and J. Walker. 1994. *Rules, Games, and Common-Pool Resources.* Ann Arbor: University of Michigan Press.

Portes, Alejandro, Manuel Castells, and Lauren A. Benton, eds. 1989. *The Informal Economy: Studies in Advanced and Less Advanced Countries.* Baltimore: Johns Hopkins University Press.

Portes, Alejandro, and Saskia Sassen-Koob. 1987. "Making It Underground: Material on the Informal Sector in Western Market Economies." *American Journal of Sociology* 93: 30–61.

Reiss, Albert J., Jr. 1986. "Co-offender Influences on Criminal Careers." In *Criminal Careers and "Career Criminals,"* ed. Alfred Blumstein, Jacqueline Cohen, Jeffrey Roth, and Christy Visher. Washington, D.C.: National Academy Press.

Reiss, Albert J., Jr., and David P. Farrington. 1991. "Advancing Knowledge about Co-offending: Results from a Prospective Longitudinal Survey of London Males." *Journal of Criminal Law and Criminology* 82: 360–95.

Robertson, R. 1995. *Globalization: Social Theory and Global Culture.* London: Sage.

Salagaev, Alexander. 2001. "Evolution of Delinquent Gangs in Russia." In *The Eurogang Paradox: Street Gangs and Youth Groups in the U.S. and Europe,* ed. Malcolm W. Klein, Hans-Jurgen Kerner, Cheryl L. Maxson, and Elmar G. M. Weitekamp, 195–202. Dordrecht, Netherlands: Kluwer.

Sampson, Robert J., Jeffrey D. Morenoff, and Felton Earls. 1999. "Beyond Social Capital: Spatial Dynamics of Collective Efficacy for Children." *American Sociological Review.* 64: 633–60.

Sampson, Robert J., Steven W. Raudenbush, and Felton Earls. 1997. "Neighborhoods and Violent Crime: A Multilevel Study of Collective Efficacy." *Science* 277: 918–24.

Sarnecki, Jerzy. 2001. *Delinquent Networks: Youth Co-offending in Stockholm.* Cambridge: Cambridge University Press.

Sarnecki, Jerzy, and Tove Pettersson. 2001. "Criminal Networks in Stockholm." In *The Eurogang Paradox: Street Gangs and Youth Groups in the U.S. and Europe,* ed. Malcolm W. Klein, Hans-Jurgen Kerner, Cheryl L. Maxson, and Elmar G. M. Weitekamp, 257–72. Dordrecht, Netherlands: Kluwer.

Sassen, Saskia. 1991. *The Global City: New York, London, Tokyo.* Princeton, N.J.: Princeton University Press.

———. 2002. "Governance Hotspots: Challenges We Must Confront in the Post-September 11 World." In *Understanding September 11,* ed. Craig Calhoun, Paul Price, and Ashley Timmer, 106–20. New York: Social Science Research Council.

———. 2002–2003. "Globalization or Denationalization?" *Social Science Research Council Items and Issues* 4, no. 1 (Winter): 15–19.

Short, James F., Jr. 1980. "Political Implications of Juvenile Delinquency: A Comparative Perspective." In *Critical Issues in Juvenile Delinquency: Facing the Last Quarter of the Twentieth Century,* ed. David Shichor and Delos Kelly, 297–316. Lexington, Mass.: D. C. Heath.

———. 1996. "Personal, Gang, and Community Careers." In *Gangs in America.* 2nd ed., ed. C. R. Huff, 221–40. Thousand Oaks, Calif.: Sage.

———. 1997. *Poverty, Ethnicity, and Violent Crime.* Boulder, Colo.: Westview.

———. 1998. "The Level of Explanation Problem Revisited: The American Society of Criminology 1997 Presidential Address." *Criminology* 36, no. 1 (February): 3–36.

———. 2001. "Technology, Risk Analysis, and the Challenge of Social Control." In *Contemporary Issues in Crime and Criminal Justice,* ed. Henry N. Pontell and David Shichor, 213–30. Upper Saddle River, N.J.: Prentice Hall.

———. 2002. "Foreword: What Is Past Is Prelude: Gangs in America and Elsewhere." In *Gangs in America III,* ed. C. Ronald Huff, vii–xx. Thousand Oaks, Calif.: Sage.

Short, James F., Jr., and Lorrie A. Hughes, eds. 2006. *Studying Youth Gangs.* Walnut Creek, Calif.: AltaMira.

Short, James F., Jr., and John Moland. 1976. "Politics and Youth Gangs." *Sociological Quarterly* 17: 162–79.

Short, James F., Jr., and Fred L. Strodtbeck. 1965/1974. *Group Process and Gang Delinquency.* Chicago: University of Chicago Press.

Spergel, Irving A. 1995. *The Youth Gang Problem: A Community Approach.* New York: Oxford University Press.

SSRC (Social Science Research Council). 2001. *Social Science Research Council Items and Issues* 2, no. 3–4: 1–14.

———. 2005. *Items and Issues* 5, no. 3.

Stiglitz, Joseph E. 2002. *Globalization and Its Discontents.* New York: Norton.

Sullivan, Mercer. 1989. *"Getting Paid": Youth Crime and Work in the Inner City.* Ithaca, N.Y.: Cornell University Press.

Suttles, Gerald. 1968. *The Social Order of the Slum: Ethnicity and Territory in the Inner City.* Chicago: University of Chicago Press.

———. 1990. *The Man-Made City: The Land-Use Confidence Game in Chicago.* Chicago: University of Chicago Press.

Thornberry, Terence P., Marvin D. Krohn, Alan J. Lizotte, Carolyn A. Smith, and Kimberly Tobin. 2003. *Gangs and Delinquency in Developmental Perspective.* New York: Cambridge University Press.

Tilly, Charles. 1995. "State-Incited Violence, 1900–1999." *Political Power and Social Theory* 9: 161–79.

Tonry, Michael, ed. 1997. *Ethnicity, Crime, and Immigration: Comparative and Cross-National Perspectives.* Vol. 21 of *Crime and Justice: A Review of Research.* Chicago: University of Chicago Press.

Venkatesh, Sudhir A. 1996. "The Gang in the Community." In *Gangs in America,* 2nd ed., ed. C. Ronald Huff. Thousand Oaks, Calif.: Sage.

Venkatesh, Sudhir A., and Steve D. Leavitt. 2000. "Are We a Family or a Business?: History and Disjuncture in the Urban American Street Gang." *Theory and Society* 29: 427–62.

Vigil, James Diego. 2003. "Urban Violence and Street Gangs." *Annual Review of Anthropology:* 32: 225–42.

Vigil, James Diego, and Steve C. Yun. 2002. "Southern California Gangs: Comparative Ethnicity and Social Control." In *Gangs in America,* 2nd ed., ed. C. Ronald Huff, 139–56. Thousand Oaks, Calif.: Sage.

Warr, Mark. 2002. *Companions in Crime: The Social Aspects of Criminal Conduct.* Cambridge, UK: Cambridge University Press.

Wilson, James Q. 1975. *Thinking about Crime.* New York: Basic Books.

Wilson, William Julius. 1987. *The Truly Disadvantaged: The Inner City, the Underclass, and Public Policy.* Chicago: University of Chicago Press.

———. 1996. *When Work Disappears: The World of the New Urban Poor.* New York: Knopf.

# Contributors

**LUIS BARRIOS** is associate professor of psychology and Puerto Rican studies at John Jay College of Criminal Justice. He is coauthor of *Between Black and Gold: The Street Politics of the Almighty Latin King and Queen Nation*, and the coeditor of *Gangs and Society: Alternative Perspectives*.

**DAVID C. BROTHERTON** is a professor of sociology at John Jay College of Criminal Justice and the Graduate Center/CUNY. He is coauthor of *The Almighty Latin King and Queen Nation: Street Politics and the Transformation of a New York City Gang*.

**JOHN M. HAGEDORN** is a fellow at the Great Cities Institute of the University of Illinois-Chicago. He is the author of *People and Folks: Gangs, Crime, and the Underclass in a Rustbelt City* and coeditor of *Female Gangs: Essays on Girls, Gangs, and Gender*.

**CAMERON HAZLEHURST** is an adjunct professor in the Humanities Research Centre at the Australian National University. He is coeditor of *Gangs and Youth Subcultures: International Explorations*.

**JOACHIM KERSTEN** is a professor of sociology in the Department of Social Sciences at the University of Applied Science Villingen Schwenningen Hochschule für Polizei Baden-Württemberg. He is the coauthor of *Der Kick und die Ehre—Vom Sinn Jugendlicher Gewalt*.

**JOAN W. MOORE** is a distinguished professor emeritus of sociology at the University of Wisconsin–Milwaukee. She is the author of *Homeboys* and *Going Down to the Barrio.*

**JOHN PITTS** is Vauxhall Professor of Socio-Legal Studies and the director of the Vauxhall Centre for the Study of Crime at the University of Luton, Bedfordshire, England. He is the author of *The New Politics of Youth Crime: Discipline or Solidarity.*

**JAN RUS** is an anthropologist who has worked in highland Chiapas, Mexico, since the early 1970s. Since 1985, he has been the coordinator of the "Taller Tzotzil," a native language publishing project for Maya writers and community activists. His latest book is *Mayan Lives, Mayan Utopias: The Indigenous People of Chiapas and the Zapatista Movement* (2003), with Shannan Mattiace and R. Aída Hernández Castillo.

**SASKIA SASSEN** is Ralph Lewis Professor of Sociology at the University of Chicago and Centennial Visiting Professor at the London School of Economics. Her new book is *Territory, Authority, and Rights: From Medieval to Global Assemblages.* The coedited *Socio-Digital Formations: New Architectures for Global Order* was published in 2005. She has just completed for UNESCO a five-year project on sustainable human settlement for which she set up a network of reseachers and activists in over thirty countries.

**JAMES F. SHORT JR.** is a distinguished professor emeritus of sociology at Washington State University. He is the author of *Poverty, Ethnicity, and Violent Crime,* among many other important works.

**DIEGO VIGIL** is a professor of social ecology at the University of California-Irvine. He is the author of *Barrio Gangs* and *A Rainbow of Gangs.*

**LOÏC J. D. WACQUANT** is a professor of sociology at the University of California-Berkeley and affiliated with the Centre de sociologie européenne du Collège de France. He is the author, with Pierre Bourdieu, of *An Invitation to a Reflexive Sociology* and the forthcoming *In the Zone: Life in the Dark Ghetto at Century's End.*

**JOCK YOUNG** is a professor of sociology at Middlesex University. He is the coauthor of the influential *The New Criminology* and the author of *The Exclusive Society.*

# Index

The University of Illinois Press
is a founding member of the
Association of American University Presses.

---

Composed in 10.5/13 Adobe Minion
with Meta display
by Jim Proefrock
at the University of Illinois Press
Manufactured by Sheridan Books, Inc.

University of Illinois Press
1325 South Oak Street
Champaign, IL 61820-6903
www.press.uillinois.edu